CATCHING
WHIMSY

CATCHING WHIMSY

365 DAYS *of* POSSIBILITY

BOB GOFF

NELSON
BOOKS

An Imprint of Thomas Nelson

Catching Whimsy

Copyright © 2024 by Bob Goff

All rights reserved. No portion of this book may be reproduced, stored in a retrieval system, or transmitted in any form or by any means—electronic, mechanical, photocopy, recording, scanning, or other—except for brief quotations in critical reviews or articles, without the prior written permission of the publisher.

Published in Nashville, Tennessee, by Nelson Books, an imprint of Thomas Nelson. Nelson Books and Thomas Nelson are registered trademarks of HarperCollins Christian Publishing, Inc.

The author is represented by Alive Literary Agency, www.aliveliterary.com.

Thomas Nelson titles may be purchased in bulk for educational, business, fundraising, or sales promotional use. For information, please email SpecialMarkets@ThomasNelson.com.

Unless otherwise noted, Scripture quotations are taken from The Holy Bible, New International Version®, NIV®. Copyright © 1973, 1978, 1984, 2011 by Biblica, Inc.® Used by permission of Zondervan. All rights reserved worldwide. www.Zondervan.com. The "NIV" and "New International Version" are trademarks registered in the United States Patent and Trademark Office by Biblica, Inc.®

Scripture quotations marked ESV are taken from the ESV® Bible (The Holy Bible, English Standard Version®). Copyright © 2001 by Crossway, a publishing ministry of Good News Publishers. Used by permission. All rights reserved.

Scripture quotations marked MSG are taken from *THE MESSAGE*. Copyright © 1993, 2002, 2018 by Eugene H. Peterson. Used by permission of NavPress. All rights reserved. Represented by Tyndale House Publishers, Inc.

Scripture quotations marked NKJV are taken from the New King James Version®. Copyright © 1982 by Thomas Nelson. Used by permission. All rights reserved.

Scripture quotations marked NLT are taken from the Holy Bible, New Living Translation. © 1996, 2004, 2015 by Tyndale House Foundation. Used by permission of Tyndale House Publishers, Inc., Carol Stream, Illinois 60188. All rights reserved.

Any internet addresses, phone numbers, or company or product information printed in this book are offered as a resource and are not intended in any way to be or to imply an endorsement by Thomas Nelson, nor does Thomas Nelson vouch for the existence, content, or services of these sites, phone numbers, companies, or products beyond the life of this book.

ISBN 978-1-4002-2814-0 (audiobook)
ISBN 978-1-4002-2815-7 (ePub)
ISBN 978-1-4002-2698-6 (HC)

Library of Congress Control Number: 2024945952

Printed in the United States of America

24 25 26 27 28 LBC 5 4 3 2 1

To Sweet Maria Goff and our kids and their spouses and their kids and their kids.

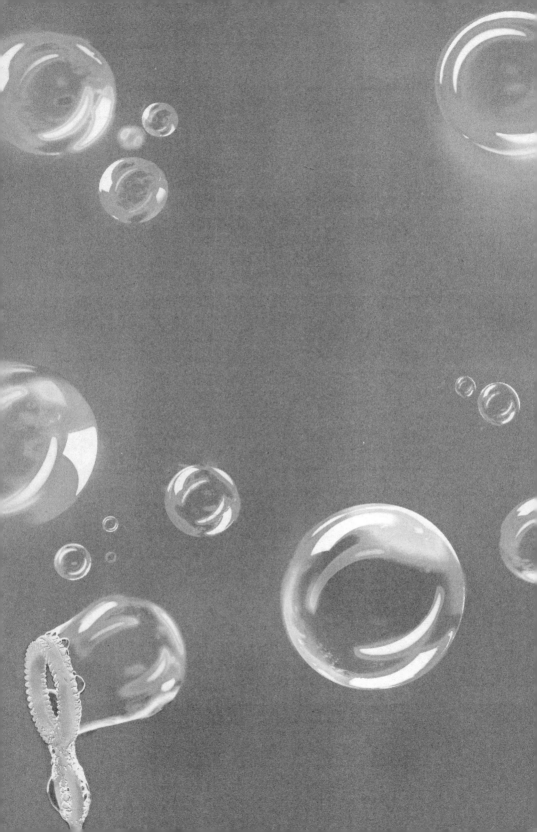

INTRODUCTION

Why a devotional called *Catching Whimsy*? A couple of reasons. First, we can't catch what we don't chase. I want to provide you with some daily thoughts to help you chase after a more meaningful life, experience a more engaged faith, and approach the challenges that will likely come your way with greater intention and confidence than perhaps you have experienced in the past.

Next, I want to give you a daily tap on the shoulder to remind you that God is over the moon about you and your beautiful, often complicated life. He is not looking for the easiest path forward for you but the most purposeful and lasting one.

Finally, I want to whisper some truth, hope, and whimsy into as many of your days as you will allow me to, with the hope that some truths you find in these pages will turn out to be louder than all the other noise competing for your heart and attention every day.

Whimsy isn't something we just stumble into, happen upon, or that sticks to us unnoticed like a dryer sheet. It is something we need to chase after every day with intention, resolve, and tenacity, not unlike a child trying to catch a bubble as it floats in the air. It's not easy to do, but you can spot someone who has caught up to whimsy a mile away. It shows up as joy and hope and generosity and selflessness and endless amounts of curiosity.

In the past few years, the idea of catching something has gotten a well-deserved bad rap. I want to reclaim the phrase and suggest that some things, like whimsy and wonder and passion and the ability to give and receive extravagant love, are worth catching. The truth is each of us are only one or two decisions away from a more beautiful and winsome life; we just need to decide to access it through a door God leaves ajar for us each day.

A while back, I wanted to find a book that emphasized the love and radical acceptance Jesus demonstrated in His life, but I couldn't find one that spoke about it using plain and simple language and that offered the message in a relatable context. I couldn't relate to twenty-dollar words and the theologically complicated and lengthy explanations I found. I didn't want to know what the words in the Scriptures meant in Greek or Aramaic or Hebrew about dealing with the lovely people I encountered on Sunday mornings; I wanted something that would help me live out the impossible demands of Jesus on a Tuesday or Wednesday evening with the difficult, sometimes prickly people I assume are just as insecure as I am, but maybe less adept than me at hiding it. So I decided to write what I couldn't find.

For the past decade and a half, I have been writing books about loving people the way Jesus did and I have attempted to communicate Jesus' messages the way He did—with stories. The Scriptures say Jesus never spoke to anyone without telling them a story or two, and I think I know why. We remember the stories we are told much longer than all the information that comes our way. For this reason alone, I have organized this daily devotional around telling stories that *connect to faith*, rather than merely giving information *about faith*.

I have also written these devotional passages and the stories they are wrapped in to point you toward certain questions to consider. When I have written in the past about how to move from merely thinking about doing big things to acting on those ambitions, I have asked my readers to tease out answers for themselves to questions like these: What do you want? Why do you want it? And what are you going to do about it?

My hope is that the passages in this book will help you not only ask these questions of yourself but also find a more courageous and authentic path forward, as well as unlock answers to the questions that have snagged you and kept you stuck in place.

But don't stop at simply finding answers. Finding answers might lead you to a more informed life, but not necessarily a better or more obedient one. It is what we do with the information we amass that says the most about who we really are. When we stop at finding the answers instead of actually doing something with them, we run the risk of getting stuck in an endless cycle of planning that doesn't lead to action.

My hope is that when you turn each page of this book, you will not merely agree with the words I have written but replace that endless cycle of planning with doing something about what you believe. I hope you will entertain the possibility that God does not want us to spend our lives caught up in figuring out His will for us but instead wants us to find a new gear to access a more loving and adventurous relationship with Him, one full of connection and wonder and possibility.

Hear me when I write that despite all the Bible verses you will find in these pages, this is not a religious book. Instead, these pages are filled to the brim with ideas drawn from the many books and letters that make up the Bible. C. S. Lewis famously wrote, "One road leads home and a thousand lead into the wilderness."[1] For some of you, the verses you will find in these pages might be familiar; for others, they may be new.

Whatever your background and experience with faith, both good and bad, I hope you will find both comfort and acceptance in God's words to us in the Bible and in the application of them to your life, because words without application are merely more noise in an already loud room. I hope these words will lead you to a quiet place, a deep level of gratitude, and perhaps even lead you home to a renewed sense of whimsy.

Let's go catch a couple of bubbles of truth together. Let the chase begin!

JANUARY

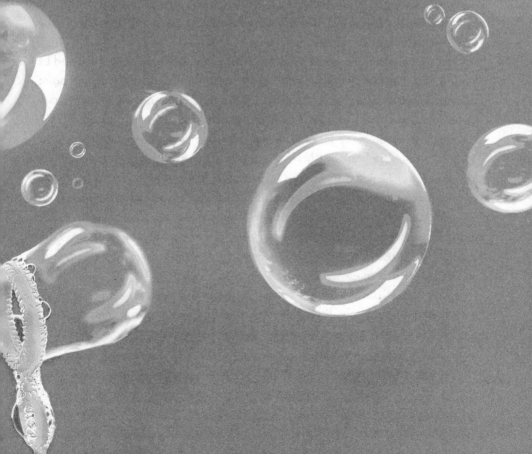

AMBITIONS AREN'T BAD WHEN THEY'RE DRIVEN BY LOVE

I urge you to live a life worthy of the calling you have received.
EPHESIANS 4:1

Have you ever felt selfish about pursuing an ambition? It's easy to equate ambition with selfishness. Don't take the bait. Ambition and selfishness are entirely different things. Give this a try: Write down your ambitions using four columns. In the first column on the left side, write down your highest lasting values. These will be the things that express your faith, your hopes, and what you want to be remembered for long after you are gone. In the second column, write all your ambitions, and draw a line connecting these ambitions to your high and lasting values. In the next column, write down the reasons you are uniquely equipped to do these things. And on the far-right side, in the final column, list the reason(s) you think you shouldn't pursue an ambition or why you think it might be selfish to do so.

It's easy to see our ambitions with a critical eye. But look at your list and be honest with yourself. Are you avoiding an ambition because it's truly selfish or because you have a boatload of self-doubt? Remember, it's not selfish to exercise your gifts and chase the opportunities God brings your way.

I'm a guy who gets a lot of calls after putting my cell phone number in the back of millions of books. When I did it, I didn't know if I'd get one call or one thousand, but I knew I wanted to be available. What if you were to say to the world, "I want to be available to the things that God has already put inside me"?

We can't always control the opportunities that come, but we can decide to make ourselves available when they do. Start today by saying, "God, I am available to those things that might come my way that uniquely sync up with what You already made me good at."

It is not selfish to take the beautiful ambitions God has uniquely called you to and do the heavy lifting it takes to accomplish them. In fact, it might be selfish not to.

Get busy. Start making your lists, and add a dash of whimsy to them.

MEASURE IT TWICE; CUT IT ONCE

Plans fail for lack of counsel,
but with many advisers they succeed.
PROVERBS 15:22

We all need a plan to succeed, yet it can't be all planning and no strategy. It can't be all strategy either; we must figure out the moving parts along the way.

Omar Bradley was an army general in World War II who famously said that amateurs talk strategy while professionals talk logistics. I agree. But the truth is we can't do without either; we need the right amount of both. As you think through what worthy ambitions you want to pursue next, you will need one scoop of strategy and two scoops of logistics.

Try this exercise. Talk about this year as if it already happened and you are reviewing it. What would you say about it? Most of us wouldn't say, "I really didn't do anything, and that was exactly what I was aiming for." Instead, we might list the things we can envision having completed.

But don't just stop at listing the tasks you want to have completed; think about who you would want to help you with the logistics of making it happen. Get those people on board right now, so you can avoid the year-end review where you kick yourself for not having the right team together to execute your ideas.

There is an old woodworking saying: "Measure it twice; cut it once." Once you have a viable plan, ask yourself who you need in your life to help you measure it a second time and who can help you cut it once.

RELATIONSHIP AUDIT: KEEPING OUR ACCOUNTS IN THE POSITIVE

So that we may not cause offense, go to the lake, and throw out your line. Take the first fish you catch; open its mouth and you will find a four-drachma coin. Take it and give it to them for my tax and yours.
MATTHEW 17:27

Even the early followers of Jesus had to engage with the day-to-day matters we deal with. They had plenty of things to manage, including their finances. There was a tax collector who came to check in on Jesus. You can think of it as the first time Jesus was audited. The collector said, "There's this two-drachma tax. Did you pay it?" One of Jesus' friends said, in effect, that Jesus did pay His taxes. They had nothing to hide, but they did have some accounting to do.

Audits can be a real hassle and something to avoid when it comes to paying taxes. But auditing our lives is actually a great thing to do. Just like we account for our income and losses every year, we should regularly be looking at where we are with our family, faith, friends, generosity, availability, and more.

The first thing God did in Genesis was create, and the second thing He did was hover over what He had just created. Do the same in your life. Hover over your family for a moment. Ask yourself, *What does each family member need that only I can give them?* Next, hover over your faith, and ask yourself, as you look back over this past year, *Has my faith grown, or is it staying about the same?* Don't beat yourself up with your answer; understand yourself better with your response. Now, hover over your friends for a moment. Do an audit on each relationship. Who are the people you are pouring into? Is there a quick call you can make to speak some words of truth over them? Finally, hover over yourself, and ask yourself what you want to do in this coming year.

Adopt a practice of setting aside time every year to audit the various areas of your life. For each of these areas, ask yourself, *Just as God is providing what I need, how can I be a part of providing what the people around me need?* God is probably not going to give you a fish with a $20 bill in its mouth, but He might have already given you a friend who needs just the right word, in just the right season.

Ready to begin your audit?

MOTIVATION MATTERS

Let us not become weary in doing good, for at the proper
time we will reap a harvest if we do not give up.
GALATIANS 6:9

I have had plenty of passing interests and habits, like my brief fascination with making saltwater taffy. But some habits—the ones that are genuinely good for my heart, soul, and those around me—I want to keep around longer. I want these to etch a fresh groove in my mind and become a fundamental part of my life. But how do we make these new ideas for our lives stick?

The key isn't just creating new habits; it's understanding the underlying reasons for developing those habits. If you haven't been able to stick to a new habit, it might be because you haven't found it worthwhile in the grand scheme of your life. In the sea of possibilities, it didn't have enough buoyancy to rise to the top. To lift your new idea to the top, you need to get clear about the compelling reasons for it. A truly good reason isn't simply that someone told you to do it; that's compliance, and compliance won't stand up to the test of time and life as it happens. Instead, you need reasons that speak to the deepest parts of you and will truly motivate you.

If I say, "I'm going to run every morning," for example, my underlying reason might be that I want to be healthy and able to be present in people's lives. It's the foundation of a habit that makes it meaningful, not the decision to merely have a new practice. Remembering these foundational reasons will provide you with the momentum and enthusiasm to carry it through.

One last thing: don't be too hard on yourself. You're going to slip up, and that's okay. Adopting new practices isn't about adding one more thing to fail at; it's about risk and extending yourself some grace.

So, as you endeavor to form new habits, get clear on your reasons for each habit and then surround yourself with people who genuinely encourage you and remind you why it's worth it.

Establish something new, whimsical, and lasting in your life.

TELL OTHERS WHO THEY ARE BECOMING THROUGH GOD'S EYES

Do nothing out of selfish ambition or vain conceit. Rather, in humility value others above yourselves, not looking to your own interests but each of you to the interests of the others.
PHILIPPIANS 2:3–4

Did you know helping others find their way forward can help you find your way forward as well? In his letter to the Philippians, Paul told the early church that one way to live out their faith was to do it the way a friend of his, Timothy, did it—by taking a genuine interest in the people around him.

When you take a genuine interest in others, you stop telling them what you think they ought to do, and instead find yourself reminding them who you think they are becoming. Every day, we can tell the people around us about the things they might not see in themselves.

For instance, Jesus didn't say to Peter after he had denied even knowing Him, "Peter, you're such a wimp." Instead, He reminded Peter of who he was becoming, telling him, "Peter, you're a rock." He took a genuine interest in Peter at a time when Peter thought he was a failure. Jesus thought Peter had a bright future, not a sordid past. God didn't see a loser revealed; He saw a leader emerging.

We will become what the people around us say we are. Don't take my word for it, look at the Scriptures. Peter became a rock, Moses became a leader, King David became humble, Rahab got brave, Nicodemus became faithful, Paul got loving, Jonah wasn't fish bait anymore, the leper got healed, the woman at the well changed, the centurion was amazed, Matthew the tax collector reformed, the prodigal ran home, the criminal next to Jesus woke up in paradise, and you arrived on earth as a son or daughter of the living God.

This is what happens when people start seeing themselves the way God does.

Let's be a part of helping those around us see what God sees in them.

DELIGHT IN SMALL BEGINNINGS—GOD DOES

Do not despise these small beginnings, for the
LORD rejoices to see the work begin.
ZECHARIAH 4:10 NLT

We all sometimes feel a little hopeless. Maybe there was something you wanted badly, but it didn't materialize. Perhaps it was a relationship or a promotion or an opportunity that didn't come together. Or it could be that what you hoped for was something more intangible. Maybe you wanted to develop character qualities like more patience or kindness or compassion or empathy. But just when you thought you were making progress and seeing these attributes emerge in your life, you had a setback, an argument, an unkind word or thought.

In the South, there is a saying that makes a lot of sense to me: "Be where your feet are." The best way to reset from a time of disappointment or hopelessness is to understand clearly where you are now and where you're trying to go. God's got some big hopes for the person you are turning into. Resist the urge to fake it or rush it. Understand where you are starting from and be willing to take small next steps toward your worthwhile goals. Experience the journey by trying to understand it. This way, when you come to something discouraging, you won't lose your equilibrium. You will have the confidence that comes from knowing the adventure you are on and knowing where you are headed.

The prophet Zechariah told his people not to despise small beginnings because God delights in seeing the work begin. When my grandson took his first step, I didn't see him trying and say, "I've seen better." Of course not. It was his first step, and I delighted in it. Continue to take small steps in Jesus' direction. When you mess up, sure, call yourself out, but don't beat yourself up. God isn't looking for a string of successes; He delights in our attempts.

What small move do you need to make toward Jesus today? Do this with a ton of expectation and one step at a time, beginning with where your feet are right now. The angels are leaning over the rails hoping you will. Now go catch some whimsy!

IN JOY AND SADNESS, HE IS OUR COMFORT AND FRIEND

Praise be to the God and Father of our Lord Jesus Christ, the
Father of compassion and the God of all comfort, who comforts
us in all our troubles so that we can comfort those in any
trouble with the comfort we ourselves receive from God.

2 CORINTHIANS 1:3-4

One of Jesus' disciples, John, wrote about when one of Jesus' friends, Lazarus, died. When Jesus arrived at the place where Lazarus's family lived, Mary, Lazarus's sister, ran out to meet him and let him know her brother had already died. Here's the amazing thing about Jesus: He could have brought Lazarus back to life that very moment. Jesus had even told His disciples what He was going to do. Jesus' life was all about overcoming death, setbacks, and disappointments, and with a snap of His fingers He could have had Lazarus standing right next to them.

Instead, He stopped and wept with Mary. Jesus' plan to bring Lazarus back to life didn't undo or upstage the pain Mary had experienced in losing her brother and Jesus didn't overlook it; He entered it. He wasn't late to the funeral; He was right on time for the sadness.

God cares about us and all our experiences, good and bad. As much as we would like to, sometimes the first step isn't to fix the painful things in our lives or anyone else's, but to mourn them. Don't get me wrong, I don't think we're meant to permanently dwell in mourning, but it's an important first step in our own healing and the healing journey of others we are privileged to walk alongside.

I know it can sometimes feel like God has gone silent in the middle of something incredibly painful. Perhaps when God is quiet in these times, it's because He is sad too. The quiet doesn't mean He's not there. He was with Mary, and He will be with you in your pain as well.

Invite Jesus into the grief; He is already there waiting for you.

FROM SANDY SETBACKS TO A FIRM FOUNDATION

Everyone who comes to me and hears my words and does them . . . he
is like a man building a house, who dug deep and laid the foundation
on the rock. And when a flood arose, the stream broke against that
house and could not shake it, because it had been well built.

LUKE 6:47–48 ESV

Jesus told a story once about two men who built houses. One man built his house on the sand, and when the storms came his house fell apart. The other man built his house on a rock, and when storms came that man's house stood strong.

Out of all the types of buildings Jesus could have talked about to illustrate this idea of having a strong foundation—barns and silos, official-looking offices, garages—I don't think it's an accident that Jesus chose to talk about a house. A home can represent our families, what we value most, and the things we have worked to build with our ambitions. Jesus explained to His followers that building something lasting with our lives begins with a foundation that is as strong as rock, one built on loving God, loving others, and being generous with our time and gifts.

It is an exercise worth doing to list the things you value most in your life—not cars and boats and savings accounts but people, places, and character traits you want to be remembered for. Next, list the impediments you keep running up against, the self-defeating habits, the letdowns you have experienced, and the hurts you have felt. You're not going to make any headway without getting real about where you are, but setbacks don't need to become campsites for us. Ask God for the courage to invite the disappointments out of the shadows. Once we see these perceived impediments clearly, we can do something about them. We can recognize them as the sand that they are and start building our foundation on something stronger and more trustworthy.

Jesus didn't give an epilogue to His story, but I can imagine it going something like this: The man who built his house on the sand said, "I'm going to get rid of a couple of old habits. I'm going to take what I can learn from the storm and start building again." Just when we start to think we've dug ourselves a pit, we realize instead we're prepped to lay a new foundation.

Have a little courage. Rebuild your foundation. You've got this.

QUESTION WITH HOPE AND WHIMSY: GOD IS ALREADY AT WORK

As he went along, he saw a man blind from birth. His disciples asked him, "Rabbi, who sinned, this man or his parents, that he was born blind?" "Neither this man nor his parents sinned," said Jesus, "but this happened so that the works of God might be displayed in him."

JOHN 9:1-3

Think about the miracle when Jesus spat on the ground and made some mud to heal a blind man. The first questions the onlookers asked were, "What caused this man to be blind? Who sinned?" I think my question would be, "Why did you just hock some spit and rub mud in the poor guy's eyes?" What if we changed the questions we asked? What would happen if we replaced some of our initial questions with these: "What is Jesus doing, and what is He going to do next?" This is a small but important shift in the way we perceive what is happening around us.

Sometimes the events in our lives are opportunities for God to show up, and I have learned to trust that He always wants to show us more of who He is. When things have been awful in my life—when there's been a big setback, when a friend has died, when we have experienced a loss—sometimes it feels like God has gone below the surface, but what I think is happening is that He is on the search for us.

Think of the things happening in your life right now and invite God into them. Ask yourself, *Is there something God might be doing in this right now? And what might He do next?* This isn't merely putting a happy face on difficult circumstances, and it is not a trite exercise to look for the silver lining. It's a shift in perspective to consider, "Are the fingerprints of Jesus visible yet in this situation?"

In the opening paragraph of the book of Acts, Luke encouraged his friend Theophilus to look for "many convincing proofs" that Jesus was still alive (v. 3). Maybe you're going through a hard time right now. What if you were to change your viewpoint to one like Luke encouraged? What if, instead of wondering why things are happening, you gave that question a quarter twist and started thinking, *Maybe these things are happening so the works of God could be put on display in my life. What might He be doing now, and what might He be doing next?*

God is constantly searching for the most authentic version of us. He wants us to let Him know when we feel joyful or gut-punched. Even in the most challenging circumstances, God is at work. And when we see Him at work, perhaps we will get a glimpse of what God will at some point put on display for everyone to see.

Look for God to show up today. Be authentic with Him!

TRUST THE MASTER PLANNER FOR THE PERFECT BLUEPRINT

LORD, I know that people's lives are not their own;
it is not for them to direct their steps.
JEREMIAH 10:23

The Princess Louisa Inlet is a beautiful place. Some time ago, I heard *National Geographic* called it the eighth most beautiful place in the world, and I believe it. What makes this place so striking are the steep granite cliffs leading to glacier fields that stretch hundreds of miles. When we purchased the forests in this area decades ago, the intent was to protect them for generations to enjoy. A few years after the purchase, we thought perhaps we could build a lodge on one corner of the property. We drafted some initial plans, which then turned into a massive roll of blueprints. Once we figured out the details, we went to the builders who would be helping us with our big roll of plans, and they began a long and expensive process of blasting a flat spot equal to the footprint of our big roll of plans. It took more than a year of blasting through the granite to complete a building pad big enough. It wasn't long before I realized I had gotten things completely backward. It would have been much more sensible to first figure out how much room we actually had for a building pad and then draw up a set of plans to fit what we already had.

The reason I am telling you this is that we sometimes get caught up in our own ideas and draw up a big roll of plans for our future before we bring it to Jesus. Don't get me wrong, I am a fan of plans, because a hope without a plan is only a wish. Yet, consider the words and promise from the prophet Jeremiah six hundred years before Jesus arrived: God already has plans for us that are good and lasting and important.

These days, when we are considering building something new, we make the biggest flat spot we can and then draft up the plans to work with what we have—not what we wish we had—to build on. We make the building fit the pad rather than making the pad fit the building.

What flat spot do you already have that you can invite Jesus into to build something beautiful and lasting on?

STEP OUT OF FEAR AND INTO FREEDOM

So if the Son sets you free, you will be free indeed.
JOHN 8:36

A friend of mine plays guitar for a band. When his crew was coming through town to play at a sold-out arena, he called and asked if I wanted a ticket to the show. I felt like a kid who had just found one of Wonka's golden tickets. When I got inside the arena, I started walking up to the nosebleed section. At the top of the stairs, a guy stopped me and looked at my ticket with his flashlight. He told me I was in the wrong section. I wondered how far away the seats actually were. The man then pointed downward and said this ticket would get me on the main floor. I was thrilled. "Are you kidding me?!" So I walked down all the stairs until I got to the floor, where another usher looked at my ticket and said, "Oh, you're in the wrong section." I thought, *Ah, shoot, I'm going to have to go back up to the rafters.* But then I thought, *I'm going to get my steps in, so it's cool.* Then the guy said, "Actually, with this ticket, you can go into the mosh pit." I wasn't sure what that was, but I was game. I arrived next to the stage where the mosh pit was, and two guys looked at my ticket and said, "You know what? This is an all-access pass. You can go anywhere you want with this thing."

Too often, we don't live with the freedom of an all-access pass. We get hemmed in by our circumstances and the people we spend the most time with. Maybe for you it was your parents. They were amateurs when you arrived on earth at a hospital or by stork. They didn't know what to do with you. Perhaps they just didn't want you to get hurt or were dealing with fear, and spoke a lot of no's over your life. "Don't do this." "Don't do that." "Be careful." Little by little, the world you thought was filled to the brim with freedom was displaced by one marked by caution and limitations. Your parents weren't trying to mess you up, but maybe you adopted a mindset that dismissed freedom as something unavailable to you.

The truth is, you have an all-access pass to more freedom than you might think. You can live with freedom in relationships, freedom to go deeper, freedom to ask questions of God. Experience that freedom right now in your life.

You have a magnificent invitation to go deeper, make courageous changes, and expand your faith. What's your next move?

SHARE THE LOVE

I thank my God every time I remember you.
PHILIPPIANS 1:3

We are all reflections of or reactions to the people we grew up with. If you had parents who raised their voices to each other, because that was how they navigated difficult circumstances, this might explain why you raise your voice. The corollary might be true as well, and you get quiet like a church mouse when there is conflict. This is likely a reaction to what you experienced growing up.

Go through the people in your life who have shaped you. Start with the earliest memory you have of somebody. I had a first-grade teacher named Mrs. Martini (an awesome name for a teacher). She made me feel like I had more educational game in me than we both knew I had. When I graduated from law school, I gave my diploma to Mrs. Martini, who was late in her life by then, and I had the opportunity to thank her for the impact she had on me. Because of the way she believed in me, I never lost hope that I could be that guy. I wasn't dumb, but I always felt dumb. I became a reflection of what she had seen long before.

Do a gratefulness audit today. Start by writing down the names of the people who have intersected your life and have impacted you and look them up. Drop them a note or send them a pizza with "thank you" spelled out with pepperoni. It won't be hard to find them or get their email address. Let them know the specific difference they made in your life. Then, move on to the important work of being that person in somebody else's life that you needed in yours. This isn't the Academy Awards where we merely thank people from afar; we also get to become the up-close encouragers of others. Expressing encouragement doesn't need to be a grand, gigantic gesture either. It could be one or two words spoken at the right time.

Find someone who needs a kind word from you. Be their cheerleader and reflect Jesus' love to them. I bet you will be the one person in the past decade who has singled them out and done that. You just might start a chain reaction with the power to change the entire world.

Ready? Go find that person today.

SHOW WHAT YOU REALLY BELIEVE BY HOW YOU LOVE

If you keep my commands, you will remain in my love, just as I have
kept my Father's commands and remain in his love. I have told you
this so that my joy may be in you and that your joy may be complete.
My command is this: Love each other as I have loved you.

JOHN 15:10-12

Jesus once asked Simon Peter, "Who does everybody say I am?" It was an honest question, and Simon Peter responded, "Well, some say You're a teacher." Jesus was indeed an awesome teacher. He had all kinds of things to teach and say to those around Him.

Simon Peter said, "There are other people who say You are a prophet." And Jesus was all of that too. He told the people what God wanted of them.

Then Simon Peter volunteered, "I think You are God." And Jesus said, using different words, "You are right."

Jesus said, "Don't tell anybody."

I'm sure Peter was thinking, *What in the world?* I don't think Jesus was asking His friends to keep a secret. I think He wanted to *show* people who He was, not just *tell* people.

Sometimes we think what we need to do is give people more information about Jesus when what they need is evidence of what we believe unveiled in our lives. The truth is most people have all the information they need; what we need are examples. And you and I get to be those.

Everyone has something they say they believe; however, it is what we do, not what we say we believe, that defines us. Every selfless act of love is a declaration of faith. Every day, your actions and mine are saying to the world, "This is what we believe to be true about who Jesus is," and every time we do something unselfish, we move everyone a little closer to Him.

How will you declare your faith today?

AIM FOR AMAZING

The whole earth is filled with awe at your wonders . . .
PSALM 65:8

We all know what a maze is. Perhaps you have been in a corn maze at a fall festival or in a boxwood hedge maze in England. You enter a narrow area, which leads to other narrow areas, and follow a path not knowing where it will lead. Mazes are all about confusion. This is where the root of the word *amazing* came from. The definition was revised over time to also include a sense of childlike wonder. Think of *amazing* as equal parts confusion and delightful wonder. That's what I think we should be aiming for in life.

Depending on our beliefs, biases, and the stories we have adopted for ourselves, some of us will aim for small, safe, predictable results. Others will swing for the fences and be huge risk-takers. What if, instead of shooting for something really big or something really small, we aim for our lives to be amazing?

Doing a big thing like climbing Mount Everest isn't necessarily an indicator of someone who is living an amazing life. It is equally likely this person is on a hedonistic bender or just looking for applause or approval. People who think they have everything figured out are also usually not living amazing lives. They're living according to their prescribed box of how things should go in their own minds and possibly missing out on even greater things God has in mind.

To live a truly amazing life, you must leave room for the delightful wonder ushered in by a lack of certainty about the result. When you don't know precisely what will happen moment by moment, when you follow a path God leads you to without telling you everything that will happen along the way, you open yourself up to amazing. No matter your age, you've got twenty pounds of goodness to be collected for release into the world and a five-pound bag of time to fit it in.

**Surround yourself today with people who are aiming
for amazing and make room for the right stuff.**

DON'T LET THE BAD STUFF STICK

Then they brought him a demon-possessed man who was
blind and mute, and Jesus healed him. . . . All the people were
astonished and said, "Could this be the Son of David?" But when
the Pharisees heard this, they said, "It is only by Beelzebul,
the prince of demons, that this fellow drives out demons."
MATTHEW 12:22-24

There was a man who was blind and mute, and the people around him said he was demon possessed. When Jesus drove this spirit out of the man and healed him, the people were amazed. If we had been there, I bet we would have been amazed (and perhaps a little freaked out) too. But someone came up to Jesus after He had performed the miracle and said, "Oh, I know what's going on. You're doing this by the power of the devil."

There will always be skeptics around us, people who won't be impressed with what God is doing or who misunderstand you and dwell on the negative. Don't become distracted by this. Keep your eyes fixed on Jesus. That's what Taylor, an illusionist who is also one of my closest friends, did. We were on a bus tour from city to city with our friends when someone at one of our shows said they figured out how he did his sleight of hand. Even though they had it all wrong, Taylor didn't take the bait; he just encouraged the angsty guy to keep pursuing wonder and brought peace to the negativity.

Some people have their heads in the game and are constantly amazed by what God is doing in the world, while others keep saying, "But what about this? And what about that?" Don't let this throw you off. I'm not saying that you need to avoid skeptical, negative people completely, but do pay attention to the fruit that negativity is bearing in their lives. If what you're seeing is not what you want for your own life, be careful of the time you give them. Love them, bless them, but consider giving them more distance and a little less airtime in your life.

Spend time with a positive person today.

HE IS WILLING—JUST ASK

A man with leprosy came and knelt before him and said, "Lord,
if you are willing, you can make me clean." Jesus reached out
his hand and touched the man. "I am willing," he said. "Be
clean!" Immediately he was cleansed of his leprosy.
MATTHEW 8:2–3

One of Jesus' miracles was healing a man with leprosy. At the time, everybody thought leprosy was highly contagious and kept their distance. But in this story, when a leper saw Jesus and said, "If you're willing, You can make me clean," Jesus didn't shy away or keep His distance. Instead, He responded, with no hesitation, "I am willing." Isn't that beautiful? Let this phrase sink in for a second. *Jesus is willing.*

Here's the thing: Jesus was not only willing for the man with leprosy, but He's willing for you—right now, immediately, no hesitation. He's not pouting about your failures; He's willing about your future.

Perhaps you feel contagious pain or doubt or fear or frustration. All you might need to do to combat these feelings is to have an honest conversation with God and make the same statement to Him that the leper did: "If You are willing, You can make me clean." Make this a declaration of faith, not a question about it.

Jesus is willing with your relationships, to sort them out, to give you clarity and perspective, to bring the right people into your life.

He is willing with your job, to give you a better or different one, or to give you a better or different perspective on the one you have.

He is willing with that friend of yours who is facing what seems like an overwhelming difficulty, to bring them comfort and to show them what to do next.

**Take what is troubling you right now and say
these words over it: "He is willing."**

IF IT'S NOT JESUS, IT'S JUNK MAIL

In the beginning was the Word, and the Word was with God, and the Word was God. He was with God in the beginning. Through him all things were made; without him nothing was made that has been made. In him was life, and that life was the light of all mankind. The light shines in the darkness, and the darkness has not overcome it.
JOHN 1:1-5

When Jesus was traveling, teaching, and performing miracles, people were on the lookout for where He would be. They wanted to find ways to be close by. They cracked the code that being near Jesus is always a good idea, because where Jesus is, people get healed; redemptive, grace-filled things happen; and a new perspective on life emerges. It was true then, and it remains true now.

But how do we know where Jesus is going to be? The answer to this question doesn't need to be a big theological one. It rests on the idea that God is in all things, and nothing happens that is independent of Him. This was the message John was passing along when he said that Jesus has been around since the beginning, and He is in and with everything. The trick for us, then, is to see where Jesus already has been and where He is now.

I don't know about you, but I get a lot of mail—by the foot. What I do first is read the upper left-hand corner to see who it's from. If it's from somebody I don't know or some company I've never heard of, I know it's junk mail and I don't open it; I just throw it away.

We need to do something similar with the messages we receive in this life. You will know the message coming your way is from Jesus if it lines up with what you read in the Scriptures about the big life He talked about. That's a return address you can trust. Stop reading the junk mail that gets delivered to you every day.

Let Jesus be the focus of your thoughts, and no matter what it is you are doing, keep your head on a swivel and look for evidence of Him in everyone and everything.

GO A LITTLE DEEPER AND SEE WHAT HAPPENS

When he had finished speaking, he said to Simon, "Put out
into deep water, and let down the nets for a catch."
LUKE 5:4

There is a story in the Gospel of Luke about Jesus walking along the shore of the Sea of Galilee. He spots two boats. He climbs into one and pushes out into the water to teach from there. What is interesting is what He does next. He asks a fisherman named Simon, who is washing up his nets nearby, to come fishing with Him. Luke went on to say that Jesus told him and his crew to push out a little deeper.

The guys doing the fishing no doubt thought this idea was a bad one. After all, they had been fishing all night and had zero in the fish count. But the Scriptures say the fishermen pushed out deeper anyway. Guess what happened next? They caught so many fish that other boats had to come help them haul in the catch and started sinking because of the weight.

This all happened because Simon, who later became known as Peter, was willing to go a little deeper than he had before. What do you suppose would happen in your life if you pushed out a little deeper in a couple of areas? How might you push out a little deeper in your faith? What about pushing out a little deeper with your career? What might happen if you pushed out a little deeper with your friends or family or your hopes?

It could be that you have been pushing up against a mountain of resistance for a long time. Forget all night; it has felt like years. Perhaps it feels like your relationship or career or love net is empty. You aren't fishless, but life feels hopeless. It certainly can feel counterintuitive to trust that there is more during these times, but trust Jesus when He invites you to lean in to Him and push out a little deeper.

If you knew it was Jesus calling you deeper, would you go? If you really believed He would be with you when you got there, you might just make that move.

Today, make that move and follow Jesus.

QUITTING CAN BE A SUPERPOWER

Jesus straightened up and asked [a woman caught in the act
of adultery], "Woman, where are they? Has no one condemned
you?" "No one, sir," she said. "Then neither do I condemn
you," Jesus declared. "Go now and leave your life of sin."

JOHN 8:10–11

Did you know January 19 is Quitter's Day? This is evidently the day when most people bail on their New Year's resolutions.

I grew up hearing various axioms from my parents. Some were good and helpful, and others were just annoying. One of their all-time favorites was "Goffs aren't quitters." I learned later that my parents had inadvertently lied to me, because Goffs indeed *are* quitters. Let me tell you what I mean.

Quitting important, necessary, lasting things might be a bad idea, but quitting the right things is a really great idea. I now quit things all the time and let my kids know that Goffs *are* quitters. The more I quit doing things that are distractions, the better my life becomes.

There are a couple of times in the Bible when Jesus told people to quit doing something. He said to the woman caught in the act of adultery to knock it off. Jesus saved her from the crowd and told her to quit doing what she was doing. He said the same thing to the guy at the Pool of Bethesda, who once was paralyzed but now wasn't.

Here's my question for you. What do you need to quit? Is it a job or a relationship or a hurt or a grudge? Sometimes leading means leaving. Is it your time to quit something you have been hanging on to?

I get it. Quitting something you are good at can be hard, but don't let your caution get in the way of your obedience. Keep being strong and courageous and when you quit, go big.

**Today, stop taking half measures or spending
your time practicing your announcement speech.
Just say "I'm out" and call it good.**

GOD KNOWS THE PLAN, EVEN IF WE CAN'T SEE IT CLEARLY

For now we see in a mirror, dimly, but then face to face. Now I know in part, but then I shall know just as I also am known.
1 CORINTHIANS 13:12 NKJV

I don't know how many weddings I've gone to where someone read 1 Corinthians 13: "Love is this, love is that." You too? Don't get me wrong, weddings are terrific, as are wedding cakes and this familiar verse, too, but right *after* where the reading at the wedding usually stops is a verse that feels hopeful and insightful and relevant. It describes doing life with God as looking "in a mirror, dimly, but then face to face" (NKJV). We usually get the fuzzy outlines of our faith before we get to actual faith, yet sometimes there is a subtle pressure to declare we have clarity when things are still a little fuzzy for us. If you have ever picked up someone else's prescription eyeglasses by mistake, you know what I mean.

I don't know if you had a Polaroid camera when you were growing up, but if you did, you know that when you press the button and a thin cardboard film grinds out from the front of the camera, the emulsion is murky. It takes a little while before the image develops with clarity. A lot of us are tempted to take the photo by the corner and wave it in the air, thinking this will make the image develop faster. It might feel like you are helping, but you're not. The same is true of our faith and wanting to see things develop more quickly.

Is faith easy? Of course not. Will we know all the moves to make and when to make them? One hundred times, no. The reason is simple: we're looking through the mirror dimly. Rather than faking it and pretending you have clarity on things you are only guessing about, bring those things to Jesus and ask Him to help you work through them.

Remember, even though sometimes practicing our faith is like looking through a mirror dimly, God's promise is that if we'll stay at it, we'll eventually get to see Him face-to-face.

Get your mirror out today. What do you see and what is obscured from view? Don't be impatient. Oftentimes clarity takes a while to develop.

TIRED OF EXCUSES? PUT THEM ON NOTICE AND FLY FREELY

We have different gifts, according to the grace given to each of us.
ROMANS 12:6

Excuses are like ears; everybody has a couple of them (except Van Gogh, but you know what I mean). You might be saying to yourself, "I've got a few big ambitions. I just don't have the resources or the time or the creativity to take the next step." I get it. These may feel like realities, but these excuses don't need to continue to be impediments for you.

Make an inventory of what you already have available to you, including your unique interests and abilities. Do you take joy in serving people? Are you pretty good at teaching? Perhaps you are an awesome encourager (keep it up), or you leak generosity, or you are a natural leader.

Once you've identified your gifts, consider connections and opportunities you have where you could express those gifts. Start with these statements as you take your inventory: "Here are the people with knowledge and expertise in my life. Here are some people who are awesome at encouraging me. Here are some opportunities that are in front of me: an interview, an address, a phone call." Do you see what I'm getting at? You probably have a lot more than you thought you did.

Now list a handful of ambitions you've been stalled on. Overlay on top of these ambitions the opportunities you just identified and the relationships and knowledge you have in your back pocket but perhaps have not accessed yet. Now, go back and identify the factors you have believed are limiting you from pulling off your big ideas and call them out. Put these limiting beliefs on notice that they no longer have control over you. Don't limit what God can do in and through you with your magnificent, once-in-history combination of gifts and abilities. And don't worry about having it all figured out in advance; you'll connect the dots as you go. We're going to build this plane while we're flying it.

Keep your eyes open, make a plan, and then get busy executing it.

IT'S TIME TO SET THINGS RIGHT

Therefore, if you are offering your gift at the altar and there
remember that your brother or sister has something against
you, leave your gift there in front of the altar. First go and
be reconciled to them; then come and offer your gift.

MATTHEW 5:23-24

I was speaking at a small church. Before I gave my sermon, I had everybody turn on their cell phones, stand up, and walk outside so they could make a call to anyone they might have something against. The people in the pews looked a little confused when I told them not to come back if they were unwilling to square up with whoever that was. This is actually something Jesus commanded us to do. Sure, it can feel uncomfortable to do the difficult things Jesus demands. But He is not looking for our approval; He wants our obedience.

Eventually, the members of the church filed back in (some did not), and we worshiped with the freedom and clarity Jesus said would be ours if we sorted out some of what we have been carrying with us. I haven't been invited back to that church a second time and I understand why. Jesus didn't say obeying Him wouldn't be awkward; He just said it would work.

Reconciling broken relationships is a hard but necessary thing. Don't get me wrong. There are some people who are unhealthy and, in some rare instances, dangerous for us to be with, but most people we get sideways with have a much less dramatic backstory. Maybe they were rude or unkind or insensitive, or maybe they misunderstood us or misrepresented something to us or even betrayed us. But we are still called, if it's safe to do so, to put down our offering and square up with the people in our lives before we head back to worship. This wasn't my idea; it was Jesus'.

Reflect on the relationships you have that are strained or broken. Are there some relationships that need to be tended to? Don't let them fester. Pick up the phone, drive over to where they work, find them at church or a bar or at the bowling alley, and try to square up with them. Don't feel ashamed. Difficult relationships happen to all of us.

What difficult relationship will you tend to today?

STOP BEING BOSSY AND START HELPING

In the same way, let your light shine before others, that they
may see your good deeds and glorify your Father in heaven. Do
not think that I have come to abolish the Law or the Prophets;
I have not come to abolish them but to fulfill them.

MATTHEW 5:16–17

I spent most of my career as a trial lawyer and have heard every lawyer joke there is. They still make me chuckle a little. I know Jesus loves kids, but He didn't seem to be fond of lawyers. When you find Jesus saying, "Woe to you," a reference to a lawyer usually isn't far away.

It feels a little close to home to read this in the Scriptures, but it is true, and I think I know why. It's not the profession that is the problem; it's the people who beat other people up with religious rules and laws.

Jesus takes it seriously how we treat the rules He made for living beautiful, meaningful lives, and He cares about how we caretake His promises. But He doesn't ask us to be the hall monitors of other people's conduct as we are figuring out our own. He asks us to be light in an otherwise dark world.

Maybe the reason Jesus talked so much about being a bright light was to keep us focused. If we remain intent on doing beautiful things in the world, we won't become distracted by what others are doing. This doesn't mean we are indifferent to what is happening around us. In fact, it is just the opposite. We will be so aware of our own need to be an example of our faith that we will stop being enforcers of everyone else's.

Let your light shine brightly. You'll know you are doing it right when others see your good deeds and give the applause to God, not you.

**Who can you reach out to today with love and
acceptance rather than words of correction?**

IDENTIFYING THE PROBLEMS TO FIND THE SOLUTION

But let all who take refuge in you be glad; let them ever
sing for joy. Spread your protection over them, that
those who love your name may rejoice in you.

PSALM 5:11

Here's the thing about joy: You can't catch it, net it, or manufacture it. You can only experience it. It will never trespass nor arrive uninvited. It loves to be welcomed and will leave only if it is being ignored.

So how do we welcome this elusive joy into our lives? It feels at first counter-intuitive, but one way to welcome joy is to reflect on the things that *do not* bring us joy. Maybe you feel a little bit off in some of your relationships and you're not quite sure why. Who are the people involved, what are the circumstances, and when can you almost predict that you will feel your joy ebbing? We need to figure out how and where we get robbed of joy so we can take the necessary steps to prevent ourselves from being ambushed again.

Most of us have heard of the *David*. Michelangelo carved this magnificent statue out of a huge piece of marble. What many people don't know is the *David* was carved two degrees off-center. It worked out fine for hundreds of years, but now his ankles are cracking. It stinks to be a marble statue sometimes, right? The reason I want you to think about marble statues and broken ankles is that we all can get one or two degrees off-center from our joy without noticing right away. But over time, the misalignment will show up as cracks in our relationships with people and how we deal with ordinary setbacks that come our way.

If we want to push back against those things that are stealing our joy, we need to ask ourselves, *What is it that is getting between me and my joy? What is it that's just a degree or two off-center?* Once you see it, you can understand it, and then you can take it to Jesus with humility and ask Him to intervene. This is what taking refuge in Him looks like.

Ask those questions today.

LOVE NEVER FAILS, EVEN WHEN WE DO

Jesus answered, "The work of God is this: to
believe in the one he has sent."
JOHN 6:29

Sweet Maria Goff and I have a daughter named Lindsey. She didn't arrive by stork, which was a little disappointing to me and way more painful for Sweet Maria. When we held her, we immediately loved her, even though she had arrived only a moment before. Years later she put a large and expensive dent in my car, but I love that girl on the other side of that failure just as much as I loved her the day I met her. And that's how God feels about you and me. He delights in us. He doesn't care what we have done, currently are doing, or might do in the future. He just wants our hearts.

In John 6:28–29, Jesus' disciples were asking a practical question: "What do I do so that You will love me more?" and Jesus told them, "Your job is to believe in the one God sent." In other words, Jesus' big idea is that our one and only job is to keep our eyes fixed on Him. He is not an umpire, calling balls and strikes on us and all the things we do. He's more of a base coach, seeing where we are and where we could be and continuing each day to lead us toward Him.

His goal is not that we would be more successful; He wants us to be more *His*. This is how real love works. Love finds people and sees the beauty in them that they sometimes don't see in themselves because they put a big dent in something. I want my love to be released in that same way.

My love for Lindsey isn't the over-under on what she has done right or what she's done wrong. I just love her. And that's how God loves you.

**Delight in God's love today. See things in people
that they don't see in themselves.**

WHEN IN DOUBT, OPEN THE DOOR AND INVITE PEACE IN

Jesus came and stood among them and said to them, "Peace be with you."
JOHN 20:19 ESV

Have you noticed that after Jesus rose from the dead, He appeared to people several times, often greeting them by saying, "Peace be with you"? If Jesus showed up in a room with me like He did with some of His followers, I might need to change my toga, and yet He brought calm to the most startling of circumstances.

The first time Jesus appeared to His disciples, Thomas wasn't with them. Then He appeared a second time when Thomas was in the room. Jesus wanted even the guy whose nickname was "the doubter" to experience peace. Maybe that's you today and you've got a little Thomas in you. God is more than okay with that; He wants to bring His peace to your honest doubts.

Jesus often talked about His "shalom" (or His "peace") resting on people and places. Shalom is more than a polite greeting or parting comment. It is God's eternal and mysterious peace. How can we experience the kind of peace Jesus talked about today? First, we need to know what peace actually is.

Peace is not something that happens externally; it is an inside job. We can be in a crowded place surrounded by many loud voices and still feel totally peaceful. In the same way, we can be in a quiet, beautiful place and not feel any peace at all. Peace arrives or escapes based on our state of mind. So if we want to experience Jesus' peace, we need to be intentional about what we're focusing on, whether we're hanging on to His love moment by moment or spiraling into negative "what if?" thoughts.

Whether it is a relationship that needs repair or a decision that feels daunting, go back to Jesus a second time like Jesus did for Thomas. Leave the door ajar for Jesus to enter every room in your life and every decision that needs to be made with His peace. Peace be with you in this important work; may His Shalom be upon you and with you as you invite Jesus into your doubting places.

**If you are feeling distracted or anxious today,
get real and be honest with God.**

NAME YOUR FEARS AND THEN HAND THEM OVER TO GOD

I pray that out of his glorious riches he may strengthen
you with power through his Spirit in your inner being, so
that Christ may dwell in your hearts through faith.
EPHESIANS 3:16–17

I'm not afraid of very many things, except sharks and spiders and snakes (which is totally normal) and venom-spitting koala bears (there is no such animal, but if there were, I know I would be afraid of them). Some people are afraid of being late or misunderstood or canceled or shunned. Some people are afraid they will lose their job, and others are afraid they will keep it. Think about it for a minute. What are you afraid of today? The way to take away the power fear may hold over us is to name what it is we're afraid of, understand the origins of our fear, and then take these fears to Jesus to overcome.

Most of us can come up with a list of our concerns and fears, but what may take a little more digging is figuring out where these fears originated. If it is a fear of rejection you harbor, go back to your earliest memory of being rejected. See yourself in that time and at that place and remember what it felt like. That was you back then, but it doesn't need to be you right now. You have changed and grown and learned what to trust and who to trust. You might ask Jesus to help you find your confidence in Him and His promise that He's not going anywhere, ever.

What fears are standing in your way? Do you struggle with a fear of failure? Maybe it's a big, public screwup that you're afraid of, or perhaps it is the thought of an even bigger private mess-up that is holding you back. Whatever it is, do the work to determine where that fear came from, so that you can then ask God to help you sort out what is true and what is not true and what a good plan might be moving forward to break free from those fears.

Fearlessness is the opposite of being ignorant of the circumstances. It's saying, "Notwithstanding the circumstances, I serve a mighty Lord, and He can handle this."

Run after fearlessness with all you've got.

KEEP SHOWING UP; YOU'RE THE ONLY YOU THERE IS

Do not be anxious about anything, but in every situation, by
prayer and petition, with thanksgiving, present your requests to
God. And the peace of God, which transcends all understanding,
will guard your hearts and your minds in Christ Jesus.

PHILIPPIANS 4:6–7

I went golfing not long ago for the first time in a couple of decades, and I saw some golfers in front of us breaking their clubs in half because they ended up needing to take a swing or two more than they were hoping for. I guess a lot of people fear mediocrity. They think of mediocrity as being small and insignificant and getting the participation ribbon as an embarrassment rather than an acknowledgment. But what if we came up with a new perspective and set of metrics for what a win looks like? What if we flipped the script and understood that God is not keeping score the way we might be tempted to, but He delights in our attempts? Run up to someone today who is trying something new and say to them, "Wow, look at you! You participated and had the guts and the grit to show up. Way to go!"

For some, this is how they interact with people every day, yet when it comes to themselves, they can't seem to access these same affirmations. But Jesus doesn't grade our lives on a curve. He doesn't compare you to Einstein, or some famous movie star, or a country singer, or Mother Teresa. Instead, God delights in you for your "you-ness." I know that's not a word, but it ought to be.

All your giftedness and your peccadillos, your insecurities and your joys—keep bringing them to the world every day. Own them and wear them with confidence and humility. Acknowledge right now that God is over the moon about you. Give yourself a high five for trying something new, making the call, initiating the conversation, spinning the wheel. Your early steps and attempts may not seem like very much in the world's eyes, but every time we shrug our shoulders at what God is doing in and through us, we turn the wine back into water.

**God has created something magnificent in your life.
Have a little patience with yourself as He continues to
unfold it so you can release it into the world.**

THEY WILL KNOW YOU BY YOUR SUPERNATURAL LOVE

And if the Spirit of him who raised Jesus from the dead is living
in you, he who raised Christ from the dead will also give life to
your mortal bodies because of his Spirit who lives in you.

ROMANS 8:11

It is easy to be mistaken about who Jesus is in our busy and sometimes fraught lives. Oftentimes, we mistake Him for somebody who is measuring and keeping a tally of our good conduct. I promise you this: Jesus didn't come to die so we would behave better. He doesn't want us to be a better version of ourselves either; He wants us to be a more accurate reflection of Him.

You are the best evidence to the world that Jesus was raised from the dead. People can see it in the way you choose to treat those you encounter, the way you exhibit grace that is otherworldly, love that is supernatural, peace that is unexplainable. What does your life look like to the people around you? Do you look like Jesus, or are you just another person running scared and trying to get ahead?

You will know you are tending your fire well, for example, if you find yourself putting a check on how you treat the clerk at the store. Sure, you got in the wrong line at checkout, and it feels like your clothes are going out of style while that clerk makes painfully slow progress and turns a couple-second task into a couple-minute one. Do you go with your first instinct and blow a gasket? Or do you find another response and be kind and patient?

If you want a different outcome than what you've been seeing, adopt a new strategy. Decide in advance that you're going to go with your second reaction, not your first one. Your lesser angels will send in retread plays whenever frustrating situations happen, but your better angels will shake it up and remind you that the power that lives within you is the same one that raised Jesus from the dead. That plays out in your life when you respond to people differently than you might have before.

Get out there, chase after some whimsy, and go make a difference.

THERE IS NO LOVE WITHOUT JUSTICE AND NO JUSTICE WITHOUT LOVE

Whatever you do, work at it with all your heart, as
working for the Lord, not for human masters . . .
COLOSSIANS 3:23

We have all had someone who has disapproved of us. I remember the first witch doctor case I was going to take to trial in Uganda, which was a death-penalty case against a man who had attempted to sacrifice a child. Human sacrifice involving children was a practice common in the country, but no one had ever taken on a perpetrator before because they thought the witch doctors would put a curse on them. But these were innocent children, I was a lawyer, and not taking action was not an option.

As I was preparing to leave for Africa, a leader in a faith community said, "You know what? I just don't approve of what you are doing."

At first, it felt like a gut punch, but as I thought about it more, I realized I was not looking for this person's approval; I wanted to make a difference.

I remember writing myself these words that night: "There is no love without justice and no justice without love."

Certainly, get good counsel for your life, but don't get head-faked by what the peanut gallery has to say. Keep your eyes fixed on Jesus and do the things He said to do. And if you're trying to figure out if this is something God wants you to do, take the apostle Paul's advice: check everything you do against Scripture. You will always find that Jesus wants you to love people extravagantly, extensively, decisively, and exhaustively.

Whatever it is God has made you good at, do it with gusto like you're serving the Lord. He has given us approval to do beautiful, lasting, and sometimes unlikely things. We can stop asking everyone else for permission.

**Look for God's approval today,
not everyone else's agreement.**

LOVE HAS ALREADY PAID THE BILL

> A certain man gave a great supper and invited many, and
> sent his servant at supper time to say to those who were
> invited, "Come, for all things are now ready."
> **LUKE 14:16–17** NKJV

Someone took me to a fancy restaurant, you know, the kind where they put the napkins in your lap and call you Monsieur and Madame. After an appropriately long wait so we would know they were in no hurry, the waiter brought leather-bound menus to our table, and I opened mine to a long list of fancy entrées. This place had everything: surf, turf, the works. I knew it must be nice, because I couldn't make out from the over-the-top descriptions what any of the items were. "Carefully and meticulously tossed shina soba, lavished with camembert topping." Did that mean mac and cheese?

The most concerning part was that there was no price next to any of the entrées. I guessed this was one of those places where, if you needed to ask what it costs, you were at the wrong place. Can you imagine if I had opened the leatherbound menu at the fancy restaurant to see it full of dishes like pancakes and waffles, Cap'n Crunch cereal, and a quart of milk? It would be my dream ending for the story but perhaps not what my host intended for me.

Jesus invites us to a banquet. On the menu aren't just the things we want but the things He wants for us. He has already covered the costs, because even if we were the richest person in the room except Him, we wouldn't be able to pay even a small portion of the bill for our lives. We can go to the table He has set for us and order off the kids' menu or bring our own bagged lunch, or we can bring our appetite and choose something more special that Jesus has prepared for us. The entrée He has for us is a life packed with meaning, laden with opportunity, and steeped in love.

Here's my question: Are you settling for crumbs when God has something much bigger for you? God wants to fill you with more than you could imagine for longer than you could hope for.

**Start looking through God's eyes at what He's setting
in front of you and accept His invitation today.**

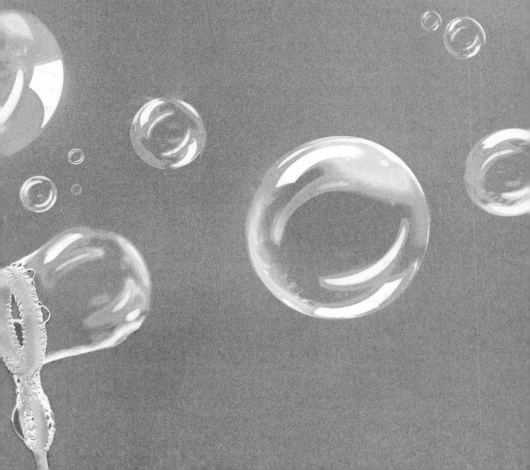

FEBRUARY

SLOW IS FAST AND FAST IS SMOOTH

He says, "Be still, and know that I am God; I will be exalted
among the nations, I will be exalted in the earth."
PSALM 46:10

I have a pretty short list of things I have wondered about that I haven't experienced yet. Some of you wonder what it would feel like to take a ride in a hot air balloon or scream with your hands over your head on a roller coaster. My list is a little different. I wonder what it would feel like to fall into a pit of quicksand. I know it sounds crazy; quicksand is not the kind of thing you find close by. Nevertheless, I have been studying up, so I will know what to do if it happens to me by mistake or I do it on purpose. From what I'm told, the more you try to get out of quicksand, the deeper you sink in. It also doesn't occur very quickly, but "slow sand" doesn't sound as ominous, so they keep the name for the movies.

Feeling stuck and slowly sinking is not an experience limited to being stuck in quicksand. We can find ourselves stuck in relationships, jobs, and even a crisis of faith where we feel like we're slowly sinking with no escape route. Here's a pro tip if you fall in quicksand: don't try so hard to get out. I know it sounds counterintuitive, but perhaps you need to push back against the alarm bells you have been listening to that tell you to strive, hustle, and look like you have it together. Stop trying so hard to make it all happen right now; our instinct to overachieve may be killing the authentic version of us that is itching to impact the world over a longer time.

Admit it, we can get so busy trying to help God that we miss out on what God is already doing in and around us. If our head is constantly down, striving and hustling, we might miss the new opportunities, the delightful new friendships, and the beauty God has placed in our paths. I am not saying that tenacity or hard work is bad. These can be good and honorable and redemptive. But for some of us, we need to come clean and realize that, in all our thrashing about, we are sinking down more in the muck than we are getting out of it. If this is you, God's word might be this: *Be still, and know that I am God.*

Be honest with yourself as you reflect and ask whether there are areas in your life where you might be trying too hard. If you are feeling stuck, experience some freedom today by pausing a bit. Let God's wind blow your hair back like a dog with its head out the car window.

**Replace striving with peace today, and you
will experience more freedom.**

YOU WON'T FIND GOD ON GOOGLE MAPS; GOD IS WHERE THE HELPERS ARE

The King will reply, "Truly I tell you, whatever you did for one of the least of these brothers and sisters of mine, you did for me."
MATTHEW 25:40

In Matthew 25, Jesus dropped us a pin for where we can always go to meet Him. If you are looking for Jesus, He says you need to find hungry or thirsty people, sick or strange ones, naked people, or people in jail. If we are going to do this, we are going to need to get out of the church building after we worship together, leave the home where Bible study is held, and engage the opportunities around us. God said He doesn't inhabit dwellings made by men, but He always inhabits those people who are doing His work.

Find opportunities to get in the blast radius of where Jesus said He can always be found. If our heads are on a swivel and our hearts are willing, we can lift our eyes and see the opportunities that already have us surrounded. Feed hungry people by loading up your car with food and handing it out under bridges, in parks, or where the homeless gather. Give thirsty people water bottles. Find a hospital or eldercare facility where sick people could use a boost. Seek out someone you have avoided because they were a little strange and engage them with love. Give your best to someone who needs clothing. Visit a jail or prison and befriend a couple of inmates. You don't have to wonder whether it will work out well or not; Jesus said He will be there every single time as you do these things.

The crazy part of the economy God operates within is that He does not need our help, but He does want our hearts. When you find your place to serve, don't make a big deal about it. You don't need matching hoodies or wristbands or team cheers. There is nothing wrong with these things, but don't let them distract you from looking for what it is God was up to long before you arrived on the scene. Replace the selfies with "them-ies" (again, not a word, but it should be).

See what God has invited you into and come as an engaged guest, ready to assist in what He is already doing rather than coming with a plan for how you would do it better.

DON'T EDIT THE EXTRAORDINARY OUT OF YOUR LIFE

Do not add to what I command you and do not subtract from it,
but keep the commands of the LORD your God that I give you.
DEUTERONOMY 4:2

It is tempting to add a little of our own life experiences, viewpoints, and opinions to what God has to say in the Scriptures. It's even easier to trim out the parts we don't fully understand or would rather not obey.

Thomas Jefferson did a little cutting and pasting of his own when it came to the Scriptures. He literally took a razor and cut out the parts of the Bible involving anything seemingly supernatural. This included the resurrection. Jefferson kept the moral lessons and principles but would cut out the miracle just before the lesson. Not surprisingly, the Jefferson Bible is pretty thin.

I haven't found any verses of Scripture I disagree with, but there are plenty I haven't applied to my life in the way God would have me do. I have not always loved my enemies, remained patient and kind, or not wanted to even the score after being wronged.

How about you? If you can identify with this, perhaps you are as tempted as I am to edit out the miraculous or extraordinary things God could be doing in your life. Resist the urge to get an invisible razor to cut out the hard parts of faith or paste in parts that aren't there.

Often, it is easier to wrap our minds around a leadership or life principle than to fully embrace the miraculous, but don't take the bait. The parts of Scripture that are hard for us to embody are often the most powerful ways God can show the world His awe-inspiring, whimsical love.

Assume God is at work in, through, and around you as you live out of the fullness of what His Word says.

Keep your head on a swivel; God is constantly on the move.

BE THE RIGHT KIND OF CRAZY

Two demon-possessed men coming from the tombs met
[Jesus]. They were so violent that no one could pass that way.
"What do you want with us, Son of God?" they shouted. "Have
you come here to torture us before the appointed time?"
MATTHEW 8:28-29

When Jesus arrived at various locations by the Sea of Galilee, it wasn't long before big crowds showed up. Jesus sometimes paddled out in a boat to teach, and other times He went up a hill. On one hillside, He famously taught about how the people listening could be like lights in the world and how a city on a hill could not be hidden. It wouldn't be a reach to imagine He gestured toward the only city on a hill nearby, which was straight across the lake from where He was standing. That city was called Hippus and was part of ten Greek cities spread across a couple of countries, referred to collectively as the Decapolis.

Just below Hippus, there were a couple of violent, crazy men hanging out among dead people and pigs. Dead people, pigs, and non-Jewish people they called Gentiles were huge triggers for the Jewish people, who had strict laws about not being around things they considered unclean. These guys represented all the bad stuff and more. They were also demon possessed, so there was that too.

The religious people thought Jesus' message was just for the Jews, so when Jesus sent the demons into a herd of pigs and cured the men, it was a big deal. What the history books show is that these men went on to carry the message of Jesus not only to the Jewish people but also to everyone else. This was the flag-in-the-sand moment, when Jesus' message spread from Hippus to the entire region, and it all started with two crazy guys Jesus healed in a cemetery on the other side of a lake.

Jesus doesn't just pick fishermen who can't get the nets on the right side of the boat. He uses people as unlikely as me and you and two crazy guys to carry His message to the world. Even if you are not living in a cemetery full of pigs by a lake, God has uniquely picked you to carry His message.

Bring the right kind of crazy to everybody around you today, and trust that through you, God will impact the world. It has happened before. Just ask two guys standing by the lake.

UNLOCKING OUR AMBITIONS

Let your eyes look straight ahead; fix your gaze directly before you.
PROVERBS 4:25

I wanted to learn how to pick a lock. I'm not sure why really. Perhaps it was all the time I have spent at San Quentin prison where I have taught classes for many years. So I purchased a transparent lock on Amazon, found a bobby pin, and started carefully pushing up on each of the pins, just like in the movies. And it worked; eventually, the lock sprang open. Then I decided to make it a little more challenging and put the lock underneath the table, so I couldn't see its inner mechanisms as they moved. Opening a lock this way takes a lock picker's touch.

Oftentimes, we need a lock picker's touch when it comes to getting moving on our ambitions. With every new year come new ambitions. The trick is figuring out how to take an ambition you've been batting around and act on it. I get it. There can always be more planning and tweaking, but at some point, we need to decide it is ready enough. Otherwise, what should be a launchpad for your imagination will begin to look like a parking lot for your ideas. If your ambitions are stuck behind bars, perhaps what you need to do is hone your lock picker's touch and move forward, even when you can't see how everything will work. Ask yourself, *What is keeping me from rolling my idea out right now?*

Sure, it's understandable to hit some snags and say, "I'm out." Maybe you were looking for validation you didn't receive. Perhaps someone you trusted let you down or you harbor a confirmation bias against success that you haven't understood. I get it. But stop giving other people and your own latent biases that kind of control over you and your beautiful ambitions. If what you are looking for is applause, join the circus, but if you are looking for meaning and purpose, lift your ambitions up to Jesus and get after them. You are not going to get it right all the time, or even most of the time, but keep at it. Remember, you are developing a lock picker's touch.

Write down four or five ambitions you've been thinking about, and drill down into them. Don't just say, "I want to be happy." Ask yourself, *What does happy look like to me?* Does that mean winning a million dollars? Does it mean learning to sail? Does it mean reading a book?

GET BACK ON TRACK SO YOU CAN LOVE EVERYBODY ALWAYS

Whoever conceals their sins does not prosper, but the one
who confesses and renounces them finds mercy.
PROVERBS 28:13

Depending on your faith tradition, there are different parts of the year you might use as times of self-evaluation and spiritual preparation. One way to do this is to look at what's working and not working in your life.

Ask yourself, *How is my life working for the people around me?* If your life isn't working for the people around you, I've got a news flash for you: it isn't working for you either. For example, you might have a career that takes you everywhere but home. Maybe it's working great for you because you get to be in many places, receive loads of affirmation, and have the money to pay the bills, but if you ask the people you live with, "Is this working for you?" you might be surprised by the answer. It is an honorable thing to provide for your family, but ask yourself if you are providing them what they actually need, which is you.

Don't be put off by discovering there are areas in your life that would benefit from a tune-up. If you try to conceal those areas, you'll not only be hiding from others but also hiding from yourself. And you will miss out on a great chance to experience the clarity that comes when you are honest about where you are. At the same time, doing this exercise doesn't need to devolve into an existential crisis. Keep yourself focused and develop a plan. We need to see things clearly in our lives so we can begin to understand them and bring them to Jesus.

Is there something you need to confront? Is there something you need to confess? Maybe finances have been hard, or relationships, or perhaps it is your day job. Name it, take a close look at it, and bring it to Jesus. And remember that you're bringing it to Jesus not only to confess but to find safety. You're seeking His help in developing a plan to get back on track.

**Remember, your goal is to be ready and
equipped to love everybody always.**

BREAKING UP CAN BE FOR THE BEST

Now the Lord is the Spirit, and where the Spirit
of the Lord is, there is freedom.
2 CORINTHIANS 3:17

Did you know the Declaration of Independence is only thirty-six sentences long? Isn't that awesome? Think about it. We broke up with an entire country and started a new one in fewer sentences than there are in one of my shortest devotional messages. What if we took a cue from that document and reduced a few of the things that feel large and overwhelming in our lives down to a more manageable size? If we did, I bet it would be easier to understand and then break up with some of what has been taking up too much space.

What do you need to break up with today? Maybe it's a job. Sure, it was great the day you started and may have been a perfect fit for who you were at the time, but, wonderfully, you have changed and, predictably, the job didn't, or it didn't change enough to keep up with who you turned into. Break up with it. I know it feels like a huge decision, but chunk up some of your hesitations into smaller pieces and it won't feel so big. The people you love will still love you. If you have kids, they're not going anywhere either. The sun is still going to rise in the morning, and God will still protect you. You won't even need thirty-six sentences to pull off a perfect breakup with your job. Perhaps you can communicate it in just two words and slip yourself and your boss a note: "I quit."

It is not just careers; it can be other obstacles we allow to get in our way. Is your big fear that you will be misunderstood? Is it an insatiable need for approval or acceptance or success or popularity that is tripping you up? If you find yourself paralyzed in your decision-making or constantly giving people too much agency over your life, it may be time to part ways with these habits.

When we break up with a few of the distractions that have been drowning everything out, we create a beautiful, quiet spot where God can meet us once again. Find that place.

**Ask God what He wants you to leave behind as
you continue your adventure with Him.**

YOU HAVE TO FACE YOUR GIANTS BEFORE YOU DEFEAT THEM

David said to Saul, "Let no one lose heart on account of
this Philistine; your servant will go and fight him."
1 SAMUEL 17:32

If you have read the Scriptures, it is likely you have heard of the Philistines. The Philistines were a seafaring nation of people who tried to invade Egypt, but it didn't work. So they moved a little bit north and started taking ground in the southern part of Israel, now called Gaza. Israel's army went out to meet the Philistines in the Valley of Elah. Goliath, a Philistine who stood nine feet, nine inches tall, would storm out onto the field twice a day to taunt the Israelite army and challenge them to send out their biggest warrior to fight him in a winner-takes-all battle.

Meanwhile, Jesse was living a humble life raising sheep. Several of his sons had joined the Israelite army to battle the Philistines, leaving only the youngest, David, to take care of the sheep. One day, Jesse asked David to take food down to his brothers, and when David got there, he saw the Israelites shaking in their armor.

David had gotten pretty good at throwing stones with his sling as he learned to protect the sheep, and he decided to take on Goliath's challenge. Saul's armor did not fit David, so he walked out on the field without it. David didn't start hurling rocks at the whole Philistine army; he picked the biggest target and hit what he was aiming for right in the forehead. You remember how the story ended, with David winning the day.

Giants come in all types. Perhaps fear of failure has led you toward a habit of deferral. Whatever your giant is for you, name it. You need to know what you are up against before you can do something about it. What giants are keeping you shaking in your shoes today? What feels like a nine-foot-nine obstacle standing between you and the big life filled with the kind of joy and peace and freedom Jesus talked about?

Call out that giant today and take the shot.

GOD DELIGHTS IN US AND LOVES KEEPING HIS PROMISES

The Lord delights in those who fear him, who
put their hope in his unfailing love.
PSALM 147:11

Guess what? God doesn't just like you. He delights in you and wants you to delight in Him. I like more things than I don't by a wide margin. I like sunny days and surfing and puppies, but the idea of delighting in something the way God delights in us simply doesn't compare. How God feels about us is far beyond happiness, pleasure, or approval.

The Bible is filled with many terrific stories that show us the way God delights in us, including one about spies. After a generation of wandering around in the desert, twelve spies were sent out from the Israelites' camp to check out the land God had promised them. Ten of the spies came back bad-mouthing the land. The Israelites were filled with fear as the ten reported how much bigger and more fortified everyone was in the promised land and how they wouldn't be able to take it.

But Joshua and Caleb returned with a completely different take and were brimming with hope. They didn't bemoan their condition; instead, they rejoiced in it. Here's why. They knew God delighted in them and in the land He had led them to. In their words, "Because He delights in us, the land is as good as ours already." They were full of faith and vision.

Sadly, the Israelites listened to the ten spies who were afraid to enter into what God had promised them. Forty years later, after the ten spies had passed on, Joshua, who by then had taken over for Moses, led the next generation into the promised land.

What seems improbable, perhaps even impossible in your life right now? What are you leaning away from? Don't allow your joy to be skipped by a generation or two.

Lean in. God delights in you, and He loves keeping His promises.

DISTRACTIONS ARE A DIME A DOZEN: STAY FOCUSED ON GOD'S AMAZING PLAN FOR YOUR LIFE

Do not conform to the pattern of this world, but be
transformed by the renewing of your mind.
ROMANS 12:2

The thing that most often keeps us from growing is distraction. I wrote a book called *Undistracted*, and much of the difficulty I had in finishing it was, wait for it, I got distracted. I have a friend, Ian Cron, who talks about the Enneagram, which is a personality trait–identifying system. The person who identifies as a seven in this system is described as the enthusiast, and, not surprisingly, all indicators point to me being a flaming seven. He tells me it's ironic that someone wired like me and so prone to distraction would write a book called *Undistracted*. This was not by mistake. Authors get to write the books they need, and they are not alone in this. You also get to give yourself the reminders you need every day.

Try this exercise: ask yourself, *What are the things distracting me right now?* Write those things down and keep track of them for one week. Next, come up with a practical strategy to deal with your distractions. For instance, if emails are distracting you, declare email bankruptcy in an auto-reply and step away for a while. If the television is interfering with your focus, unplug it.

Satan doesn't want to destroy you; he wants to distract you. And the reason is simple: destroying you is one and done, while distracting you is the un-gift that keeps taking.

If you are distracted, the people around you will be distracted, your family will be distracted, and the other people you love will be distracted. And the cost that is heavier than all that? When we are distracted, we lose sight of the path God has laid out for us.

If you're struggling with distraction, figure out who and what the culprits are and put some guardrails around them.

Whatever it is that eliminates the distractions and gets you to the feet of Jesus, do lots of that.

WHY NOT DAZZLE GOD WITH YOUR FAITH?

[Jesus] said, "I tell you, I have not found such great
faith even in Israel." Then the men who had been sent
returned to the house and found the servant well.

LUKE 7:9–10

The eighth miracle Jesus performed of the thirty-seven discussed in the Bible involved a centurion who had a servant who was paralyzed. Instead of waving his arms or shouting commands about what could be done about the situation, the centurion simply told Jesus, "All You need to do is say the word and he'll be healed." That centurion had an amazing amount of faith. As a matter of fact, Jesus only said He was amazed two times in the Scriptures, and this was one of those times. And with that, the centurion went back to his house and found the servant healed.

Isn't it terrific that faith could do that? Jesus has been doing and continues to do miracles in the world all the time, but we often overlook what He is doing because we don't recognize, as the centurion was able to, that Jesus has all the power needed to direct all the outcomes. It would take some real faith in the most challenging of circumstances you are facing to declare, "You know what, God? All You would have to do is say the word." But why not start doing just that today?

Do you have a strained relationship? Ask Jesus to just say the word. Is it a difficult job you are struggling with? Acknowledge that all Jesus needs to do is say the word. Is it haunting shame from the past that is dogging you? Ask Jesus to say the word.

So, what will it be for you? What is it that you need to be trusting God for today? Where do you need to bring all your belief, even though everything inside of you would otherwise feel like you were asking for too much from God? Try replacing that thought with a desire to amaze Jesus one more time.

**We are just one short statement away from
getting there: "Jesus, say the word."**

HUMILITY DOESN'T KEEP SCORE. WHEN YOU PUT OTHERS FIRST, EVERYONE COMES OUT AHEAD

Greater love has no one than this: to lay down one's life for one's friends.
JOHN 15:13

One of the things God constantly does is drop people into our path whom we need to help us grow. He doesn't pass us messages; He gives us friends. Sometimes the people we're doing life with are the ones we need to grow the most through and with.

Think about how God could help you go deeper in your friendships. Think of it as an exercise of worship. Here is the math: God makes you, He makes somebody who ends up in your circle of friends, and then He allows you to grow deeper in that friendship if you are willing to risk it. Laying open your life can look like a lot of things. You can do it by confessing things to each other you need to confess or by getting real about the things you need to get real with, and pointing out where you see Jesus showing up in your life and your friends' lives.

Now that we've looked at laying open our lives, let's consider what it means to lay down our lives. John said, "Greater love has no one than this, that someone lay down his life for his friends" (ESV). What is something practical you can do for a friend today? In Jesus' reverse economy, laying down our lives for our friends sometimes means taking cuts to the back of the line rather than taking cuts to the front. Perhaps it will look like putting somebody else in front of yourself to let them receive the praise and accolades. This isn't false humility; it's true humility.

As we grow in our faith, we will see the opportunities both to lay open our lives to our friends and to lay down our lives as we elevate our friends above ourselves. This will help us grow closer to God.

**Every selfless act of love is a decalaration of faith.
Lay down your life today in words and deeds,
and everyone will know what you believe.**

ALWAYS LOOK FOR HOPE IN THE HARD TIMES

I know how to be brought low, and I know how to abound. In any and every circumstance, I have learned the secret of facing plenty and hunger, abundance and need. I can do all things through him who strengthens me.
PHILIPPIANS 4:12–13 ESV

It is easy to be grateful when things are wonderful, but we need to learn how to be grateful when times are difficult too. I had a lodge I worked on building for twenty years burn to the ground. It was gone in twenty minutes. That was a gut punch. Everything that was special to our family, every memento, every photograph, all gone.

It probably wasn't a house that burned down for you. Maybe it was a relationship, or perhaps it was a career choice. Whatever it was, how do we stay grateful in the middle of these big setbacks we all face in our lives?

It's about perspective. Hard things happen for any number of reasons, but one of the outcomes is that we get the opportunity to be more conformed into God's image. That sounds like a big theological statement, but here's the deal. You and I end up looking a lot more like Jesus when we recognize our desperate need for Him—and tragedy exposes our needs.

Sure, we have all experienced disappointment, but rather than remaining glum, we need to learn how to get past the moment of total letdown and move on toward the bright hope that Jesus offers for the future. If you want a different outcome, adopt a different approach when you encounter a setback. Ask yourself, *How can this difficult thing equip me for the next hard thing?* Then get curious about what God will do next.

Don't try to cover over the blemishes in your life or green-screen them. Finding gratefulness in the middle of hard things doesn't mean ignoring those hard things but instead engaging them and harnessing all the good that can be found as we grow and change. What are some of the hard things you've experienced? What went wrong, and how did you feel about it?

Is there more you can learn from that experience as you move forward?

MAKE LOVE YOUR STRATEGY

Dear friends, let us love one another, for love comes from God.
Everyone who loves has been born of God and knows God.
1 JOHN 4:7

I haven't found one thing in the Scriptures that directly addresses dating. Isn't that strange, given there's no more common thing that intersects our lives with joy and butterflies and anticipation? Dating can be a complicated push and pull where we feel drawn to someone and curious about them but at the same time terrified, not knowing where things are leading. We shuffle our feet a few relational inches closer to a person and see if they reciprocate by shuffling theirs closer toward us or further away.

As soon as Sweet Maria walked into the room when I was in law school, I was smitten and, within minutes, was picking out names for our kids. Because she was in the same room, I suppose I just figured we were dating. I went over the top on Valentine's Day with an eight-foot-tall card with a one-foot-square stamp I had made. It turns out this was way too much way too fast, and Sweet Maria initiated the "let's just be friends" discussion.

I wanted to be respectful but had a much deeper relationship in mind. Without considering how over-the-top this would be once again, I showed up on Maria's doorstep with all the materials to make a teddy bear. My motives were noble. I wanted her to like me, I wanted to do something together, and I wanted it to be something that would make a great story later. This was my version of dating, and it involved big, grand, over-the-top expressions of affection and near restraining-order-level pursuit.

Sure, love can sometimes be this way, but it doesn't always have to look grand. If we simply bring our authenticity to every new and existing relationship we have, we'll know we are walking in the same love Jesus pursues us with.

Keep bringing the most authentic version of who you are to all your relationships. This is the grandest of all gestures you could ever make and the greatest gift you could give to the people you love.

**Make love your strategy. And don't forget
to bring along a little whimsy!**

A NEW CAMERA ANGLE ON YOUR LIFE

*And why do you worry about clothes? See how the flowers
of the field grow. They do not labor or spin.*
MATTHEW 6:28

We often adopt behaviors in our lives without knowing why. Usually, our odd behaviors point to deeply held, underlying beliefs, unmet needs, and deep biases. Here's an example.

Two high values in our family are independence and not imposing on anyone to meet our needs. That's why Goffs drive our own cars. We also take our own Uber rides and travel alone in a state of absolute contentment and delight. We do this because we want to be independent of other people's timetables and schedules and ever-changing circumstances. It's not only that we are impatient, but we also just want to do things in the order we want. We don't want to get to the airport too late or too early; we just want to get there without having to think about it.

When I am speaking at events, I only fib about one thing: when my return flight is leaving. I always say it is wheels up an hour before it really is. That way whoever ends up driving me to the airport isn't racing along the interstates, with me barely making it. I think if I don't give someone else control of my schedule, I can avoid a lot of unnecessary stress (and I'm right).

Here is why all this maneuvering is a problem for me and might be a problem for you. God wants us to be dependent on Him. It's easy to confuse being self-reliant in the right ways with being independent when it comes to the exercise of our faith. Here's a trick for distinguishing between the two. Take a look at how you spend your days, the nature of your conversations, the ways you engage with or avoid people. Are you impatient or bored or indecisive? I promise you these are attached to something else in your life. The path toward faith is best lived when we understand why we are doing what we are doing.

**Find out why you are spending your days engaging with
or avoiding people in certain ways, and you will find a
new camera angle on your life worth exploring.**

ASKING FOR HELP TAKES COURAGE

Come to me, all who labor and are heavy laden, and I will give you rest.
MATTHEW 11:28 ESV

The thing about having kids is that it is an eighteen-year experiment of life in constant motion. This was especially apparent to me one day when I was once again in a hurry and attempting to get our young children into their seats in the minivan. Most days it felt like I was trying to get three spring-loaded snakes into a can—once I got them inside the can, I needed to put the lid on fast—so I became adept at buckling the last one in while, in the same movement, sliding the minivan door closed as I started making my way back around the car to my seat. This day was no different, and as I slid the door closed and started my sprint to the driver's seat, I suddenly realized I could go no farther. I couldn't quite figure out why. My eyes followed my shirt out toward my arms, and I noticed four of my fingers had just been closed inside the door.

All of this happened in an instant, and the sensory pain signals had not yet made it from my squished fingers to my brain. But all of that would soon change. My mind raced over how I could fix the dilemma. I knocked on the window to get the kids' attention, then tried to wave and point to the door handle, which was out of my reach. The kids waved back at me and smiled. It was a long couple of minutes before Sweet Maria pulled into the driveway, saw me hanging from the door, and set me free. I don't hold a grudge, but I don't miss that minivan.

Are you feeling stuck and unable to get free? It's probably not your fingers shut in a door, but maybe it's in your relationships or your faith or your ability to dream big dreams. Perhaps you have so many things going on that you can't seem to come up for air, much less call out for help. And even if you did, it feels like no one would hear you, or they would just wave back at you like my kids did. The fix isn't to grow more arms to juggle more activities or extra legs to run even faster. Why not ask a friend or two for some help?

Make a call, send a text, tell a friend about the pinch points in your life. God opens doors all the time.

GOD LOVES OUR NEW BEGINNINGS, NO MATTER HOW MANY

Therefore, if anyone is in Christ, the new creation has
come: The old has gone, the new is here!
2 CORINTHIANS 5:17

Have you ever had a dream or ambition and told yourself, "Okay, I'm going to begin working on this really soon," only to defer or dismiss the idea yet again? Perhaps you immediately started thinking about all the times you've tried before. Maybe, like me, you set your sights on doing the Keto diet but ended up doing the Cheeto diet. Or maybe you were looking for permission or approval and bailed on the launch of a new ambition before you even rolled out your rocket ship of ideas onto the tarmac. Or maybe you revisited all your weaknesses and thought, *Who am I to be pursuing something this big and grand?*

I have thought of all these reasons not to act and dozens more, and probably you have too. What has helped me is to reframe what I am doing not as failing again but starting again, and this makes it somehow easier for me to press forward. It feels like finding a cheat code for life and a fresh start on a worthwhile endeavor.

I love that God's promise to us is this: we are new creations. When Paul was writing his letters to the Corinthians, he explained to the new church that we aren't stuck with all the previous versions of ourselves.

God made us so we could fall asleep, wake up, and try again. In this way, each day is a beautiful reset. When you start over, don't allow yourself to pitch a tent in the shame or regret or disappointments of the days behind you. Say to yourself, "New day, new me. I'm beginning again."

Pick something big and grand and lasting, and give it everything you've got. Don't allow yourself to be distracted with half measures, moving the peas around on the plate doing something small and safe and temporary.

Remember, you are the daughter or son of a huge and dangerous and infinitely kind God, and we don't need to scare so easily anymore.

HOW COMFORTABLE ARE YOU WITH UNCERTAINTY?

By faith Abraham, when called to go to a place he would
later receive as his inheritance, obeyed and went, even
though he did not know where he was going.
HEBREWS 11:8

Some people have a strained relationship with ambiguity. They want all their ducks lined up, alphabetized, and labeled. They don't like hearing something is "just around the corner," because it means they can't see it right now and this rattles them. But the truth is, most of us can't forecast the future with absolute accuracy, so we are going to need to get a little more comfortable with uncertainty than perhaps we have been.

I was talking to a few friends of mine who love certainty and spend quite a bit of time organizing their lives and everyone else's around them. They were describing how wonderful they thought it would be to go into a room they saw advertised where there is no sound, no light, and that holds a salty zero-gravity pool where they can float and experience complete sensory deprivation. They grinned and rubbed their hands together, imagining with delight this experience of absolute certainty about what would and would not be happening around them.

If they could have read what was in the thought bubble over my head, they would have seen that this sensory-deprivation room described Dante's nine circles of hell to me. No interactions? Zero gravity, floating in an abyss? Total silence and absolute certainty? No thanks. I would rather be left in a darkened room they called the "ambiguity room," and have someone whisper to me, "There might be someone in the room with you" before they locked me in. Just imagining the countless possibilities would light me up.

What's your relationship with ambiguity? You might be like me and love ambiguity. My wife, Sweet Maria, on the other hand, would say she and ambiguity are seeing other people. Whether you love it or hate it, we have to learn to live with a lot of uncertainty in our lives. We don't get to find out in advance how things will work out. In fact, the only thing that is certain is that we will be at the feet of Jesus someday and have both a delightful and difficult conversation with Him about our complicated and unpredictable lives.

If God wanted to make everything in the future plain and fully transparent to us now, He certainly could, but He usually doesn't. So today, as we encounter ambiguity, let's learn to delight in the possibilities uncertainty provides for us to grow and learn.

Uncertainty leaves just enough room for hope and whimsy.

START PURSUING PURPOSE BEFORE YOU TIP OVER TRYING TO FIND BALANCE

It is useless for you to work so hard from early morning until late at night, anxiously working for food to eat; for God gives rest to his loved ones.
PSALM 127:2 NLT

Many of us ask how to balance work and life, and it is a fair question. There was a time when I spent so much time trying to find balance in my life I almost tipped over. Balance implies a set of scales with equal amounts of working on one side and pursuing pleasurable things—like vacations, time off, down-time—on the other side. You put some work on one side of the scale, and you need to balance it out with some fun on the other side. What if, instead of trying to find balance in our lives, we pursued purpose?

I totally get the desire to find this kind of balance. We can't spend all our time working. Think of work as carbs. I don't know anyone who eats a stack of pancakes every day. Eventually, you would stroke out or explode if you did. Your life isn't Waffle House, and you were not designed to be open for business twenty-four hours a day, seven days a week. We do need to put some guardrails around the time we spend working. But I'm not sure trying to equal out the scales between work and play is the answer. The truth is, only faith-infused purpose has the ability to be the great balancer.

Replacing balance with purpose is not for rookies and it isn't going to happen with the snap of your fingers. It will start, but not end, with identifying the most purposeful endeavors for you to invest your time in. Ask yourself if what you are considering is loving and lasting. Does it merely change your life for the better today, or could it impact someone else's life forever? When your activities check these internal boxes, you will tap into an entirely new economy of reward and joy and peace that transcends work, activity, and acknowledgment.

At some point we need to get off the hamster wheel and take agency in our lives to pursue more of what is purposeful and lasting. As we do that, we will find a new definition of balance in our lives.

What will be your next courageous move toward purpose that will outlast you rather than balance, which is certain to escape you?

DON'T BREAK PEOPLE; START THEM

Therefore encourage one another and build each
other up, just as in fact you are doing.
1 THESSALONIANS 5:11

Across from a retreat center I own, we built an equestrian facility. I didn't really know much about horses, but I knew I wanted many of them so our guests could take them on trail rides and participate in equine therapy and feed them carrots. What I didn't realize initially was that having fields and hay and a big barn was a magnet for people who wanted to give away their horses to me. When the first horse arrived, I thought, *How nice of them*, until I tried to put a saddle on the new addition and take it for a ride. Then I received a second and a third and a fourth "free" horse. Each one was worse than the previous one. Good heavens, my "free" horses all bucked and jumped and snarled, and when I did eventually get a saddle on them, I was everywhere, including up and off. I immediately understood why these unruly horses were given to me for free; they were so mean they made hornets look cuddly.

One day, I pulled our farm manager aside, shaking my head, and said, "We've got to break these horses and get them in line." He squinted his eyes at me in the afternoon sun, pushed his cowboy hat up a quarter inch like the sage cowboy, Curly, in *City Slickers*, and corrected me with the kindness of Mother Teresa and the wisdom of Solomon. "Bob, we don't *break* horses here. We *start* them."

Starting a horse is about getting them familiar with the rider, the saddle, the inputs, and the expectations; it's about building a relationship. Breaking a horse, on the other hand, is about compliance rather than about trust. That'll preach.

I wonder what would happen if we started more people in their faith rather than thinking we need to break them of their bad habits to comply with Jesus. My guess is we would form stronger bonds with God and one another if we did. God wants a relationship with us based on trust and built over time. We should do the same with the people we encounter today.

Don't break people; start them.

WILL YOU DRAG ANCHOR OR SET THE HOOK?

We also glory in our sufferings, because we know that suffering
produces perseverance; perseverance, character; and character, hope.
ROMANS 5:3-4

Sweet Maria and I live down by the water in San Diego, and we enjoy watching the boats pull into the harbor. They will usually circle the bay a few times as they decide where they will drop their anchor. What happens after they have picked their spot distinguishes the experienced sailors from the novices.

There is a big difference between the boats that just drop anchor in the bay and those who set the hook. While both approaches look the same on the surface, merely dropping the anchor will give you a big piece of metal on the sand that has not dug into anything. Everything is fine until the winds and waves come. Then these boats drag their anchors and end up on the beach in front of our house. On the other hand, the captains who set their hooks dig their anchors into something firm by putting the boat in reverse and giving the anchor a tug when they arrive in the bay. When the storms come, the anchors, which are already dug in, don't drag to shore. In fact, these anchors dig themselves in farther and provide greater protection and staying power the more the wind and waves rise.

You might be facing headwinds right now. But you get to decide whether you will drag anchor or set the hook. It is easy to drag anchor if you are spending time with people who are acting religious but don't follow Jesus. Sure, everything might look the same on the surface, but when you only have the appearance of faith, when the winds come you'll easily be dragged away. If you set the hook, however, if you dig deep and develop more than a surface-level faith, you'll be ready for the storms. And the apostle Paul said the suffering you endure will produce perseverance, and perseverance is going to result in character, and character has the power to turn into hope in your life and in the lives of the people around you.

Much of what we experience we won't fully understand this side of heaven. The promise of Scripture is that if we dig deep in our faith and continue to endure, God will make something useful out of our pain.

In short, set the hook.

YOU WILL BE REMEMBERED FOR YOUR LOVE, NOT YOUR OPINIONS

A wise man will hear and increase learning, and a man of understanding will attain wise counsel.
PROVERBS 1:5 NKJV

I'm a lawyer. I get paid to have opinions, and I have hundreds of them. I have opinions about things I know a lot about and opinions about things I know very little about. The hard truth is no matter how confident I am, many of my opinions have proven to be misplaced over time.

It's easy to confuse those opinions emerging from our hopes or imaginations with those born of truth and supported by our experience. While there's no shame in telling people what you imagine might be a good idea, don't confuse your gut reactions with a well-formed, trustworthy, truth-based, and experience-based opinion.

If someone is suffering deep grief or sadness, it would be a kindness to say, "This must be such a painful time for you," rather than, "I know exactly how you feel." Get real with yourself and with the people around you. Talk about what you know to be true rather than what you think might be true, and people will trust you more when it really counts.

Wise people are easy to identify, because they usually won't bring a boatload of opinions into conversations. They will talk about their lives, their experiences, and their faith. And they won't just talk about what they think God's position is on a topic; they will point it out in Scripture so you can be sure.

The only thing as good as finding wise counsel is being a person of wise counsel. And every new day is an opportunity to try out for the part.

It's your move.
Will you be a wise person who hears and learns today?
Or will you settle for merely having a lot of opinions?

DO YOU NEED A TALLER HEDGE?

Above all else, guard your heart, for everything you do flows from it.
PROVERBS 4:23

I took a break from speaking and canceled everything on my calendar at the beginning of one year. A short time later, it seemed the world stopped spinning from a pandemic, and the remaining events I still had were also canceled. I was sad about the problems being faced worldwide but also was silently delighted to be out of work. One event in Arizona, though, didn't cancel, for some stubborn reason. I guess they didn't have the same problem everyone else on earth had, or maybe they were just pretending not to. I didn't feel comfortable getting on a commercial airline, and I estimated the drive from San Diego to Arizona would take only a couple of hours, so I decided to hop in the car. Boy, did I miss that one. After a punishingly long drive to the event, I spoke that evening and then turned around and drove home, finally pulling back into San Diego at 3:00 a.m.

The next day I was beat and went out on my back porch to take a nap on the warm bricks. I am not usually a napper but I was whupped. I was in one of those deep, drooler sleeps when something woke me up. It was a woman standing over me. "I'm here to render help," she said, locking her intense eyes with my groggy ones. My first thought was, *Who in the heavens are you?* And my second thought was, *Why are you speaking in King James English?*

Evidently, this overeager woman had been walking down a path behind our house on the bayfront when she looked over my hedge, saw me lying down, and assumed I was having a stroke. She jumped over the hedge separating the walking path from us, ran across my lawn, up some stairs, across another lawn, up some more stairs, and up to the porch, where she was ready to do mouth to mouth and chest compressions on me. What I learned that afternoon was this: sometimes what we need is a taller hedge.

We all experience trespassers in our lives. Some come in the form of in-laws, or strangers, or fans, or work colleagues, but we need to find a way to guard our tender hearts and lives while these people are navigating their complicated ones.

What hedge do you need to grow a little taller in your life? What boundaries would serve you in your faith and your relationships?

ASK GOD'S HELP WITH THE BLUE-SKY PIECES

And we know that in all things God works for the good of those
who love him, who have been called according to his purpose.

ROMANS 8:28

When you're working through something tricky in life, one good way to organize your thoughts is to think about it like a jigsaw puzzle. The first thing you do when assembling a puzzle is find the four corners, right? In the same way, when you're stuck on something in your life, the first thing you should do is pause and think of the top four objectives or organizing principles you value, such as kindness, availability, loyalty, and honesty. Or these might be faith, family, friendships, and finances. The list of your high values will no doubt be much longer but try to pick just four things that are toward the top.

Once we find the corner pieces, most of us try to find the edges. Think of the edge pieces as the connecting ideas and habits you either have or want to have to help you go after the important high-value corner pieces you are aiming for.

Next, if you are like me, you will find the puzzle pieces that look like a fence or a large tree or something else recognizable and sort them into piles of matching pieces. Think of these piles as your ambitions, encompassed in the space between the high-value corners and the connecting ideas and habits in your life. Think of the individual pieces in the piles as the skills or opportunities you already have.

This is a systematic and helpful approach to understanding what we are doing and why we are doing it. When we try to move forward without understanding those things, it's like starting a puzzle with the blue-sky pieces, which leave you without identifiable clues about how they fit into the bigger picture and will likely just leave you confused.

What puzzle are you working on in your life? Perhaps it is a confusing relationship or what you do for a day job. Don't just drop off all the pieces with Jesus and expect Him to put it together for you.

**Use the life experience and intellect God has given you to
get as many pieces as you can in the right place, and then
ask for His wisdom to sort out the blue-sky pieces.**

WHEN YOU'RE LEARNING SOMETHING NEW, LET LOVE LEAD

Don't let anyone look down on you because you are young, but set an example for the believers in speech, in conduct, in love, in faith and in purity.
1 TIMOTHY 4:12

I remember taking my first deposition as a young lawyer. A deposition is where lawyers ask someone questions under oath while a stenographer types everything they say. At the beginning of the deposition, there are admonitions given to the witness about how the deposition process will unfold. Sage lawyers have these admonitions memorized, but I was new to it. I had practiced for hours the night before, but I just couldn't memorize all the words, so I decided I would write everything down, give the page I had written to the witness, and have them sign it. It would be simple enough, right?

I walked into the room filled with twenty grizzled lawyers. I put my carefully worded document on the table, slid it across to the witness, and said, in my most confident voice, "I usually have people sign these admonitions in advance of the deposition instead of having me say all of them for the record." Another lawyer picked my paper up, gave it a quick glance, and threw it back my way. "We came here to answer questions, not sign papers," he growled. "What's your next question?" Yikes. I didn't have a next question, or a first one. I didn't know whether to scratch my ear or wind my watch and, honestly, I could have used a pair of large Depends.

Something akin to this happens to all of us regularly; the only difference is the context. We take on a big challenge or risk trying something new, and it takes a horribly wrong turn. Your rookie moment might happen in a board room, or you might have a house full of bored kids. When you feel outmatched, ill-prepared, and like you are going to flop, think about Paul's encouragement to his young friend Timothy. Be an example of kindness, love, faith, and purity.

Don't let anyone look down on you because you are new or young or inexperienced at something. Do your best and remember to be kind to the people you encounter, especially if they are also trying something new.

Today is your day to roll out your extraordinary brand of kindness into the world.

EMPTY TALK CAN WOUND, BUT WISE WORDS CAN HEAL

What goes into someone's mouth does not defile them, but
what comes out of their mouth, that is what defiles them.
MATTHEW 15:11

My people came from County Cork in Ireland. It's an area where potatoes are grown in fields laced with four-leaf clovers and is also the location of Blarney Castle. There is a piece of limestone that was put into a wall of Blarney Castle ages ago, and the story that circulated is if you kiss this stone, you get the gift of gab. In other words, you can talk for a long time about things that don't matter.

The story goes that every time Queen Elizabeth sent one of her people to capture the castle, they became engaged in such long conversation about nothing that the capture was never completed. The Queen kept asking for reports and became so frustrated that she said, "It's all blarney!" And the rest is history.

I know a couple of people who I am guessing must have given that stone a kiss or two, because they spend a weird amount of time talking about things that just don't matter. All talk is not bad. We all know a few "verbal processors," people who need to talk through information and emotions to make sense of them. Then there are others who just talk way too much and about things that don't matter to anyone but themselves. Pro tip: don't be that guy. When it comes to your speech, exercise discretion, because Jesus said what comes out of our mouths matters.

I also know a couple of people who feel weirdly comfortable being as quiet as the dead and not contributing anything to a conversation. Don't be that guy either. Instead, be known as a person who is both candid and measured with their words. Your words last much longer than the conversation, and they can bless or scar the people on the receiving end.

Whether you have the gift of gab or tend to be stingy with your words, spend your time today talking about things that matter. Filter out all the filler from your conversations.

**Talk honestly about faith and feelings and setbacks,
and watch your relationships go deep and wide.**

READ THE ROOM AND REMEMBER LOVE COVERS ALL

If an unbeliever invites you to a meal and you want to go, eat whatever is put before you without raising questions of conscience.
1 CORINTHIANS 10:27

I was speaking at a terrific school filled with amazing educators in North Carolina, and afterward the headmaster offered me a ride back to my hotel room. I got in the passenger side and was surprised to see a brake pedal by my feet. It turns out he also teaches students how to drive. As we drove down the highway, my headmaster friend told me about the things he teaches the students and how he can tap the brakes from the passenger side when necessary to give a student driver an extra margin of safety. As I looked down at the brake at my feet, my curiosity got the best of me, and I couldn't resist the urge to step on it. I'm not sure why, I think that's just what flaming Enneagram sevens do when they are curious. It turns out I hit the brake a little too hard, and we shot across several lanes and ended up stopped on a wide spot on the road. I wasn't sure if we were still friends at that point, but he asked me what I was thinking. I tried to come up with an intelligent answer, but the fact was, I was just curious and wasn't thinking my actions through.

Paul wrote a cautionary chapter to his friends in Corinth about thinking their actions through before they did something they would regret. Their situation had to do with someone inviting them over for a meal. He didn't tell them to depose their host before they ate; he didn't say to ask if the food was gluten-free, or soy based, or vegan, or vegetarian. He said to eat whatever was put before them and not get hung up on theological questions about what food was okay and what food was not.

What are a couple of the conversations you have found yourself in where you've said something you regret or pushed someone away simply because you didn't think things through before you spoke?

Are your words and choices drawing people toward Jesus and giving away more love and acceptance, or do you need to lightly tap the brakes and rethink your approach?

IF A DOOR CLOSES, LOOK FOR A WINDOW

Give thanks in all circumstances; for this is the
will of God in Christ Jesus for you.
1 THESSALONIANS 5:18 ESV

We talk a lot in faith communities about open and closed doors. I'm not a big fan of that way of thinking. It's easy to encounter a difficulty while pursuing a desire you perhaps have had for ten years and then bail because you think, *God closed a door.* For instance, how many times have you heard, "I applied to medical school, but they said no and so God must have closed that door"? It's a more likely bet that some guy named Billy, MD, said, "You can't get in." That doesn't mean you shouldn't go to medical school; it just means you're not going to medical school where Billy works. Be slow to elevate someone's misplaced, inaccurate, or lame decision to divine revelation.

Stop thinking in terms of open doors and closed doors. That kind of thinking will just mess with your head. God is not that cryptic. He doesn't play hide-and-seek with our hopes and dreams. Instead, He places beautiful desires in our hearts to love people and to engage the world. Don't turn all this beauty into a cosmic game of rock, paper, scissors.

I do some work in a place called Luzira Maximum Security Prison in Uganda. I began to visit this prison after I tried a case and placed a guy on death row. When you go into Luzira, you enter through a barred door, and then that door closes behind you before you can go through another door. If I were waiting for God to close one door before He opened another door, I'd always be stuck just outside of where I wanted to be, never fully entering in. Walk through the doors in front of you, and if one seems closed, find a window that is ajar to climb through.

Open doors are great, but when you encounter a couple of closed doors, remember why you started down that path in the first place and renew your resolve to get there.

Find a couple of friends who will help you stay on track and remind you who you are and the contribution you are about to make.

MARCH

WHAT IF WE JOINED IN A CONSPIRACY OF KINDNESS AND ADVOCACY?

I have no one else like him, who will show genuine
concern for your welfare. For everyone looks out for
their own interests, not those of Jesus Christ.
PHILIPPIANS 2:20–21

These days we hear the word *conspire* quite a bit. But did you know the original word doesn't mean a sinister plot hatched in a dark, windowless room? It simply means taking a deep breath together. Isn't that beautiful? A conspiracy doesn't have to involve political intrigue; it can be about two people taking a breath together and supporting each other. What if we joined in a conspiracy of kindness and advocacy?

Imagine your spouse or loved one is dissatisfied with their job. Instead of dismissing or ignoring their feelings, ask them what opportunities they believe are just out of reach and how you can support them in reaching those goals. If you know a college student struggling to choose a major, ask them what truly excites them, what they love, what sparks their interest. Or maybe you know a child having trouble making friends in school. Ask them about what kind of friend they're looking for and suggest fun activities they could engage in together. By helping others discover their ambitions, we unlock something beautiful in them and in ourselves.

Take a genuine interest in the lives and aspirations of those around you, whether they are good people, people you disagree with, or even difficult people. Identify a few people, and ask them what they want, what they love, and what genuinely excites them.

Look beyond fleeting desires like a vacation or a new car and explore ambitions that will have lasting impact. You will be joining the conspiracy of kindness and advocacy and offering God's love in a way people don't often see it.

Now it's your turn. Take a breath, take time, and take an interest today in the people God has already dropped in your path.

WE MIGHT NOT KNOW THE WHY, BUT WITH GOD WE KNOW IT'S GONNA BE GOOD

I am the LORD, the God of all mankind.
Is anything too hard for me?
JEREMIAH 32:27

During His three years of public ministry, Jesus performed thirty-seven miracles, depending on how you count them. But counting the miracles is less important than trying to understand what was happening around the miracles. For instance, everyone remembers the first miracle, when Jesus turned water into wine at the wedding. What happened just before the miracle? According to the Scriptures, Mary told those present to do whatever Jesus told them to. These are words worth keeping in mind as we navigate our lives. Do whatever He tells you to do in your career, in your relationships, in your decisions, even if you don't understand why.

Doing whatever Jesus tells us to do will require that we stop merely talking about what He meant and start doing what He said to do. This means cutting whatever ropes have us moored to the safety of the dock and pushing out a little further into the sea of opportunities He has made available. Will it be risky? You bet. Is there a possibility you will fail? Certainly. Will you question whether you are making the right moves? Of course you will. Do it anyway.

Listen today for what Jesus is telling you to do. While it may not be mystical or mysterious or what you first think of when you think of the miraculous, it will be important. I may have never seen anyone raised from the dead, but I have seen dead marriages restored, dead-end careers abandoned, and relationally dead people engage others with the kind of selfless love that can only come about through the power of God.

While we may not initially understand what Jesus asks us to do, most of the time clarity comes later. In our obedience, we allow God to use us to achieve something miraculous.

Today is your day to be a miracle in someone's life. Sure, the outcome will be uncertain, but do whatever He tells you to do anyway.

GOD DOESN'T WANT PERFECT HUMANS; HE WANTS HUMAN HEARTS

God chose the lowly things of this world and the despised
things . . . so that no one may boast before him.
1 CORINTHIANS 1:28–29

In high school, I used to get free rides on the bus to the ski slopes. My deal with the bus company was that I could ride for free if I would clean up the trash on the bus before I left. I was returning from a ski trip one day when I found a beat-up book on the floor of the bus that said on the cover *Good Book*. *I could use a good book*, I thought. As I flipped the pages, I found the same stories repeated a couple of different times by guys named Matthew, Mark, Luke, and John. I didn't know if those four guys were on a sports team together or what, but I thought having them each telling the same stories made it an average book, at best. I figured this must be the kind of book my friend Doug would read, since he was the only Christian I knew then.

Later that week, Doug and I were out in the woods shooting our pellet guns at some old cans. When I noticed Doug wasn't walking next to me any longer, I turned around and saw him standing behind a tree and pointing his pellet gun at me. I had apparently become the next can. When I turned to defend myself, he shot me. We covered the hole in my belly with a piece of paper and old leaves and ran back to his house. Doug got some tweezers and poured mouthwash into the wound. As he did, he started telling me about Jesus. I didn't think you were allowed to shoot pellets at your friend if you went to church, but if that was part of it, I was in. We eventually got the pellet out, put a Band-Aid on it, and swore we'd never tell anybody. I figured, if God could let a screwed-up guy like Doug follow Jesus, maybe there was room for an even more screwed-up guy like me.

Sometimes we think it is the person who has it all together that God will use in big ways, but the opposite is often true. Paul said God uses foolish things (and people) so that no one can boast.

**Who is someone you can thank for loving you the way
Jesus does, even if they haven't been perfect?**

DON'T GET DISTRACTED BY ASSUMPTIONS; SURPRISE EVERYONE BY PRESSING ON

Fools base their thoughts on foolish assumptions, so their
conclusions will be wicked madness; they chatter on and on.
ECCLESIASTES 10:13–14 NLT

I have spent most of my life moving fast. I think fast, eat fast, and talk fast. For two decades, I even commuted from San Diego to Seattle and back home for work each day. That was a lot of moving around by any measure. Nowadays, I travel overseas most often for our nonprofit, Love Does, which operates in many places, such as Afghanistan, Somalia, Iraq, and a dozen other countries. I try to get to the various countries to check in regularly and, as a result, I still do a lot of moving around, so much so that my family often assumes I'm not home. That is an assumption I am trying to change.

You can tell a lot about what's going on in your life by the assumptions people start to make regularly about you. If you sense things are off and not quite what you want them to be, a good thing to do is identify the most common assumptions people make about you and start working to change them.

If you have a reputation for being short and abrupt with people, blow their socks off by slowing down and asking them how they are or even getting the checkers or chess set out and playing a game with them. If you have a reputation for being predictable and stoic, dye your hair pink and hand out balloons to your coworkers.

Not long ago, I was at home on the back porch midweek, something that historically hadn't happened often. My son Adam called on the telephone and asked what I was doing. I told him I was just at home on the back porch, and he said, "I assumed you would be at home." What a change from how things used to be! He didn't see me silently pumping my fist in the air. I had started to change my life and, as a result, I had changed the assumptions my family made about me. I'm not fully there yet, but I am on my way.

**What assumptions can you change about your life that will bring
you closer to God, closer to your family, and will help you become
a more accurate reflection of who you want to become?**

THE BEST REPLACEMENT FOR DISTRACTIONS: PURPOSE

Set your mind on things above, not on earthly things.
COLOSSIANS 3:2

When our kids were little, I walked into the house one Saturday morning to see them staring at the TV. "Hey, you guys, what are you going to do today?" There was no response. "Kids? Hello? What are you guys up to?" Lindsey or Richard might have mumbled something in response, but it was hard to hear over the noise of the TV. Later that evening, we had a family meeting around the dinner table. We knew we needed to change, because the television was becoming a distraction from more important things. We decided as a family that we'd give up our television for a few months to see what happened. And you know what? There were all kinds of things that filled up the space that was left!

The kids started a lemonade stand on the weekends. They hopped over the wall to play with the neighbor kids and invented their own plays and performances. Sure, they got bored a few times, but that was okay too. Having time to be bored made them think about other ways to spend their time and helped them come up with some of their most creative ideas yet.

The Bible talks about how important it is as followers of Jesus to keep our minds and hearts clear from the things that would distract us from the very best things God has for us.

After a few years we decided to have a television in our house again, because it was something fun for the kids to do with their friends. But you know what? This time we weren't distracted by it.

You may not have to give up television like we did, but it's helpful to ask yourself, *What is distracting me? What is taking me out of conversations or relationships? What things might be getting in the way of my being creative?* Once you figure out what those things are, lose them. You will find yourself setting your mind on things above, rather than on earthly distractions.

Today is your day to put a flag in the sand and start all over again. Kick distraction to the curb and fill your beautiful life with whimsy.

TEST THE OPINIONS YOU TAKE TO HEART

Now the Berean Jews were of more noble character than those in Thessalonica, for they received the message with great eagerness and examined the Scriptures every day to see if what Paul said was true.
ACTS 17:11

I was talking to a guy I had just met and somehow we got on the topic of sailing across the Pacific. He told me about the course I should steer to get the greatest amount of wind and what sails I should bring to go as fast as possible. He even had opinions about the food I should bring along. It was both funny and fascinating because I had done the crossing twice and have given very little thought, if any, to many of the things he felt strongly about. When there was a pause, I asked how long he had been sailing. He looked a little surprised and shot back, "Oh, I've never left Iowa."

You will probably meet many well-intentioned people who will offer their opinions on almost every aspect of life. If they are giving you relationship advice, have them tell you about their experience with friendships and dating. If it is financial opinions someone is floating your way, ask them to tell you about their experience in wealth and investments. Test everything. You're not trying to pick a fight; you are attempting to gather context for their comments.

If the guy with loads of opinions about relationships is on his third marriage, it gives you context to understand his opinions better. If the one giving you financial advice is just emerging from his third bankruptcy, he might have some great things to offer but probably isn't the guy you want to get wealth-building advice from without some serious grains of salt added to those opinions. Putting opinions through this kind of stress test will give you more touch points so you can decide how much weight to give them.

The same holds true when it comes to matters of faith. You will hear lots of opinions about how to follow Jesus more closely, how to serve people better, how to be kind and loving, and when to rest. Weigh how much stock to put in their advice by the outcomes you see in their lives. Test everything against what the Scriptures say.

Be careful whose words you take to heart.

JUST ON THE OTHER SIDE OF CONFESSING OUR FAILURES IS A BOATLOAD OF FORGIVENESS

Whoever conceals his transgressions will not prosper, but
he who confesses and forsakes them will obtain mercy.
PROVERBS 28:13 ESV

In the lead-up to Easter, we enter the season of Lent, a time of preparation, self-evaluation, and reflection. During this season, take a close look at your life and consider what's working and what isn't. If you are like me, there are aspects that are no doubt going great and others that might need some attention. This can be hard to do sometimes, as it isn't always comfortable revisiting our failures. Still, we need to face these realities head-on if we are to keep moving forward.

Think about what you've found challenging recently. Confess it to God and perhaps to a safe friend or two, and then make a plan to change a few things. We need to be proactive in addressing the areas in our lives that aren't working. Insight without action won't produce any change.

If you find yourself struggling to figure out how to address the gridlocks in your life, as most of us do, bring these things to Jesus. Drill down and get as specific as you can. Don't do this for God—He already knows—do it for yourself so you can keep it real. Ask Him for guidance and clarity on what needs to change.

This is your opportunity to come to Him honestly, seeking His help to mend what isn't working to find a path forward. There is a boatload of forgiveness waiting just on the other side of your admission of failure.

**Don't wait any longer. Bring your concerns to
Jesus today, and work toward becoming the
humblest and most aware version of yourself.**

ASK GOD FOR HELP AND SEE WHAT HAPPENS

*Immediately the boy's father exclaimed, "I do
believe; help me overcome my unbelief!"*
MARK 9:24

A father brought his son to Jesus and said, "My son is suffering. He's having seizures. He falls into the water, and he falls into the fire." You can imagine the kid was probably pretty beat up, and I bet his parents were too. The boy's dad explained, "I took him to Your disciples, and they couldn't fix him." Jesus' disciples were in the middle of an argument at the time with the teachers of the law. I wasn't there, but I would guess they were arguing about why they weren't able to cast out the demon that was causing the boy's issues.

I wonder if the disciples were so distracted by wanting to prove a point they became separated from their ability to make a difference in the moment. Perhaps they had become so wrapped up in their arguments they forgot what it was all about: bringing a needy young man directly to God.

The Gospel of Mark says Jesus cast out the demon from the boy and told His disciples that it could only have come out through fasting and prayer. Casting out a demon is outside of my life experience, but what is within my life experience—and maybe within yours—is what Jesus pointed out was at the core of what was happening: the disciples' focus was off. Instead of being distracted by seeking an audience's approval, they needed to be focused on cultivating a greater dependence on God.

Do you have something in your life that seems insurmountable? Whatever it is, go straight to Jesus with it. Follow His instructions for becoming more dependent on God through prayer and fasting. Prayer and fasting aren't about tradition; they are about acknowledging and obeying God.

Skip a meal or two. Let the hunger pangs remind you of your deep need for God. Then pray for help. It doesn't need to be a fancy prayer laced with big words. Sometimes "help me" is the most honest prayer you need to say today.

Ask for just a little more faith, and see what God does next.

UNDERSTANDING THE PAST FREES US FOR OUR FUTURE

Am I now trying to win the approval of human beings, or of God? Or am I trying to please people? If I were still trying to please people, I would not be a servant of Christ.
GALATIANS 1:10

When I was in kindergarten, the school put me in a program for gifted and talented kids. I can only imagine how proud my parents were that I had been selected. Unfortunately, I only lasted for one half of the first day. They kicked me out of kindergarten, not just for the day, but forever.

I had never been to school before, so when I ended up in the principal's office and my mom came and picked me up, I was only aware in a general way that I was in trouble. After a long time inside the house alone, I went into the backyard where my mom was midway up a ladder with a paintbrush, painting the stucco. She looked down and said, "I am so disappointed in you," and then went back to painting. We never spoke about it again.

Now, I'm not faulting my mom for being disappointed. She probably had every right to be. But what was inadvertently planted in my life that day were seeds of rejection. I began to view love as something that could be given or withheld based on my behaviors. I saw love as a weapon and not a gift.

If you can identify with experiencing this feeling, pull on the thread a little bit, and ask yourself, *Where did this sense of rejection come from?* We don't need to be afraid to ask the ones we love, "Hey, here are the parts of what happened that I don't understand. Tell me about it." That doesn't sound like an accusation; it feels like somebody taking a step toward understanding. Do it with your palms up and be generous with your forgiveness while you do.

Paul wanted his friends in Galatia to remember that the approval they should pursue can only come from God. And that is what we need to keep in mind on our journeys out of past rejection.

Let God rewrite the narrative and then let His love and acceptance point you in a new direction as you cultivate a new sense of fearlessness and dependence on Him.

WE'RE ALL MESSY SOMETIMES; EMPATHY IS A BALM WE ALL NEED

Rejoice with those who rejoice; mourn with those who mourn.
Live in harmony with one another. Do not be proud, but be willing
to associate with people of low position. Do not be conceited.
ROMANS 12:15-16

There are countless ways people express their joy and hundreds of words in various languages that mean "joy." I'm not a big fan of trying to figure out words in different languages, probably because I'm still wrestling hard with English. I had to giggle a little when I read that in German, the word *freude* (pronounced "froy-da") means joy. There is, however, another German word, *Schadenfreude* (pronounced "shah-din-froy-da"), which sounds similar, and also like a disease a little penicillin might clear up if you caught it early enough. But *Schadenfreude* actually describes someone taking joy at another person experiencing setbacks and bad circumstances.[1] You know this type of person. They may try to cover their twisted delight by feigning concern, but not far under the surface you sense they are quietly pleased things have melted down for someone else. One last hard-to-pronounce word and I'll be done. This word is the opposite of *Schadenfreude*, and the word is *Freudenfreude* (pronounced "froy-din-froy-da").[2] This word is about the joy we get when we see other people succeed.

Paul talked to his friends in Rome about both ends of the joy spectrum and our personal reaction to other people's joy or suffering. He encouraged us to lean into empathy. Empathy requires a willingness to identify with the painful parts of someone's story. Standing with our friends in their messy times, without assuming we are there to fix things, shows them the kind of love and solidarity we all need. And celebrating our friends' big successes, surprise wins, and victories not only lifts them, but also lifts us.

Here is where we get practical. Is there someone you need to celebrate with today? Give them a call, send them a cake, or decorate their car. None of us will be remembered for our accomplishments; we will be remembered for our love.

Make your move today. Let your joy, empathy, and celebration off the leash and see what happens in your life and in the lives around you.

THE PHONE IS RINGING—PICK UP AND ANSWER THE CALL!

We constantly pray for you, that our God may make you worthy of his calling, and that by his power he may bring to fruition your every desire for goodness and your every deed prompted by faith.
2 THESSALONIANS 1:11

What does "calling" mean anyway? We have all heard people talking about how God "called" them to do this or that. I always cock my head to the side when I hear a young guy tell me "God called me to go surfing in Tahiti" in a support letter. Hmm. . . . We all get a lot of calls on our phones, but what does it mean to be called in the way people in our faith communities describe it?

Paul usually used this reference to mean doing what is most important to God. In the book of John, the disciples asked Jesus a similar question: "What is our work?" Think of this sincere question as a different way of asking, "What's our calling?" Jesus told them that their work (calling) was to believe in the One God sent. Stated differently and simply, Jesus told His friends our work, our calling, our focus is faith and relationship with Him.

Here's the thing. While according to Jesus our work and calling is faith, He also created for us big and wondrous lives filled with the opportunity for purpose and meaning and massive creative contributions. By being available to the things God has already placed inside you—the interests and gifts that point to the bigger callings simmering within you—you honor God. Go be a doctor or plant seeds at a farm, bag groceries or study the cosmos. These can all be honorable efforts. You shouldn't live someone else's calling or let others dictate to you what yours is. Aim for living a life that aligns with what you have been uniquely invited into with your gifts and abilities and interests and uncertainties and peccadillos.

Remember, it is not selfish for you to pursue the beautiful ambitions God has uniquely called you to—catching whimsy is strategic. Don't shy away from the hard work required to share your message with the world.

Good luck and saddle up. Go live a life worthy of the calling you have received.

SOMETIMES GETTING A LITTLE MUD IN OUR EYES IS JUST WHAT WE NEED

[Jesus] spit on the ground, made some mud with saliva, and put it on the man's eyes. "Go," he told him, "wash in the Pool of Siloam" (this word means "Sent"). So the man went and washed, and came home seeing.

JOHN 9:6-7

My grandfather was from Ireland and owned a pub. When I was young, he would make us root beer floats, and we would raise our glasses mostly filled with ice cream to toast each other. "Here's mud in your eye," he would say and throw back a big swallow from the glass, leaving a coating of foam and ice cream around his lips. I didn't put it together until decades later that this toast referred to Jesus healing the man born blind.

There are several places in the Scriptures where Jesus engaged with blind people. Sometimes He touched them, other times He just spoke and their sight was restored, and still other times He put mud in their eyes. I bet these interactions left not only the blind people but also the onlookers more than a little puzzled.

We all have questions when things happen in our lives that we don't understand. Sometimes, the puzzling things serve as an opportunity for God to show up and even show off His massive bent toward grace. Other times, He simply wants to be quietly grieving alongside us about the brokenness in this life. The tricky thing is that sometimes—a lot of the time—we won't know for sure why things are revealing themselves in our lives the way they are. It is natural for us to want to find a shelf to put information or circumstances on to understand them. But the truth is, sometimes we need to build a new shelf for things that don't make sense to us and be prepared to never know the exact reasons for them on this side of heaven's veil. I bet the blind guys in the Bible who were healed would agree.

Think about a situation in your life that you don't understand. How might God be using it to display His love and grace? And if you can't see that clearly right now, how might you choose to trust God with it?

God is on the move in your life today. Be attentive to where He is showing up. Here's mud in your eye!

LOVING LIKE JESUS MEANS LIVING WITH INTERRUPTIONS

A furious squall came up, and the waves broke over the boat, so that it was nearly swamped. Jesus was in the stern, sleeping on a cushion. The disciples woke him and said to him, "Teacher, don't you care if we drown?"

MARK 4:37-38

Life can be filled with deep meaning, purpose, and expectation, or it can be filled with just a lot of busyness. Sometimes, amid the frantic nature of life, when we're being pulled in multiple directions, it helps to slow down and reflect on a few of the miracles God has done.

Several of the Gospels tell the story of people Jesus healed of sickness or demons or unclean spirits. Despite Jesus having done many miracles in the daytime, the Gospel of Matthew suggests that people tracked Him down at night too. Maybe you can relate. Do you work hard all day and then find yourself spending much of the evening doing more of the same? I know Jesus didn't mind the interruptions, but for many of us, while we are delighted to help, it can be a lot of a good thing—kind of like we're drowning in chocolate.

Often this happens at a time when I don't have a surplus of energy or time to give away. What do we do when we feel exhausted from a busy day, and yet people find us with their needs? I have found the best way to respond in the moment when I feel tapped out is to bring those burdens, as well as the difficulties others bring to us, directly to Jesus rather than shoulder them myself. But how, exactly, do we do this?

First, invite Jesus into the depths of what might be happening in your life today. If you are feeling a little beat up or beat down by the number of people coming to you for help, get specific about how you are feeling and what specifically is a pinch point in your life. Next, bring the need that just came your way directly to Jesus and see what He does next to give you the strength you need to continue to show up for the people around you.

Jesus isn't looking for stoic, go-it-alone people. He wants us to find our resilience in our dependence on Him.

LET LOVE BE THE LOUDEST VOICE IN YOUR LIFE

*Don't have anything to do with foolish and stupid arguments,
because you know they produce quarrels.*
2 TIMOTHY 2:23

I can't watch scary movies. I'm not sure why, because I know it is all make-believe and filmed in a studio with actors, using ketchup instead of blood. But, still, it doesn't feel like entertainment to me; it feels like trauma is about to happen. On the few occasions when I did watch a scary movie, I was up all night afterward with my eyes wide open, wondering who or what was hiding under my bed or in the closet. Deeply disturbed, I would think to myself, *What was that noise? Am I safe? Did I lock the doors?* It made me want to sleep in a suit of armor holding a baseball bat—you know, just in case.

Because I know scary movies are bad for me, I don't watch them. It is not a moral judgment or religious belief, or because I am more temperamental or fragile or broken than others. I just know scary movies distract me on a good day and freak me out on a bad one. The same is true about arguments. Sure, I could enter into controversy—I was a career trial lawyer and that is what we do—but I know the effect it has on me, so I don't do it anymore. The math is that simple.

Arguments can be hard to avoid, though, especially these days. I don't know if there has been another time in history when there have been so many people with so many scary videos and inflammatory opinions to share. For many of us, it is a parade of the horribles on a loop every week, and being surrounded by these things can feel like watching scary movies. It puts us on edge and can be a huge distraction. I applaud people's zeal, even when it's misplaced, but I just know getting caught up in arguments will distract me from things that matter more, like hope, joy, love, and anticipation. I don't listen to the loudest voices anymore; I listen to the truest ones.

**Who and what are you allowing yourself to be exposed
to that is not good for you? When you catch yourself
engaging those things, take a step back.**

FORGIVENESS IS AN UNLIMITED RESOURCE WITH JESUS

Then Peter came to Jesus and asked, "Lord, how many times shall I
forgive my brother or sister who sins against me? Up to seven times?"
Jesus answered, "I tell you, not seven times, but seventy-seven times."
MATTHEW 18:21-22

A friend of mine was having a surprise celebration. I tried to RSVP to the event a couple of times but didn't want to leave a message on the machine, because then it would give away the surprise. When I finally got through to the host a day or two before the special day, they said, "Oh, sorry, but you can't come." I got uninvited to one of my closest friends' gatherings, and I was a little miffed. Upon reflection, though, I realized miscommunications like these can happen easily. When something like this happens to you, resist the urge to overreact. Misunderstandings simply happen. Don't let them get you off course with people who are important to you.

I have come to realize that sometimes we need to revisit hurtful situations and recast what happened. One approach I have found helpful is to consider what the kindest explanation is for the misunderstanding, instead of assuming the worst one. Maybe the person who hurt us was distracted or made an oversight. By accessing this perspective, we free ourselves from judgment and hard feelings, allowing God's forgiveness to work in our hearts. I'm not suggesting we ignore heavy issues or let bad conduct slide. On the contrary, we should dive deep into these weightier matters but do it with humility and grace.

As we journey through this Lenten season, let's prepare our hearts by resurrecting something that has died—a broken relationship, a lost opportunity—and addressing it courageously and with kindness. Maybe give somebody a call and suggest starting over or addressing the past. Don't wait for others to take the first step. Ask God to work miraculously within you and in your relationships, and be brave enough to change. Will it be a little scary to do this? Yes. Is it possible it won't even repair what was damaged? Of course.

**Be willing to fail trying; it will change
something inside of you when you do.**

LOVE IS THE BEST LEGACY

One generation commends your works to
another; they tell of your mighty acts.
PSALM 145:4

My grandparents lived in a castle, and I had a room in it. Can you believe that? Sure, some people would call my grandparents' house in San Jose a tract house, but my grandparents told me they lived in a castle, and I believed it. They painted their castle bright pink with white trim, because they told me these were the colors of all true castles.

My grandparents were poor—I mean really poor—and lived on a few hundred dollars each month from social security. But as far as I knew growing up, they lived like a king and queen. Every night my grandparents would eat TV dinners. They told me someone in their castle, evidently named Swanson, made all their meals and delivered them on aluminum trays. I believed that too. I marveled at how they would peel back the tinfoil on their TV dinners to expose the apple cobbler so it would brown on top. With all of that processed frozen food, they both probably had more sodium in their bodies than Lot's wife, but from my vantage point, they were living the dream, in a castle, with all their meals prepared for them, and they also made me feel like royalty with the way they loved me extravagantly.

If I got the sniffles, I would get to spend the night at my grandparents' castle, and my grandmother would butter my toast, then cut it into triangles. She said the toast cut on the diagonal would make me better more quickly and that it was a long-standing castle recipe. It is now decades later, and whenever I get sick, I always butter my toast and carefully cut it into triangles. And you know what? It works. Love has this kind of healing power.

When you are gone, what is going to remain? What traditions and stories of love and hope will be your legacy? Take one more step today in creating the collage of memories that will become ground zero for the beautiful traditions you are remembered for. Make it the bread-and-butter expression of your faith.

**Every day is a new page for you to color in
with a handful of joy-filled crayons.**

DON'T FAKE FAITH; LIVE OUT LOVE

They said, "All right, say 'Shibboleth.'" If he said, "Sibboleth,"
because he could not pronounce the word correctly, they
seized him and killed him at the fords of the Jordan. Forty-
two thousand Ephraimites were killed at that time.
JUDGES 12:6

I have a couple of friends who moved to the South and started saying "Y'all" and "Welp" and "Golly" a lot more than they did before—which was never. It reminds me of a surprising story buried in the book of Judges about a pronunciation test used to see if someone was the real deal or just faking it. The blockade guards would ask the people trying to cross it to pronounce a word. If they didn't pronounce it correctly, they were killed on the spot. Pretty harsh, right? This wasn't just a random high-stakes quiz used on a few people; it was a big operation with even bigger consequences for the forty-two thousand men killed for pronouncing the word the wrong way. Forget cancel culture. These people were permanently canceled.

The word was *Shibboleth* (shib'–o–leth). The good guys pronounced the word with a "shib" sound, and the imposters pronounced it with a "sib" sound. The people were in the middle of a battle and needed to know who was really part of the group and who was just pretending.

This wasn't the last time language was used to check someone out. They did something similar in one of the world wars when the enemy learned to speak like Englishmen. They could tell it was the enemy by talking about trucks. In the UK, they call a truck a "lorry," so if someone posing as British said "truck," they were exposed as one of the bad guys trying to fake their way in.

In his letter to the Galatians, Paul said the thing that shows your faith is genuine is your expression of love. There is only one way to know whether someone truly believes, and that is seeing if they work out their faith in love. This is the Shibboleth of our faith.

People are listening to what your actions say, not just your words. What are you saying to the world today?

ALL YOU HAVE TO DO IS SAY YES

"Come, follow me," Jesus said, "and I will send you out to fish for people."
MATTHEW 4:19

When my son Adam was in high school, he learned how to fly an airplane. Adam got his pilot's license just a short time before his junior prom. Things have changed quite a bit since I was in high school. Back in my day, a young guy would summon all his courage and just ask the girl to go to the prom. In my case, it was more of a beg than an ask, and the conversations were brief. She would say no, and I would end up going solo. One girl, Paula, surprisingly did say yes, but then she got a better offer a few days later. These days the big ask-the-girl-to-the-prom moment is a battle of who can come up with the most over-the-top way to make the request. They are jokingly called "promposals." I'm not dissing the creativity on display; it is truly impressive.

Adam didn't have a girlfriend at the time, but there was one girl he thought would be the right one to ask, even though he barely knew her. He got permission from her parents (a gutsy move on their part) for him to take her up in his $100-per-hour rented airplane. As he flew over the beach at sunset, she saw the words a couple of his buddies had written in the sand in twenty-foot-tall letters: "Go to the prom with me?" I suppose if she had balked, he could have gone into a couple of steep dives and asked again, but all this got me thinking.

All Jesus said when He first met a handful of men He didn't know at all, from what we can tell, are two words: "Follow Me." It wasn't a silly prom He was inviting them to; it was a beautiful life. And it wasn't just for one night, but literally forever.

"Follow Me" isn't a promposal Jesus makes to us; it is a much bigger ask. Think about the extravagance of God sending us sunrises and sunsets and calm lakes and roaring seas and ultimately His Son. His pursuit of us is much more than any promposal; it is the ultimate act of creativity and imagination and sacrifice ever put on display, and all we need do is say yes.

Jesus is inviting you on an adventure with Him. Are you ready to go? And who do you want to bring along with you?

LET THE WORD LIGHT UP YOUR PATH SO YOU CAN LIGHT UP THE WORLD

All Scripture is God-breathed and is useful for teaching,
rebuking, correcting and training in righteousness.
2 TIMOTHY 3:16

I know a lot of people who are more likely to use the Bible as a doorstop or coffee coaster than a guide to living. Sure, they agree with it in a general, safe way and might even be influenced by its generally acceptable message of love, but when it comes to living into the challenging demands of the life Jesus talked about, or even knowing what those demands are, they are largely indifferent.

The Bible records Jesus talking to some people who acted religious, said all the right things, and even asked lots of questions to set Jesus up. But they didn't know the Scriptures and, as a result, they hadn't experienced the power and confidence that comes from knowing them. Don't get me wrong. I don't mean you need to whack everybody over the head with Bible verses—nobody likes that—but think of how much more confident, encouraged, and peaceful you would be if you could deal with all that life throws your way with the power and perspective God left in His words for us.

Do you find yourself asking for permission to do the things God already said you had permission to do? Don't beat yourself up; get to know the Scriptures. Or, are you feeling rudderless or sad or fearful? Get familiar with the encouragement God left us in the Scriptures for those times. Know the Word and you'll find the power.

But don't just stop at familiarity. I have met plenty of people who know all the doctrine but are living out lousy theology. It is never about all the things we know and even believe; it is what we do about what we believe.

Get to know the Scriptures and live according to what you read. When those around you meet you, they will bump into Jesus, not just a pile of your opinions.

LET GOD UNCOMPLICATE YOUR LIFE— HE REALLY WANTS TO

I do not understand what I do. For what I want
to do I do not do, but what I hate I do.
ROMANS 7:15

I don't know many people who set out to live a bad life, who want to hurt people and damage relationships. It is certainly the odd person who would aim for a shallow, unpredictable, noncommitted relationship, yet this is where so many of us end up. How come? The answer is as simple as it is complicated because we are both simple and complicated people. We have conflicting desires and motivations, and we spend a weird amount of time toggling between our better and lesser angels.

Paul said what he wanted to do he didn't do and what he didn't want to do he did. I can relate to this, and I bet you can too. So how do we get out of this cycle? First, we need to develop an understanding of our underlying tendencies, get real about what unmet needs are tied to our disappointing responses, and realize we are all deeply flawed in one area or another.

Sweet Maria calls the areas in our home where we ditch things that we don't have a place for "hot spots." We have these hot spots in our lives too. They can be our blind spots, our sometimes-inexplicable actions and over- or underreactions. We need to get these complicated and sometimes conflicting emotions out on the table so we can understand what they are connected to and where they might be coming from. We can't just ignore them and hope they'll go away. We have to face them and see them clearly, so we can take them to Jesus to heal them.

Only then can we start replacing our natural reactions with supernatural ones, our defeatist views with winning ones, or our deep hurts with immeasurable hope.

Take a page out of Paul's playbook and spend a few minutes today writing down those things in your life that are inconsistent with the person you want to be. Think about what is driving the behaviors you want to change, and then take these things to Jesus and ask Him for the strength and resolve to take courageous steps toward a new and different response.

**We are all becoming the next version of ourselves.
Take aim at the person God is hoping you will be.**

GOD PICKED: "EVERYBODY'S IN"

Better is one day in your courts than a thousand
elsewhere; I would rather be a doorkeeper in the house
of my God than dwell in the tents of the wicked.

PSALM 84:10

In Haiti, there is a famous citadel that was built by twenty thousand workers over the course of fifteen years. It was protected by 360 cannons and held enough food for five thousand people to live for a year. But here's the thing. No one ever moved in and lived there. This sounds strange until we look at the fortresses we build in our own lives to keep out unwanted people, controversy, and annoyances.

We build castles all the time, out of our jobs and our families and the things we've purchased. Sometimes we even make them out of each other. Some of these castles are impressive too. But Jesus told His friends we aren't supposed to spend our lives building castles; He said He wanted us to build a kingdom to dwell in instead. And there's a big difference between building a castle to impress people and building a kingdom to dwell in.

You see, castles have moats to keep creepy people out, but kingdoms have bridges to let everyone in. Castles have dungeons for people who have messed up, but kingdoms have grace. There's one last thing castles have: trolls. You've probably met a couple; I have too. Trolls aren't bad people; they're just people we don't really understand.

Here's the deal: it's how we treat the trolls in our lives that will let us know how far along we are in our faith. If we want a kingdom, then we start by drawing a circle around everyone and saying they're in. Kingdoms are built from the people up.

**Continue building God's kingdom today one
conversation and selfless act of love at a time.**

LET JESUS BE YOUR COPILOT

Two are better than one, because they have a good return for their labor.
ECCLESIASTES 4:9

"Do you want to meet a U-2 guy?" someone once asked me. "Sure," I said, "When is Bono available? I'll bring my guitar." But then I learned that I was meeting a guy who flew the U-2 spy plane. A friend had somehow talked him into taking one of my books up in his plane on its release date to take a photograph in the cockpit. I squinted as hard as I could at the photo to see what country he was over at the time. I was envisioning he was somewhere over North Korea, but it was more likely Bakersfield, California. Either way, it was a cool photograph.

Because the pilots wear space suits with helmets and sit in a tiny cockpit, they don't have the ability to turn their heads, so they don't have the peripheral vison needed to see where the runway is underneath them as they get close to landing. Other experienced U-2 pilots drive souped-up Camaros with U/VHF radios to follow the planes and talk the pilots through the last few feet of the landing.

My new friend asked if I wanted to go in the car with him. "Let me think about it and get back to you," I said. Not! "Let's go!" I yelped as I waved my arms in the air. For landing after landing, I sat in the passenger seat as we tucked ourselves under the U-2s, speeding down the runway within a dozen feet of the airplanes' tail pipes at well over one hundred miles per hour.

Like the U-2 pilots, none of us can fly high, go far, or land our complicated lives alone. No matter how much experience you have or how skilled you are, sometimes you just need someone with a different perspective to help you see more clearly. But you don't need strangers, rookies, or fans to give you input— you need Jesus. He shows up in the words found in the Bible and maybe in a few friends who also love Him and are more knowledgeable and experienced than you are. But don't stop at finding that person to help you; be that person to someone else.

Thank someone today who is helping you land your faith and reach out to someone who could use a person like you in their life as they try to land one of their ambitions.

SOMETIMES WE NEED TO CUT AWAY OUR PARACHUTE AND KNOW GOD IS OUR BACKUP

By dying to what once bound us, we have been released
from the law so that we serve in the new way of the
Spirit, and not in the old way of the written code.
ROMANS 7:6–8

There are two ways to skydive, and they are both great in their own ways. One method is where you are attached to someone who knows what they are doing, and you are along for the ride. The other method is where you learn to solo free-fall. This sounded a lot more interesting and challenging to me, so I took a couple of classes and learned the steps and maneuvers.

Skydivers make their jump with a main parachute and a backup parachute. After the main parachute deploys, you are supposed to look up to make sure the canopy is fully open and none of the lines are looped over the top. You might think that a single line over the top is just one line out of hundreds, so what's the big deal? But the answer is, it *is* a big deal. With a line over the top of the canopy, the parachute will still fill with air and fly, but not the way it was designed to. And while it feels like you are in good shape at five thousand feet over the ground, you will discover at fifty feet that the parachute isn't slowing you down and you will likely crater when you hit the ground. It feels a little counterintuitive, but if there is a line over the top, you need to cut away the old parachute, start your free fall all over again, and pull your backup one. The second free fall in the middle is the key. If both the main and reserve parachutes are out at the same time, they will wrap together, and then it is game over.

Here's the point. Just because something looks right doesn't mean it is working the way it was intended to. Sometimes you need to cut loose what isn't working and start over. This is what Paul was getting at when he talked about cutting away things that were part of our old life.

In what area of your life have you been flying with a string or two over the canopy? Maybe it's a wrong relationship or a bad job. You know something isn't right, but it's close enough and certainly better than being alone or jobless, right? I get it. Cutting something loose will throw you into a free fall for a moment, and it feels risky, but the truth is that it is much riskier to keep things the way they are.

Make a courageous, authentic move today, and cut loose whatever is keeping you from living fully into this one beautiful life God has given you.

IF YOU LISTEN TO A PARABLE AND ONLY HEAR A STORY, CHECK YOUR HEARING

Then Jesus said, "Whoever has ears to hear, let them hear."
MARK 4:9

I have a friend who worked in the White House during one of the administrations. I won't tell you which one, because I'd lose half of you before we get to the story. The truth is that whatever major party has been in control of the government, I have found some exceptionally kind and talented people who have pitched in, even when others in leadership were unimpressive. Two things these people have in common is, first, they love this country and, second, they are all pranksters and filled with a little mischief. It's not just those in the executive branch either. I know one guy in another branch who buried the word *ripcord* in a report on a dare. Another staffer would get on someone else's computer and send messages to other staff to liven things up a bit. These were not security breaches. They were innocent, fun pranks with an inside meaning to a small group of friends.

God wasn't trying to prank us with the stories in the Scriptures, yet much of what Jesus said intentionally had hidden meanings. Take the parables, for instance. When someone asked why He used them, He said it was so people *wouldn't* understand. Huh? The fact is, the messages Jesus was communicating were for everyone, but He knew that some people just wouldn't get it and would walk away scratching their heads, while other people who were leaning in and seeking to understand would get it. This is what He meant when He said, "Whoever has ears, let them hear." It wasn't a reference to guys like Van Gogh; it was a message for guys like me, perhaps someone like you.

Parables were intended to make a lot of sense to some people and no sense to others. Are we going to be open to what God has for us so the stories He told begin to make sense and the truths take hold in our lives? In other words, do we have ears to hear what God has told us to do when it comes to the lessons He wants to teach us?

Your life is a parable. It will make sense to some people and not to others. You are not the average of what everyone thinks of you; you are God's unique creation and gift to the world.

GOD DESIGNED US FOR COMMUNITY; ISOLATION IS NOT GONNA CUT IT

Breaking bread from house to house, they ate their food with gladness and simplicity of heart, praising God and having favor with all the people. And the Lord added to the church daily those who were being saved.

ACTS 2:46–47 NKJV

Many of us are addicted to speedy results. Fast food, fast cars, fast passes, diamond lanes. We like the rush of having things come together in a hurry. I have a friend who wrote a book about how you can manage people in one minute, and he sold millions of them. Cottage industries of time-motion consultants help businesses with their efficiency, speed, and productivity. Running Start programs help high schoolers get into college early to knock out course requirements. Our society values running full out, pedal to the metal, and right now. But this wasn't part of the culture when Jesus walked His dusty streets. Instead, there was a high value around gathering, storytelling, breaking bread, and having things in common. In the second and fourth chapters of the book of Acts, it says the disciples were committed to this and, as a result, their numbers were added to daily. I don't think people were constantly joining because they wanted the falafels. They did it because they desired community, and community is not something you can rush.

Being a part of an intentional community means digging in and staying a while. We will become part of the communities we spend the most intentional time with. So when you find a community you want to invest in, make sure you don't simply attend. You must participate to show up fully, and to do this, you will have to slow yourself down. You will need to do the unhurried work of meeting with people and breaking bread together and spending your lives together. I promise you, it's worth it.

If you are not part of a community, find one. If you can't find one, create one. Start today. Who is going to be your first call?

**Pick up the phone. Here's your script:
"Hey, let's start a community."**

THE MORE WE TALK TO GOD, THE CLEARER THINGS BECOME

Rejoice always, pray continually, give thanks in all
circumstances; for this is God's will for you in Christ Jesus.
1 THESSALONIANS 5:16–18

We have drilled many water wells in Uganda. When a bore hole goes in, a pump with a handle is installed at the top of the well pipe and it is primed with some water. As the handle is pumped, the water comes out initially as a small, muddy stream. The recharge rate—how quickly surrounding water under-ground makes its way to the bore hole—becomes faster every time the well is used. The more you pump the handle, the clearer the water becomes. The same is true in our faith. Among the most effective ways to recharge our faith is to talk to God. This is what gets the spirit of whimsy and the joy Jesus brings flowing. Priming the pump might look like reading the Scriptures or walking in the woods. For others it might be reading books or even writing a few.

Paul told his friends in Thessalonica to pray without ceasing. What does that mean to you? Does it mean to close your eyes and bow your head when you're driving down the road? I hope not. Does it mean to pray when you're taking a walk? Perhaps. I think praying without ceasing means being mindful of the people and circumstances around us, as well as the presence of Jesus, and inviting God to whisper into whatever situation we are currently in. Like a well, the more we pray, the faster we recharge and the clearer things become.

I married Sweet Maria thirty-six years ago, and I love talking to that girl. When I wake up in the morning, I want to start talking. We talk several times in the afternoon and again all evening. While she doesn't always want to talk to me (imagine that), God always wants to talk to you, and not just a little bit. He wants to talk to you without ceasing. He loves it. It's a little like when you haven't seen a friend for five or ten years and it feels like you pick up the conversation right where it left off. That is what it's like with God.

**Today, recharge your relationship with God simply by talking
with Him. Remind yourself of the honor of being in the
presence of the One you are praying to. Pump that handle.**

NEW DAY, NEW YOU

You were taught, with regard to your former way of life, to put off your old self, which is being corrupted by its deceitful desires; to be made new in the attitude of your minds; and to put on the new self, created to be like God in true righteousness and holiness.

EPHESIANS 4:22–24

When I was a young lawyer, I bought an old Victorian house that had a walk-in vault. Sweet Maria and I were broke and my law firm was just getting started, so there was nothing to put in it except Pop-Tarts and our kids' favorite toys. It turns out this Victorian was once owned by Wyatt Earp, the famous Tombstone sheriff known for his shoot-out at the O.K. Corral. This might explain the walk-in vault and the hitching post out back.

For as long as there have been things of value, there has been a need to protect them. We have to be on our guard when it comes to the things that are most important to us. And for those of us who follow Jesus, one important thing to guard is our identity as a new creation.

Being a new creation is not easy work. Just when we think we have a couple of things figured out about ourselves, we change. Paul described this to his friends from a city called Ephesus, saying that all of us are new creations every day, that we're continually being renewed and are putting on what he called "a new self." I like that idea. Think about it this way: new day, new me and new day, new you. Every day we should be growing and on our way to becoming a newer and better version of ourselves, closer to how God made us to be. The simple truth is that we can't claim to be new creations if nothing in our lives changes and everything remains the same.

Look at your life. Are you keeping up with the growth and changes God is developing in you? Take notice of where you're learning new things or trying new adventures or seeing with new perspectives, and welcome those changes with joy and anticipation.

Join all of heaven in celebrating the newest and humblest version of you as you draw closer to Jesus.

THE ARMOR OF GOD WON'T WEIGH YOU DOWN, BUT FEAR WILL

Finally, be strong in the Lord and in his mighty
power. Put on the full armor of God, so that you can
take your stand against the devil's schemes.
EPHESIANS 6:10-11

I was driving our Suburban back from our retreat center on a rural road far away from any city when I came around a corner and saw a man walking barefoot down the middle of the road. It wasn't clear to me what was happening, so I hit the brakes and slowed to a stop.

The guy heard my car and turned around, as creepy as a barefoot guy can be. He started walking toward the car, and as he did, he pulled out a ten-inch knife with his right hand. I was more than a little freaked out and concerned about what would happen next, but then I realized this guy had brought a knife to a car fight.

Paul told his friends not to be afraid when they faced opposition but instead to live in the strength and power God gives us. He called them to stand against their enemies by putting on the full armor of God. What does that mean?

Putting on the armor of God means realizing you are sitting inside of six thousand pounds of protection, and darkness has got nothing you're afraid of. It means you are strong enough to face your biggest challenges, look them in the eye, and then, with the power and protection Jesus gives you, beat them back. Putting on the armor of God is more than a slogan cross-stitched onto a pillow at a Christian bookstore; it is the anthem we live by as we die to fear and intimidation and the constant pull to conform.

**God doesn't want you shaking in your armor anymore.
He wants you to live like you are protected by a
fearsome God. What will you do today to suit up?**

LEAD WITH CURIOSITY

A fool takes no pleasure in understanding,
but only in expressing his opinion.
PROVERBS 18:2 ESV

We all bring a set of perspectives to every conversation or human interaction we have. If we looked carefully, we would see that some of these perspectives we have are built upon truths while others are built upon biased information.

In high school, my favorite musician was a guy named Randy Stonehill. He was one of the early contemporary Christian music artists and would walk on stage wearing jeans covered in patches. I remember thinking then that he must be an old guy. I knew this because he wrote a song called "Turning Thirty," in which he reflected on his earlier life when he was in his prime in his teens and twenties.

How can someone be so old and still so cool? I wondered. I didn't know anyone who was thirty at the time. Now that I'm an old guy who is more than twice as old as the person Randy was singing about, I have a new perspective on his song. All my kids have turned thirty, and some of them did it quite a while ago. The perspectives we bring filter and shade the information we receive.

Everyone seems to have a different perspective on many of the common things we experience in life. We love, we suffer loss, we laugh, we bear up under misunderstandings. The perspectives we hold are born out of the breadth or limited universe of our experiences. Someone may have what we consider to be a misguided set of opinions or engage in conduct we find offensive or off-putting.

This conduct and our reactions to it are a collision of two people with different perspectives and lived experiences with a particular situation. Before you form an opinion about something that you experience, consider the perspectives you bring with you.

Don't ask people for their opinions today. Ask them
about what their unique perspectives are.

IF YOU WANT TO BE LIKE JESUS, BE AVAILABLE

And this is the confidence that we have toward him, that if
we ask anything according to his will he hears us.
1 JOHN 5:14 ESV

Most of us get a lot of telephone calls, but having put my cell phone number in the back of several million books, I get more than a lot. These calls don't bother me at all. I have been so inspired by the people I have had an opportunity to have a quick conversation with. I will admit, though, that I get some unusual telephone calls and some requests that make me scratch my head.

I received a call from a woman recently. It went something like this:

> Me: Hello, it's Bob here.
> Woman: Bob, the devil is in my bathroom.
> Me: I know exactly how you feel. I had teenage boys too.

I resisted asking her whether the devil was doing number one or number two. It just seemed like too much information. I told her to give her best friend a call and invite her over. This is the kind of thing you don't want to face alone. A few hours later, the same woman called me back and said, "Devil's gone," and hung up. While it left several of the large questions I had unanswered, I was fine with it. We don't need to have all the details or know all the reasons for everything. We can just celebrate that the right kind of availability will often result in the right kind of outcomes.

There is a misconception about availability and how we need to guard it like it's ours rather than give it away like it's God's. The truth is, the right kind of availability has the power to multiply our time, not reduce it. If you think about it, Jesus was even available to the two guys on crosses next to him. If He could do that while being crucified, surely we can make some time for the people around us.

**Today, just love people and, as much as
you can, be available to them.**

WITH JESUS AS YOUR COMPASS YOU WILL ALWAYS KNOW WHERE TRUE NORTH IS

*Whether you turn to the right or to the left, your ears will hear
a voice behind you, saying, "This is the way; walk in it."*
ISAIAH 30:21

Have you ever held a compass? It can look a little like a watch with a floating red arrow inside, and it shows North, South, East, and West. What many people don't know is there is a difference between true north and magnetic north. True north is where North is on a map. Magnetic north is the direction a compass points when it lines up with Earth's magnetic field.

The thing about magnetic north is that it can be at a different place depending on where you are on Earth and it shifts over time as Earth's core changes. So if you navigate toward magnetic north, thinking you are heading toward true north, you might think you're going the right way but end up in a totally different place, scratching your head about what happened.

When you're figuring out what you want to do with your life and where you want to go, the most important thing you can do is know what your true north is. God created you to do good and wonderful things in the world, but He didn't put you here to do them alone. He gave you Jesus and some other trustworthy guides to help get you headed in the right direction.

Your true north will be things like your family, your friendship with Jesus, and your relationships with those who love you and want the best for you. There may be some things, though, that seem like true north but are really magnetic north, so it's important to figure out the difference.

As you move along life's journey, if you periodically look up to align your trajectory toward true north, you'll stay on track. So pick your direction, understand what true north is, bring a couple of friends along with you, and stay the course.

God wants you to find His way today and walk in it.

APRIL

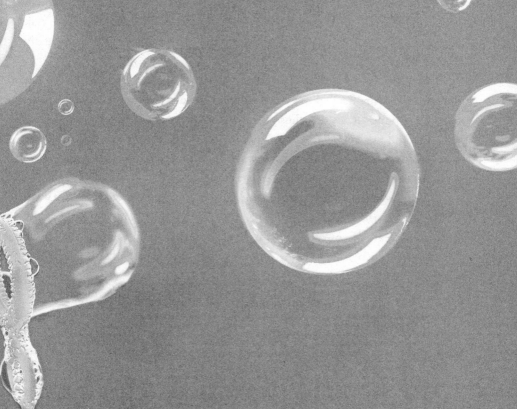

APRIL 1

FIGURE OUT WHAT YOU'RE AIMING FOR, SPOT WHAT IS AIMING FOR YOU, AND CHART YOUR PATH

But the LORD God called to the man, "Where are you?"
GENESIS 3:9

We have a lodge in a remote part of Canada. Getting there involves either a long seaplane trip or an even longer boat ride. When the weather is down and a seaplane can't fly, we navigate a boat through the fog and snow almost entirely by radar. There are three settings for the radar: short, medium, and long. The short-range radar tells us what is immediately in front. This helps us spot logs that lie just a few inches above the surface yet expand fifty feet below. Hitting one of these logs will sink most boats, so we have to be on the lookout for them, similar to how we need to be on the lookout in life for those things that are necessary to either immediately avoid or engage.

Think of things like unhealthy habits or relationships or activities which, if left unaddressed, will eventually drive a wedge between you and God. Ask yourself what area of your life warrants closer examination. We will usually miss or collide with what we don't look for.

The medium setting on the radar picks up on things one to five miles out, things we are headed toward or that are headed toward us. This helps us navigate around or toward those things with intention. Do a quick audit of your life and ask yourself, *What is coming up in the next few weeks or months that I need to tend to? What are some practical, courageous next steps I can take to prepare for and move toward those opportunities or needs?*

The long-range radar can't look around corners, but it will look forward all the way to the horizon. Think of it like zooming out and looking at the next many years of your life. This is when we ask questions about the legacy we want to leave behind when we are no longer present in body but with Jesus in spirit.

If we spend all our time looking downrange, we will probably hit something right in front of us. On the other hand, if we are only looking right in front of us without lifting our eyes to see where we are headed, we won't have an accurate perspective and framework through which we can achieve our long-term goals. We need to learn to toggle between these three points of view—short-, medium-, and long-range—so that we can have an accurate picture of where we are now and where we are going.

Remember, God isn't looking for the easiest path forward for us, but the most lasting one.

WHEN YOUR HEART IS HURT, CALL ON KINDNESS AND GRACE

While [Jesus] was still speaking, Judas, one of the Twelve, arrived. With him was a large crowd armed with swords and clubs, sent from the chief priests and the elders of the people. Now the betrayer had arranged a signal with them: "The one I kiss is the man; arrest him." Going at once to Jesus, Judas said, "Greetings, Rabbi!" and kissed him.

MATTHEW 26:47-49

Jesus was betrayed by a warm greeting and a kiss. This is where we get the "kiss of death" idiom. Judas Iscariot kissed Jesus as a way of identifying Him to the soldiers who came to arrest Him. This is one of the world's best-known betrayals, and one that felt intensely personal. Have you ever experienced betrayal?

Most of us have not experienced a Judas-level betrayal, but we probably have experienced some amount of betrayal. The heartache that comes from a betrayal of any size is piercing, far more so than a garden-variety misunderstanding. And that's because, unlike a misunderstanding, a betrayal feels hugely personal. When trust is broken, hearts are broken.

Do we ignore betrayal and try to move on from those feelings, or do we engage with it? Here's what I've learned to do. First, identify the wrong without initially calling out the wrongdoer. Once we understand what happened, we can bring it to God to fix. Maybe it was a misplaced assumption someone made, or gossip they engaged in involving you. You talk to the person creating the problems later. Don't make the already muddy waters more complicated to navigate by engaging interpersonal dynamics before you fully understand what happened. Create needed distance from the people or the event to give yourself some clarity. Then, once you've wrapped your head around the truth of what happened and have given yourself the space to envision a productive and God-honoring path forward, invite reconciliation. If the other person is unable or unwilling to engage in restoring the relationship, continue to move forward with your beautiful life.

Always take the path of kindness and grace.

DON'T BE HIGH MAINTENANCE
WHEN YOU CAN BE LOVE

But when you are invited, take the lowest place, so that when your
host comes, he will say to you, "Friend, move up to a better place."
Then you will be honored in the presence of all the other guests.
LUKE 14:10

I know quite a few people in the hospitality industry. We were swapping stories, and a few of them told me about a small group who arrived at their place on the East Coast in a couple of black Suburbans as my friends stood on both sides of the road, waving their arms and shouting, "Welcome!" The chauffeurs stepped from behind their wheels and opened the doors. The group got out, gave my friends a polite "hello," and then asked, "Who will be hanging up our clothes?" My friends honestly thought they were kidding at first, but it became evident they were serious. "That would be you!" one of my friends said with a grin.

Another guest came with someone who was there to respond to their special requests. I heard this person drove an hour to get water bottled from a certain manufacturer. On one level, it was all fine, I suppose. I thought, *Whatever blows your hair back, I guess.* But there was another side to the split screen in my mind where I was silently thinking, *Are you kidding me?* And then I thought to myself about how difficult I must be from time to time too.

I don't care who you are or what you have accomplished. None of us need cupbearers or fanfare. It is easy to hear these extreme examples of people who have unusual requirements and poke fun at their absurd behaviors, but we would be well served to recognize we all have the capacity to be more than a little high maintenance from time to time. The trick is to recognize it when it happens and remember that bright lights don't need spotlights and we can make a big difference without being two handfuls of work for those around us. Before we ask someone to meet one of our perceived needs, what if we stay alert and spot the needs of a few people around us?

**Let's find our comfort and joy in losing all the trappings
of power or success or influence and replace them
with an attitude of caring and self-sacrifice.**

BE QUICK TO HEAR, SLOW TO SPEAK, AND SLOW TO ANGER

*Know this, my beloved brothers: let every person be
quick to hear, slow to speak, slow to anger.*
JAMES 1:19 ESV

Speaking comes easy to some people. I once was invited to go on two twenty-day speaking tours, which works out to be about forty days and forty nights of speaking. It sounded so biblical, so full-on Moses, so Jesus, to do something like that. I couldn't say no. If Uber Eats had delivered wild locusts and honey to the bus, I would have put on a camel-hair toga and met everyone at the door each night.

I enjoy how my friends in the South poke fun at people who are talkative. "He could talk the legs off a chair." "She speaks ten words a second, with gusts to fifty." "He's a chin musician." "He shoots off his mouth so much he must eat bullets for breakfast." These are just a few that make me chuckle.

With lots of practice, I have found I am one of those people who enjoys speaking. I even tracked how quickly I speak once by transcribing one of my talks. It turns out I speak at a cadence of about 15,000 words per hour, more if I have had a couple of Red Bulls (which should be labeled a heart attack in a can). Depending on who you talk to, you'll find the average person speaks at least 7,000 words a day and hears between 20,000 and 30,000 words during a twenty-four-hour period. I have met a couple of you, and those numbers are way low.

Notwithstanding the tens of thousands of words spoken by each of us, I read somewhere that out of all those words, most people only speak on average about 500 to 700 words of actual importance and value each day. Crazy, right? All the rest are just extra words. That's a whole lot of fluff by any measure.

It's a new day. Keep track of your words today. Find more authentic, important, meaningful words to put out there into the world. Your words don't need to be hip or snappy, but just as honest and vulnerable as you can make them.

Be quick to hear, slow to speak, and slow to anger.

WHEN WE'RE DROWNING IN DOUBT, JESUS REACHES OUT HIS HAND AND CATCHES US

Immediately Jesus reached out his hand and caught him.
"You of little faith," he said, "why did you doubt?"
MATTHEW 14:31

We have all met people who act like they are certain about everything. You know the type: they say they know the reason God is doing everything in their lives, and what is going to happen next in your life, my life, and everyone else's lives. I think they use the appearance of unreasonable levels of certainty to hide even greater amounts of insecurity. Every time they blow smoke with another self-important fib about what they are certain God is doing, another person is misled into believing they must not have what it takes. Meanwhile, the insecure person feigning confidence pretends to have all the answers, despite not understanding the questions.

Wouldn't it be something if we had a gauge on our foreheads that let everybody know how full or empty of belief we actually are? I wonder if the people who read as the most confident and assured from the outside might be running on reserves, their show of confidence just a cover.

I know for me, my faith and belief fluctuate daily, depending on my heart and the issues and circumstances at hand. I can relate daily to how Doubting Thomas must have felt. Torn between belief and disbelief and wanting more proof, more clarity, and greater assurance. It is not lost on me that Jesus reached out to Thomas in the midst of his disbelief, not in the center of what he was already certain of.

It's natural to have doubts. God knew we would all have them. What I bet God thinks is sad and amusing is when we pretend we know what we are only guessing about.

Remember that God loves you and delights in you whether or not you fully understand the unseen things He is doing right now.

Ask Jesus to help you with those parts of your life where you want to believe more than you do.

JESUS LOVES US ANYWAY

For I am convinced that neither death nor life, neither angels nor demons, neither the present nor the future, nor any powers, neither height nor depth, nor anything else in all creation, will be able to separate us from the love of God that is in Christ Jesus our Lord.
ROMANS 8:38–39

I'm a softy for a good story. One of my favorites is a years-old movie called *The Mission*. In it, a soldier who brought pain and injustice to many indigenous people is trying to make personal amends for the damage he has done. He begins climbing the rocks beside a waterfall hundreds of feet high, pulling behind him the heavy load of all the armor he once wore. When the soldier reaches the top of the waterfall, drenched, weak, broken, his adversary finds him and, in a dramatic moment, draws his knife and moves toward him. But instead of killing the soldier, unexpectedly and contrary to what would have been fair, he cuts off the burden the soldier had been hauling and it falls away. This is what Jesus' level of forgiveness looks like.

Forgiveness takes as many shapes as there are mess-ups we can engage in. What always remains the same is the power that is available if we are willing to allow Jesus to cut loose all the shame and regrets and sadness we have been carrying.

When I was growing up, one of my father's favorite sayings was, "You need to accept the consequences of your actions." I wasn't sure exactly what he meant, but I figured it had to do with taking responsibility for what I had done. I get that now and agree, but I also think we can get so caught up in beating ourselves up over what we did that we overidentify with what got us in trouble rather than listening to Jesus, who says He loves us anyway.

There are certainly consequences to our decisions, but two things are not true. First, those consequences do not separate us from the love of God and, second, they should not separate us from one another.

Don't believe the lie that you are who you used to be; you are His.

BE THE KINDNESS, BE THE HOPE, BE THE COOKIES— BE THE AROMA OF CHRIST

For we are to God the pleasing aroma of Christ among those who are being saved and those who are perishing.
2 CORINTHIANS 2:15

When we have guests coming over, Sweet Maria will whip up a batch of cookies or scones and pop them in the oven. There is nothing that says you are welcome more than something baking in the oven. The aroma of caramelizing, artery-clogging, heart-stopping sugar wafts down the hallways in the house and into every room.

We could wreck this picture by talking about the science of smells and benzene rings that are small and light enough to travel through air, but who cares, right? It is rarely information we need; it's inspiration we crave. It is the aroma of the cookies, not the explanation of science, that welcomes us.

Kindness, empathy, and curiosity about another's life experience are all part of what the Scriptures call the aroma of Christ. These things have the ability to fill the room with Jesus and fill our sometimes-weary hearts. These are the ingredients from which we build the bonds of deeper friendships and memorable experiences.

I've never met a cookie I didn't get along famously with, as the aroma reminds me that I am in the vicinity of revisiting joy once again. Let's be that for other people. Let's stop settling for just being the teacher but instead be the kindness, be the hope, be the cookies—be the aroma of Christ.

Who can you call today to spread the aroma of Christ? What handwritten note can you drop in the mail? What kind word can you give to someone who needs to receive one?

CUT THE SEAWEED LOOSE FROM YOUR LIFE SO YOU CAN GET BACK TO SMOOTH SAILING

Therefore, since we are surrounded by such a great cloud of witnesses, let us throw off everything that hinders and the sin that so easily entangles.
HEBREWS 12:1

Just after I graduated college, my friend Doug had a great idea: "What if we sailed a boat across the Pacific Ocean to Hawaii?" There's a sailboat race that happens every other year called the Transpac, and my friends and I piled into a boat we could barely fit in and readied to set sail across the high seas.

The race began, and I noticed that our boat was getting slower and slower. But I couldn't figure out what was happening. If you've never been sailing, let me give you your first lesson: Under every sailboard is a keel, which is a long, tall fin sometimes filled with lead that stretches far down into the water and helps the boat stay upright. Without the keel, the sailboat would tip over when the wind blows against the sail. But when you have something sticking out of the bottom of your boat, every stray piece of seaweed floating in the water has a chance to get wrapped around the keel, and this can slow your boat down.

As we pulled into the harbor when the race was over, 2,700 miles and some change later, I saw that we had been dragging a massive piece of seaweed behind us—across the entire Pacific Ocean. It wasn't any surprise that we were one of the last boats to finish the race.

We had stayed so focused on what was happening on the surface that we didn't stop to think about what was happening under the surface. Our lives can be similar. If we're so focused on how we look on the outside but don't take time to understand what is happening underneath, it's going to really slow us down.

What in your life is acting like kelp around a keel? Who or what is causing you to slow to a crawl in areas where you should be running? Are there relationships you need to change? Is it time to quit the relative safety of the job you have outgrown?

Lose the kelp that has accumulated around you, and ask God to help you navigate a newer, faster direction in your life.

DON'T SETTLE FOR THE ORDINARY WHEN THE EXTRAORDINARY IS RIGHT AROUND THE CORNER

For God has not given us a spirit of fear, but of
power and of love and of a sound mind.
2 TIMOTHY 1:7 NKJV

I remember lying in bed the night before law school started. Tears were streaming down my cheeks, because, at orientation that day, the faculty had given their draconian version of a pep talk by saying that every third chair was eventually going to be empty because one-third of the class would flunk out the first year. No matter what end of the row I started, as I counted silently toward myself—one, two, three, one, two, three—I was always the third guy.

My first thought was to defer law school and start some other time when I had my act together. Isn't this what a lot of us do when that fear of failure kicks in? We settle for the dissatisfaction of what we know rather than the ambiguity of what we haven't tried yet. But settling for the ordinary when the extraordinary is right around the corner doesn't get us anywhere.

How about this? Instead of avoiding distress, confront it. Rather than fostering a sense that failure might be near and doom is just around the corner, name what your fear is and call it out. Once it is out in the open, not only can you begin to understand it, but you also take away the power it has over you.

Identify what is keeping you back today and bring that to Jesus. Tell God what you are afraid of. Take Paul's words to his younger friend Timothy to heart: "For God has not given us a spirit of fear, but of power and of love and of a sound mind."

Experience the freedom that comes from calling out what you fear as specifically as you can and then bringing it to Jesus today. Ask Him for the guts and the grit to do something about it.

BEFORE YOU ASSUME THE WORST, CHOOSE LOVE, ALWAYS

It always protects, always trusts, always hopes, always perseveres.
1 CORINTHIANS 13:7

Our son Richard met a really nice girl on the playground in the fourth grade. He was running after a ball near a chain-link fence and somehow got tangled up and stuck underneath it. Ashley came along and helped him wiggle his way out. For the next decade, Richard and Ashley were a thing and went everywhere together.

It was during high school that Richard and Ashley asked Sweet Maria and me if we could meet with them over dinner. They said Ashley's parents would be coming too. There was no topic they indicated they wanted to talk about, so we were scratching our heads, wondering what it could be about. I have to admit, our minds were racing with all the possible topics. Were they planning to drop out of high school? Did they get kicked out of high school? Was there a fender bender they needed to let us in on? Maybe they were going to elope? When we arrived at dinner, they said they had wanted to invite us into their relationship to be transparent with us. What a beautiful way to honor their relationship and their families who loved them and were always so proud of them.

Family relationships can be tricky. Sometimes we don't have all the information about what's happening, so we make assumptions that send us down the wrong path. If you find yourself on edge and at times unsettled about what's going on in your family, you are in good company. But what if we reacted differently? When there isn't clarity in a situation, why not assume the best?

What would it look like for you to assume a better motive in what might feel like a strained or confusing relationship? Sure, that person may have been off-putting, or come across a little coarse or harsh, but choose to believe the best in them, not the worst, and watch God change your heart.

Love always protects, always trusts, always hopes, and always perseveres.

APRIL 11

PRIDE WILL KEEP YOU IN PRISON, BUT HUMILITY IS THE GATEWAY TO WISDOM

When pride comes, then comes disgrace, but with humility comes wisdom.
PROVERBS 11:2

Brandon was the first friend I made at San Quentin. Years earlier, he was involved in an argument that went way wrong and he took a friend's life. Everyone lost. Brandon lost, the victim lost, the spouses lost, as did all their respective children. It is a cautionary tale about the importance of keeping a tighter grip on the reins in our lives.

After many years and much personal change, maturity, and coming to faith, Brandon was released from San Quentin. A few days later, the police arrived with handcuffs. They arrested Brandon and took him back to San Quentin. He asked the same question you would have: How come? Get this, they said they did the math wrong. The guard told Brandon he owed them 110 more days.

How would you respond to this news? You thought you were free, thought you had paid your debt, and assumed the odometer had been reset to zero, only to find out this was a false summit and there is more hill to climb. At a minimum I would want to punch a wall or give a loud primal scream.

When I called Brandon, I asked how he was holding up behind prison bars again. I was bracing myself for some sharp language but was floored by his response. "Sure, I'm disappointed," he said, "but you know, I'm glad I have 110 more days to say goodbye to these guys here in prison." There was no bitterness or angst or bile or sour words. This is what happens when someone has truly changed. This is what humility turning into wisdom looks like.

What about you? When the unexpected negative turn in your life happens, how will you respond? Will you respond from a place of pride and anger or will you invite humility and patience to the discussion? When we do, they always show up with wisdom and kindness.

Think about the setbacks or disappointments you are experiencing. Can you dig deep and find the kind of courage and grace and humility and wisdom Brandon was able to access to meet your situation with resolve and perspective?

It won't be bravado or grousing that will get you there; it will be tremendous humility and a big dollop of faith.

> Do you keep putting yourself back in jail for something in the past? Are you giving the shackles a forwarding address so your past can find you? It was a typo that cost Brandon his freedom a second time. What is it that is costing you yours?

CULTIVATING GRATEFULNESS IN HARDSHIP MOVES US CLOSER TO THE GOOD THINGS HE HAS PLANNED FOR US

I consider that our present sufferings are not worth comparing with the glory that will be revealed in us.
ROMANS 8:18

It is easy to be appreciative when life presents us with a windfall, like a surprise million-dollar check, but what about those moments when life takes an unexpected nosedive, and we find ourselves in chaos and turmoil? How can we cultivate gratefulness when it seems like God allows difficulties to be our greatest teachers?

Paul told his friends that these hard things happen so that we can be more conformed to God's image. That sounds at first like a big theological statement, but the truth is, it *is* a huge theological statement. Hard times shape us more than we realize. We either become a reflection of our pain or a reflection of our hope.

We have all experienced setbacks. Gratefulness happens when we understand what happened, confront our feelings that rose up in response, and then chart a course toward the future. This isn't the end; it's the dawn of a new beginning orchestrated by a loving God. This is not to say we should simply ignore the pain in our lives. Masking our pain is like applying Bondo to a dent in the car. It's temporary and superficial and eventually will fall off. Instead, God wants to perform metallurgy, causing a deep transformation within us that turns our wounds into tools for His work.

Revisit a difficult conversation, situation, or circumstance you have struggled to get past. How did it make you feel? Can you learn more from it? Can you bring it to Jesus and say, "Change me. Grant me patience, clarity, and wisdom, so I don't repeat those mistakes and can take comfort in knowing You have something better planned"?

Learn from the past, and let it shape how you live more courageously and winsomely today.

THERE'S NO SUCH THING AS TOO LATE WITH GOD

One of the criminals who hung there hurled insults at him: "Aren't you the Messiah? Save yourself and us!" But the other criminal rebuked him. "Don't you fear God," he said, "since you are under the same sentence? We are punished justly, for we are getting what our deeds deserve. But this man has done nothing wrong." Then he said, "Jesus, remember me when you come into your kingdom." Jesus answered him, "Truly I tell you, today you will be with me in paradise."

LUKE 23:39–43

Jesus was flanked on each side by criminals. Luke focuses on one of the thieves, who eventually had a change of heart and said to Jesus, "Remember me."

Ninety-nine out of one hundred religious people would have vetted the thief before giving him an all-access pass to eternity in paradise. They would have asked, "Do you really believe? I heard what you were saying a few minutes ago." Or, "What were you in for anyway? I'm asking for a friend." Or perhaps the discussion would have devolved into something unrelated about the death sentence. Yet Jesus had none of these lengthy discussions. He took into account just two key words from the thief: "Remember me." And Jesus' brief and comprehensive response was something like, "I don't need to. See you in a few minutes. You'll be with me for eternity later today."

Sometimes we are waiting for God to make a move toward us before we make a move toward Him. When we do make a move, we often do it tentatively, worried it's too late or that we will not say the right things, or we operate under the misunderstanding that it will be our fancy or many words that will get us God's attention.

Maybe you think you have messed up and need to do something big and grand to get Jesus' attention. Remember this: two words—"Remember me"—is all it takes. And be ready for His response, because Jesus has already tipped His hand. He will say to you, "See you forever."

What will your few simple words to Jesus be today? "I'm in." "I'm yours." "Let's do this."

GLOW UP YOUR LIFE WITH GRATITUDE— AND BE SPECIFIC!

Every good and perfect gift is from above, coming down from the Father of the heavenly lights, who does not change like shifting shadows.
JAMES 1:17

Gratefulness starts by reflecting on the things God has done and recognizing His "good and perfect gifts." The first chapter of the book of James talks about God being the origin of every good gift; our job today is to recognize them and call them out. This doesn't mean to walk around with a giddy, dumb look on your face as if you are vaguely grateful for everything in general. Get clear about exactly what you are grateful for. For example, "I'm grateful for my oldest child, for their uniqueness, for the things that have driven me crazy about them, and all the energy they bring into every room." Or, "I'm grateful for this job I have and the opportunity it gives me to grow. The difficulties are making me stronger, and my courage is expanding by the day." If we get more specific, we will become more grateful, because specificity and gratitude travel together.

Gratefulness can be difficult, though, when it comes to some of the harder aspects of a person or a situation, but people—and life—are multifaceted and complicated. It's like when our lodge burned down and we started the almost decade-long process of rebuilding. As we were picking out new marble for the countertops at an industrial showroom, I saw a slab with an elaborate swirl in it. Sweet Maria has much better taste than me and the colors and pattern were too wild, but the marble guy said, "You know what makes that piece of stone so unique is also its weakest point." That'll preach. We can be thankful for both the good, easy-to-love sides of people and the hard, more flawed sides of them. Those weak points might just be evidence of what makes them unique. As you're working on increasing your gratefulness today, replace a vague concept of gratefulness with a specific sense of gratefulness. Do this, and you will begin to see more of the good things God has dropped in your life, His perfect gifts from above, coming down just for you.

What are you grateful for today? Get as specific as you can and you will see the unique ways God has been showing up in your life.

WANNA LOVE LIKE JESUS? BE AVAILABLE

For God so loved the world that he gave his one and only Son, that whoever believes in him shall not perish but have eternal life.

JOHN 3:16

It isn't lost on me that Jesus was the most famous person ever to walk the earth, yet He was almost always available. He no doubt had a long list of big things to accomplish in His three years of living a very public life, like rescuing everyone who would ever live from an eternity of isolation from God. It included small tasks as well, like telling someone on the fringe of society they, too, were in the center of His radical acceptance.

But most of the time, Jesus was surrounded by people who would do anything to be anywhere close to Him. They stood at the doors He walked by, dropped in through roofs He was standing under, and pressed in on Him from all sides, yet this didn't make Him shy away from people. Instead, He took an interest in a centurion's sick servant, noticed a woman who grabbed a small corner of His shirt when He walked by, and engaged a short guy named Zacchaeus who climbed a tree just to get a peek at Him.

The key to being intentionally available is to decide in advance what it is we want to be available to. We can be like Jesus and use our availability to engage incredibly important and lasting things, which will impact countless lives in the short time we are given this side of heaven, or we can make ourselves constantly available to mind-numbing distractions, petty grievances, passing fancies, and unimportant arguments. Think about it. Being intentional about what and who we decide to be available to will be one of the best predictors of the legacy we will leave behind.

Today, pay attention to what and who you're making yourself available to. At the end of the day, evaluate whether those things match up to what is lasting and important. If they do, keep up the great work. If they don't, start over tomorrow and be more purposeful with your availability.

For God so loved the world, including you, that He made available His one and only Son. Have that mean something more to you today than it did yesterday.

CLEAR YOUR DECK AND MAKE ROOM FOR JOY

There is a time for everything, and a season for
every activity under the heavens.
ECCLESIASTES 3:1

We are prone toward imbalance and disorder. For you physics enthusiasts, it is the second law of thermodynamics that the more time goes by, the greater the disorder. I tried to explain this to my parents when they told me to clean my room, but they still didn't give me a pass on all the LEGOs on the floor. Still, the principle remains true. We tend toward disorder and decline. But we don't have to just accept or submit to this eventuality.

During storms, the cargo on a ship will sometimes shift, causing the boat to list to one side. This kind of disorder makes it more likely for the boat to flip over. Rather than just accepting this to be inevitable, the crew can decide to right the ship by moving a few things around on the deck. We can do the same thing.

Think of your own "ship's" cargo as all those things you have accumulated: commitments you have made, careers you are engaged in, relationships you are maintaining. Take a hard look at how full the deck on your boat has become over the years. If yours looks like mine, you ran out of deck space a long time ago and now have cargo containers of obligations stacked on top of other cargo containers of responsibilities.

Life can leave us listing to one side. If this has happened to you, right the ship by sorting out or tossing overboard those commitments that once served an important purpose in your life but no longer do. It might be the nonprofit board you serve on, the event you volunteer at, the gala you always attend, or the annual trip you always take. Perhaps the season has passed for these things, and they no longer need to be a focus for you. Clear some space. Identify those things that give you joy and are filled to the brim with purpose and intention and move those to the center. There is a time for everything, and sometimes righting the ship means clearing the decks.

**Rather than moving a relationship or a habit or a job around
to a different part of the boat, let's clear the decks today.**

BALANCE OUT THE NEGATIVE WITH TRUTH IN KINDNESS

Do not let any unwholesome talk come out of your mouths,
but only what is helpful for building others up according
to their needs, that it may benefit those who listen.
EPHESIANS 4:29

When I wrote my first book, it was posted for sale on Amazon. There, readers who like a book can give you up to five stars if they loved the book and as few as one star if they hated it and offer a few words about what they thought about it. One of the first reviews that came in rated my book only one star. I was gutted. The person said it wasn't a very good book and I should stick to being a lawyer. Even millions of copies later, I still think about that one-star rating. How come we are wired this way?

The reason we react the way we do to adverse inputs is complicated and would take a team of shrinks to fully explore, but there is a concept known as a negativity bias which, in a nutshell, explains that negative things have a greater effect on us than positive ones. Think of when you have a conversation with a friend. Dozens of nice and affirming things could be said, but if one comment strikes you wrong, it might wreck your whole day. We come by this negativity bias honestly; it is in our primal nature to learn to give added weight to the negative.

If the guy in the cave next door had a great couple-year run inviting animals to stop by to pet them on the nose but then has a bad couple of minutes with a T. rex who stayed for dinner—because the guy *was* dinner—we put extra emphasis on that one negative event and our gene pool grows while the other guy's is digested. But while these instincts can serve us in the fight to survive, they stop serving us when we allow them to keep us from moving forward.

What we say can have a big impact on the people around us too. For this reason, Paul told his friends not to let any unwholesome talk come out of their mouths, but only to say what is helpful for building others up according to their needs. I understand why, because one misplaced word can become a huge distraction to others.

No, I'm not saying you need people who will only blow sunshine your way. You do need truth tellers, but you need truth tellers who are also kind and have your best interests in mind.

> Surround yourself with the people who will help
> you see your life, your friendships, your faith
> accurately, and who will do this out of love.

APRIL 18

FORGIVENESS IS A BIG DEAL TO GOD; FORGIVE LOTS, AND THEN SOME

Then the master called the servant in. "You wicked servant," he said, "I canceled all that debt of yours because you begged me to. Shouldn't you have had mercy on your fellow servant just as I had on you?"
MATTHEW 18:32–33

Every time I read the parable of the unforgiving servant, I see myself in it. Maybe you can see a little of yourself too. You know the story. A guy owed ten thousand talents. Think of this debt as about a quarter of a billion dollars. The servant asked the king for more time to square up the debt. Instead, the king went over the top and forgave the entire debt before the servant could even finish begging for a break and a payment plan. But check out this plot twist: the newly forgiven servant then turned around and put the squeeze on someone who owed him a day's wages, or what is only about one hundred dollars. The king heard about it and came after the servant for all that he had previously forgiven and then some.

What is the point of this story? Simple. Forgiveness is a big deal to God. He gives it and He expects it, and not in small, TSA-sized quantities. He wants you to go full Costco on it. The grace we get should turn into more grace.

The idea of forgiveness wasn't new to those hearing this parable at the time. According to Jewish law, every seven years, debts were forgiven. It was like a chapter 7 bankruptcy without the bankruptcy part. It was a total do-over, a refresh, and a brand-new restart.

Who do you need to forgive today? Who needs to catch a break from you? This isn't about paying it forward or paying Jesus back for what He did for you; you don't have that kind of coin. This is your reminder to remember what He's done for you. Then do the right thing in response as you interact with the people around you.

Make the call, send the note, take the shot. It takes guts, but you will be changed from the inside out as you make bold moves in the direction of forgiveness.

SEARCH YOUR HEART FOR THE GOLD

The purposes of a person's heart are deep waters,
but one who has insight draws them out.
PROVERBS 20:5

Not far from where I grew up is a place called the Winchester Mystery House. It is a huge home and has 160 bedrooms, 40 staircases, 47 fireplaces, and 13 bathrooms. This place was built by the inventor of the Winchester rifle, and he spent much of his fortune building it. Evidently, he believed that as long as he kept building this house he wouldn't die. Things didn't turn out the way he was hoping, and he died, but he gave the house and a pile of cash to his widow, who also believed she wouldn't die if she kept building (all evidence to the contrary).

What makes the Winchester Mystery House even more odd is that there are stairways that go nowhere, rooms with no windows, and still others that have no doors. The construction feels haphazard at best. It is as if they were so busy building, they didn't stop to have a plan. Sometimes we do the same thing in our lives when we confuse having a lot of activity with leading a purposeful life.

Do a quick audit of the things you are spending your time and money on. Are you choosing the steps you are taking with intention, or are you just doing whatever you feel like doing in the moment? This exercise isn't about beating yourself up but instead uncovering where you might be doing a lot but not doing something useful, like old man Winchester.

If you are building a business, are you thinking long term? Do you have an heir and a spare? If you are building a marriage and a family, how is it going? What kind of relationships are you aiming to have, and how are your choices working in that direction?

No matter what it is you are aiming for in your life, wade into the deep and lasting purposes Jesus said were available if we would build a life with a great deal of intention—with Him at the center.

Search your heart.

FILL YOUR LIFE WITH DECISIONS, NOT DISTRACTIONS

Be sober-minded; be watchful. Your adversary the devil prowls
around like a roaring lion, seeking someone to devour.
1 PETER 5:8 ESV

I took my boat out for a ride one early morning. After taking in a stunning sunrise, I drove back to the dock, walked up to the house, and sat down in my favorite chair, where I start each day. As I looked out across the water, I saw a boat on the other side of the bay that was the same shape and size as mine. I got my binoculars out to take a closer look, and to my chagrin, I realized it looked like my boat because it *was* my boat. I had become distracted when I got back to the dock and had forgotten to tie the boat up. Instead, I'd hopped out and just walked away.

Distractions result in drifting every time, whether it is a boat or an ambition. You will know you are drifting in your ambitions when you have no completion date for the next step. You will know you are drifting in your relationships when you settle for shallow talk and avoid the deeper dive into things that matter the most. You will know you are drifting in your relationship with God when you think about matters of faith but rarely find yourself acting upon those ideas.

I have a friend who got distracted while making her family a Thanksgiving meal, and instead of turning the oven to the bake setting when she slid the turkey in, she turned it by mistake to self-cleaning mode. The oven door locked, and she watched helplessly as the twenty-pound bird was incinerated over the next hour.

Distraction will always leave us hungry, and we will be tempted to fill that hunger with things that are not helpful to us. This is why the apostle Peter warned that the devil prowls around like a lion looking for someone to devour. Where you find distraction, you'll often find the devil.

Fill your life with decisions, not distractions. Decide right now that you will not be distracted by a bad decision, a misstep, or a bad job.

**Replace distraction with direction. You won't get it all done in a
day, but you will find greater purpose and clarity in your life.**

THE POWER OF LOVE IN OUR LIVES IS THE SAME POWER THAT RAISED JESUS FROM THE DEAD

I pray that the eyes of your heart may be enlightened in order that you may know the hope to which he has called you, the riches of his glorious inheritance in his holy people, and his incomparably great power for us who believe. That power is the same as the mighty strength he exerted when he raised Christ from the dead and seated him at his right hand in the heavenly realms.

EPHESIANS 1:18–20

The same Spirit that raised Jesus from the dead dwells in us, offering us a new way of living if we are willing to step into it. When we do, people can see it in the way we treat others and respond to everyday situations, as we are attentive to the needs of those around us and we show kindness and patience, even when it's challenging. So when you are confronted with impatience or angst from others, remember that it is the spirit of this world you are encountering. Don't take the bait. Instead, choose to respond differently, and go with your second instinct—the one led by the power of God's Spirit.

Prepare in advance how you are going to show Christ living within you. I've done this by giving myself specific reminders of how I want my life to show this. Here are a few I've found helpful: "I'm working on patience. That's what the resurrection of Christ means in me." "I'm going to work on being more available to people. That's what the resurrection of Christ means to me." Write a few sentences of your own about the power that raised Christ, which lives in you, and how you want your life to show this to others.

Approaching each day with enthusiasm, anticipation, and a determination to live in alignment with the resurrection power of Christ will lead us to respond to people in a way that reflects the love and grace of Jesus. All of that power is there; we just need to decide to tap into it.

As we step into this post-Easter season, let's treat every day like it is game day and our opportunity to show the world that Jesus' power within us is alive and active.

DELIGHT IN BRINGING PEOPLE A BOATLOAD OF JOY AND HOPE—GOD DOES

*I always thank my God as I remember you in my prayers,
because I hear about your love for all his holy people
and your faith in the Lord Jesus. . . . Your love has given
me great joy and encouragement, because you, brother,
have refreshed the hearts of the Lord's people.*

PHILEMON 1:4–5, 7

Some people pop their *ps* when they use the phrase "people pleaser," as if it is a loathsome disease. But people pleasing has gotten a bad rap, in my opinion. Frankly, I am a lot more concerned about people who are indifferent to the opportunity to please a couple of people in the right ways.

Don't get me wrong. I'm not going to get confused and distracted by bowing to the wishes of others or altering what I do for applause, but I delight in bringing people a boatload of joy and hope. If there's an opportunity to do that, to bring a smile and a little dash of whimsy to my fellow humans in the middle of their day-to-day struggle, I am going to jump at the chance.

Paul was in jail in Rome when he wrote to his friend Philemon, who was a wealthy businessman. He said that Philemon's love had given him great joy and encouragement, because he had refreshed the hearts of the people he was with. Philemon had been wronged by someone he trusted, and Paul wanted to remind Philemon of the importance of mercy and forgiveness in our faith.

We get to live into these words from Paul and choose to be people who are filled with love. When we do, the people we encounter will walk away encouraged.

**Do you have an opportunity today to bring someone
in your circle a little delight? Take a short detour
from your regular routine and show that person
they are seen and known and loved.**

IT'S HARD TO SET YOURSELF ASIDE FOR OTHERS; DO IT ANYWAY

Agree with each other, love each other, be deep-spirited friends. Don't push your way to the front; don't sweet-talk your way to the top. Put yourself aside, and help others get ahead. Don't be obsessed with getting your own advantage. Forget yourselves long enough to lend a helping hand.

PHILIPPIANS 2:2–4 MSG

We need to be careful about what we say. Here's a pro tip for you if you want to do a better job forging new friendships and preserving the ones you already have: add a beat or two between when you think about saying something and when you say it. When someone says something you're not sure about, ask yourself, *Is there any part of this I can identify with?* It might not be something you agree with, but perhaps you can identify with the underlying intent. I'll give you an example.

If someone feels zealously in favor of a highly politicized issue you feel mostly against, see if you can identify with what it feels like to have a deeply held opinion, to be all-in on a topic. Sure, you might think they're wrong about this specific issue or the conclusion they reached, but you can still love them and be deep-spirited friends with them. Do what Paul said and put yourself aside for a moment. Will this be hard to do? Of course it will. Do it anyway. Then, as you continue talking, ask about the experiences the other person may have had that contributed to their opinion. Be genuinely curious about how they got there.

This is going to feel impossible to do if you are just thinking how absolutely wrong they are or how skewed their opinions are from reality. That's why Paul called on us to come into community with the goal of exhibiting love and putting ourselves aside, rather than with a desire to push ourselves ahead. This will take having a humble enough view of yourself and a high enough view of the other person.

It's easy to want to dominate and control the conversations we are in. Resist the urge to take over. Everyone has a right to an opinion, but neither having an opinion nor being offended means you are right. You might just be louder than everybody else around you.

If you find yourself in a conversation today that you feel unsure of, pause and think about how you can put yourself aside and approach the other person with curiosity and humility.

SWAP OUT JUDGMENT FOR LOVE AND CURIOSITY, AND SEE WHAT HAPPENS

Do not judge, or you too will be judged. For in the same
way you judge others, you will be judged, and with the
measure you use, it will be measured to you.
MATTHEW 7:1–2

It's easy to judge others because we came from the factory prewired to make judgments. It is how we survived, dodged dinosaurs, learned who to trust and who to keep at a safe distance. And it's how we created safe communities of people to live with. The truth is, the judgments we make are loaded with our known and unknown biases. For instance, I have gray hair, and in some cultures, this is valued as reflecting wisdom and trustworthiness. In others, dyeing a man's hair with henna to give it a red appearance is thought to have religious significance. In still other cultures, youthfulness is more highly valued and people dye their hair black to look younger.

Beyond culture, our lived experiences will also give our judgments a big shove in one direction or another. If someone with big hair or thick glasses or with an accent or who hails from a certain country did something either wonderful or horrible in your life, you might bring that experience to the interactions you have with a person or group of people with those same characteristics. In this way, our instinctive reactions are overcome by our lived experiences and become biases.

To avoid getting caught up in unfair judgments about other people, we need to figure out what beliefs we hold that are sabotaging our development. Then we can overwrite those judgments with the words of Jesus, words about rejecting comparison and judgment and swapping ivory-tower opinions for countless kind actions. Let's apologize for the times when we have let our judgments cause us to ignore the creative hand of God at work in people's lives.

Today, try showing love, acceptance, and the deepest level of understanding you can muster to replace the temptation to judge someone. Then stand back and watch God do something beautiful.

REIN IN NEGATIVE TALK, BUT LET LOOSE WITH LOVE

Those who consider themselves religious and yet
do not keep a tight rein on their tongues deceive
themselves, and their religion is worthless.

JAMES 1:26

I love Mexican food, and in San Diego, we have lots of it. I am kind of a DIY guy, and at my favorite Mexican food restaurant, I particularly like it when they bring me fajitas with all the pieces of a meal that I get to assemble myself.

The server will bring over the still-sizzling pan and put it down in front of me, popping and radiating with heat, kind of like a space shuttle reentering the atmosphere, loaded with cooked chicken. The server always cautions me to be careful and not to touch the pan because it is very hot. The warnings are always welcomed, even though the danger is obvious.

James, the half-brother of Jesus, gave the people following Jesus some obvious advice, too, which we should welcome. He said that we should be careful what we say. James talked about how what we say can get us in trouble if we are not careful. It would be like touching the sizzling fajita skillet with our tongue.

Even though we know what we say can have a big and negative impact on the people around us, some of us are careless with our words anyway. It's important to be careful about what we say because harsh, hurtful words can cause people to take their attention off important things like hope and faith and patience and kindness and Jesus.

James linked what we say to what we believe, and he is right. We can't pretend we love God, then run our mouth with words that are not honoring to Him.

Make it your goal to steer clear of words that hurt or divide or accuse. Keep a tight rein on your tongue.

THERE IS FREEDOM ON THE OTHER SIDE OF GUILT

And when he had given thanks, he broke it and said, "This is
my body, which is for you; do this in remembrance of me."
1 CORINTHIANS 11:24

Once, at the end of a very consequential case I brought to trial in a court in another country, the judge signed the decree and then did something I will always remember. He took the pen, broke it, and threw it off the table as he said, "What has been done today will never be undone."

That was certainly a solemn moment. It was also an accurate picture of the entire gospel message: God took His son, broke Him, threw the pieces off the table, and, regarding everything that has the power to separate us from God, He said, "What's been done today on the cross will never be undone."

We have all experienced guilt for mistakes we have made. Sometimes it comes out as lament or regret or sometimes a confusing cocktail of conflicting emotions that feel, in a word, yucky. But with guilt also comes a way forward, a brokenness of our spirits that can humble us enough to push us to make much-needed changes.

Don't let your guilt box you in or bring you to a standstill. Don't let it keep you from the freedom on the other side. Think about that gospel message when Jesus sat with His friends and broke bread: "What's been done today will never be undone." Jesus freed us up from having to live in that place of feeling bad, separated, and broken. It's not that we're going to be impervious to those feelings, but there is freedom if we will reach out and grab an armful.

Let Jesus reach His strong hand in your direction and welcome you to the next steps of the journey. Let love and grace kick to the curb the guilt that is blocking your way forward.

**Don't wait another day to realize what God has done to save you
from your mistakes, and then live into the freedom He's given you.**

PEOPLE ARE NOT PROJECTS

"If a man owns a hundred sheep, and one of them wanders
away, will he not leave the ninety-nine on the hills and go to look
for the one that wandered off? And if he finds it, truly I tell you,
he is happier about that one sheep than about the ninety-nine
that did not wander off. In the same way your Father in heaven
is not willing that any of these little ones should perish."

MATTHEW 18:12–14

Jesus spoke to His friends about sheep and what to do when they wandered. He did the math so everyone would realize that it is so important to the shepherd to find the one, he would leave the ninety-nine to look. But before a shepherd can pursue a lost sheep, the shepherd needs to know it's lost.

When a kid gets lost at the beach in Brazil, everyone claps their hands and shouts out, "Lost, lost, lost!" until one of the parents comes and finds them. Isn't this a beautiful custom? So many people get in on this that it can sound like a Taylor Swift concert. Unfortunately, this isn't what happens when we become lost most of the time. In fact, sometimes we don't even realize we are lost, and others don't either.

How often does someone in our circle of friends or our community of faith lower the periscope and quietly go missing because they are lost and wounded and hurting? There are as many reasons as there are hurts to explain why. Shame, confusion, anger, frustration, garden-variety embarrassment, and transition are just a few.

If you want to show someone who is hurting the love and grace you believe in, go find them today. Certainly pray, but don't just put your hands together in prayer. Clap your hands a little and draw the right kind of quiet and empathetic attention to them as you run in their direction. And when you arrive at their side, don't come with an agenda. Love doesn't need one, and whatever you come up with won't be good enough anyway. Remember, people are not projects.

**Find one or two friends you have lost touch with and make the call,
drop the note, hand deliver the flowers, or bring the Dippin' Dots.**

BRING PEACE WITH YOU AND HARMONY WILL HAPPEN ON ITS OWN

If it is possible, as far as it depends on you, live at peace with everyone.
ROMANS 12:18

I have a friend named Joanna who is accomplished in so many areas, it's almost unbelievable. She is a pediatrician, a clothes designer, a wife, a concert violinist, and so much more. I asked Joanna to come to San Quentin with us and to bring her violin to play for the guys in the class I teach there. Always kind, she agreed and flew out from Chicago to make some new friends.

As an afterthought, I remembered that one of the guys in my class was allowed to have a violin in prison. I got word to him to bring his violin to our monthly gathering and told him I had a friend who was bringing hers.

The day of the class, my friend in prison arrived with his violin already out of its case. He quickly tuned it and started playing a song. Joanna grinned, tapped her foot, and nodded her head in approval. When he was done, she asked if he would mind if she played along with him. "Sure," he said, not knowing anything about Joanna or her skill level. She slung her violin under her chin, grabbed her bow, and nodded to him to start. My guess is that he was slightly off in his tuning, but Joanna didn't say a word. She just adjusted her fingers down a sixteenth of an inch to sync up with his instrument. She played a few notes with him, then started harmonizing and adding to what he was playing. We were no longer in prison. Carnegie Hall could not hold all the love and joy on display as Joanna met his notes with hers. We all soared. None of us needed to know the harmonic details of what Joanna was doing; we could just tell that it sounded right.

In the book of Romans, Paul encouraged his friends that, as much as it is in their power to do so, they should live at peace and in harmony with one another. Rather than telling someone who is a little out of tune to fix themselves first, what if we learned to make a couple of small adjustments ourselves to accommodate them? This isn't going light on doctrine; it's going big on Jesus.

Who do you need to harmonize with today?

MARK YOUR DAYS WITH LOVE

*A thousand years in your sight are like a day that has
just gone by, or like a watch in the night.*
PSALM 90:4

We all measure time differently. When I was a lawyer, we kept track of our time in six-minute increments. When our kids were young, we wanted to give them something within their experience to measure time, so when we were on a car ride and they would ask, "Are we there yet?" instead of saying, "Fifteen minutes," which wouldn't mean a lot to them, I said we were seven bags of microwave popcorn away.

Another interesting way to measure time is in watches. This is something you do when you're sailing. I have sailed to and from Hawaii a couple of times, and each time our crew of only six would divide into watches, each four hours long. Usually, the watches switch off at 4:00 a.m., 8:00 a.m., noon, 4:00 p.m., 8:00 p.m., and midnight. There are no clocks on the boat, and it doesn't really matter, because it is more fitting to listen to the ship's bell count off the time. The ship's bell rings once at the end of the first half-hour of a watch, and every half-hour after that it adds one more bell. If you looked at your watch at 4:00 a.m., you would hear eight bells, which let the previous watch know their shift was done. At 4:30, there would be one bell, at 5:00, two bells, at 5:30 a.m., three bells, and so on, up to eight bells, which would indicate the end of another watch.

I don't know how many bags of popcorn or bells you and I have left in our lives and how many watches we will be allowed to stand. But it's not the amount of time that matters so much; it is what we do with that time.

While you are able, stand your watch with love. Look for opportunities to extend acceptance, offer hope, increase delight, and meet the needs you see around you.

**Mark the time and your days with love and, while
you make the popcorn, listen for the bells.**

DON'T SETTLE FOR LESS THAN JESUS—EVER

People will be lovers of themselves, lovers of money, boastful,
proud, abusive, disobedient to their parents, ungrateful, unholy,
without love, unforgiving, slanderous, without self-control, brutal,
not lovers of the good, treacherous, rash, conceited, lovers of
pleasure rather than lovers of God—having a form of godliness
but denying its power. Have nothing to do with such people.
2 TIMOTHY 3:2-5

We've all heard about "the most interesting man in the world." People still delight in attributing amazing and unobtainable attributes to him. "The circus ran away to join him." "The dark is afraid of him." "He once parallel parked a train." These imagined exploits are fun and I like to hear the big talk about this fictional person, but that's all it is, just big talk about things that didn't really happen. Enter stage left into history Jesus of Nazareth. He and His Father made the world and everything in it. He turned water into wine. He raised people from the dead, and then He died and was raised from the dead as well. Jesus wasn't made up or imagined but was actually here. What is there not to like or admire about Jesus? He was truly the most interesting man in the world.

Sadly, the reason a lot of people shy away from Jesus is that the people who say they believe in Him don't appear to be different from anyone else.

In his second letter to Timothy, Paul wrote about pretty unflattering attributes some people will have in the last days. He said they will talk a big game about what they believe but, when you blow the foam off the top, there will be nothing there. Paul sounded harsh, but he didn't say to reason with these people or to dismiss what they are doing. He told his friends to have nothing to do with them. Yikes.

Unlike the fictional most interesting man in the world, we are reflections of and representatives of the One who is truly the most interesting Man in the world. Be mindful of what you do with that responsibility and who you hang with.

**Living into the difficult demands Jesus makes of us requires that
we stand apart while everyone else is trying to stand out. It's
your move. What is your next step in the direction of Jesus?**

MAY

GOD'S NOT LOOKING MERELY FOR COMPLIANCE; HE WANTS OUR HEARTS

Let us run with perseverance the race marked out for us, fixing
our eyes on Jesus, the pioneer and perfecter of faith.
HEBREWS 12:1-2

We got a puppy when the kids left the house. It seemed like a good idea at the time. We thought it would keep us company and not monopolize the bathrooms or leave dirty dishes in the sink or borrow my truck and return it on empty like our kids did. The dog arrived at the house, and it was a truly wonderful couple of hours—until the puppy took a dump on the carpet. But, hey, puppies are just that way on the first day as they get their bearings, right? Wrong. This dog was evidently incontinent, and the only thing he missed for the next few years was the lawn. He could walk past four IKEA rugs to do his thing on a Persian rug. It was truly remarkable.

We don't always mess things up in the same way this dog wrecked our house, but we do keep repeating the same failures. Yet God is good and patient and still loves us. He wants our attention and obedience, but when we foul up, He doesn't wish He had not invested so much in us. Instead, He delights in us. He is not looking merely for compliance; He wants our hearts.

We can be a lot harder on ourselves and on one another than God is. We see someone mess up, and we quickly form a long list of judgments without knowing any of the underlying emotions, circumstances, and habits driving their conduct. When Paul talked about throwing off things that hinder us, one of the first things he said that needs to go is our tendency to meet people's mess-ups with judgment about their conduct rather than concern about their hurting hearts. Resist the urge. Instead, know where to fix your eyes.

When I met Sweet Maria, I couldn't keep my eyes off her. She could be in a room filled with other people, but I would be locked in on her, noticing all her movements, her laugh, and her kindness. I know what it feels like to have my eyes fixed on someone, and Paul said to fix our eyes on Jesus in the same way.

**Resist the distractions of comparison and criticism today
and fix your eyes on Jesus, the perfecter of your faith.**

SOMETIMES BEING LIKE JESUS MEANS CARRYING A BACKPACK FULL OF BURDENS FOR A FRIEND

Carry each other's burdens, and in this way
you will fulfill the law of Christ.
GALATIANS 6:2

When I was thirteen years old, I got on my bicycle and rode to the beach. There is nothing remarkable about this, except that the beach was sixty miles in one direction by backroads. I wasn't allowed to go alone, of course—that would be irresponsible—so my parents had me bring my older friend with me who was fourteen years old. No doubt, he could bring a rich depth of life experiences to the table and give me the sage advice I would need if something went terribly wrong on the trip.

I had stuffed some supplies such as water and food, a jacket, a tent, a deck of cards, and a spare tire in a backpack for the trip. This was long before fancy saddle bags that strapped to our bicycles. It wasn't until we were halfway to the beach that I realized I had packed way too much for the trip. I took a turn a little tight and crashed, which sent me and my backpack sprawling. My friend offered to offload some of what I was carrying and put it in his backpack.

We eventually got to the beach, spent the night in a single-wide trailer somebody gave us the key to, and rode home the next day. I am still a little fuzzy about why my parents allowed me to go on this adventure. Perhaps they thought that burning off a little extra energy would do me, and them, some good. I think God was using this time in my life to help me understand the value of carrying other people's burdens, because He allowed someone to carry mine when I really needed it. I have a set of metrics I use now to know if a new acquaintance will go the distance. It is not how fun or smart or engaging they are; it is how well they bear others' burdens. The people who have mastered how to carry burdens for others always make great friends.

Who do you know today who could use a hand or a shoulder to carry some of their burdens? Once they come to mind, make the call, and show up.

FILTER OUT THE JUNK MAIL TO CREATE SPACE FOR GOD

Check out everything, and keep only what's good.
1 THESSALONIANS 5:21 MSG

I don't know about you, but I receive a lot of junk mail—so much that it fills up quite a lot of space on the counter each day. Junk mail is a lot like the various voices we have trying to sway us one way or the other every day. Sometimes it's the media we're consuming, and sometimes it's the opinions of our friends and family.

Sure, some of it may be helpful and good, but a lot of it can turn out to be the opposite. Let this serve as a gentle reminder to refrain from lending an ear to voices other than that of Jesus. Treat the false ideas that come your way as though they were junk mail, destined for the wastebasket.

Follow in Paul's footsteps, who advised examining everything in the light of Scripture. Dive into the Bible each morning, not just to read through pages but to seek answers by asking, "What do the Scriptures say about this topic?" And do not rely solely on what someone else says the Scriptures say either. Take the time to read it for yourself, so you're not easily led down a false path. In the book of Matthew, Jesus Himself warned the people: "You are in error because you do not know the Scriptures or the power of God."

By silencing the voices that do not align with God's message, much like Jesus silenced the demons, you will create space within your heart to hear what God is saying. In the book of Galatians, there is a warning to flee if even an angel from heaven preaches a different gospel.

We can only recognize a counterfeit gospel if we are intimately acquainted with the genuine one.

Spot the junk mail in your life today and stop opening it up.

THE JUICE IS WORTH THE SQUEEZE AND THE REWARDS ARE WORTH THE RISK

Then I heard the voice of the Lord saying, "Whom shall I send?
And who will go for us?" And I said, "Here am I. Send me!"
ISAIAH 6:8

Does the situation you are struggling with feel too big for you to handle? Perhaps you are waiting for someone else to step up and lead. You have a vision for change but don't feel qualified to be the one pushing things forward. Maybe you feel like the young man in 1 Samuel 3:4, hearing the call of God but feeling confused about where to go. Or you're like the one in Isaiah 6:8, feeling inadequate for what is before you.

Are you tempted to give the verse a twist and say, "Here I am, Lord. *Send them!*"? Or are you like Moses, asked by God to lead but feeling inadequate because you get easily tongue-tied? Dig a little deeper. Take a breath. If any of these sound like you, summon some divine courage and consider going all in. Tell God, "Here I am. Send me."

Where is it that you feel stuck? What is it that you have tried without seeing the results you were hoping for? We all face the decision at one point or another over whether to press forward or bail. What would it mean for you to resist the urge to call it a day and, instead, continue pushing a little deeper into your relationships, your faith, or your career?

Going deeper takes vulnerability, and none of us gets there without substantial personal cost. But the juice is worth the squeeze, and the rewards are worth the risk.

What move will you make today? Figure out what it will take for you to continue pushing in the direction you have been called.

Know that if Jesus is calling you deeper, you can trust that He'll be with you every step of the way.

WE'RE DESIGNED FOR COMMUNITY; THERE'S NO NEED TO GO IT ALONE

They devoted themselves to the apostles' teaching and to
fellowship, to the breaking of bread and to prayer. . . . All the
believers were together and had everything in common.
ACTS 2:42-44

Years ago, I was scuba diving in Canada with my friend Doug. We were hoping
to spear a fish or two for dinner. It is a good idea to dive with a buddy, so you
can be there for each other if something goes wrong. Doug was following me
with a speargun in his hand. I was mindful that an accidental misfire on his
part would prove to be both awkward and painful for me, so I was separating
myself from him by a safe distance.

Unfortunately, the regulator on my oxygen supply unexpectedly failed.
One breath it was oxygen filling my lungs, and the next breath it was all salt
water. I was deep under water at the time and could have really benefitted from
having Doug nearby to buddy breathe with me (to share the air supply by passing the mouthpiece back and forth), like we had practiced in training, but no
luck. There was no option other than to head for the surface fast. Fortunately,
the small amount of compressed air in my lungs expanded as I bolted for the
surface, which got me there safely.

Here's why I tell you this story: some of us are in the habit of going it
alone. Sometimes it works out well and you avoid getting speared in the back
(or in other parts). But the problem is that God made it so we would thrive in
community. The choice is not binary. In other words, it's not a choice between
being with everybody all the time or being with nobody ever.

The young church in the book of Acts understood the idea of being together
and having things in common. They had a common love of God, even though
they no doubt had different ways of expressing that love. And because this amazing community was operating in this fashion, their numbers grew every day. Who
wouldn't want in on this level of kindness, connection, and service to others?

**Join a community today. Find a shared
experience, and see what happens.**

FAITH AND HOPE ARE JUST WAITING TO HIT A HOME RUN IN YOUR LIFE

In Lystra there sat a man who was lame. He had been that way from birth and had never walked. He listened to Paul as he was speaking. Paul looked directly at him, saw that he had faith to be healed and called out, "Stand up on your feet!" At that, the man jumped up and began to walk.

ACTS 14:8–10

The adventures of the young Christians are recorded in the book of Acts. In one passage, Paul was telling people about Jesus and the power He could have in their lives if they wanted Him to be in charge of everything. There was a lame man listening intently to Paul's words. We're not sure how Paul knew, but my guess is that the lame man made some strong indications he believed Jesus had the power to heal him. So Paul called out to this man, commanding him to stand up, and to everyone's amazement, he did. Sometimes all it takes for a miracle to happen is a word spoken in faith and authority.

In my book *Love Does*, I shared a story about how I wanted to get into law school, but I wasn't qualified. I told the dean of the law school about how in the Bible there were loads of examples of people who had faith in God's power to make things happen and how they were healed even at just a few words from the apostles. So, I asked the dean to just say the words, "Get your books," and I'd be in. Inexplicably, that dean let me in, and for thirty years I delighted in being a lawyer.

What about you? Could you trust God enough to believe He can heal the most challenging parts of your life today? We are not testing God when we do this; we're genuinely relying on and trusting Him. It's about recognizing that He has power and authority over our broken relationships, the jobs we want to keep, or the ones we want to lose.

What is it that you need to trust God for? Where do you need to bring all your belief, even if everything inside you says what you are aiming for might be too much or too crazy?

Acknowledge that God has the authority to make things happen with just a word.

FOLLOWING JESUS THROUGH THE FOG

If any of you lacks wisdom, you should ask God, who gives generously to all without finding fault, and it will be given to you.
JAMES 1:5

I've sailed along the coast of California quite a few times. Thick fog banks can roll in sometimes, making the coastline largely disappear. This can be disorienting and a little bit scary, but if you look closely and focus, you'll find that you can still make out some recognizable features.

There isn't always a lighthouse to illuminate things as you might hope, but as you squint and look more closely, a little at a time you will start to recognize outlines of features on the shore. "Oh, I know what that is. . . . I know what that is too." And it won't be long before you are able to weave these sightings together and figure out where you are.

Keeping your eyes fixed on Jesus is similar. For me, like the apostle Paul wrote, living a life of faith can be like looking through a mirror dimly most of the time. I can kind of make out some shapes, and I have an idea of what might be there, but it's hard to feel certain about exactly what I'm looking at. Is that how it is for you, too, sometimes?

Here's a trick for finding some clarity: Look a little closer. With all that life throws at us, it gets more than a little murky sometimes. Get real about what is murky in your life and bring it to Jesus.

It's okay to have conflicting feelings and huge uncertainties when we're looking through the mirror dimly. Acknowledge those uncertainties and seek answers in the Scriptures.

**If you're feeling a little unsure today,
ask Jesus for more clarity. And keep staring
in His direction until you see Him face-to-face.**

DODGING HORNS WITH LOVE AND GRACE

Love your enemies, do good to those who hate you, bless those who curse you, pray for those who mistreat you. If someone slaps you on one cheek, turn to them the other also.
LUKE 6:27–29

We have a farm adjacent to The Oaks, our retreat center. I didn't grow up around sheep and goats and horses, so it has been fun to add to our collection of animals each year. My favorite barnyard animals so far are the Scottish Highlands cattle. We call them "fuzzy cows" because both the male and female cows have horns and they look a lot like a pet with long hair and bangs hanging between their eyes.

A person who raises cattle brought some baby fuzzy cows to us, and we were thrilled. He said he also had a full-grown female Highland cow we could have if we would like to give it a home. "Is it nice?" I asked, knowing we have quite a few people who visit and like to pet the cows. "Of course, just like a pet, super friendly," he promised. When the cow came off the trailer, it made a beeline for me and gored me with one of its horns. I looked down at my torn shirt and the small hole just below my ribs and said to the guy, "Hey, I thought you said this was a nice cow?" He shot a wry smile in my direction and said to me in his big Texas accent, "She don't know she has horns." Please, no mother-in-law jokes here.

Some of the most difficult people we encounter don't think they are being a pain. Sure, there are mean and unruly people who do hurtful things on purpose and others are just plain ornery. But far more common is a person like you or me who pokes someone's feelings without knowing we are doing it.

It's important to have truth tellers in our lives, but it's even more important to have grace givers. Today, when you encounter someone who is a little prickly, don't throw holy water at them or start a fight with communion crackers. Be that grace- and love-filled person that you know you also need sometimes, and you will leave a tremendous legacy behind.

Remember this: most people who say or do something off-putting just don't know they have horns.

SLOW DOWN, SHOW UP, AND BE AN AMBASSADOR FOR CHRIST

We are therefore Christ's ambassadors, as though God were making his appeal through us. We implore you on Christ's behalf: Be reconciled to God.
2 CORINTHIANS 5:20

I have served as the Honorary Consul for the Republic of Uganda for twenty years—yes, it's as unusual as it sounds. I'm not the US diplomat to Uganda; rather, I'm the Ugandan diplomat to the US. I stroll into embassies, and when they see my Irish face, they ask, "Where's the Ugandan guy?" To their surprise, I respond, "I'm the Ugandan guy." You might be wondering what a consul does. Basically, when someone can't get what they need, they reach out to the ambassador in Washington, DC. If they can't reach the ambassador, they come to the consul for help. So the consul is like a backup ambassador in some ways.

Consider this idea of ambassadorship. It can mean a lot of things, but among them is that you're the available person. If somebody needs something—perhaps they need help getting a visa—they will call and ask. As Christ's ambassadors, we need to be available, but we also need a message of safety. We need to have a reputation for being the safe person people can bring their concerns, questions, and needs to. Being Christ's ambassador doesn't mean being the top dog; that role belongs to Jesus. Instead, it means that we're available and safe and offer protection.

I don't always get it right, but I make a point of regularly trying to offer safety and availability to people. I spend many Wednesdays at Disneyland, specifically on Tom Sawyer Island. It is a place where I am accessible and ready for anyone at the park who wants to talk. I've also given my cell phone number to millions of people on the back page of my books, and I'm always delighted when one of them calls to chat. Don't merely claim availability; make yourself accessible and be prepared to provide both kindness and substance when people reach out in need.

You are God's ambassador. You are the consul for those who couldn't reach someone else in a time of need. When people encounter you, let them find acceptance and protection and safety.

Slow down, ditch the hurried glances at your watch, and convey the message, "I'm here for you."

FORGIVE EXTRAVAGANTLY, JUST AS JESUS FORGAVE YOU

"If you forgive anyone's sins, their sins are forgiven; if
you do not forgive them, they are not forgiven."
JOHN 20:23

After a few years of being married, Sweet Maria and I bought a thrashed two-bedroom house we couldn't afford. There was a hole in the floor where a heater was at one time located, lots of dry rot, and some wormy-looking things in the bathroom walls. It was gross, but we didn't have any money to fix it up, so we camped out as best we could.

We read somewhere that if you only had a few bucks to spend on your house, a trick was to paint the front door and put a new doorknob on it. It would be the first thing someone saw or touched and would make them feel welcomed, getting their attention off of how beat the rest of your house was. So we budgeted for a month and found a guy to spray the front door we had sanded down. He put four coats of shiny black paint on the door, and we splurged by dropping eighty dollars on a brass doorknob.

Our son Adam was learning how to write his name in preschool at the time. The day the shiny black door was installed, Adam evidently wanted to surprise us and show us what he had learned, so he scratched his name with a nail on the glossy, perfectly painted door. He certainly got our attention. When I got home from work, I stepped out of the car and walked up to my brand-new door and saw in huge capital letters the name ADAM.

I'll admit I was disappointed when I first saw the scratched-up door I had sacrificed a lot to make perfect. But, at the same time, I loved Adam, was eager to forgive him, and was also a little proud. This is how God feels about you and me. He made a perfect place we scratched up, but He doesn't just stand there, seeing our failures and grumbling under His breath about how badly we failed. He sees the bright promise of what is within and ahead of us and He is proud of us. (I'm waiting for Adam to purchase his first home so I can scratch DAD into his door.)

Let's give away extravagant amounts of forgiveness to those who have messed up, seeing not their mistakes but who God is making them into.

TAKE INVENTORY OF THE INGREDIENTS GOD HAS ALREADY GIVEN YOU—YOU PROBABLY HAVE ENOUGH TO MAKE A CAKE!

His divine power has given us everything we need
for a godly life through our knowledge of him who
called us by his own glory and goodness.
2 PETER 1:3

I have been teaching a class at San Quentin for many years. There is a guy in my class named Chris. Chris's problem is that he doesn't like prison food. He has another bigger problem, however, which is that he is going to be in San Quentin for a long time. So, what did he do about that? He figured out a way to make food he liked.

Chris is ingenious. He knows how to get what he needs. He got a hot plate for his coffee and rewired it so he can warm other things up. It gets so hot it burns off a half inch of the wire every time he uses it, so he keeps buying new ones, but now he can prepare food in his cell. I asked Chris what the coolest thing was that he has ever made in his cell, and he told me he once made a cheesecake. I couldn't make a birthday cake with a stainless-steel, Le Cordon Bleu–approved kitchen and a keg of marzipan, but Chris figured out what was available to him and made a whole cheesecake. I had him write down the recipe for me so I would remember. Here's what you do.

You get six sticky buns from the mess hall, bring them back to your cell, and tear them up. Then you mix in a cup of melted butter. There are no stores to go to, of course, so Chris has friends bring him the small rectangles of butter that are served with their food. After mixing these ingredients and a couple more together, he adds two cups of cream cheese. It turns out there are some guys at San Quentin who get bagels and cream cheese, and Chris got his hands on fourteen cream cheese packets. The last step is to chill the cheesecake. To do this, Chris's friends take the ice out of their drinks and run back across the yard to his cell before it melts. There Chris piles the ice on the cheesecake. It's a little nasty, but, hey, it works. Your life can too.

Simon Peter wrote in his second book that God has already given us everything we need to lead a beautiful life. Take inventory. What opportunities are already waiting for you? What community of people has God already dropped in your lap? Remember, God doesn't pass us messages; He gives us each other.

**Find a couple of good friends and
let them know what you need.**

SOMETIMES WE NEED TO QUIT SOMETHING GOOD TO MAKE ROOM FOR SOMETHING GREAT

"I have the right to do anything," you say—but not everything is beneficial.
"I have the right to do anything"—but not everything is constructive.
1 CORINTHIANS 10:23

If you want to become the newest, healthiest version of you, it is going to require making more room. To do this, you might need to quit a few things. It could be a habit, a relationship, or even your job. I'm not suggesting you quit your marriage—if it's tough, hang in there. But most other things are fair game. Maybe you have outgrown your current job. What was good for you when you started may not be great for you today. The promise of Scripture is that people change and become new creations, and that's a good thing.

Those of you who have spent some time with me know that I pulled into my driveway one day, after doing some "let's go save the whole world" stuff, and in the window of my home was a Help Wanted sign Sweet Maria had put up. She wasn't saying she needed help; she was saying, "Buddy, you need help. You are missing it."

In a moment of vulnerability, she told me, "I feel like you just picked everybody else on earth except me." This came from the person to whom I had said, in front of a bunch of people, "I will sacrifice everything for you." I realized I had lost the plot. It wasn't over bad things; it was all the good and important things that distracted me. I had been focused on kids, refugees, people in tremendous need. But I was drowning in the chocolate sea of good intentions. I had forgotten to care for the ones I love most.

Some of us are so busy helping others that we neglect those under our own roof. I realized I was that guy. And I can still slip into being that guy from time to time. If your life is so full that your family is suffering, it's time to think about what you can let go of to prioritize what's most important.

**So, what will it be? Don't just agree with me;
quit something today. Ready? Go.**

DON'T GET FAKED OUT BY FOOL'S GOLD, BUT INSTEAD BECOME RICH TOWARD GOD BY LOVING OTHERS TODAY

"But God said to him, 'Fool! This night your soul is required of you, and the things you have prepared, whose will they be?' So is the one who lays up treasure for himself and is not rich toward God."

LUKE 12:20–21 ESV

I own a gold mine in the Sierras. It has been handed down in my family for generations. There is not an ounce of gold in it, but there are quite a few critters residing underground in there. If spiders and squirrels were gold nuggets, I'd be a rich guy, but sadly, the gold mine is all webs and no cheddar.

Years ago, I decided to explore the mine. Walking in felt like entering an *Indiana Jones* movie set. I took a stick, wrapped an old T-shirt around it, doused it in kerosene, and made my way inside. The small tunnel instantly filled with smoke, which I don't remember happening to the hero in the movies. I bailed on the rustic idea and upgraded to a flashlight. I'm glad I stopped when I did, because the shaft the miners dug back in the 1800s suddenly went straight down twenty feet. When I got to the bottom, the tunnel went level for a few yards, then continued up and to the left. Here's why there were so many twists and turns. This mine was loaded with iron pyrite. It's called fool's gold because it glitters like gold but has no value. As they were searching for what was valuable, the miners needed to remove a lot of worthless things that looked enticing.

As you search for meaning, purpose, and success, it is tempting to think you will arrive there by accumulating cash or material items. But if you follow this path, you will find yourself living less in the present and more in the future, just like the rich man Jesus talked about in one of His parables. The rich man thought it would be a good idea to build larger buildings to store up more for later. It's not a bad idea to do some planning for the future, but Jesus was saying that if you want to be rich toward God, don't get faked out by what isn't valuable and lasting.

Look for the needy and hurting and lonely people. God is everywhere and in everything, but He promised He could easily be found in the least, the overlooked, the hurting, and the hopeless.

QUIT STARING IN THE REARVIEW MIRROR AND FOCUS ON THE ADVENTURE IN FRONT OF YOU

"Forget the former things; do not dwell on the past."
ISAIAH 43:18

There are moments in our lives when we will inevitably make the decision and perhaps say out loud, "Okay, I'm going to start anew." But then, moments later, you may hesitate and think, *Wait, I've tried this before and it didn't work out.* If you can identify with these feelings, here is the good news: God promises that we are new creations, if we want to be.

One aspect of starting anew involves overcoming the discouragement caused by previous setbacks and failed attempts. When you say, "I'm starting again," the word *again* can be painful, because you recall all the obstacles that got in your way the last time. What if, instead of beating yourself up again, you shake the Etch A Sketch of those failures and move on? Dwelling on the past does nothing to prepare you for right now. Certainly, learn from those experiences, but remember that God has greater plans for you than you may realize, and some of those plans take time to unfold.

I remember wanting a particular job that I never got despite trying over and over. It turned out not getting that job prepared me for an even better opportunity. On reflection, I don't know why I wanted the job so badly, because I would have been horrible at it. I thought I had been prevented, but I had been protected.

What do you need to let go of? If you find yourself stuck in a job where you no longer need to be, quit. If you are hesitant to make the call to your boss, give me a ring at 619-985-4747, and I will quit for you.

Embrace an "every day is new" mindset. The rearview mirror in your car is for combing your hair, not for being stuck looking back at your life. Take a lesson from Isaiah, when God said to "forget the former things."

Don't dwell on the past. Instead, focus on what
lies ahead and live with anticipation.

INFORMATION DOESN'T CHANGE PEOPLE; JESUS DOES

Seated in a window was a young man named Eutychus, who was sinking into a deep sleep as Paul talked on and on. When he was sound asleep, he fell to the ground from the third story and was picked up dead.

ACTS 20:9

If you have as much trouble as I do paying attention when there is a lot of information coming my way, you are in good company. In Acts 20, there was a gathering of believers, kind of like what some people now call a Bible study. Paul was the guy leading, and he evidently had a lot to say because he just kept talking and talking and talking. You know the type: great guy, but he just kept circling the field without ever landing the plane.

Eutychus, a young guy at the meeting, looked around for a spot where he wouldn't stand out. It was probably a warm Middle Eastern night, and he eyed the sill of an open window. That would do. He sat and listened to Paul speaking, and listened, and listened, and listened some more. I bet he wondered, *When is this Bible study going to end?* He could feel his eyes rolling back in his head and fought to stay awake. The next thing he remembered, he was coming to in the street outside of the building with Paul holding him in a bear hug. He had fallen out of the window and hit so hard, he died. It was the first recorded death by Bible study, but it wasn't the last. And get this: after Eutychus was raised from the dead, Paul went back upstairs and kept preaching through the entire night. Geesh!

The fact is, we are carpet-bombed with information every day, with only a tiny amount of it changing anything substantial in our lives. Information doesn't change people; Jesus does. What we really need, more than a list of instructions and hours of preaching, is an experience of the compassion and life-changing acceptance Jesus offered and a loving and accepting community to thrive in.

Find someone today you can engage with genuine interest and curiosity about their journey. Don't give them more information; love on them the way Jesus did.

SPREAD JOY LIKE BUTTER ON TOAST

May the God of hope fill you with all joy and peace in believing, so
that by the power of the Holy Spirit you may abound in hope.
ROMANS 15:13 ESV

It's tempting to compare how you are feeling with how other people seem to
be feeling. This is particularly true when it seems like everyone around you is
a lot happier than you. Know what I mean? Why not switch up the metrics
you are using to measure your level of happiness? Let's look instead at joy and
find a more accurate measure of the many ways you can experience a joyful,
meaningful life.

Real joy won't look like confetti, superficial hand-waving, and forced
laughter. It will be an inner sense of contentment punctuated by unrelenting
anticipation. It will also look like peace and the assurance that you are where
you need to be. In the Scriptures, you will find the promise that joy can be
found in rejoicing with those who rejoice and grieving with those who grieve
and celebrating what God has created in and around you.

Jesus told His friends that He had spoken various things to them in order
that His joy would be in them and so their joy would be made full. Do the
same for the people around you. Discover your part in this grand symphony of
life. You may be on the kettle drums or the piccolo, but whatever your role is,
let's make some noise about it.

Gather your family, create a band, or just clap pots and pans together. Let
the world know about your joy; don't keep it a secret. But remember, it's not
about just making noise; it's about sharing the experience of joy together. As
you do this, you'll be living fully into the expectation of joy.

**You are holding your permission slip in your hand to live
a more joyful and whimsical life; all you need to do is
enter into the place you have already been invited.**

A FEW FAITHFUL FRIENDS CAN BE THE BALM YOU NEED IN LIFE

Though one may be overpowered, two can defend themselves.
A cord of three strands is not quickly broken.
ECCLESIASTES 4:12

If someone stands just a few inches too close when they are talking to you, it's a little creepy, right? I find myself slowly moving backward to create some much-needed personal space. People get in our spaces for several possible reasons. The best reasons are to give us a welcomed hug or to show trust or project a ton of support, but there are other less noble reasons too. The person might be crowding our space because they lack people skills or are trying to assert a dollop of power in a misplaced attempt at asserting dominance. Some of us react to these more negative experiences by creating a no-fly zone around ourselves that extends beyond the encounter. The truth is, we need the right people around us—just in the right ways.

Ecclesiastes is a book Solomon wrote about getting right with God and getting right with each other. He said the best way to do life is together. He said two people back-to-back defending themselves have a big advantage over one person alone, and three don't stand a chance of being broken. I think King Solomon was on to something here.

Find two or three people to draw close to. Go for the three-strand cord, but don't get too carried away. Having fifty people in your life is not manageable. Even Jesus had a cord of three strands among the twelve friends who were always with Him.

Draw close to a couple of safe people today; go a little deeper with them. Give them the biggest lung-popping, non-creepy bear hug you can muster. God wants us to grow in community. Sure, there will be a couple of people you will need to air-gap along the way. They're not bad people; they may be just standing a little too close.

Don't settle for a life full of side hugs and shallow conversations. Lean into the closeness a few good friends can bring.

PUT SOME WHEELS ON YOUR FAITH AND TAKE THE TIME TO LOVE SOMEBODY

Dear children, let us not love with words or
speech but with actions and in truth.
1 JOHN 3:18

It's easy to go through life navigating the many demands placed upon us by making our lives small and our viewpoints narrow. It can feel like we are Pinocchio and everyone else has a string tied to us that they can pull. The reaction to all the inputs can be to keep our heads down, work on what our own challenges are, and not take the time to engage in the many difficulties others are encountering. After all, who has the time? The answer is simple: we do—if we will make it. It is not lost on me that the first thing God did when He was creating the world was make time, but this is sometimes the last thing we will do for one another.

Think for a moment what it would look like to lift your eyes from life's many demands and take a genuine interest in others' lives. Find some people today, and ask them these questions:

"What is it that you want?"

"What is it that you love?"

"What is something that would light you up?"

Then, ask yourself what you have, who you know, or what you might do that could be helpful to them as they pursue what God has placed in their hearts.

Some people think pointing out that someone's tires are bald is being helpful, and in a very limited sense it is. Why not go change their tires instead? They'll get some much-needed tread, and you will have put wheels (literally) on your faith. It is only when we get skin in the game that we experience the kind of lasting impact Jesus talked to His friends about.

I want to be remembered for the love I expressed, not the ideas I had and didn't act on. How about you?

If you want to be remembered for your love, take a genuine interest in the lives and ambitions of the people around you.

REBOOT YOUR FAITH AND GET BACK IN TOUCH WITH YOUR CHILDLIKE WONDER

And he said: "Truly I tell you, unless you change and become like little children, you will never enter the kingdom of heaven."
MATTHEW 18:3

Jesus isn't wowed if we are smart or can memorize loads of Bible verses. What delights Him is simply that we are His. If big words or ideas help you understand Him more, go for it. But He takes particular delight when we demonstrate our childlike faith toward Him and the people around us.

In Matthew 18, while Jesus' friends were arguing about who would get the big chair next to Him, I wouldn't be surprised if He put a kid on His knee as He said, "I tell you the truth, unless you change and become like a child, you'll never enter the kingdom of God."

At one time I thought all you had to do to enter God's kingdom was just pray a prayer, but evidently there's more. Jesus wants us to have a childlike faith. This means loving the people who are difficult to love, playing with those who don't play well with others, and accepting our own deep flaws.

What can you do today to cultivate in yourself a childlike faith? If you think you've lost it somewhere along the way, do what you would do if you lost your car keys and think about where you last saw it. Return to those places and to those people, and ask Jesus to meet you there.

Invite someone who is a little prickly to go with you to get a kite, skip a couple of rocks across a pond, or break out your roller skates. Even if you end up with a few bruises, you may find yourself walking about with a much-needed reboot of your faith.

How will you go about catching whimsy today?

LET YOUR LIFE BE THE STAINED-GLASS-WINDOW REMINDERS OF GOD'S LOVE

For where two or three gather in my name, there am I with them.
MATTHEW 18:20

I didn't grow up in church, but I know a lot of people did and continue to gather together in places of worship. Some churches have a traditional appearance and tall white steeples with bells. Others are more contemporary and might look like rented storefronts or parking lots or community centers or coffee shops or diners.

It doesn't really matter what your church looks like. Jesus never asked anyone to spend boatloads of money building giant buildings; He is neither disappointed nor impressed by our buildings. He delights in our efforts to create and experience spaces that help us to love Him back. That is the only math in the equation.

God loves being together with His people, whom He calls His bride. And He doesn't care *where* it happens that we meet; He just cares *that* it happens.

God invites us to gather anywhere and everywhere. Jesus said He would be present if there were two or more gathered around Him. So go build a great big building or meet at the corner coffee shop or under an overpass or up in a sycamore tree. Either way, Jesus promises He will be there.

Today, gather with whoever is around you to worship God, and don't worry about what your surroundings look like. Let your lives and your stories be the stained-glass-window reminders of God's tremendous love as you share what He has done in your lives and give thanks for His goodness and faithfulness.

**God has already shown up
and is waiting for you to do the same.**

STAY CAPTIVATED BY PURPOSE

So [Nehemiah] sent messengers to them with this reply: "I am
carrying on a great project and cannot go down. Why should
the work stop while I leave it and go down to you?"

NEHEMIAH 6:3

Nehemiah was the cupbearer for a Persian king in what is now modern-day
Iran. Being a cupbearer was an important and risky job. Anyone who had it
in for the king using poison would take out the cupbearer every time, so the
level of trust between the king and the cupbearer was huge. As a result, the
cupbearer was on the inside track for many of the king's conversations.

When Nehemiah was the cupbearer, the Jewish people were no longer
being held captive in Babylon and had started returning to Israel. Due to his
proximity, Nehemiah had the king's ear and, in a moment of boldness, asked
the king for permission to leave and rebuild the temple walls in Jerusalem,
which had been knocked down. It would have been easier for the king to tell
Nehemiah, "Nope," and save himself the hassle of looking for a new cupbearer.
But, instead, he said yes, and Nehemiah went.

It took Nehemiah just fifty-two days to get the walls around Jerusalem
rebuilt. I know comparison isn't fair, but I spent six months remodeling a
bathroom. While he was in the middle of those fifty-two days, several people
came by with invitations and requests, and each time, Nehemiah responded
the same way: "I'm doing important work, and I can't come down." Nehemiah
knew what he was doing, why he was doing it, and he wasn't going to let anyone
get him off task.

What can you give your undivided attention to today? Be prepared for
many people to come along with great intentions but massive distractions, and
when they do, just say, "I'm doing important work, and I can't come down."

**You have important work to do. You will know you are
chasing down the right things with your time because
these things will be both lasting and loving.**

TRUST THE AUTHENTICITY OF AMBITIONS THAT LEAD TO JOY AND LOVE

I know that there is nothing better for people than
to be happy and to do good while they live.
ECCLESIASTES 3:12

Someone told me when they returned from a trip to the beach that they got a bad rap. I wondered what they had been wrongly accused of. Or, maybe the rap they were talking about was the music some kids listened to in my neighborhood where I couldn't make out the words. They immediately corrected me. "No, no, I mean I got a bad wrap. You know, like turkey, veggies, and mayo at lunch."

In some circles, "positive thinking" has gotten a bad rap and is dismissed as shallow or superficial. The bad rap may have come from the inspirational "you can do this" messages people give while flexing their muscles and teaching an arena full of overly enthusiastic people. This can feel shallow and overly hyped. But it's way different than the deep-seated joy that bubbles up in our lives when we have a positive view of what God is doing in the world. Don't wrap (see what I did there?) insincere and aimless motivational positivity together with the deep spiritual awakening that springs from the fact God has created the wonder and mystery of each day in the hopes that we will fully enter in with anticipation, celebration, joy, and hopefulness.

You will no doubt come across people whose words and enthusiasm about God feel artificial, contrived, or saccharine, and they might leave you feeling skeptical. But don't let their poor choice of words give a bad rap to the joy God is inviting you into today. Instead, surround yourself with positive voices who speak words of truth and affirmation.

We will in large part become whatever we spend the greatest amount of time looking for. If it is discouragement or cynicism or negativity you are looking for, you will find it. Similarly, if it is hope and joy and meaning you set your sights on, this is what you will find.

Solomon got it right when he wrote, "There is nothing better for people than to be happy and to do good while they live."

DON'T LET COMPARISON STEAL YOUR LUNCH MONEY

Each one should test their own actions. Then they can take
pride in themselves alone, without comparing themselves to
someone else, for each one should carry their own load.
GALATIANS 6:4–5

When we were growing up, my parents would have my sister and me stand up as straight as we could against the doorjamb at the kitchen door that led to the garage. They would put a pencil on top of our heads and measure our height. Once they made their mark, they would carefully date it, and we would all stand back and see how much we had grown.

Even though I was taller than my sister, whenever we stood back and looked at our marks on the doorjamb, she was always one quarter inch taller than me. How could that be? I felt like I could look down at the top of her head when we were standing next to each other. I would stand extra tall for the next measurement, and, without fail, she would once again prove to be taller than me by a quarter of an inch. It wasn't until years later that I figured out her secret—she had been standing on her tiptoes every time. If this doesn't sound like a sibling move, I don't know what does.

We have all met someone who wants to be a little more right or a little more funny or more athletic or smart or engaging than we are. They leave us feeling like we don't quite measure up. The fact is, it is exhausting trying to always be a quarter of an inch taller or better than everyone else. When you meet someone like this, glance down and look to see if they are up on their tiptoes. They probably won't be wearing ballet slippers, but if you look closely enough at the dynamics of the communication that is happening, both audible and inaudible, you will probably see them lifted just slightly on their toes. This might give you greater empathy for them and also lead you to give yourself a break from the competition, because no matter how you slice it, it is exhausting to spend most of your life on tiptoes. Don't become like that. Don't let comparison steal your lunch money any longer.

Starting today, call comparison out wherever you see it. Let it know you aren't going to try to measure up to its unfair expectations.

PRUNE YOUR FOCUS: FINE WINE TAKES TIME AND ENERGY

"I am the vine; you are the branches. If you remain in me and I in
you, you will bear much fruit; apart from me you can do nothing."
JOHN 15:5

We have a beautiful family living at The Oaks. Justin and Stefanie stand at
the intersection where caring, compassion, bravery, and courageous action all
meet. After the loss of two of their children to a rare disease, they needed a
new start, and we were fortunate enough to be on their radar. I invited them
to move from Chicago to Southern California and promised we would give
them their own house in a vineyard on the property to live in. What I didn't
tell them was that they would have to build the house and plant all the vines.
Yet, as always, they transformed everything they touched.

The vineyard now has seven varieties of grapes and produces fifty thousand
bottles of wine each year. I tell my friends to act surprised at Christmastime
when they receive bottles of wine from me. I know very little about grapes
and even less about wine (I'm a Dr Pepper guy). What I have learned, though,
has fascinated me, and I can understand why Jesus used grapes and vines as
examples of how faith works.

Vines take time, attention, and pruning. Plant a radish seed, and you will
have a radish in twenty days, but it takes years for a grape on a vine to produce
good wine. During these years, you need to constantly prune away the volunteer shoots, focusing the vine's energy into the grapes and not just growing
more leaves. In the same way, we need to be intentional about where we're
putting our energy and what we're growing in our lives. Otherwise, distractions
will pop up and steal our focus, taking away from the most important things.

Ask God to show you what He wants to grow in your life. Then, make a
list of some things that are taking your energy from that focus, and rework your
schedule so you can direct your energy back to the fruit God is developing in you.

**This is your time, this is your life, this is your
vine to tend to. What will you do today?**

THE MOST DIRECT PATH TO GOD IS THROUGH JESUS

He guides me along the right paths for his name's sake.
PSALM 23:3

You might think the shortest distance across the Pacific Ocean is a straight line on a map, but the fast way across isn't a straight line. It is actually an arc or an ellipse. There is a complicated explanation for it called spherical trigonometry, but who cares? The simple reason is the earth is curved, and the map is flat. Mariners call this shortest path the great circle route.

The Pacific Ocean is a big place, but this is important to be aware of when you are crossing the great circle route from Los Angeles to Hong Kong, because this is the narrow band of water that all container ships take to save time and fuel. There are scary stories of container ships pulling into the harbor in Hong Kong with a sailboat mast hanging from the anchor.

Late one evening, as my friends and I made our way on the great circle route during one of our ocean crossings, a light appeared on the horizon. To make sure this ship knew we were in front of them, we called on the radio, "Ship on the horizon, we are a small sailboat in front of you and want to make sure you see us." There was no answer. "Ship on the ocean, do you see us?" No answer. Every fifteen minutes we called out to the ship whose lights were getting brighter as it quickly closed on our position. Nothing.

I was down below on the radio once again trying to raise the ship on the VHF when I heard laughing on deck. How could these guys be laughing during such an urgent time? I charged up the companionway to take names and numbers. Everyone was pointing toward the horizon, as it had become apparent it was not a ship headed our way, but the moon rising through the clouds.

Life can be confusing. The decisions, the changes in direction, the surprises—all these underscore our need for God, who doesn't control us but is with us and guides us through whatever circumstances we find ourselves in. He leads us along the right paths for His name's sake, and the shortest path— the great circle route—to God is through Jesus.

Ask Jesus to be at the center of the path for you and you won't get fooled by all the distractions around you.

LIVE IN HOPE AND LOOK FOR VIRTUE

Blessed is the one who does not walk in step with the wicked or stand in the way that sinners take or sit in the company of mockers.
PSALM 1:1

Diogenes was the founder of cynicism. He made his own clothes, pushed back on society's rules, and lived a simple life. He called a large water barrel home. When he was tired, he slept, and when he was hungry, he ate. He walked the streets of Athens with a lamp raised high in his outstretched arm at high noon each day. When people asked what he was doing with his lamp lit during the day, he replied that he was looking for virtue. I like Diogenes's style and I bet we could have been friends. Anyone who jumps the tracks of what is typical and opts for a life of looking for virtue is worth understanding a little more.

There is a big difference between Diogenes's original brand of cynicism and modern-day cynics who grouse and gripe about everything. For today's cynics, all ideas and viewpoints except theirs are bad ones. Every other way to live life is suspect and worth ridiculing and putting down. If you want to live a life like a modern-day cynic, go ahead, but don't expect people to want to hang around you. Go old-school Diogenes and spend your days looking for virtue, and you will lead a beautiful life and leave a lasting memory.

Paul must have had similar thoughts when he said to let your conversation be always full of grace, seasoned with salt. He knew the way to connect with people involves looking for virtue in people and situations, not looking to constantly ridicule.

Keep it positive. Stay engaged. Push back against the chaos you face in life with love and anticipation and focus. Keep your eyes fixed on Jesus, look for virtue, and keep encouraging people the way Jesus did. He encountered difficult people but was unrelenting in His optimism. It wasn't positive thinking He was doing; He was positive about His purpose.

Any way you slice it, modern cynicism is a punk. It is usually fear masquerading as confidence. Don't take the bait today.

Lift your lamp high, look for virtue, and keep your eyes on Jesus.

WANNA BE LIKE JESUS? KEEP SHOWING UP

*I needed clothes and you clothed me, I was sick and you looked
after me, I was in prison and you came to visit me.*
MATTHEW 25:36

I heard from an inmate who was doing time at a supermax facility. These are places used to protect the most violent and dangerous criminals from the even more violent and dangerous criminals. Not surprisingly, these are not happy or comfortable places. They can require twenty-three hours a day of solitary confinement, and the interaction between inmates is limited.

The guy in the cell next to my new friend slid a Bible under the bars of his cell. My friend told me he immediately slid it back. The next day, the Bible came sliding under his bars again, and he slid it back again. This went on for six months; it was like shuffleboard for felons. One day, though, when the Bible slid over, he didn't slide it back. Instead, he told me he read it, the words resonated with him, and he came to faith.

The men I've met in prison are each on their own journey. It is often one of growth and taking responsibility and needed introspection and sometimes faith. I have come to know these men not for what they once did in their past, but for who they are becoming. Sometimes, what they need is just some encouragement—which might look like another inmate sliding a Bible under the bars of their cell—and other times what they need is someone to see them, to talk with them, to be a kind and listening ear during a time of intense loneliness.

After I had become a regular at San Quentin, the guys there made a frame for me in the wood shop. The back of the certificate is signed "residents of San Quentin," and it also has Matthew 25 on it: "I was in prison and you came to visit me."

There is power in showing up. Some people are behind actual steel bars, and others who appear to be free are equally imprisoned.

**Keep showing up for whoever the imprisoned ones are in your life.
Keep sliding hope and joy and genuine interest under the door.**

DON'T LET YOUR FAITH START TO SMELL LIKE MOLDY CHEESE

"Yet I hold this against you: You have forsaken the love you had at first."
REVELATION 2:4

One of my first jobs in high school was working at Hickory Farms. It's a place that sells lots of cheese. It was almost too much for my silly adolescent mind to handle when I stumbled on an advertisement for a job where your role was cutting the cheese. I felt uniquely qualified to do this important work, and being paid the minimum wage, which was two dollars an hour at the time, was icing on the cheesecake, so to speak.

On the first day of training, the store manager (I guess you could call him the big cheese) told me my first assignment every shift was to "wake up the cheese." *Huh?* I thought. My mind was racing. How was I supposed to wake up cheese? Yell, "Hey, Jack!" or "Gouda morning!"?

The thing about cheese, in addition to tripling the chances you will have a heart attack, is that it grows mold when it is exposed to the air. It turns out, waking up the cheese means cutting off all the mold that grew on the cheese overnight. When I arrived in the morning, the mold would look a little nasty, but once I cut the veneer of mold off, it was like the cheese had been minted all over again. It reset the clock. This wasn't deception; it was healthy maintenance.

We all need a reset from time to time. Think about all your firsts—your first day of school, first date, first time driving alone. We remember these first moments and can almost feel the excitement of those times, but no one remembers their fifth day at school or the tenth date or the third year driving. At some point, the novelty wears off and things become ho-hum to us—we lose that first love. Cultivating a sense of wonder can bring us back to our joy like it was the first time. It wakes us up and cuts through the distractions in our lives. Make today the day you return to the first day you felt God's love. Did you feel engaged, protected, pursued?

Return to that earlier version of your faith before it became so complicated. God is waiting right there for you.

DON'T JUST KNOW ABOUT JESUS— GET TO KNOW HIM

"Now this is eternal life: that they know you, the only true
God, and Jesus Christ, whom you have sent."
JOHN 17:3

There are lots of strange things that have happened in recent years. One unexpected outcome from having written some books and spoken at a number of gatherings is that Sweet Maria and I have stalkers. They aren't dangerous and don't want to hurt us, but their enthusiasm to meet us has made an impression.

One morning before dawn, I walked downstairs and there was a guy sitting in my chair on my back porch. "Hello," I said tentatively as I opened the door. You can tell someone is a stalker when, just like this guy, they say, "I'm not a stalker." *All evidence to the contrary*, I thought. He said he had read one of my books about someone getting engaged on our porch and wanted to experience it. My immediate thought was that all he was about to experience was a restraining order, but I was kind. We all need to work on our people skills, some of us more than others.

Another time, I arrived home from an out-of-state trip and, as I walked into the living room to say hi to Sweet Maria, I received a call from a woman. "That's a nice blue shirt you are wearing," she said. I looked down at my blue shirt and then out the window and saw the glow of her cell phone where she stood in the bushes. Yikes!

I suppose we all do things from time to time that people might feel are stalker-ish. I guess sometimes you're the hunter, and other days you're the duck. What I don't want to do is to stalk Jesus. Here's what I mean. Jesus doesn't want us to merely gather lots of information and details about Him or make late-night calls. Jesus stalkers might know all the stories and parables and miracles but not really know Jesus, and I bet that creeps Him out a little too.

**Decide today that you are not going to merely find out more
information about Jesus, but you will get to know who He is.**

LOVE WITH AN AGENDA ISN'T LOVE

Jesus replied, "Blessed are you, Simon son of Jonah, for this was not
revealed to you by flesh and blood, but by my Father in heaven."
MATTHEW 16:17

Have you met people who are more interested in sharing the gospel with
strangers than showing it to them? Here's what I mean. These people have a
boatload of answers they're eager to confidently share but don't follow up with
actions that communicate love, which is what it takes to make the message
stick. Fancy words are not the metrics by which Jesus measures our faith.
Just look at the religious people Jesus walked right by and the outcasts and
mess-ups He chose instead to carry His message. Faith is what we do about
our accumulated beliefs by releasing them into the world through many acts
of unselfish love.

What takes real guts and maturity is living out what we believe with kindness and vulnerability in the murky and difficult waters of everyday life. When
a person has blown it, they usually don't want someone to give them big, high-
minded explanations of what they did wrong. Sometimes the best advice we
can give each other is a hug. Don't play the role of the sheriff who is there to
straighten everyone out; immerse people in kindness. This is how we release
the gospel into the world in a lasting way.

Here is the simple reason why much of what some people call evangelism
isn't effective: when love has an agenda, it isn't love anymore. It's a program,
and we don't need any more programs. Jesus didn't have one, and His disciples
didn't either. They just had seven days a week to love and care for the people
in front of them. If we can lose all the tricks and gimmicks surrounding our
faith, we will be able to see it better for ourselves and, with acts of selfless love,
communicate what we believe in an effective way to those around us.

We don't lead people to Jesus; Jesus leads people to Himself. We just get a
front-row seat to watch it happen if we're willing to release all the other well-
intentioned but often contrived approaches.

**Just go love everybody today. Jesus will let
people know what the return address is.**

BE KNOWN FOR YOUR FAITHFULNESS

For it is not the one who commends himself who is approved, but the one whom the Lord commends.
2 CORINTHIANS 10:18

What defines your character? It's not just about being able to point to five pictures of yourself doing virtuous acts or reading your own news clippings. It's about being known at the city gates as a dependable person. Do people speak of you and say, "If he says he'll be there, he'll be there" or "If she commits to showing up, she follows through"? Develop a character and reputation for this kind of truthfulness, not based on a modified version of the truth but based precisely on what you promised, even when it becomes inconvenient.

This reminds me of a time I had promised I would return to speak at an event in Orlando, Florida. As the time drew near, I found myself already in Orlando but needing to return to San Diego to attend to something before this event. It seemed nearly impossible to pull off all this traveling, with the flight between the two cities spanning more than five hours each way. I was tempted to back out. I even inquired if the event was still happening, but the response was, "It's still on." So, I decided to keep my word and responded with my cheeriest voice, "I will see you there." I made all the complicated necessary arrangements to fly home and then back to Orlando, only for the event to eventually be canceled. Ugh.

You might be thinking, *See, Bob? You should have just canceled in the first place!* But despite how things turned out, I still think I made the right decision, because this was about what God was shaping in my life, not about the event itself. I don't know what was going on with the event organizers in Orlando. They might have had a perfectly good reason to cancel that day. I just needed to be faithful to what I knew God was working on in my life by keeping my commitment. It doesn't make me a hero to see life this way. It makes me someone determined to fulfill what God has set specifically for me. Don't be sidetracked by what goes wrong on the surface as you're following Jesus' lead.

Focus on letting God work within you. Understand why you're doing what you're doing and find delight in it.

JUNE

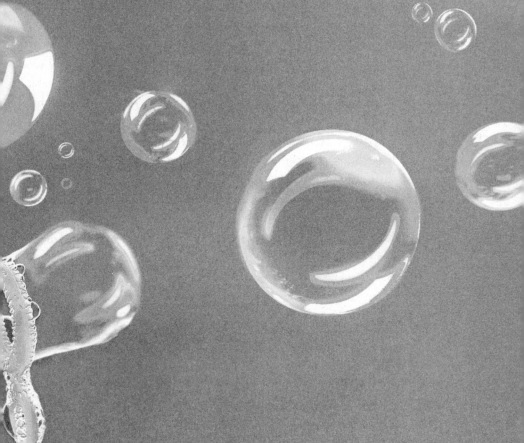

JESUS ALREADY GAVE US HIS PEACE—WE JUST HAVE TO CREATE SPACE FOR IT

"Peace I leave with you; my peace I give you. I do not give to you as the world gives. Do not let your hearts be troubled and do not be afraid."

JOHN 14:27

Growing up, I missed most of the sixties, as I was a very young boy during that decade. But I've heard it was common then for everyone to call out, "Peace!" while flashing a victory sign. But real peace isn't something you can claim externally; peace is an inside job. So, how do we find peace if it feels like it has been eluding us? One thing we might try is to create a safe place. Here's an example of what I mean.

There were two countries in a dispute with each other over the name one of the countries would be known by. It was high stakes, because one country's admission to NATO was being denied while the dispute festered. I knew the person heading one of the delegations negotiating the dispute, and I put on an event where I had more than a thousand people sign a table encouraging peace. Before the event ended, I sawed the table in half and shipped half of the table to each of the two sides, calling them both not to merely *come to the table* but to *bring the table*.

Creating a safe place means curating an environment where others feel okay to say how they feel without fear and feel seen without judgment, even during difficult conversations. Remember, peace isn't just the absence of conflict. It is having a space filled with protection, and we have the ability to create those safe places.

When we bring peace into the room, especially if we are in the middle of conflict, hearts are less troubled and fear diminishes. It becomes an environment where we can tackle difficult issues in a loving and secure place. This isn't the kind of peace the world gives. It's the kind of peace Jesus gives.

Today, experiment with peace. You won't get it right all the time, and that's okay. Fail trying.

GOD NEVER SAID TRUTH WOULD BE COMFORTABLE

> I warn everyone who hears the words of the prophecy of this scroll: If anyone adds anything to them, God will add to that person the plagues described in this scroll. And if anyone takes words away from this scroll of prophecy, God will take away from that person any share in the tree of life and in the Holy City, which are described in this scroll.
>
> **REVELATION 22:18–19**

Many years ago, I started writing the Bible. Let me clarify what I mean. I replicated the Bible as a Word document and began annotating it with the stories and lessons I have learned along the way. These devotionals are among them. I changed the color and the font of what I wrote so as not to run afoul of what seems like pretty harsh prohibitions in the Bible about adding to or subtracting from the Scriptures. It did make me wonder, though, why God feels so strongly about people adding to or taking away from what is written in the Scriptures.

It seems like, for as long as God has been talking to man, we've been wordsmithing what He had to say. We add or subtract a little here or there, thinking we are bringing clarity or making the Scriptures more relevant or not as judgmental or more inviting or easier to follow, but this was never God's goal. He isn't looking for a bunch of coauthors. And while He is a fan of making faith simpler to understand, He has never tried to make it easy.

The troubling fact is that we all make additions to or subtractions from the Bible more than we are likely to admit. I have ignored some of the more difficult parts of Scripture. Love my enemies? What if I just tolerate them or maybe just ignore them? And the creepy people—not them, right?

Take a hard look at the parts of the Scriptures you either don't get or don't want to follow.

Ask yourself what might happen in your life if, instead of making up your own version of the Bible, you went with Jesus' version.

IF YOU CAN'T HEAR THE VOICE OF GOD, IT'S TIME TO CARVE OUT A QUIET PLACE IN YOUR LIFE

Before daybreak the next morning, Jesus got up
and went out to an isolated place to pray.
MARK 1:35 NLT

When I was in law school, I needed to find a quiet place to study. I went to a nearby university that had a medical school and loads of crowded rooms. It seemed wherever I went there were people laughing or talking or riffling through their school papers, so I walked down the stairs to the basement level where I finally found an incredibly quiet spot. It smelled a little odd and stuffy, but I was grateful to have found a solitary place. I returned several days a week with my stack of notes and books, put my head down, and got a ton of work done.

After about a month of cramming where it was dead quiet, someone with a name tag on their white jacket asked me what I was doing and if I had permission to be there. I made a rousing opening argument about how this place was a state school, that I was a taxpayer (or would be someday when I wasn't broke), and that the room was empty and I needed a quiet spot, so I should be allowed to stay.

When I finished, the guy pointed to a sign on a door, shook his head, and left. I had been studying next door to the morgue. This explained quite a few things.

Sometimes the room we're in can be too loud, and God won't try to shout to us over all the noise. He will lead us beside quiet waters, but He won't force us to follow Him there. It could be that all the noise has been scaring away the breakthrough you have been looking for.

**Find a quiet place today. Go there and do some business
with God. Perhaps if you quiet your mind enough to hear
the birds singing, you will hear God speaking.**

WHEN LIFE GETS TOO SALTY, CHECK THE RECIPE

Be very careful, then, how you live—not as unwise but as wise,
making the most of every opportunity, because the days are evil.
EPHESIANS 5:15–16

Auditing your life and becoming aware of where you are spending your time and who you are spending it with can be incredibly clarifying. Here is one way to figure out where you're at and what needs to be adjusted in your world. Grab a paper plate and draw the major pieces of your life like pieces of a pie, showing how much of the whole they make up.

Ask yourself:

How much time am I spending sleeping?
How much time am I spending intentionally with the people I love?
How much time am I spending merely in proximity to my family but not
*   engaged?*
How much time am I devoting to reading or quiet reflection?
How much time am I spending having fun or working on a hobby?

Next, give your paper plate to someone who knows your life well to see if they agree with the size of the slices you've drawn for the different categories. Take a second paper plate and draw the slices according to what you would like your life to look like. Then tape both to the wall so you can see the difference.

Paul told his friends to be very careful about how they lived. He wanted them to be wise and make the most of every opportunity. Ask yourself what it is you can let go of in order to move closer to the second paper plate's version of life. Rather than being constantly distracted by the next thing, clear the decks. Understand the life you have been living and the life you want to live in the future.

Get your paper plates out. I'll do the dishes.

CHOOSE GRACE
AND YOU WILL ALWAYS BE RIGHT

> But in your hearts revere Christ as Lord. Always be prepared to
> give an answer to everyone who asks you to give the reason for the
> hope that you have. But do this with gentleness and respect.
> **1 PETER 3:15**

A lot of people refer to Peter's teaching about always being prepared with an answer for people who ask about your hope. Too often, though, they use it as a reason to get in someone's grill to stick up for Jesus, even at the cost of loving others well. They're forgetting the rest of the verse: "But do this with gentleness and respect."

We need to watch out for this unbalanced way of living out our faith. We are all called to operate out of both gentleness and respect, or, put another way, with grace.

In John 1, the Scriptures say Jesus Christ came "filled with grace and truth." I like that He came with equal parts grace and truth. And it was 100 percent of both, not 50 percent of each. Here's the thing to remember about the apostle John's words, though: grace came first.

Think about a time when you have been right about something and someone else has been wrong. Regardless of how right you were and how wrong the other person was, let grace come first. Now, think about a time when your feelings have been terribly hurt or you have been completely misunderstood. Even in that situation, let grace come first.

**When Jesus was on the cross, He didn't vet the guy on
the cross next to Him. He just said, "See you in paradise."
He let grace come first. Let's choose to do the same.**

TRUST GOD, EVEN WHEN YOU'RE DRIVING WITH THE HEADLIGHTS OFF

"For every animal of the forest is mine, and the cattle on a thousand hills. I know every bird in the mountains, and the insects in the fields are mine."
PSALM 50:10-11

There's a region in Uganda called Karamoja, and it is a land locked in time. The Karamojong people believe all cattle in the world are owned by them. I know a couple of Texans who feel the same way—you know who you are. In Karamoja, they have no hesitations about stealing cattle from other clans and view this as returning the cattle back to themselves. Cattle are the currency used in the region. We use dollars; they use cows. They attack weaker clans and take their cattle. The more cattle a clan has, the more power they have.

Many of the Karamojong are also armed with old rifles and AK machine guns. It's not a good idea to drive at night when you're in their region because the Karamojong will shoot at the headlights of any car. I was visiting the first lady of Uganda, who had a compound in Karamoja, and our conversation went long. While she had hundreds of Ugandan military people to protect her, I was going to have to drive through the night to get back to where I needed to be, and I was a little uptight. The potholes were the size of small swimming pools and this made the effort challenging. Kind of like playing Marco Polo with your eyes closed while everyone else poolside is armed.

There are times in our lives when we feel like we're driving without headlights. We generally know where the road is, but, at best, we can only make out some of the edges. It is in these times that we need to remember what Psalm 50 tells us about God owning all the cattle, and even the insects and all the birds. He owns it all, and He not only knows our needs but has the power to offer us protection. The Karamojong would understand this; we need to as well. No matter our circumstances, God's promise is that He will provide us protection. He owns everything, rules everything, and knows everything.

What is an area in your life where you feel like you are driving in the dark and need God to remind you of His tremendous love and protection?

THE GRACE OF GOD IS BIGGER THAN OUR COMPLICATED LIVES

See to it that no one falls short of the grace of God and that
no bitter root grows up to cause trouble and defile many.
HEBREWS 12:15

Most of what we do are reactions to the people and experiences in our past. The trick is to figure out who or what you are reacting to. Learn your tells. For instance, when you have a disproportionate reaction to something, you probably aren't just reacting to what is happening right then; you are reacting to your entire life. Perhaps it was an abusive relationship or a huge financial setback or lingering relational ambiguity or a reminder of when you were rejected or ignored or taken for granted. Does any of this sound familiar? Your deep-seated emotion may strike you at first as an irrational overreaction to a set of circumstances, but peel that back a little and you will find an unresolved adjacent issue. Once we take a hard look at the root causes, we can develop a plan to replace half-truths or outright lies with absolute truth.

Figure out what is lying underneath your feelings and call it out. If rejection is your button, as it is mine, call it out. Remind yourself that what is happening likely isn't rejection; there is probably something more complicated going on in the other person's life and they don't have the capacity right now to reciprocate your interest in friendship. Then, replace a negative spin with a positive assumption. Recognize the other person's life might be as busy and full of conflicting emotions as yours and mine are, and the off-putting behavior you noticed is not a rejection of you—it is simply evidence of a complicated and busy life.

Today, try to identify someone who is reaching out to you but perhaps you have been too busy to reciprocate. Let them know it means a lot to you that they would reach out.

Find someone who has been a little distant and drop them an unassuming note, just thanking them for being around and wishing them well this week.

DON'T EXAGGERATE SO MUCH YOU NO LONGER RECOGNIZE THE TRULY AMAZING THINGS IN LIFE

You, God, are awesome in your sanctuary; the God of Israel
gives power and strength to his people. Praise be to God!
PSALM 68:35

How many times have we heard someone take a sip of a smoothie and say, "This is amazing," or see a view or hear a song and say, "That was amazing"? There is a kind of word inflation that can happen over time. A bag of chips isn't just nice, it's "awesome." So is the trip to the market or to summer camp. How was your time? "Awesome."

I'm not saying we need to be wordsmithing for others, but when we dig a little deeper into what we are saying, what we actually mean is that the time went well, or the camp met our high expectations and hopes for the week. If we don't recognize when word inflation is happening, it's no wonder we get a little confused when we then go to sing a song about how we serve an "awesome God" or about "amazing grace." The words we're using have lost their power, and we no longer recognize the weight of truly awesome and amazing things. What if we were to recalibrate our words to save a few of the big-sounding ones for the things that are truly big deals?

Try to go a day without any of the hyperbole we can easily slip into. "It was the best!" "I've never seen anything like it!" "It's unbelievable!" "It was amazing, totally awesome." Don't get me wrong. I'm not trying to be a bummer; I'm just aiming for accurate. If we do these things, then when we see God doing something truly amazing or awesome in our lives or in someone else's, we can call it what it is. And that, my friends, would be something God might, indeed, find awesome.

**Be picky about the words and phrases you use and
you will uncover new and more valuable meaning
in what you communicate to others today.**

LEARN WHEN TO LOOK BACK SO YOU CAN KEEP MOVING AHEAD

I remember the days of long ago; I meditate on all your
works and consider what your hands have done.
PSALM 143:5

I once heard a friend say, "I never look back." I think I get what he was trying to say, but I actually think we should look back a lot. We just don't need to obsess or get stuck staring at what we see behind us. We need to know when it is helpful to look back and when it isn't.

There is a book in the Bible called Deuteronomy. It's the fifth book and its name literally means "the words of Moses." You will remember, he was the one with the tablets with commandments written on them. Moses told his friends they should look back constantly in order to understand the goodness of God in their lives. He said the same thing twice in the book, once in chapter 6 and once in chapter 11. So I think he really meant it, and we should do this with a ton of intention.

Of course, there are times when looking back won't be helpful. There is the story about Lot's wife in Genesis 19, for example. In short, Abraham's nephew, Lot, lived in a city that was going to be destroyed by God. As the angels led Lot and his family away, they told Lot's wife not to look back. When she disobeyed, she turned into a pillar of salt. It was a bad day all around.

If looking back has been helpful to you, do that. You will know it has been helpful if you gain new insights for how to live the next steps of the journey. If, on the other hand, looking back is causing you to become distracted or so wounded that you can't receive what God has for you now, then take a lesson from Mrs. Lot and stop looking back.

**God's deepest desire is that we would know Him and
experience His love for us. Look in whatever direction
gives you access to what God has for you today.**

WHATEVER JOB YOU HAVE, REMEMBER JESUS IS YOUR REAL BOSS

Whatever you do, work at it with all your heart, as working for the Lord, not for human masters.
COLOSSIANS 3:23

Most of us have had good jobs and bad jobs. The thing about bad jobs is that they prepare us for better ones. It's easy to think that having a job that matters means doing big things like inventing something new or creating an app everyone uses or doing something you will one day be famous for. But work of any type, no matter how tedious it can sometimes be, matters. It is as honorable to plant the seeds and tend to the fields as it is to bag the groceries or stand your post at a cash register.

Whatever it is you do, don't grumble as you do it. Will there be parts of your job you don't like? Of course there will. Are there things you will be asked to do that are uninspiring? Yep, that too. But bad-mouthing your job or resenting your boss or your burdensome work projects won't get you where you want to go. Think of Paul's words to the Colossians about carrying out each task with enthusiasm and doing them as if you were serving the Lord.

I'm not big on going into Greek words to explain what we are experiencing, but I will make an exception for the word *enthusiasm*. It literally means "the God within." Enthusiasm in this context isn't about wild arm-waving; it's about doing your work as an expression of what God is doing inside of you. If you're feeling lackluster about a challenging project or dealing with an ungrateful person, perhaps it's time to tune up your perspective and ramp up your enthusiasm. Approach your tasks as if you're doing them for Jesus Himself.

Enthusiastically jump into your day today with the expectation that God is with you and in you and around you. If you do, you will experience your faith in new and beautiful ways as it is expressed through your honorable work.

You matter and your work does too. Do it with joy and whimsy and an unreasonable amount of anticipation.

LIFE WITH GOD MEANS LIFE IN COMMUNITY

Build houses and settle down; plant gardens and eat what they
produce. Marry and have sons and daughters. . . . seek the peace
and prosperity of the city to which I have carried you into exile. Pray
to the Lord for it, because if it prospers, you too will prosper.

JEREMIAH 29:5–7

You are probably familiar with Jeremiah 29 and God's promise that He has a
solid plan for us, but there's more to that passage than you might think. It goes
on to say with more detail that the plan is to "build houses and settle down.
Plant gardens and eat what they produce. Marry and have sons and daughters."
This isn't just about starting a family; it's about growing a community. What
does it mean to grow a community? It starts with seeing who God has already
placed in your life.

Sometimes we shy away from the people who are right there with us,
because engaging with them means confronting sadness or awkward relational
issues. I'm generally the "happy guy," and I tend toward avoiding difficult
conversations. It's easier to ask, "Where are the balloons?" than to ask, "Where
is the pain?" If you can relate to this, Jesus might be asking you to embrace a
different approach, to grow by slowing down and addressing some of the more
complex issues.

For those of you on the other end of the spectrum, who always want to
go a mile deep on everything, consider chilling out a bit. When you do, you
will give people the opportunity to arrive at depth with you rather than feeling
pulled there before they are ready.

Community is something worth pursuing with gusto. It's not easy, but
it can be incredibly meaningful, because God always seems to do His most
significant work within the context of community.

**Take a look around you and see who is already nearby. It's easy
to overlook the people right beside us because they've become
so familiar to us. But God has put them there for a reason.**

CALL IN THE COURAGE, BRING THE LOVE, DISCIPLINE YOUR MIND, AND GET READY FOR BLASTOFF!

For the Spirit God gave us does not make us timid,
but gives us power, love and self-discipline.
2 TIMOTHY 1:7–8

What does it look like to launch something? Snowboarders might interpret "launching" as hitting the half-pipe at a whopping forty miles an hour and blowing everyone's minds with some aerials. That's not the launch I'm referring to here. Let's talk about what it would take for a successful, purposeful launch of your dreams and ambitions.

Before every launch is a reset from the last one with loads of intention. Learn the lessons from what you've tried previously before you roll your new ambitions out onto the tarmac. Think of rocket ships. They don't just shoot into the sky; they are aiming for an altitude, an orbit, and eventually a landing. A launch without direction is just a lot of smoke and flames. We've all experienced those kinds of launches, and that's definitely not what we're going for.

Launching something successfully also requires preparation and prioritization. Astronauts don't just hop into the capsule and press the Go button. There is a lot of planning, and then, eventually, someone lights the fuse and there is liftoff. But some of us get hung up with never-ending planning. We think talking about doing something is the same as doing something but, sadly, it's not. Certainly, plan and meet and discuss if that is helpful for you and gives you clarity, but at some point, we need to roll out the idea, turn on the engines, and see where it goes.

Paul reminded his young friend Timothy that living the big life Jesus talked about is not for the weak-kneed and promised that God would give us the spirit of courage we need to get the job done. Be humble today as you learn and incorporate the lessons from previous launches, but don't be timid. Be filled with hope but even more filled with love, and cultivate the self-discipline Paul said was ours for the taking if we wanted it.

**What is it that is holding you back from shooting for the stars today?
Call in the courage, bring the love, and discipline your mind.**

LET YOUR WHIMSY LEAD TO RADICAL LOVE

The Word became flesh and blood, and moved into the neighborhood.
JOHN 1:14 MSG

I know a few people who are busy and in demand, even a couple who draw pretty big crowds wherever they go. Some of these people have layers of people between them and the people who want to connect with them. They have executive assistants, and those assistants have other assistants. They have bodyguards and tour managers and schedulers and drivers and sometimes travel with an impressive entourage of people who surround them and keep everyone else at bay.

I know a couple of pastors who also have this going on. I'm not knocking this idea and the need sometimes for protection and support, but I look at the life of Jesus and see the opposite. He was radically available to everyone.

Have you ever wondered why Jesus made Himself so available? I think it was His defining message, that God made Himself available to us, skin to skin, through His son, and wants us to make ourselves available and obedient to Him. We can't decide how rich we will be or how handsome we are or how long we will live, but we can decide how available we will be and the kinds of things we will make ourselves available to.

At the Oscars, the stars are separated from everyone else by velvet ropes hung from shiny chrome stanchions. The popular people get on one side of the ropes, and everybody else can snap pictures and watch from the other side. That might work for the movies, but it doesn't create relationship. It intentionally or unintentionally promotes a caste system where the people who self-identify as the cool kids huddle up with one another. Sure, there might be the token photo of someone kissing a baby, but the barriers are still in place.

What would it look like for you to get on the other side of the ropes today?

Who in your neighborhood or workplace or circle of influence would be blown away if you made yourself available to them?

THE BEST WAY TO EXPRESS YOUR FAITH IS TO GO OUT AND LOVE LIKE JESUS

The only thing that counts is faith expressing itself through love.
GALATIANS 5:6

God champions the unlikely ones, whoever they may be. In Matthew 25:40, Jesus emphasized that whatever you do for the least of the people you meet—the overlooked, the unnoticed, the unlikely—you do for Him. In your workplace or in the classroom or at the park there might be someone sitting alone, perhaps socially awkward or hesitant in conversations. Engage them with love and with no agenda. Help them with the hard parts of their lives.

Finding Jesus is impossible without finding those in need. Sure, it's easier to tend to your own needs, but how much richer would life be if we did what Jesus said we were designed from the factory to do, which is to love the weak, the hurting, and the isolated?

Who comes to mind for you as you consider who to reach out to? Remember, God doesn't confine Himself to the popular kids' table; He's also at the other table off to the side with the forgotten, the estranged, and the lonely.

Maybe you're thinking about finding someone who is hungry or thirsty, but consider this. You won't know if someone is hungry or thirsty if you don't ask. It's when you extend curiosity and kindness and empathy that you are likely to encounter Jesus through those around you.

How can you start today? It's refreshingly simple. Seek out the person who is not surrounded by a large community of friends. Engage with someone online who would be blown away if you reached out to them with a message of gratefulness.

Express your love to those on the margins, outside the mainstream circle. These small acts of kindness are more than gestures; they are declarations of your faith.

GOD'S THE ONLY AUDIENCE YOUR GENEROSITY NEEDS

"But when you give to the needy, do not let your left hand know what
your right hand is doing, so that your giving may be in secret. Then
your Father, who sees what is done in secret, will reward you."
MATTHEW 6:3-4

Who comes to mind when you think of someone who is incredibly generous? I
have a friend who had a practice where, when anyone said they liked something
of his, he would give it to them. Crazy? Maybe not.

One time I was in his office, and someone famous came in. This person
told my friend that he was stepping down from the important position he had
held on Capitol Hill for a long time. He unclasped his wristwatch, slid it off,
and gave it to my friend, saying as he did, "I wore this watch every day I held
the post, and I want you to have it." A short while later, the famous person left
and, within a few minutes, another person walked in who wasn't famous at all.
He shook my friend's hand and noticed the new watch on his wrist. "That's
a nice watch you have there," he said in passing. Without a word spoken or a
moment of hesitation, my friend took the watch off his wrist, gave it to his new
guest, and said, "Hey, I really want you to have this," never even mentioning
the rich history of the watch.

Generosity is a beautiful way to walk out the love God calls us to, and there
are a lot of different ways you can practice it. I heard someone once describe
generosity as having many levels. The lowest level, they said, is when you hand
something to someone directly and openly. The highest is when they never
know it was you.

This is akin to what Jesus meant when He told His disciples to be generous,
but to do it in secret. Like you, my left hand always knows what my right hand
is doing, but just because I know about it doesn't mean I need to tell people
about it.

Today, do something secretly incredible in someone's life. Perhaps someone
will tell you, "I like your watch." The next move is yours to make.

Give me a call later today if you need to know what time it is.

STARTING ANEW MEANS YOU DIDN'T GIVE UP

"But as for you, be strong and do not give up,
for your work will be rewarded."
2 CHRONICLES 15:7

I once decided to try jumping a motorcycle. I charged up a hill at full speed and managed to launch myself thirty feet, but there was one problem—the motorcycle only went twenty feet! I crashed, luckily sustaining only minor bruises. Rather than thinking, *Jumping motorcycles isn't for me*, I realized I had more to learn. I needed to gain some more practical knowledge and start anew.

Starting anew means leveraging the knowledge and experiences you've accumulated over time to equip yourself for a more successful outcome in the future. For example, I discovered that if you want to lift the front wheel of a motorcycle, you need to accelerate, and the torque will lift you up. If you want to land safely from a higher jump, applying the brakes in midair helps bring you down. I didn't know these techniques initially, but I'm learning.

Throughout your journey, you will encounter setbacks, things that don't go as planned. When faced with these challenges, revisit the rules you established during your initial attempt. But be cautious not to build a fortress of rules around your heart. Instead, start anew with wisdom.

Take the information you have put together from trying, failing, and getting back up, and ask, *Is there anything I've learned that will equip me for a more successful ending next time?* Then, remember why you started in the first place. Recall your ambitions and the overarching reasons that fueled your desire for change. Revisit them, plant a flag in the sand, and declare, "New day, new me. I'm starting anew."

You have heard the saying that we miss 100 percent of the shots we don't take. Here's a pro tip for you today: Take the shot. It is a new day with familiar challenges. Start all over again. Learn from your mistakes and make the leap.

THE WORLD IS FULL OF NOISE; FIND A QUIET PLACE AND GOD WILL MEET YOU THERE

"Find a quiet, secluded place so you won't be tempted to role-play before God. Just be there as simply and honestly as you can manage. The focus will shift from you to God, and you will begin to sense his grace."

MATTHEW 6:6 MSG

John Cage, a famous musician, had finished a new work after five long years and planned to play it onstage in a huge concert hall. He got the word out to everyone who followed his music, and they filled the hall with anticipation. Eventually, John walked across the stage to a huge Steinway grand piano, which had been rolled into place the night before. The piece he would be performing was called *4'33"*.

He flipped up his tails and sat at the piano as everyone leaned in, anticipating the beginning of an amazing musical experience. For the next four minutes and thirty-three seconds, he sat in silence, his hands in his lap. After the first few minutes, which felt much longer than a few minutes, someone fidgeted, another person sneezed, and someone even yawned. "When is the song going to begin?" was the question racing on a loop through everyone's minds.

At the end of the piece, the musician rose to his feet and left the stage. What? Some people felt deceived, but others who were keen to experience something new felt engaged. During the silence, they had heard the rain on the roof, the wind blowing, even the noise of people leaving the room bewildered. It was a grand experiment in silence.

If you are like me, you feel uncomfortable with silence. I fill quiet moments with music or conversation, or sometimes I drum my fingers on the nearby table. But there is value in exploring the beauty of absolute silence. Even Jesus practiced quiet. Though He and His disciples were constantly in the middle of a barrage of people and needs, Jesus still set aside the time to invite His disciples to come with Him to a quiet place and rest.

Find a place of quiet today and come rest awhile.
Experience the quiet, listen to the wind and the rain,
and listen for Jesus' voice of love and acceptance.

IT'S A GOOD DAY TO DECIDE

If serving the LORD seems undesirable to you, then choose for yourselves this day whom you will serve, whether the gods your ancestors served beyond the Euphrates, or the gods of the Amorites, in whose land you are living. But as for me and my household, we will serve the LORD.

JOSHUA 24:15

College is a fun time for some and a painful time for others. It's when many of us sort out who will be our traveling companions on the journey of life. For instance, at Seattle Pacific University, there is a set of tall cafe tables in the Gwinn Commons. If you were seen sitting there, it meant you and whoever you were with were "a thing." For those who need a clearer signal, there is also a phrase used to describe the event when people go next level in their relationship: the "DTR" (define the relationship).

Jesus was always asking people questions to clarify where they were in their relationship with Him. He had the DTR with a rich young ruler and with another fellow who had just lost a family member. Even with a guy on a cross next to Him. I imagine the DTR he had with a guy named Saul was a hard conversation.

Saul was the guy holding everyone's coats while they killed Christians. He even got permission to arrest Christians wherever he found them. One day, though, while Saul was on his way to Damascus, Jesus showed up and asked him why he was doing the things he was doing. This was his DTR.

Saul lost his sight during the encounter, and a couple of his friends got him to town. It was in the dark place that Saul figured out that everything Jesus had said was true. Saul was so impacted by his DTR that he stopped being the enemy of Jesus' friends and tried instead to join them. He even changed his name to Paul.

Have the DTR conversation with Jesus today if you haven't before or haven't in a while. Decide that what you have is special and you are going to pursue it with everything you've got.

LOVE WITHOUT AGENDA AND GOD WILL DO THE REST

"But what about you?" he asked. "Who do you say I am?" Simon
Peter answered, "You are the Messiah, the Son of the living God."
MATTHEW 16:15–16

Caesarea Philippi is in the mountains in the northern part of Israel at the base of Mount Hermon. It is a place where lots of different gods were worshiped, so it makes sense that Jesus would use this place to ask His disciples and Simon Peter in particular, "So, who does everyone think I am? And who do *you* think I am?" When Simon Peter nailed it and said Jesus was the Messiah and the Son of God, Jesus told him that this truth was something only God could reveal. Then Jesus told His disciples not to tell anyone.

The disciples had heard "don't tell anyone" from Jesus before, when He had healed a leper, two blind men, and Jairus's daughter. I don't think the idea was to keep the fact that Jesus was God a secret. Instead I think He wants us to *show* people what we believe rather than merely *tell* them.

Everybody has an opinion; few have an experience they can directly tie to the opinion. Let's talk about what we have experienced directly from God rather than give people our opinions or the party line or merely talk about what we have learned about God in a book.

Today, ask yourself who you think Jesus really is. Was He a great teacher? He certainly was. One of the best ever, in fact. Was Jesus a prophet? He was a prophet in the way He taught with authority and foresaw what would be happening next.

If you are like me and have concluded Jesus is God, thank the Holy Spirit who made that known to you. But don't worry about making the case for Jesus to your friends.

Remember, we don't lead people to Jesus; Jesus leads people to Himself. All the pressure is off. Now, just go love everybody.

DON'T LET YOUR MESSES KEEP YOU DISCONNECTED

Cast your cares on the Lord and he will sustain you;
he will never let the righteous be shaken.
PSALM 55:22

I was on the road in another country and rushing to get to the train station, pulling my luggage full of clothes that were in need of a good washing. This disorganized pile of dirty clothes was clanking along behind me on loud and wobbly luggage wheels when the handle I was pulling broke. I hate when that happens, because the only way to move the luggage then is to wrap your arms around it and hold it to your chest like a koala bear holding onto a eucalyptus tree. It's a visual of the problem some of us have going through life without a handle on our fears and concerns and insecurities. When people meet us, instead of meeting who we really are, they meet the bundle of dirty laundry we've been clutching to our chests. It is the things we carry that often come between us and separate us from the good things God wants for us.

When we have unresolved things in our lives—and we all do—we just keep bumping into each other's baggage rather than engaging with each other. The fix is to do the heavy lifting required to get a handle on those unresolved things.

Understanding what we are holding tightly to our chests is worth all the time and energy we can scrape together. We won't be successful in lightening our load until we realize we have one, and trauma will try to trick us into believing we can just suck it up and gut it out rather than figure it out. But that's just not true. Jesus invited all of us who are weary and carry heavy burdens to come to Him and He promised He would give us rest.

Making ourselves available to the unresolved parts in our lives is necessary to see them clearly, find healing, and eventually release them. Only then can we stop being separated from the people God has put in our lives.

What baggage are you carrying today? Ask God to help
you get a handle on those things holding you back from
experiencing the big life God invited you into.

GOD DOESN'T NEED YOU TO BE CONTROLLING— HE WANTS YOU TO BE A FRIEND

Then James and John, the sons of Zebedee, came to him. "Teacher,"
they said, "we want you to do for us whatever we ask."
MARK 10:35

In Mark 10, the two sons of Zebedee tried to control Jesus. They approached Him and said, "We want you to do whatever we tell you to do." *Wait, what?* Jesus didn't say that, but I would have. Rather than scolding them, Jesus gently redirected their misguided intentions.

Let's be honest. Sometimes don't we also tell our friends we want them to do exactly what we tell them to do? We're just a little less obvious about it. Most of the things I try to control are rooted in my own insecurity and nurtured by chaotic life experiences I don't quite understand. Control wants dominion over outcomes and individuals. You will know if you have been on the receiving end of this kind of relationship when outcomes are dictated, rather than discussions invited.

Let's do the opposite of controlling people in our relationships. Let's strive to cultivate genuine, positively influential friendships. A true friend will want to understand your desires and guide you toward success without imposing their will on you or trying to control you. Let's work on being this kind of friend and adopt a more considerate and lasting approach than control can ever offer. Act like a guest in others' lives, not an owner telling everyone how to remodel the room.

We should also be looking for this kind of friend. Make sure you have a couple of people you can get super real with, who will push you to be the best version of yourself but won't try to take over. These people won't tell you what to do, but instead will remind you of who you are becoming.

Friendships will always be tricky but choose to fill your life with a couple of genuine, influential friends who will journey with you toward authenticity and fulfillment. Start today.

THE PLOT IS STRAIGHTFORWARD: WE CAN DO ALL THINGS THROUGH CHRIST

I can do all this through him who gives me strength.
PHILIPPIANS 4:13

What if we truly embraced Philippians 4:13, rather than selectively revising it to say, "I can do some things if they are easy through Christ who strengthens me," or "I can do the things I'm already good at through Christ who strengthens me"? Why do we do this kind of downgrading?

We have misgivings about "all things" being achievable. But why, if we are empowered by Christ? I think it stems from distractions that can cause us to lose the plot—and having a plot matters.

Did you ever see the TV show *Lost*? In it, people crash onto a deserted island and then try to figure out how to make their way off. They must grapple with mysterious challenges, such as a smoke monster that abducts somebody. There was no explanation of what the smoke monster was, and most people assumed they would figure it out in the next episode. Yet the explanation never came, and then two new unexplained events happened. What seemed interesting and engaging at first became less so when it became evident that there was no plot, just one random thing after another, leaving viewers frustrated and without answers.

In our lives, we need a discernible plot. We gain clarity in the challenges we face by understanding the overarching storyline of our lives. For those of faith, that plot is beautifully encapsulated in the verse, "I can do all things through Christ who strengthens me." When faced with an obstacle, you can confidently declare, "I can do all things." In other words, "I know the plot." When a relationship takes an unexpected turn, you can affirm, "I can do all things." In other words, "I can navigate this relationship too."

Grasp the powerful truth contained in the words "I can do all things," and it will change your life. Doing this requires not just acknowledging the challenges you are facing but also letting go of distractions both past and present. Understand that these distractions are meaningless smoke monsters in a plotless TV show. Fill your life with focus on the true plot that will link everything together: Jesus and the strength He gives us to do all things. Embrace this reality, and let it guide you today.

**You can do all things through Christ. Go
drive that around the block today.**

SOMETIMES THE END OF A GOOD STORY IS THE BEGINNING OF A GREAT ONE

Now to him who is able to do immeasurably more than all we ask or imagine, according to his power that is at work within us.
EPHESIANS 3:20

I sailed to Hawaii thirty-five years ago for the first time. It took a minute to get there, but when I arrived, I thought to myself, *I've got to get a place on the water here.* Then I discovered what a place on the water in Hawaii costs. I didn't bail on the idea; I tried a work-around and got on a decades-long waiting list for a boat slip at a marina in Oahu. I paid $25 a year to stay on the list and lived in constant anticipation of the day I would hear that it was my turn. It wasn't the only thing I thought about, but it came to mind surprisingly often for a guy who had lots of other things going on.

When it comes to anticipation, there is both a good version and a bad one. Good anticipation is when looking forward to something puts a spring in your step, gets you out of bed in the morning, or brings a grin to your face. Bad anticipation, on the other hand, just feels like stress. I remember in elementary school when report cards came out. It was never good news or good grades in my case. Knowing the day was drawing near for my grades to be sent home with me was never the good kind of anticipation. It felt like a fear and shame and disappointment salad.

It took thirty years, but I finally got to the top of the list. I got the slip and a beat-up boat to go in it, but I never made it to Hawaii to see it. Two years later, I sold the boat. But I got on the list again recently. I'm at the dead bottom. See you in thirty years, Hawaii. I'm living in anticipation of another shot at my place on the water.

Remember, sometimes what you think is the end of a good story is actually the beginning of a great one.

Today, focus your anticipation on God's promise to do inexplicably more than you could ever ask or imagine.

YOU'RE NOT A VICTIM OR A HERO— YOU'RE A PARTICIPANT

"Therefore do not worry about tomorrow, for tomorrow will worry about itself. Each day has enough trouble of its own."
MATTHEW 6:34

Are you a little stressed out? I know, me too. *Time* did a study recently that found that 40 percent of people in America are more stressed now than they were a year ago. That same article relayed that, according to the Anxiety and Depression Association of America, 40 million American adults—roughly 18 percent of the population—have an anxiety disorder.[1] Think of it this way. If there are five people in a boat, one of them will have a high level of clinical anxiety. I'm guessing it would be five of five if a teenager was the captain.

Here are a couple of tips for sorting out your anxiety. First, figure out what your feeling of anxiety is connected to. Resist the urge to say, "Everything," because it's not true. The source of your anxiety is probably the confluence of a couple of things, but I promise it is not equal parts of everything. Once you figure out what the anxiety is connected to, put together a list of which things you can exert some influence over and which things are beyond your influence. Give up your desire to have full control—you don't have it. Last, choose one of those things you can influence toward a more beautiful and lasting outcome and take a courageous step in that direction. In other words, do something. Don't take on the role of a victim or a hero; be a participant.

What prison are you in? Is it a bad job? A difficult relationship? Stop asking God to solve all your problems; instead, ask Him to give you context for them so you can understand them better. Then take a step toward what you can influence and trust God with the rest.

God has invited you into a big life, filled with love and joy and obedience and whimsy. If something is blocking your view of these things, figure out what it is and ask God and others for the help you need.

THE BEST WAY TO DAZZLE GOD IS TO GO BE YOU

"Look at the birds of the air; they do not sow or reap or store
away in barns, and yet your heavenly Father feeds them.
Are you not much more valuable than they? Can any one
of you by worrying add a single hour to your life?"
MATTHEW 6:26–27

Appearances drive a great deal of the assumptions people have about each other. Even the way we dress says something, whether we intend it to or not. When we began our school in Gulu, Uganda, during its twenty-plus-year civil war, we bought uniforms for the students. I didn't learn until later that the colors I had picked were those worn by a political movement whose objective was to overthrow the country. No wonder people asked questions about the school.

It's not surprising that many of us pay a lot of attention to how we present ourselves. We don't want other people to assume bad things about us based on our appearance. But there are a weird number of us going broke trying to convince people that we are what we are not. We stage photos and maneuver ourselves into locations to create a context for our lives that isn't accurate. Sometimes we use words that are designed to make us sound more knowledgeable or hip or relevant than we actually are.

This is not done without a cost, because we become strangers to ourselves while we try to impress strangers. Why not be real rather than pretending to be who we wish we were or want to appear to be? You have probably heard the saying, "Cutting the ears off a mule doesn't make it a racehorse." If you want to dazzle heaven, put the cutters down and go be you.

You don't have to pretend to be a certain way in an effort to get the acceptance and security you need.

**Look at how God takes care of the birds outside your window.
How much more will He take care of you today?**

WHY JUDGE WHEN LOVE GETS THE JOB DONE?

"Stop judging by mere appearances, but instead judge correctly."
JOHN 7:24

Someone dropped me off at Dulles International Airport on a cold, snowy winter day outside of Washington, DC. Cars were stopped, and people were unloading luggage and giving hugs goodbye. There was a police officer in a bad mood who was shouting and waving her arms at the cars. She stomped her feet as she charged from car to car, yelling loudly. We steered clear of her and pulled over fifty yards away.

I gathered my things and walked back toward the terminal in the direction of the police officer. In a moment of half passion and one quarter compassion, I walked out into the street and asked the officer if she was okay. "You seem like you are a little on edge," I said as we stood toe to toe. She looked puzzled, and I said, "You're doing a lot of yelling tonight at everyone. Are you okay?"

"Oh, honey," she said, laughing, "I'm not mad. I'm just trying to stay warm out here. It's freezing." Boy, did I feel dumb for my misplaced judgment about this person I didn't know.

We shouldn't be too quick to fill in the blanks on someone just because we think we have them figured out after a few visual or audible cues. When what we've seen going on is 100 percent of less than 1 percent, our minds fill in the other 99 percent based on our biases, beliefs, experiences, and fears.

Take, for example, seeing a large fin swimming toward you on a hot day as you float in the azure waters of the Caribbean. Some will automatically assume the fin belongs to a shark, and others will just as quickly assume it is attached to a dolphin. If you looked hard enough and long enough and gave a little more thought, you might conclude that you were safe, because a shark's tail goes side to side and a dolphin's goes up and down. Sometimes we just need to look a little longer and a little harder.

God has dropped people in our path we should be engaging, but too often we avoid them. We see a few things and decide they are a mess or are weird or scary and we don't want to get involved. Most of the time, we just don't know the whole story. Give God some room to write in the margins of the story you came up with. Who knows? You might have your perspective changed today.

Jump in. Go deep. The water is fine. It is filled with hope and joy and Jesus. Sure, there will be setbacks and difficulties too, but don't let that keep you in the shallow end of your life.

WE CAN'T HONOR GOD IF WE DON'T HONOR ONE ANOTHER

> Love one another with brotherly affection.
> Outdo one another in showing honor.
> **ROMANS 12:10** ESV

I was pulling into Chicago for a speaking event. The plane inched forward the last few feet, and a small bell rang. That was usually the signal for everyone to get out of their seats, open the overhead bins, and collect their luggage. But the captain came over the loudspeaker and told everyone to stay in their seats. I settled back and looked out the window.

Outside, there was a firetruck with its ladder extended into the air and an American flag hanging down. Underneath the huge flag was an honor guard made up of representatives from the police, fire department, air force, navy, and army, all standing at attention and saluting. A fallen soldier was being brought home.

This is what it can look like to honor someone, but it's not the only way. Honor also takes the form of kindness and empathy and paying attention or caring when there is nothing in it for you. We can't honor God if we don't honor one another.

I have met a lot of people who say they love God but don't like the people made in His image. If we want to honor God, perhaps we need to revisit the way we deal with some of the difficult, divisive, and sometimes awful people He made. We don't need to applaud behaviors we disagree with, but if we can honor the person—the divine (albeit confused) creation God made in that person—I think heaven would do somersaults.

Think about who you could outdo in showing honor to today.

Who has made a contribution to your life or the lives of the people you love the most? Drop them a note today. Love one another.

MAY OTHERS KNOW YOU BY YOUR COURAGE

When they saw the courage of Peter and John and realized that
they were unschooled, ordinary men, they were astonished
and they took note that these men had been with Jesus.
ACTS 4:13

Al was waiting on death row for the date of his execution. When the date arrived, at Al's request, our mutual friend Sam started helping him pick the way he would die and his last meal. Then the execution was delayed at the last moment. This happened three times. Eventually, Al was released into the general population and joined my class. Then one day, one of the guards took him to the front gate, gave him a debit card with $200 on it, and released him. Evidently, the case had been reversed. These days, you can find Al back in prison, but he's there mentoring others and giving away joy and hope. People can see Al's courage, and it is evident he has spent a great deal of time with Jesus. How about you? What do people see in your life?

The book of Acts tells us that after Jesus left for heaven, Peter and John helped someone who had been crippled. We never learn what this guy's name was, but I bet Peter and John knew it. After this injured man was healed and sprang to his feet, people started asking Peter and John about how God had helped him and why. The religious people in power at the time weren't happy about all this talk, and Peter and John got in so much trouble they were thrown in jail, which is something that happened to them often. A short time later, these same religious people saw their courage and immediately knew they had been with Jesus.

I wonder what people think when they meet us. Do they see courage in our lives? Who do they think we have just been with? Is it Jesus? I can honestly say I often wonder whether some of the people who yell the loudest about their opinions and beliefs have been with a cage fighter or whether the ones with the slick speeches have been with a person peddling reverse mortgages.

**Would people identify you by your biggest hang-ups or what
you do for a living, or would they see the courage displayed in
your everyday life and assume you have been with Jesus?**

LEAN INTO GOD'S SPECIAL NAME FOR YOU—YOU ARE HIS "BELOVED"

Beloved, if God so loved us, we also ought to love one another.
1 JOHN 4:11 ESV

I was talking to a friend of mine, and she surprised me by telling me she is related to the author of *The Wizard of Oz*. How cool is that? If it were me, I would be tempted to tell everyone I ever met about this branch on the family tree, but she never talks about it. It turns out the main character in *The Wizard of Oz* has a real name much longer than the abbreviated name, Oz. His full name is actually Oscar Zoroaster Phadrig Isaac Norman Henkle Emmannuel Ambroise Diggs. That's a mouthful. Evidently, the author of the book thought the name was too long (plus, the last of these initials spelled the word *pinhead*), so he simply went with "Oz" for short.

Jesus has a nickname for all of us, too, and it's not "pinhead" or "screw-up" or "letdown"; it's not "successful" or "popular" or "leader" or "influencer" either. It is much shorter than all the other names we may have given ourselves over time. His name for us is "beloved."

We have always been His beloved and always will be, but sometimes we get moving so fast, trying to earn the approval of God or strangers or girlfriends or boyfriends or spouses or parents or pastors or employers, that we don't hear Him speak this beautiful, simple, and accurate name over us.

Sit in the blessing of the name "beloved" for a moment and let it wash over you. Repeat it to yourself a couple of times. "I am His beloved," "I am His beloved." Say it like you mean it. Repeat it throughout the day and again when you wake up stressed out in the middle of the night. When the police officer pulls you over for speeding and asks for your license and registration, tell them, "I am God's beloved." Really lean into God's special name for you.

The reason to do this is both simple and hard. You and I offer the greatest blessing to the people we love when we lean into the truth about ourselves and them. So let's claim the name "beloved" and live like we believe it. Then we can do the important work of seeing others, even the difficult ones, as God's beloved too.

You are His and He delights in you. Walk in that confidence today.

CHANGE IT UP AND CHANGE OFTEN

"See, I am doing a new thing! Now it springs up; do
you not perceive it? I am making a way."
ISAIAH 43:19

We need to be ready to break up with the previous, more familiar versions of ourselves. We need to stay sharp and make ourselves more available to the next thing God is creating in and through and even adjacent to us. Don't think for a second this is going to be a fair fight. I don't see devils around every corner, but I'll promise you that darkness wants to keep you stuck, afraid, wounded, and suspicious.

If you are going to step into a new thing, you are going to have to do things a little differently. More of the same thing isn't a new thing; it's just a knockoff of what did or didn't work before. You're going to need to blaze some new trails. Even the Magi took a different way home rather than the predictable path they took on the way to Jesus the first time.

Here's the good news. Change is easier and offers more options than you might think. Did you know there are 293 ways to make change for a dollar? Sure, you could count out four quarters or ten dimes or twenty nickels or one hundred pennies, which are the more predictable, common ways to make change for a dollar, or you can mix it up a little.

You can do the same thing with how you approach potential changes you want to make in your life. Quit limiting the way you think about enacting change in your attitude, circumstances, job, friends, or any other areas of your current life. Often, we are just short a dollar or two worth of changes to make some real progress.

**Take some initiative today and try a new, creative way
of walking toward the changes you want to see.**

213

JULY

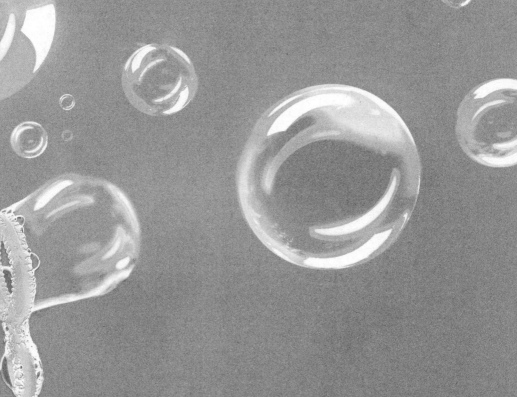

SOMETIMES LOVE IS PUTTING PRICKLY PEOPLE AHEAD OF OURSELVES

In your relationships with one another, have the same mindset
as Christ Jesus: Who, being in very nature God, did not
consider equality with God something to be used to his own
advantage; rather, he made himself nothing by taking the very
nature of a servant, being made in human likeness.

PHILIPPIANS 2:5–7

We've all met people who have a lot of attitude. You have probably seen them on a big screen: it's the rapper or pop star throwing up the sign, the football or movie star doing the strut. To put it nicely, these folks don't seem to have a self-image problem. Even though we don't know them, the vibe they give off is that everything is about them. Just listen to their interviews. They go on and on about their accomplishments or how cool they are and how there is no one equal to them. We expect them to transition at some point and say, "Well, enough about me. Let's talk about me."

Interestingly, the Bible says we can have all the attitude we want, it just needs to be the attitude of Christ. This is hard to do. It is not our first instinct to give away love when we have been wronged, to stay silent when we have plenty of choice words to say. But Paul gave us a great hack for how to stay humble. He said to consider others more worthy than ourselves.

Let's drill down and get really practical. When someone says something lame to you, silently think to yourself, *They think they are being really helpful right now*, even though they aren't. This is the new perspective having Christ's attitude will give you.

When things go surprisingly wrong, remind yourself that you aren't looking for things to be fair; you are pursuing Jesus. Thankfully, God wasn't looking for what was fair when Jesus was hung on a cross for us.

**Who is someone you can love today who is a little prickly?
How can you engage them with love and acceptance?**

FLY THE BANNER OF LOVE

Let him lead me to the banquet hall, and let his banner over me be love.
SONG OF SOLOMON 2:4

We love flags and banners at our home. When someone comes from another state or country to visit us, we fly their flag from one of our flagpoles. We love finding out what the colors and symbols mean. Not surprisingly, every flag in the world has colors and symbols that represent something. There are even flags that sailors use to communicate with one another over water. Because boats are often far away from one another when they travel, sailors used to raise flags to send messages. There is a flag for each letter of the alphabet, and each of those letters stands for a special message, kind of like a secret code.

When our kids were little, we thought it would be neat to make a family flag. We chose the nautical flag for the letter *G*—the letter for our last name—and added five stars in a circle, one star to represent each member of our family and a circle to represent that we are a family and stick close to one another. We proudly flew our flag on the flagpole in our backyard, so everyone would know what made our family special.

The Bible talks about flags and banners. Solomon wrote that God's banner for us, His organizing principle, is love. He wants love to be the most important thing we are known for, and He wants love to be the first thing people know about us when they meet us.

As you are organizing your day or your plans for your future, take some time to design and then make a flag for yourself. If you have a family, include them too. Incorporate into the flag colors and emblems that represent who you are, what you want, and what the most important things are that you would want the world to know. Then hoist that flag over your home or where you work. Let it be a reminder not only of what's important to you but also that, while we fly under the banner of love, we have the chance to live it out every day.

**Today, move through your day confidently,
knowing God's banner over you is love.**

LOVE IS MORE THAN AMAZING— IT'S EXTRAVAGANT

But God demonstrates his own love for us in this:
While we were still sinners, Christ died for us.
ROMANS 5:8

When my daughter was in high school, I wanted her to be a nun, but, unfortunately, she said she liked guys, so I gave her this tip. I said, "When the guys ask you to the prom, I want you to ask them, 'What's your definition of love?' Because they're guys, they won't know.

"Then just send them home and tell them to come back when they know what love is. If they get it right, you can go to the prom with them, but if they come back and say love is like butterflies, you can get that from bad pizza."

What would you say love is? I think love is about sacrifice and commitment. The kind of love Jesus gave away wasn't at garage-sale prices; it was extravagant and costly.

I want to be one of those people who gives away extravagant love. And I want to spend my time with people who see others for who they are becoming rather than as the sum of their mistakes.

God loves us extravagantly. He's not keeping score, shaking His head when we mess up, withholding His love, or trading it for our good behavior. Christ's death on the cross for us when we were still sinners exemplifies God's love for us—the kind of love easily identified by sacrifice and commitment.

**Who is it that you can point some extravagant
and sacrificial love toward today?**

STOP LIVING LIKE A PRISONER WHEN YOU'VE BEEN SET FREE

Now the Lord is the Spirit, and where the Spirit
of the Lord is, there is freedom.
2 CORINTHIANS 3:17

This is the month when we celebrate our freedom with big public displays of fireworks and sometimes large family events with hot dogs and picnics. Take a moment to reflect on what freedom means to you and give thanks for all the freedoms you enjoy. What a gift freedom is, isn't it? And yet sometimes you can tell somebody they're free, and they still stay stuck. They act like they either aren't free or don't know what to do with their freedom. Freedom that is not accessed, expressed, or engaged isn't freedom.

I have a friend, Mike, who tells a story about a time he was in India and his car went off the road. Somebody sent for an elephant, and it picked the car up with its trunk and put it back on the road. This was remarkable roadside assistance. Afterward, Mike was chatting with the elephant's master and asked him, "Why doesn't the elephant run away?" The owner said, "Well, ever since that elephant was young, we put a little ring around its leg. That ring was originally tied with a chain to a post, and then eventually we took the chain and the post away. But because the ring is still on his leg, the elephant thinks it's still captive."

The same thing happens to us, but it's not a ring around our leg. It's a job or debt or a bad relationship or circumstances that we think we're tied down by. We might talk a big game about freedom, but the truth is we remain captive to things we are no longer tied to.

Here is a bigger truth: you are not stuck with your job or your bad relationship or whatever you think is holding you down; you can quit it. Or maybe you need to exercise some freedom in the way you spend your time and, instead of pining away the hours, you need to stop doing things that aren't getting you where you want to go. Even in the most difficult challenges, God wants you to experience freedom.

Today, break loose from what has been holding you back.

HEROES DON'T NEED TO TALK UP THEIR VICTORIES

And their eyes were opened. And Jesus sternly warned
them, "See that no one knows about it."
MATTHEW 9:30 ESV

The first time we took our kids to Disneyland, they were very young, but they had enough excitement and anticipation to do the math of a college freshman and figure out all the details. They got incredibly specific and planned the rides we would go on, how we would get there extra early, and everything we would do in the Magic Kingdom.

When the day finally arrived, we were at the gate the moment Disneyland opened its doors. We showed the person at the gate our super expensive tickets and made our way into the park, only pausing briefly to sit on a raised planter containing a well-groomed tree that looked like a Disney character. For reasons I still don't understand, Lindsey fell off the short planter and did some face-planting of her own. A golf ball–sized lump emerged on her tiny forehead within moments, and the adventure was over before it began.

We found someone who was incredibly kind to help us and were whisked through back alleys that led to other routes. It turns out Disney has doctors and nurses and even an entire underground tunnel system for the cast members to get from one place to another. This system has multiple levels none of the guests can see. What happens under the surface at Disneyland is what makes all the things that take place on the surface so spectacular and engaging.

Like Disneyland, much of what we do in life that matters doesn't happen on the surface. To the contrary, some of the more lasting contributions we make will be done in secret. Similarly, Jesus did big things in people's lives and told them not to tell anyone about it. He also said to not even let our left hand know what our right hand is doing. Stated differently, we don't need to be the hero of the story. If we make everything about us, it won't be about Jesus anymore.

What can you do in secret today?
Heaven can't wait to see.

GOD DOESN'T NEED US TO BE REFEREES

I gave you milk, not solid food, for you were not yet
ready for it. Indeed, you are still not ready.
1 CORINTHIANS 3:2

Giving everyone my personal cell phone number has presented some interesting challenges. For instance, have you noticed how some people sound younger than they are on the phone? I thought a young person had called once—I was guessing they were in the third or fourth grade—so I did what I always do and interrupted them to ask, "Are your parents close by so you can get them on the telephone with you and we can all talk?"

The twenty-something responded haltingly, "Um, no . . . they dropped me off at college last week."

I sometimes wonder whether we sound pretty young to God. Paul talked to his friends in Corinth about how they sounded young. He told them that things like being worldly or jealous of one another or arguing made them sound and seem younger than they were. And yet we do these things all the time, don't we?

If you see things in black and white and place your highest value on being right, a great deal of your life will be wasted on arguments that don't leave a lasting impact. If you are spending your time pulling penalty cards on everyone around you, get yourself a black-and-white-striped referee shirt and a whistle, not a cross and the opportunity to carry a message of hope.

I decided a long time ago that I don't want to be a referee or merely a mascot for faith. I'd rather be a cheerleader and an example. Avoiding the acrimony in our faith communities isn't going soft on doctrine, it's going big on Jesus.

**What can you do to approach your faith and the
people around you with greater maturity?**

IF YOU'RE THE SMARTEST PERSON IN THE ROOM, INVITE WISER PEOPLE IN

Walk with the wise and become wise, for a
companion of fools suffers harm.

PROVERBS 13:20

If you want an advance glimpse at how your life will turn out, look at who you're hanging out with. Their trajectory doesn't dictate what yours will be, but it can be a strong indicator. Wise people attract and cultivate relationships with other wise people. How can you start doing this?

If you live for ninety-two years and have twelve conversations a day, that's about four hundred thousand conversations. Take advantage of the next couple of days. Have conversations and make them real ones, not "How are you doing?" or "Where do you work?" Instead, ask, "Who are you? What are the things you want in life? What does it feel like to be you? How is it really going?"

These kinds of questions will lead to conversations that tell you more about people, who they are, where they're headed, and how they think. This will help you understand which people are the ones you want to spend more time with and eventually grow to be more like.

That's what I want to do; I want twelve conversations, real conversations, every day. When you do this, you'll start surrounding yourself with people who remind you not of who you used to be but of who you're becoming. Those are the people you want influencing you.

**Make an intentional effort to walk with the wise
today, and you will start growing more into
the person you want to be tomorrow.**

CHANGE YOUR PERSPECTIVE AND CHANGE YOUR EXPERIENCE

"For my thoughts are not your thoughts, neither are
your ways my ways," declares the LORD.
ISAIAH 55:8

If I put a dot on a piece of paper, what would you see? Perhaps you have done this exercise before. For some, they would see the dot. Others would see the whole paper, and still others would see the hand holding it. If we want to live lives of impact, we need to look beyond the dot and even beyond the four corners of the paper and see God's hand holding it all. Doing this is going to require that we develop the ability to zoom in and out of our lives.

Our eyes don't come with zoom lenses like some cameras do, but our minds do. Zoom in on your life today and ask yourself what's taking up a lot of space in your thoughts and why. If your finances are constantly on your mind, ask yourself what is going on that makes this such an important theme for you. What is making you feel unsettled, insecure, or vulnerable about your money situation?

Now zoom out and think about what God says about our finances and how He will take care of us no matter what. Do the same with each additional area of your life you can think of. Hover over your family, friends, and the issues of the day that matter the most to you. What do you see when you zoom in on your anxieties, and what do you realize when you zoom out and see the bigger reality?

The quality of the lives we live depends a lot on the perspective we bring to each experience. Perfect the art of zooming in to understand yourself and your thoughts and zooming out to see the bigger picture of what God is doing and saying.

What thought pattern can you shift today based on this exercise of zooming in and zooming out?

GATHER THE GOOD AND THROW IT IN THE POT

Each person is given something to do that shows who
God is: Everyone gets in on it, everyone benefits.
1 CORINTHIANS 12:7 MSG

There is a children's story called "Stone Soup." Perhaps you have read it before. A passerby sets up a big cooking pot in the middle of a village and lights a fire. There's nothing in it other than water and a couple of rocks at the bottom. When the villagers walk by and ask what he is making, he says with delight, "Stone soup," and ladles out some of the water. Tasting it, he says, "You know, what we could use is some cabbage." The villager says, "I have some cabbage," and throws it in. Later, another villager walks by and is told, after the chef ladles out some more soup and tastes it, "You know, what we need is some carrots." You know where this ends already; the soup becomes a delicious simmering pot made up of everyone's contributions and the entire village is fed. The concept is beautiful: we all need to throw in what we've got and it will be enough.

When I think of stone soup, I think of potluck meals. Potlucks were popular with farmers in the 1800s. They would bring and trade vegetables and various other things they had grown.

In more modern times, we often organize what we'll each bring to a potluck. For example, by assigning alphabet letters. If your last name starts with the letters *A* through *G*, you bring a salad. If it starts with *H* through *P*, you bring the entrée. If it is *Q* through *U*, you bring a dessert, and if it's *V* through *Z*, you bring a bag of chips. It's a bad way to organize a dinner and a bad way to include people. Think about it. Why would you want a college kid to make the entrée? Or the Le Cordon Bleu chef to bring a bag of chips? In the same way, why would we want the person who is great with adults to serve preschoolers or the person with the winsome, childlike faith to be stuck in a board meeting?

God has created us to come together and form a beautiful community that highlights what we have each been given and can contribute.

**Ask the people around you, "What are you good at? What
lights you up and makes you spring out of bed?"**

DECORATE YOUR LIFE WITH WHIMSY

"Therefore, when the owner of the vineyard comes, what will he do to those tenants?" "He will bring those wretches to a wretched end," they replied, "and he will rent the vineyard to other tenants, who will give him his share of the crop at harvest time."

MATTHEW 21:40–41

Most of us have a place we call home, whether we own a house or condo or are renting or living in a rustic cabin in the woods. We make changes to our homes to make them feel more like ours. We hang a painting from a nail or put up a couple of posters with thumb tacks. Maybe we install a rack in the kitchen to hold our pots and pans. I have a friend who did some big renovations on her home, but she did it without telling her landlord. The improvements were awesome and delighted my friend, but evidently didn't delight the landlord. Where was the tree that used to be where the shed is? Who added the fence? Who removed the hedge?

Here's the thing. In life, whether we are paying rent or paying a mortgage, we are still the tenants. It's not our place; it's God's. If we want to move the furniture around a little, no problem. But before we start remodeling the house and repurposing what we are caretaking, we need to get permission from the owner.

How do you know what you have permission to change in your life? The answer is both simple and hard. We have permission to love and forgive and engage and be obedient and to be wise and kind. We might not have permission to build fences to separate ourselves from others. We also might not have permission to build a shed and store up things God would rather have us put into play.

Jesus doesn't need pictures of Him hung on the walls. He would rather we decorate our lives and our hearts with compassion and empathy and generosity and joy and with, yes, a touch of whimsy. This is what a good tenant would do.

Love, hope, and patience are always the best kind of accents to our lives. What can you do today to decorate your life with more of these?

THROW YOUR EXCUSES OUT THE WINDOW AND YOU'LL FEEL BETTER AND BE BETTER

One who was there had been an invalid for thirty-eight years. When Jesus saw him lying there and learned that he had been in this condition for a long time, he asked him, "Do you want to get well?"

JOHN 5:5-6

There was a pool named Bethesda, and a man had been sitting beside it for years. Jesus asked him a question: "Do you want to be well?" It's a question God asks each of us in the middle of our joy and pain and uncertainty. Jesus asked, and what He got back from the man by the pool was an excuse: "I can't get in the pool in time to get healed."

I wonder what would happen in our lives if we ditched all the excuses and answered the question Jesus is more interested in: Do you want to be well? The painful truth is that some of us haven't yet decided. We hedge and defer and are so busy grousing about our circumstances or the obstacles in front of us that we don't get around to answering the question Jesus is asking.

We all have go-to excuses. What are yours? When I say I don't have time, what I am often lacking is compassion. When I say I don't have the resources, I may be feeling insecure about my finances. Sometimes when I act disinterested in something new, I am actually afraid of failing.

What excuses are you using today with the opportunities you have?

Jesus wants us to be well, and we won't get there if we are busy making excuses that only serve to make us sick.

GOD IS OFFERING YOU AN ADVENTURE—TAKE HIM UP ON IT

"Come," [Jesus] replied, "and you will see."
JOHN 1:39

If you have read my other books, you know about Charlie, a little boy we brought from Uganda to the United States for surgeries after he was attacked by a witch doctor. One day, while Charlie was recovering, I asked him what the biggest fish he had ever seen was. He said it was a Nile perch as he stretched his pointed fingers apart ten inches. I thought I could do him one better.

There's an amusement park called Sea World not far from our house. I haven't gone there often because it costs $85 to get in. But they've got some pretty big fish there, so Charlie and I jumped in the car and went. It was late in the afternoon, and I asked the girl at the ticket window what the half-day rate was. She said it was still $85. I wondered out loud if there was another way to get in. The young lady leaned forward to me and said in a hushed voice, "Ask for a shopper's pass." I leaned forward and said, "Okay, I want the shopper's pass." She ran my credit card and wrote down the time on the top of the receipt. You get one hour to go shopping and buy a rubber tuna, I suppose, and then you have to leave. If you're not out within an hour, they run your card for the full admission.

I looked at the time she printed on the receipt, grabbed Charlie by the hand, and we started running. His feet touched down about every ten yards as we made our way across the park. We ran down the moving walkway at the penguin exhibit. We ran through a glass tunnel leading to the shark tank. We petted a couple of starfish in a hurry. And then we made our final stop at Shamu Stadium, where they have a killer whale named Shamu who does tricks. Somebody wiggled an anchovy in the air, and Shamu took to the skies like a black-and-white ballistic missile. He did about half a flip and then landed right on his back, throwing a tsunami-size wave over the edge of the pool. Charlie was drenched and I was, too, as we walked toward the exit before the hour expired. We turned around, and two sets of wet shoe tracks dotted the sidewalk as we left.

Jesus has invited us on an adventure. He didn't say what would happen;

He just said, "Come and see." It is a costly adventure, and there are no shopper's passes or shortcuts. It's not going to be a stroll in the park and we will probably be running, but His promise is that He will be with us the entire way.

Today, take Jesus up on His offer. Show up for yourself and for the people God brings your way with the kind of love and intention only Jesus can provide.

DON'T UNDERESTIMATE PATIENCE

Whoever is patient has great understanding, but
one who is quick-tempered displays folly.
PROVERBS 14:29

There was a year or two when I was often in Washington, DC, trying to help some people resolve a dispute. My attempts to help didn't work, but it was interesting to try, and I met some fascinating people. During one of the meetings, I sat next to a guy who showed me a message he had just received on his cell phone: "Do you know who Bob Goff is?" We both smiled as he told me about a guy named Greg Murtha, who had sent the text.

Greg was the phenom behind Bob Buford's Halftime program and a slew of other gatherings. He lived a beautiful, amazing life, but at the time of his text, he was battling cancer and had been through one hundred rounds of chemotherapy. He was literally writing from his deathbed. My friend texted back, "Bob is sitting right next to me." Less than a minute later, there was a new text message from Greg: "Will you ask Bob if he will write the foreword to my book?" There is only one answer to a request from a dying man. So I said I would be honored to write the foreword. Here was the problem: I had only met Greg one time.

The next day, Greg went to be with Jesus. Because I had only limited exposure to Greg and still wanted to fulfill my promise, I needed to find out more about him. So, for the next month, I went to his friends and said, "Tell me about who Greg was." And they all told me one consistent thing: Greg was a guy with immense patience.

Immense patience isn't the way most people would describe me. I make coffee nervous. But Greg proved you can be both high functioning and immensely patient.

None of us knows how long we're going to live. Assuming today goes great, what do you think? Eighty-five years? Ninety-five? One hundred and five? Wherever you are on the timeline, what are you going to do today so that you will be known as a person with immense patience?

Hurry up. (Just kidding.)

MAKE YOURSELF AVAILABLE FOR THE NEXT OPPORTUNITY TO SHARE THE LOVE OF GOD

But you are a chosen people, a royal priesthood, a holy nation,
God's special possession, that you may declare the praises of
him who called you out of darkness into his wonderful light.
1 PETER 2:9

It is good to have a strategy for loving people, whether they are doing great or are in distress. I'm never quite sure what is going to happen when I pick up my phone, but it's always an invitation to step with God into a new opportunity to love.

A guy called me to talk about life, and we were having a pleasant conversation. I asked what he was doing at the time, and I was really surprised when he said he was on his honeymoon. "Brother, I have four words for you," I said. "Put the phone down." Speaking the truth in love is a gift.

Another call I got was from a guy who found my number in the back of one of my books. "Hi. Bob?" I said hello and asked how I could be helpful. He replied, "I'm actually calling to help you." *Terrific*, I thought, *I can always use a hand*. I was about to say, "Come on over, and let's change the oil in my car." But then he continued, "That's right. You see, I'm Jesus and I have returned."

I pulled the phone away from my ear to check out the caller ID, and it said the caller's name was Matt. I wasn't sure what to say about the news of his return. "Welcome back?" "Give the Trinity a chest bump for me?" This guy was sincere, but I'm guessing a little confused.

We are all priests; most of us are men and women of the cloth, without the cloth. We may not be the smartest person in the room and we may not have the perfect answers for everyone, but we can be the most available.

**Who can you be available to today? It is beautifully
pastoral to receive a call, say hello, and see
what God has next for your conversation.**

MEET THE NEW YOU

For we know that our old self was crucified with him so that the body ruled by sin might be done away with, that we should no longer be slaves to sin—because anyone who has died has been set free from sin.
ROMANS 6:6–7

I have spent sixty-five long years with Old Bob, but New Bob I met on a flight home from Dallas after a speaking event the night before. The flight took several hours, so I thought I would write down the answers to some questions about myself: *Who is New Bob? What is he good at? Who does he want to be?* I liked the answers I saw. They were clear and gave me a target to continue to aim for. When I wrote about myself in the third person, I wrote down that Bob was a guy who wanted to be trusted and available, that he knows how to tell stories that hopefully connect with people, and that he is aware of his many shortcomings.

What would you write down about yourself if you did this exercise? Don't just wonder—try it and find out. Stop letting the older versions of you push you around. The only way to call that old version out of you is to figure out who the new version of you might be, hang a target on that person, and start aiming at it.

Do you want to see more patience in your life? Perhaps it is courage you lack? Come up with strategies to get you moving in those directions. Get creative. If you want to learn patience, only travel on the highways during rush hour. If you want to develop courage, take the trip you have hesitated to take because there are a host of unknowns.

Remember the story of the paralytic's friends who removed the shingles from a roof and lowered him down to get him in front of Jesus? Maybe we need to lower the previous versions of ourselves down by a rope to get in front of Jesus so we can become the new, healed versions of us.

What do you think God would say to that new version of you right after He gave you a hug? I bet He would say He was really looking forward to meeting you.

BE PICKY ABOUT NICKNAMES

"To the one who is victorious, I will give. . . . a white stone with a new name written on it, known only to the one who receives it."
REVELATION 2:17

Do you have a nickname? In Uganda, I have a couple of them. One of my nicknames is Babu. I would like to say it means super handsome, really smart guy, but it means elder or grandfather. Nicknames come in all shapes and sizes. Sometimes they are ironic, like when large men are called "tiny" or tall people are called "shorty." Other times they can be endearing and have pieces of our inside stories embedded in them.

Look at the characters in the Scriptures. They had plenty of name changes. Abram became Abraham, Sarai became Sarah, Jacob became Israel, and Hoshea became Joshua. The book of Revelation says that even Jesus has a new name, a name that God has given to Him and which is only known between Him and God. How cool is that?

No matter the nickname, having one usually communicates friendship, closeness, and sometimes a heap of fun. But it's also pretty weighty what our friends and family call us, because in large part we will tend to become who the people closest to us say we are. If someone calls us courageous, we will tend to be more courageous. If they call us kind, we will likely see more kindness in our lives.

So let's become more aware of what we are speaking over ourselves and over other people. When you are engaging the people around you, speak words of life and respect and honor. Be like Jesus was to Peter when he messed up but Jesus still called him a rock.

Someday we are going to find out what our special name is—known only to God. Until then, know this for certain: He calls you beloved and always will.

SHIFT TO A SOLID FOUNDATION

"The rain came down, the streams rose, and the winds
blew and beat against that house; yet it did not fall,
because it had its foundation on the rock."
MATTHEW 7:25

We live in a home that is almost one hundred years old, down by the bay in San Diego. It looks terrific from far away, but if you get a little closer and tap on the wood, you'll find that some of the boards are riddled with termites. Sweet Maria and I can almost hear them in the walls when they chew with their mouths open. Sometimes I wonder if the house is still standing because the termites have all linked arms.

What about you? Do you sometimes feel like things are ready to collapse? Like the life you're trying to build is a little too precarious for your taste? Jesus told a parable once about wise and foolish builders because He wanted us to understand the importance of the foundation on which we build our lives— that it matters. But, unfortunately, we don't always get a rock to build on.

Maybe your given family has some dysfunction, and it feels like shifting sand is constantly underfoot. Perhaps it is unresolved trauma that makes you feel like you can hear the framing in the walls of your life cracking.

Jesus offers you this hope: you may not have a rock under you, but He can be the rock you need. Together, you can build something lasting, because God can give you the firm foundation to bear the weight of what life throws at you.

**We are all under construction. If you have started out
on the sand like me and have a boatload of termites
to boot, God still says that you can make Him your
foundation and He will be your rock if you will let Him.**

DON'T SETTLE FOR ANYTHING LESS THAN LOVE

And this is my prayer: that your love may abound more and more in knowledge and depth of insight, so that you may be able to discern what is best and may be pure and blameless for the day of Christ.
PHILIPPIANS 1:9–10

On average we each make about thirty-five thousand decisions a day. We get to decide what we will remember and what we will forget, who to trust and who to beware of. We also get to decide every day whether we are going to serve God or not. Make the right decision about that, and the rest of your life will fall into place.

The decisions we make about following God sound like they are binary. In other words, we either do or we don't. But the way life and faith work, it is not always a clear choice between good and bad, right or wrong, in or out. Sure, there are some red-line topics where God spoke with clarity. In those instances, we will have to decide whether to obey or not obey. The larger part of our lives, though, is spent teasing out more nuanced matters. Should we pursue the opportunity or not? Take the chance or pass on it? Participate or hold back?

We can go with our gut on these decisions, or we can take the next step and see if there are examples or instructions in the Scriptures to give us guidance. I am pretty sure you won't find anything in the Scriptures about whether to take the job or date the person you just met, but you will find the heartbeat of God to remind you of what is highest and best.

Discerning what is the highest and best is how Paul described we should make our decisions. Letting love grow in knowledge and depth of insight is the way we get there. Does this tell you whether to take the job or go on the date? Of course not, but it might remind you of what to shoot for.

There are plenty of second-best options out there and available to you. But don't settle for second best.

**Today, when you are making decisions, ask God
what His highest and best is for you.**

KINDNESS MATTERS

Be kind and compassionate to one another,
forgiving each other
just as in Christ God forgave you.
EPHESIANS 4:32

Can we just agree that people are weird? I am. You are. Everyone you love and look up to and coexist with is. Your pastor or rabbi or counselor and your teachers and professors and mail carriers and confidants are, to a greater or lesser degree, wonderfully and irretrievably weird too. We're all sorting things out, so let's be available to the power of grace and accept ourselves and others as we do.

Sure, loving is risking that you might get caught in the crossfire every now and then when the random person is still sorting some things out. Give them a break—we all need one.

Hear Paul's words of encouragement to us to be kind and compassionate to one another, forgiving one another, just like Jesus forgave us.

The person who hurt you is working through their insecurities, and you just caught a stray as they did. And if it's you who is feeling a little weird and getting the itch to be mean or do bizarre things, try to cause as little disruption as possible while you work out the kinks.

Today, as you go about your regular routine and interact with other people, assume an attitude of kindness and acceptance. When you do, you will bring heaven to earth, even in the most challenging circumstances.

**Will leaning in with kindness be hard?
Of course it will. Do it anyway.**

KEEP YOUR EYES ON THE PRIZE

Do you not know that in a race all the runners run, but only
one gets the prize? Run in such a way as to get the prize.
1 CORINTHIANS 9:24

There is an iconic scene in the movie *Forrest Gump* that almost didn't make the film: it's the running scene. It turns out Tom Hanks and the director felt so strongly about the importance of including the running scene that they chipped in and paid for it themselves.

In the scene, Forrest runs from one coast to another several times, only stopping to eat and drink and hit the bathroom. He ran for three years, two months, fourteen days, and sixteen hours. That scene turned out to be my favorite part of the movie. Without it, the movie just wouldn't be the same.

You may be living your own running scene in your life. We all run, some faster than others. We run after our careers and our relationships. We chase down a few adventures and take some risks.

If you are raising kids, you are always on the run, and if you are a kid, you are the one being run after. If you are running a company, well, you're running too (see what I did there?). But what finish line are you running toward?

After several years of running, Forrest was in the desert with many people following him. In a dramatic moment, Forrest stopped. Everyone thought he was going to say something big and deep and important, and he did. He said, "I'm pretty tired. I think I'll go home now." Forrest knew what his finish line was meant to be.

What are you running toward? What are you running away from? Do you need to run home? We can't be all run and no stop. We need to know what the goal is, how to run to get there, and when it's time to go home. Paul wrote that in a race all the runners run, but only one gets the prize.

Be the person who gets the prize.

GET OVER YOUR OWN OPINION AND LOVE PEOPLE FOR SHOWING UP

I have become all things to all people so that by all possible means I might save some. I do all this for the sake of the gospel, that I may share in its blessings.
1 CORINTHIANS 9:22–23

I was asked to speak at a large and prestigious theological seminary gathering. This is an institution with an impeccable reputation for excellence and is a bastion of conservative biblical views and values. I am usually not someone's first pick in this space, so I was eager to show up before they discovered their mistake.

After practicing in the mirror for a week, I took the stage and said with delight and as much enthusiasm as I could muster, "I'm a Pisces!" A look of shock and mortification spread across the room in an instant. Jaws were dropping, people with forks full of potatoes dropped them in their laps. What? This is certainly not what they had expected to hear in this setting. Once I received the response I was anticipating, I clarified that I didn't know anything about astrology, wasn't a Pisces, didn't even like fish, and just wanted to see how they would react. Here's the thing. Sometimes, as people of faith, we need to work on our poker faces. People are going to say things to see if they can get a rise out of us. Don't take the bait.

In our faith communities, it is common to hear people say everybody is invited to Jesus, but when they come, do they feel welcome? More important than all the teaching coming from the front, do people meet Jesus when they come? Welcome people to church when they get there. Will they be off in their theology and doctrine? Sure, they will; you probably are a hair off too. Will they be doing some things Scripture says is not God's highest and best? Yes, just like you. Loving people like Jesus did is the kind of evangelism that beats any preacher thumping a pulpit. We can't say everybody is invited to Jesus unless we are willing to welcome them when they come.

Who can you make feel welcome today?

PAIR YOUR PLAN WITH YOUR AMBITION AND TAKE OFF

"Suppose one of you wants to build a tower. Won't
you first sit down and estimate the cost to see if
you have enough money to complete it?"
LUKE 14:28

To make progress in your life, you are going to need a plan. Some people are like bees and buzz from flower to flower, activity to activity. There's no plan other than to collect some honey along the way and get home with it. Don't get me wrong. I think that's terrific, and I've got a little bumble and a little bee in me too. But there is value in having a bit more of a plan.

Other people love a plan, but they seem frozen by the fear of not getting it right or of earning someone's disapproval with a misstep. They spend all their time concocting their plan but then never seem to get the wheels up. I'm not against planning itself, but when we defer acting once we have a plan, that will catch up to us and scuttle our God-given ambitions.

I fly a small airplane, and before I take off I punch in the frequencies of the place where I'm going to land, even though it might be hours away. This gives me one less thing to manage in the air. We need to do the same with our lives.

Each of us knows where we are in our relationships, career, and faith, and where we want to be someday. Punch in those numbers, and then head in that direction. Yes, there will likely be a few unexpected things that happen en route. Wrap your intellectual arms around this reality and get going.

What is it that you should do a little planning about today?

What next steps can you take to give wings to your idea after you have your plan in place? You are cleared for takeoff.

CHALLENGES ARE OPPORTUNITIES
TO REFOCUS AND KEEP GOING

But Paul shook the snake off into the fire and suffered no ill effects.
ACTS 28:5

I was invited to a friend's ranch to go hunting for elk. I'm not a big hunter and I figure if I don't shoot at them, then if elk ever take up arms, they won't shoot at me. Shortly after I arrived at the property, I was sitting in a car taking in the large vista when one of the other guests walked up to the Jeep I was in and threw a four-foot-long snake into my lap.

I don't know about you, but in my book, any snake that is thrown in your lap is automatically a rattlesnake. I was a busy guy for a couple of minutes, getting the snake off of me and back into the brush. After I tidied myself up, I asked the guy why he did that. All I could get out of him was that there was no need to worry, since it wasn't a rattlesnake.

The apostle Paul also encountered a snake. He was on his way to Rome when he got shipwrecked with a few hundred others on the island of Malta. Just when he may have thought it couldn't get worse, it did.

When they lit a fire to warm up, a snake bit Paul in the hand. We don't know if it was venomous, but as I said before, in my book all snakes are rattlesnakes. Everyone was expecting Paul to keel over and die, but he didn't. He just shook it off into the fire and carried on. I think Paul was so singular in his focus on getting to Rome to testify before Caesar that nothing was going to stop him—not a shipwreck, not a snake.

What is it that matters so much to you that you will give it 100 percent of your focus? With all the distractions and curveballs life throws at us, can you keep your eyes fixed on that ambition and, with God's help, continue to move toward it, even shaking off a couple of snakes as you do?

Practice being singular in focus today, keeping your eyes fixed on Jesus, and see what happens.

LEAD WITH JOY AND GET OTHERS TO JOIN THE CONGA LINE

Let them praise his name with dancing and make music
to him with timbrel and harp. For the LORD takes delight
in his people; he crowns the humble with victory.

PSALM 149:3-4

Walter escaped Uganda during a violent civil war after being arrested and imprisoned. Many years later, Walter and I became friends, and he told me about the man who saved him by putting him in the trunk of his car and driving him to the border. From there Walter made his way to Europe and then to San Diego, where we met.

The man who saved Walter's life is now a well-known leader in Uganda. I met him at a celebration where the leaders of Uganda's judiciary were all gathered. It was a very formal affair and included many speeches. There was even a traditional Ugandan band playing drums and flutes. As the music played, I stood up and grabbed Uganda's Supreme Court chief justice and started dancing. We started a conga line, and we grabbed one High Court judge after another. Within minutes, all the judges in the room were in a circle dancing and yelping, and the one leading us all was the man who saved Walter decades earlier. Leaders continue to lead with joy and courage no matter the context.

In the Bible, David was big on dancing, too, and he often had music played as he praised the Lord. No one in the Ugandan judiciary the evening of our great conga line was holding a timbrel or a harp, but the celebration lasted for hours as we expressed our joy. You may not spring to your feet in your office or classroom today, but the spirit of joy and celebration can become a larger part of your life than it has been. Let's lead with joy; let this be our lasting legacy.

What makes you want to rise to your feet and dance with joy? Find a couple of things that light you up, and make plans to do them, no matter how unconventional. Sing out loud in the car; roll down the windows and stick your head out the driver's side like a golden retriever.

**Celebrate the beautiful life God has given you by
leading some to safety with your love and joy.**

DON'T TRADE BEING UNDERSTOOD BY SOMEONE FOR IMPRESSING THEM

When words are many, transgression is not lacking,
but whoever restrains his lips is prudent.
PROVERBS 10:19 ESV

Why do we sometimes use twenty-dollar words to describe our faith experiences and expressions? It might make us sound smart or religious or holy to use academically interesting or theologically profound terms, but these highbrow words can be just as useless as the fluffy ones. What if, instead, we followed Jesus' lead and used words most people can relate to? Jesus often used illustrations the people listening to Him could connect with, pointing to sheep or to planted fields or talking about people who got mugged on the side of the road or people who have experienced both being ignored and being embraced and what that felt like. This made the lessons He was giving approachable and helped people understand the concepts He was talking about. Don't trade being understood by someone for impressing them.

If you catch yourself using big words or are tempted to launch into a discussion of the four Greek words for love as you share your faith, please do everyone a favor and don't, okay? People will be more riveted by what you are saying if you talk about someone you loved well or how someone pursued you with extraordinary tenacity. Let people know what has worked in your life and what hasn't—but mostly what hasn't, if you are interested in an authentic relationship. Tell them what you have understood from the Scriptures about how challenging it is to love out of your own ability and how infinite God's ability to love is.

Keep your description of faith simple—because it is. But don't try to make it easy—because it's not. Truth be told, living the life God invited us to is impossible, so making it out to be a cakewalk isn't as helpful as you might hope.

Your vulnerability and relatability will encourage people the most.

Bring vulnerability and relatability to every conversation you have today, and leave your fantastical experiences for another time.

MAKE SURE YOU'RE AIMING AT THE RIGHT TARGET, AND DON'T GET DISTRACTED BY THE SMOKE

> Then the LORD said to Cain, "Where is your brother Abel?" "I
> don't know," he replied. "Am I my brother's keeper?"
> **GENESIS 4:9**

When I was seven, my parents gave me a Daisy BB gun. It came with a small flask of oil, which, when you put some in a hole in the side of the gun, would make a little puff of smoke come out when it was fired. I thought that was pretty neat, so I fired it a lot, delighted by all the puffs of smoke. One day, when my dad took me on a trip to the mountains, I brought my BB gun with me. I saw a bird at the top of a tree some distance away and, for reasons I still don't understand, I took aim and shot. I was devastated when the bird fell to the ground. I panicked. I didn't know what to do. Should I give it CPR with my pinky fingers? Or blow into its beak? Sadly, I realized I had taken a life.

Even as adults, we do things we don't quite understand. We take aim at things like recognition and celebrity and approval and validation, and, to get them, we do things that are not only harmful to ourselves but harmful to others. We sacrifice things that are more important to get the little puff of smoke that approval and validation offer us.

Far from a new problem, this is an age-old one. The story of Cain and Abel is a well-known example, only it wasn't a bird that was killed, but a brother. Cain and his brother, Abel, both made sacrifices to God, but God liked Abel's more. Cain was looking for validation from God for what he had done rather than looking inward to see what God wanted to work on in him. And when he didn't get the validation he was aiming for, he killed Abel and became the first murderer in history, then lied to God about it. As a result, God made it so that Cain would spend his life wandering.

Jesus talked to His friends about aiming at different things, lasting things, more important things. He doesn't want our lives to be merely a puff of smoke. He wants our lives to be rich and meaningful.

**What is it that you need to get real with God about today?
Let Him come running to you with arms stretched wide.**

WHEREVER YOU HEAR GOD'S VOICE, GO THERE AND GO OFTEN

"My sheep listen to my voice; I know them, and they follow me."
JOHN 10:27

Margaret McCollum used to go to the subway in London every day. Here's why. Her husband, Oswald, died in 2003, but his recorded voice has been coming over the loudspeakers for as long as anyone can remember to warn people to "mind the gap."

In other words, his was the voice that reminded people that there is a small gap between the subway cars and the platform and that you could trip on it if you aren't careful. Margaret delighted in hearing Oswald's voice and never got tired of the three words he repeated over and over.

After a half century, London changed the voices that come over the speaker to electronic ones. When this happened, Margaret asked for a cassette of Oswald's announcement so she could keep listening, as it brought her great comfort.

When the company heard about Margaret and how she went to the subway each day to hear Oswald's voice, they put his voice back on the speakers in one spot in London—near Margaret's home, so she could still go hear it.

We should feel the same way about hearing God's voice. Rather than get caught up in the busyness of life or allow the voices of others to drown out what God says, we should do as Margaret did and make a point to go where we can hear Him speak to us.

Maybe you're like me and don't hear the audible voice of God. That's okay because there are all kinds of ways to hear from Him. For me, reading His words provides tremendous comfort. So does sitting in a forest. When I set aside time to do these things, I get just a little bit of what Margaret must feel every day.

**Whose voices do you fill your mind and your days with?
Where could you go to hear God's voice more clearly?**

DON'T BE KIND TO BE MEAN— LOVE DIFFICULT PEOPLE

If your enemy is hungry, give him food to eat; if he is thirsty, give him water to drink. In doing this, you will heap burning coals on his head, and the LORD will reward you.
PROVERBS 25:21-22

I know a couple of people who are really into barbeque. One friend will stay up for thirty hours to get the brisket cooked just right. When I asked him how much propane it takes to pull off a proper barbeque, he looked at me incredulously and said real pitmasters only use charcoal and wood chips, never propane.

I don't know if that is true or not. He lost me when he went into far too much detail about how the mesquite wood needs to be grown on a certain slope of a hill at a certain elevation to give off the right taste. My entire decision tree is whether to use salt, pepper, or both.

But I immediately thought about my barbeque friend, his coals, and his mesquite when I heard someone say—with a weird amount of delight—that they were being nice to a difficult person because the Bible said it was like putting burning coals on their head. It sounded like he wanted to put the difficult person on a spit to cook them up.

The truth is, we are all deeply flawed and equally in need of loads of grace. So when it comes to faith, don't be kind to be mean; be kind because we are supposed to be, because God is good and we are undeserving, and because He delights in the humble.

In Luke 6:27-29 Jesus told us to love our enemies, do good to those who hate us, bless those who curse us, and pray for those who mistreat us. God doesn't want us to burn mean people to teach them a lesson; He wants us to love them so they can see Jesus.

Who is difficult for you to get along with? Don't burn the relationship; break bread with them.

LET LOVE, HOPE, AND FAITH GIVE YOU A VOCABULARY LESSON

Unless you speak intelligible words with your tongue, how will anyone
know what you are saying? You will just be speaking into the air.
1 CORINTHIANS 14:9

One of our grandchildren pointed to a bowl of apples on the table, looked up
as if searching for a word, then carefully shaped his lips, took a small breath,
and said his first word: "Apple." Wait. What? "Did you hear that?" I said, as I
turned my head to see who had seen or heard what had just happened or if it
had somehow been captured on video so we could put it on the evening news.
Our grandchild was pointing at an apple in the bowl, and I was pointing at him
as he said it again. Then he said, "Apple!" a third time. Who was this kid? As
proud as any Jewish mother, I waved my arms in the air and began envisioning him graduating from university by age seven, earning a master's degree at
eleven, and running the earth by eighteen. I saw him being voted by his peers
as most likely to do great things and, in his acceptance speech, demonstrating
a remarkable economy of words. He would just say one—"Apple"—drop the
microphone, and walk off the stage to thunderous applause.

I shook off all my musings so I could focus on our brilliant grandson,
just as our child prodigy pointed out the window at a bird. There was now a
crowd of family members around him and, having mastered the *a* sound, we
all leaned forward with indescribable anticipation and got ready to make the
a sound with him. He took a breath, shaped his lips once again, and said . . .
"Apple," as he pointed at the bird. Then he pointed to me and said, "Apple,"
and to the dog and said, "Apple."

Here's my point. Sometimes when we don't have a lot of words to describe
what we are experiencing in our faith, we overuse the few we have. To a kid
who only knows the word *apple*, everything is an apple. The same can be true
in our faith gatherings and other communities.

**Find a couple of new words to describe what you
believe today, and you will uncover new ways of
experiencing those things that matter to you most.**

FAIL TRYING

"It is the LORD who goes before you. He will be with you; he will
not leave you or forsake you. Do not fear or be dismayed."
DEUTERONOMY 31:8 ESV

Years ago, during a trip to Washington, DC, for my work as honorary consul
for Uganda, I discovered a house for sale across the street from the United
States Supreme Court. The house was beat up and looked like it had received
its last coat of paint during the Revolutionary War. But I saw potential in it,
and the short story is, I bought it. Sweet Maria fixed up the house, with gold
curtains and tassels and wallpaper like they have in the map room at the White
House. For several years, people who make government decisions would quietly
use this place to meet. We even had a docent who made meals for guests when
they came over. I just wanted people to have a safe place for authentic conversations without having to posture or argue unnecessarily.

Then a few things changed, and it wasn't possible to use the house for this
purpose any longer. So I put it up for sale. I even threw in all the furniture. I
think I'm the only guy who has ever lost money in the Washington, DC, real
estate market. Then the new owner handed the keys over to one of the most
controversial public figures of our time. My house turned into the Death Star.
Our living room became the gathering place where truly awful plans were
hatched, and the gold curtains and tassels and wallpaper we had chosen to
adorn a place of peace became the backdrop for photographs of people who
were waging war.

Here is why I am telling you this. Sometimes what we try will work, and
other times it won't. That's just the way it goes. But I would rather fail trying
than fail watching. How about you? Have you been deferring a great idea
because you're afraid it won't work? Will your great idea work? Who knows?
Mine cratered in a spectacular way, but I'm still glad I did it. Will I get another
house in Washington, DC, and try this again? Of course not! I'm too eager to
make brand-new mistakes while trying brand-new ideas.

**What is something you have held back on, afraid
it won't work? Dust off that idea today.**

DON'T FORGET TO REMEMBER THAT EVERYTHING GOOD COMES FROM GOD

God chose the lowly things of this world and the despised
things—and the things that are not—to nullify the things
that are, so that no one may boast before him.
1 CORINTHIANS 1:28–29

God made it so that ordinary people like us could live extraordinary lives. I am certain, however, His intent was not that we would make a big deal about ourselves but that we would give the credit to Him. Maybe we aren't the smartest or the most popular or have a last name everyone recognizes and makes a big deal about, but God uses what we think of as unimportant to fake out the people who think they have all the answers. He uses the less powerful things to confuse the powerful people, and He uses the things people bad-mouth to baffle the ones who thought they had life all figured out. The reason He does this isn't to fool us or to prove any point other than this: we have nothing to boast about but Him.

I have a friend who was in a play on Broadway. I went to see it and was amazed. The choreography, the harmonies, the dazzling sets, the guy on the kettle drums in the orchestra. When the curtain came down, the entire audience sat in near disbelief of the beauty they had just experienced. What if I had run up on the stage before the cast came out and started to take a bow for what everyone had just experienced someone else doing? What if I addressed the audience and said I was so pleased that they liked the play I didn't write, the music I didn't score, the sets I didn't make, and the orchestra I didn't conduct? I would be laughed off the stage.

What good gift has God given you? Do you have a career or a reputation or loved ones or things you have accumulated or inherited? Boast about God and how He made these things possible. Don't try to take an undeserved bow. You'll just look silly.

**Today you get to play the part of the audience and rise to
your feet to applaud all that God is doing in the world.**

AUGUST

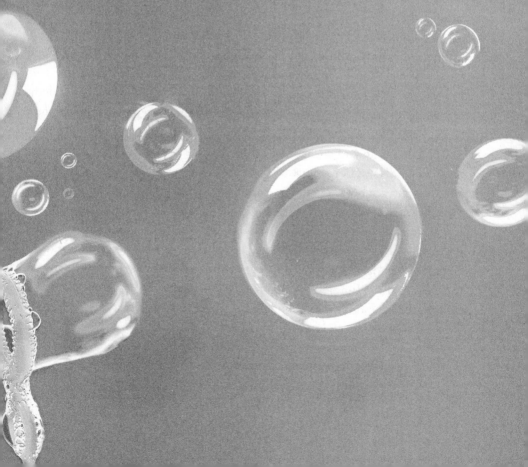

THINK BEFORE YOU SPEAK, WHICH MAY MEAN KEEPING YOUR MOUTH SHUT

*Those who control their tongue will have a long life;
opening your mouth can ruin everything.*
PROVERBS 13:3 NLT

We all know what words mean to us, but we are wise not to make assumptions that can confuse our message and put a kink in our relationships. For instance, in Uganda you would not ask someone, "How many children do you have?" High infant-mortality rates, a twenty-plus-year civil war, and other social circumstances have resulted in many of Uganda's young dying far too early. Instead, the proper question is, "Do you have many children?" With a huge, warm smile, the person you're talking to will predictably say, "Yes, I have many."

We all make a lot of assumptions about other people's circumstances, their worldviews, who they love, and a long list of other things. But we shouldn't be too quick to speak. Solomon was supposedly the smartest man to ever live, and in Proverbs 13:3 he said that those who control their tongue will have a long life, while opening your mouth can ruin everything. I agree with him. Don't be the person known for being "ready, shoot, aim" with your words.

Pro tip on how to engage the people you meet: slow it down a little and make fewer assumptions. Start with what you are positive about, which is usually this: you are both together and are learning about each other. And when the other person fails you, don't be too quick to take offense or put them down. If you must make an assumption, assume they meant well and missed. Jesus didn't block Peter when he said he had never heard of Jesus after three years of being together daily. Jesus also didn't get into a shouting match with the guy on the cross next to Him. Jesus was more likely to take someone by the hand and answer their questions than point a bony finger in their direction and assume they were beyond engaging with love. Let's do the same.

**Practice approaching your next conversation
without assumptions and with grace.**

REVERSE ENGINEERING YOUR LIFE

*Put your outdoor work in order and get your fields
ready; after that, build your house.*
PROVERBS 24:27

We built a log home twenty-five years ago. Sadly, it burned to the ground, and we needed to rebuild it. Log homes are built in a parking lot somewhere, where all the logs are cut, notched, carefully fit together, and then numbered. Then they disassemble the structure and reverse load it onto ten 18-wheelers. The idea is that the bottom log will be the first one off the truck and the top log will be the last log off the truck. It all works great unless you mix up the trucks.

Why am I telling you this? To build the life, the faith, and the relationships you want, it will take some advanced planning and a little reverse engineering. Take a little of King Solomon's wisdom and get things in order, get your fields ready, then start building. Let's say your goal is a thriving marriage. It's tempting to want to put that crowning log up first, but a marriage is like a timber home, and it is all the logs underneath your relationship that give it support. Get the trucks in the right order, offload and set up the logs of trust and authenticity that go on the foundation first, and you will really have something.

Another part of building a strong and lasting log home, though, is choosing the right kind of wood. Wood is like dessert for termites; a lodge made entirely of logs for them is like a swimming pool of Dippin' Dots for me. So if you want to build a home that is resistant to bugs, the trick is to find a type of wood that termites don't like, such as cedar. The same is true of the things we're trying to build in our lives. Build with people and things that are resistant to unnecessary drama. Choose the friends who will help you meet your largest challenges and make you resistant to the damage those challenges can present.

Think about what it is that you're trying to build today. What do you need to prioritize as you're laying the foundation for that goal? And who do you need working alongside you to help you withstand the inevitable challenges?

**God has given you agency to build something in your life that
is both beautiful and lasting. Use the right materials.**

KINDNESS COMES WITH PRIZES

A man who is kind benefits himself, but a cruel man hurts himself.
PROVERBS 11:17 ESV

Sometimes we seem to think we need to be Jesus' lawyer. Here's the problem: we're not good enough, and He doesn't need one. Maybe we think we need to protect baby Jesus in the manger, but if we read the book of Revelation, we know He's out of the crib, is as ferocious as a lion, and can do a pretty good job sticking up for Himself. Perhaps what we should do is follow the words of Peter in the Bible, when he urged his friends to revere Christ and to engage the people around them with gentleness and respect. Carving this new groove in our minds will take some humility. Come in with the mindset of a student, not a guest lecturer in someone's life.

You have seen cars with the Student Driver sign attached to the top. Most people give student drivers a little more leeway than they might otherwise. They're just learning, right? Give them a break. This is what it looks like when we approach people with gentleness and respect. Self-identify as a student husband, a student friend, a student follower of Jesus, and you will be blown away at the grace and kindness that comes your way. Go next level and start treating the people around you, even the difficult ones, as your teachers who you can learn from. You don't need to adopt their worldview or even agree with them to engage them with kindness and respect. Who knows? They may start reflecting a little grace back your way.

Find new freedom in the realization you don't need to have all the answers. Practice saying, "I don't know" in the mirror a couple of times a day. When people ask you questions about faith, don't give them some phony, prepackaged answer you don't yet believe, because they won't believe what you say either. Instead, live out your faith with kindness and engage people with love, and see what will happen.

**How can you approach people today like a student
majoring in kindness and respect?**

BE HONEST WITH GOD TODAY; HE ALREADY KNOWS THE TRUTH

But the LORD God called to the man, "Where are you?"
GENESIS 3:9

The three words no speaker wants to hear are these: *Where are you?*

I had just arrived home one day from a busy travel schedule. I jumped into my sweats and favorite hoodie and sat down in my favorite chair. Just then, the phone rang and a panicked voice on the other end said, "Bob, where are you?" I didn't put it together until a few moments later, but it turns out I had agreed months before to speak at an event in town and somehow it had not made its way to the calendar. The evening I thought was ending was just beginning.

I jumped out of the chair while still speaking to the person and yelped, "I'm on my way!"

The band was playing a couple of extra songs as I skidded to a stop in front of the venue and ran in. I was embarrassed, but the sun rose the next morning, so I know for certain the world did not end when I didn't show up on time. The same is true if we don't show up today, ready to keep it real in our faith, but God still asks the question I received: "Where are you?"

Ironically, these were the same words God spoke to Adam and Eve in the garden. I don't think God was confused about where they were, and He wasn't talking about latitude and longitude. He wanted to know where their hearts were, and He wants to know where our hearts are today.

He's asking where we are after that relationship failed or the ball was dropped or the disappointment was delivered. He wants us to be honest with Him.

Get real with God today. Answer His question with where you really are, not where you wish you were.

I'M WORTH A LOT MORE THAN THREE MILLION, AND SO ARE YOU

God bought you with a high price.
CORINTHIANS 6:20 NLT

I landed in Mogadishu, Somalia, knowing a total of nobody. I had a car pick me up at the airport to drive me to the cheap hotel where I was staying. As we were driving, I tried to make small talk with the driver, but none of the things I said seemed to land and all I would get back in response was the occasional grunt. After about twenty minutes of painful silence, the driver turned to me and said, "Three million." *Huh?* I thought. "Did you say three million? I don't get it." "That's what you're worth," the expressionless driver said as we made another right turn at a building pockmarked with hundreds of bullet holes from the decades-long conflict in the country. His statement was more than a little unsettling, especially coming from a guy I was paying thirty dollars a day to drive me around Mogadishu. Abductions are common in Somalia. When you arrive, one of the first things you give someone is the answer to a "proof of life" question.

It is many years later now and everything ended up turning out fine. I have been to our schools and safehouses in Somalia many times since that first trip, but here's why I tell you this brief story. Understanding our worth to God will help you and me not get abducted by all that the world throws at us over the course of our lifetimes.

Our value to God is immense. It was costly for God to send Jesus to earth to win us back. This is what Paul was trying to communicate to his friends in Ephesus. And this wasn't a one-and-done thing. God not only bought us back, but He adopted us into His family forever. He picked us, He bought us, He rescued us, then He adopted us. Not a bad day for us.

Today, walk into the joy and challenges of life like you are safe, you are worth it, and like God's not going to abandon you. But don't stop there.

Value the people you interact with as if they are priceless creations, too, because they are.

OPPORTUNITIES AHEAD: LOOK OUT!

So then, as we have opportunity, let us do good to everyone.
GALATIANS 6:10 ESV

We can be adjacent to or in proximity to people without actually being with them. Know what I mean? How many times do we unintentionally settle for being within a few feet of people but engaging only in small talk and not communicating anything meaningful? I get why this happens. We don't want to interrupt or pry or presume, so we sit quietly. But Jesus wants more for us than that.

Don't sit at the table and twirl your hair while staring at a screen when you're surrounded by friends. Instead, practice presence. Pursue "with-ness," and give it everything you've got. Take a genuine interest in other people. Turn to the person next to you in the checkout line at the grocery store and ask what the highlight of their day has been. You're not asking them to donate their liver to you, and you're not hitting on them. Just be interested. Here's the crazy part. Your question to them will probably be the highlight of their day.

Show up in your conversations in a new way. If you find yourself talking past someone rather than to them, don't beat yourself up. Use it as a great prompt to slow to a stop and find a new way to communicate. If you find yourself merely biding your time in a conversation, waiting to say what you have to say without listening to what the other person is saying, it's time for a new approach.

Make a rule for yourself to ask whoever you are talking to a couple of questions about what they are doing. Don't use these questions to challenge them; make it an invitation to share. Let them know you are 100 percent with them and curious about how life is going for them.

God sent Jesus to be with us, so we would be with one another. All the water is on our side of the tub.

**Engage the people around you with love
and inexplicable curiosity today.**

FIND SOMEONE PERCHED ON THE PERIPHERY AND PULL THEM INTO THE CONVERSATION

Finally, all of you, be like-minded, be sympathetic, love
one another, be compassionate and humble.
1 PETER 3:8

We all remember what it was like in high school when cliques of people hung out together. The popular or "cool" kids had a table that few were invited to join, but a lot of judgment and disapproval came from their small circle.

It always seemed to me that these cliques were comprised of insecure people who were reading their own news clippings about how hip and happening or right they thought they were. Unfortunately, this dynamic isn't limited to high school. We have all experienced the same thing in our faith communities, social communities, and workplaces.

The thing about Jesus is that He let everyone know they were welcome. His message of acceptance wasn't limited to the popular or talented people. He let a woman in need come close to Him. He invited a tax collector in a sycamore tree to dine with Him and a thief on a cross to spend eternity with Him.

Here's my question for you. Are you giving off a vibe of accessibility and availability and safety, or are you one who stands off or has intermediaries who stand between you and the people who want to connect with you?

Don't get me wrong, I get that availability can create some odd or uncomfortable situations, but Jesus evidently thought it was worth it. And my guess is that He still feels that way.

**Find someone who looks like they feel unwelcome
and pull them into the center of the conversation. It
will honor them and God at the same time.**

WHEN YOU OPEN YOUR MOUTH TO SPEAK, REMEMBER WHO GAVE YOU YOUR VOICE

Moses said to the LORD, "Pardon your servant, Lord. I have never been eloquent, neither in the past nor since you have spoken to your servant. I am slow of speech and tongue." The LORD said to him, "Who gave human beings their mouths? . . . Is it not I, the LORD? Now go; I will help you speak and will teach you what to say."

EXODUS 4:10–12

There is power in experiencing the simplicity of faith the way Jesus did. He didn't feel the need to continually dazzle people with complex theological ideas. He didn't have smoke machines or dramatic music rising in the background as He taught to get people to an emotional summit.

Sure, He taught in synagogues sometimes, but more often He was by the water or under the tree or on a gently sloping mountain. Let's do the same thing. Keep the choreography to a minimum, your words kind, and your message clear.

For some of you, I have another suggestion: Cuss just a little less, okay? I get it. There are things we get riled up about, and it can even feel poignant or relatable to drop a cuss word or two in an impassioned conversation, but all in all it's not good advocacy.

Find a way to prompt yourself not to cuss. For example, there is a guy who, for years, has given my nonprofit, Love Does, five hundred dollars every time he cusses in a conversation. I figure he must be a lawyer or a politician, or a bad carpenter who hits his thumb with a hammer often, because he's donated a ton of money to Love Does over the years.

If you want to join in on the fun, I'll get you our post office box number, or you could save a few bucks and just tone it down a bit.

Our words matter more than we think and have impacts in the world far beyond what we would imagine. Choose yours carefully today.

FAITH WITHOUT WORKS IS AS USELESS AS A PEN WITHOUT INK

What good is it, my brothers and sisters, if someone claims to have faith but has no deeds? Can such faith save them?
JAMES 2:14

My sons, Adam and Richard, have an insatiable appetite for activity. When they were teenagers, we got up early and drove an hour to jump into a wind tunnel where skydivers practice their free falls. After a few hours of mock sky-diving there, we continued another hour to a place where high-performance go-karts whip around a legit racetrack at fifty miles per hour or more, complete with chicanes and banked corners. My boys whipped me good on the track, but I sent both of them into the hay bales a couple of times just to let them know I may be slow, but I'm still sneaky.

We arrived home in the late afternoon, and I was exhausted from the non-stop fun of the past eight hours. Forty-five minutes later, the boys came into the room and said, "So what do you want to do now?" "What?" I said. "We've driven for hours, we've skydived, we've been go-kart racing, we've pounded hamburgers and donuts, and you're still bored?" Puzzled and unfazed, they said in unison, "Yes, what do you want to do now?"

Jesus isn't an overly caffeinated, Red Bulled–out adolescent like my sons were, but He asks that same question: What do you want to do now with the faith you say you have? James, Jesus' brother, asked his friends, "If we claim we have faith but don't do something with it, is it worth anything?"

Here is the crazy part. God doesn't need our help. But He wants our hearts, and He knows we will understand more about Him the more we engage our faith.

God has invited us on an adventure, not a business trip. Let's actually do something with what we believe and fight back against the boredom of a faith without activity.

Have a blast today. Sure, go search for dinosaur bones, read a book, or take a walk, but find your adventure in Jesus and express your faith in love and action.

COMPARISON IS A PUNK

When they measure themselves by one another and compare themselves with one another, they are without understanding.
2 CORINTHIANS 10:12 ESV

When I was in the fourth grade, I was covered with freckles and had braces, including headgear that strapped around my skull. While all the other kids were getting go-karts and stingray bikes, my dad got me a rock tumbler. I played a clarinet that year, not an electric guitar, but when my next birthday came around, it seemed like the trajectory of my life was about to change when I scored a skateboard.

That afternoon, while I was skateboarding with my friend Jackie in his driveway, the metal wheels spun out and I landed facefirst on the cement. I was wearing headgear, and the prongs jammed themselves so far back on my molars that we couldn't get them out. I remember Jackie with his foot on my chest and a hand on each side of the headgear, yanking as hard as he could. Just then, a group of neighborhood girls I had been hoping to get the attention of walked by. Could I look any more pathetic?

Here's the thing, though. In general, I didn't feel pathetic during those young years. I felt loved. The guys on the block played with me, my parents did the best they could with me, and my no-frills life let me grow up learning how to be completely content with who I was and how I rolled.

But then I got to high school and there were more people to compare myself to. I began noticing that other people were living lives that seemed way cooler than mine. This is when envy and comparison reared their heads in my life. As I grew less comfortable with who I was compared to who everyone else was, my insecurities swelled. This happens to many of us, no matter our age.

If you can relate to these feelings or are experiencing them today, remember this: God never compares what He creates. We are the ones who came up with the idea of comparison. He imagines and creates and calls what He creates good—and us His beloved.

If you find yourself tempted to compare your life with someone else's, don't take the bait. Comparison is a punk.

AS AN AMBASSADOR FOR JESUS, YOU REPRESENT HEAVEN TO EARTH

"You did not choose me, but I chose you and appointed you so
that you might go and bear fruit—fruit that will last—and so that
whatever you ask in my name the Father will give you."
JOHN 15:16

I have served as the honorary consul for the Republic of Uganda for almost twenty years. The consul works as the local embassy presence in a city or region. Some of the perks of being a consul are getting some cool license plates that allow you to park anywhere, including in someone's living room, I suppose, as well as an epic State Department card that will get you through customs in the diplomat line in a minute. And then there is also diplomatic immunity, which is a bonus.

Being the consul for a country means that when you send a letter to a leader from another country, the letter is not just coming from you; it's from the country that you represent. In my case, what I write would be on behalf of forty-six million Ugandans. Similarly, when you walk into the room, it is as if the entire country walked in. Being the consul for a country is a neat gig, and if you get a chance to be one, don't miss it. You might even get out of a couple of speeding tickets someday.

Paul called us ambassadors for Christ, a parallel idea to being a representative for a country. When we walk into the room, it is like all of heaven walks in with us. And when we use the language the Bible did about loving people, it is as if God is speaking through us. Our problem is that we too often identify with Jesus but don't think of ourselves as representing Jesus. It is like having a passport but never using it to go anywhere.

What would it look like today if you thought of yourself as the representative of heaven to earth? What would change in the way you deal with the people you meet, the difficulties you face, and the setbacks you experience?

**You have all the credentials you need to bring heaven
to earth today. You are Jesus' ambassador.**

GOD CREATED YOU FOR CONNECTION

And let us consider how we may spur one another
on toward love and good deeds.
HEBREWS 10:24

When our first son graduated from high school, I decided to take him and his brother on an adventure. We bought a couple of motorcycles and a map and decided to ride across North America. We didn't let it slow us down that we had never been on the highway on motorcycles before.

We started in Mexico and made our way north to Canada. By the time we got to San Francisco, we had figured out how to shift gears and everything. When we finished the trip, we could barely stand from all the seat time and walked around like cowboys for weeks, but we also felt the deep satisfaction that comes from accomplishing something together.

Our motorcycle trip wasn't just about transportation; a plane would have gotten us across the country faster. It was about companionship. Community is where all the good stuff happens. It was true for the Acts church as they broke bread and had things in common, and it is true today. But not everyone is wired to do things in groups.

If you are somebody who prefers singles over doubles, do your work alone but make sure you find a few trusted friends to talk with about what is working and not working in your life. It is in our disclosures to other people about who we are that we understand who God made us to be.

What is God revealing to you through your relationships with other people? What bold move are you going to take today to share your life more with others?

**Don't just agree that this is a good idea.
Make the call, send the text, or go to
the office next to you right now.**

GOD LOVES TO GIVE SECOND CHANCES

A man who refuses to admit his mistakes can never be successful.
But if he confesses and forsakes them, he gets another chance.
PROVERBS 28:13 TLB

I worked briefly at a gas station in high school. The job was pretty simple. If a car pulled up to the full-service island, I was supposed to lift the hood and check the oil, as well as wash the windows while the tank was being filled. Those were the days, right? I would put the gas pump hose in the tank for the customers, ask them what grade of gasoline they wanted, and then start filling it up. When the hose shut off, I would walk to the driver's side, remove the hose, collect the cash, and count out change from my pocket.

One day a car pulled up, and I sprang into action. When the tank was full, the windows washed, and the oil checked, I collected the cash, gave back a little change, and told the driver I hoped they had a memorable day. But as they drove off, I realized I had forgotten to remove the hose from the customer's Buick. I heard the bending of metal and watched in horror as the car took the gas hose and part of the gas pump with him. It turned out to be a memorable day for both of us, and I was fired immediately.

We are all going to make mistakes. Some things will go right in our lives, but more will go wrong. We don't need to keep a won-and-lost tally, and we don't need to let those things define us. Instead, use your failures to inform your next steps. I never worked at a gas station again, but I have pulled up to a couple of them over the years. Now I put my car key by the gas tank so that I will remember to remove the hose before I pull away. It just works out better that way for everyone, and there is less bent metal left behind.

What failure have you experienced that you continue to beat yourself up over? Bring it to Jesus today and ask Him to help you grow stronger and bolder because of it, not weaker and more timid.

God isn't impressed by our accomplishments or distracted by our failure; He delights in our obedient attempts.

SPEAKING TRUTH IN LOVE
HELPS EVERYBODY GROW UP

Then we will no longer be infants, tossed back and forth by the
waves, and blown here and there by every wind of teaching and by
the cunning and craftiness of people in their deceitful scheming.
Instead, speaking the truth in love, we will grow to become in every
respect the mature body of him who is the head, that is, Christ.
EPHESIANS 4:14–15

When our children were young, we would take boat trips each summer in
the Pacific Northwest. During the days, we would explore shorelines, count
starfish, catch crabs, and skip rocks. In the evenings, we would find a cove to
anchor in for the night. Where we were, the tide changes the water level twelve
feet twice a day, so even when the boat is stopped, it is always moving up and
down and spinning in circles around the anchor.

As a result, it is important to know if the boat is moving closer or farther
away from rocks along the shore. I got in the habit of waking up every few
hours at night, looking out one of the windows to see if we were drifting toward
a problem. I would usually pick out a tree on the shore or another fixed point
and see where our boat was in relation to it to get my bearings.

After a terrific summer, we returned to San Diego. In the middle of the
first night at home, I instinctively went to the window after a few hours of
sleep to see where I was, trying to find a fixed point I could recognize and
wondering why there was a swing set and a palm tree in the cove I thought
we were anchored in. It took a while before I realized I was no longer on
a boat.

Just like it was important to know where the boat was in relation to the
dangers around it, we need to know where we are in our lives. Paul wanted his
friends to avoid getting pushed around by the winds and waves of life. He said
the way to reorient ourselves is to speak the truth in love, even if the truth is
that we're drifting toward danger.

Make a quick assessment of where you are right now. Spot the rocks and
pinch points in your life, then you can take confident steps forward and bring
your areas of confusion to Jesus.

Find someone you can call or meet with and talk about the place you find yourself in. You will know they are the right person if they speak the truth to you in love.

> You are surrounded today with love and truth and massive possibilities. Figure out who you are and then take action.

WE GROW IN OUR LIVES WHAT WE PLANT IN OUR HEARTS

Remember this: Whoever sows sparingly
will also reap sparingly, and whoever sows
generously will also reap generously.
2 CORINTHIANS 9:6

There is a difference between two very similar sounding words: *further* and *farther*. Here's a quick way to know which one to use. *Farther* is used to talk about literal distances, but *further* is used for metaphorical distances.

When it comes to the relationships that matter the most to us, we want to go further and deeper, but too often we settle for simply going farther and logging more time rather than pursuing greater depth.

I don't know anyone who wants to get to the end of their life and have their spouse say, "You know, you were the best roommate I have ever had." Of course not. We are hoping for something truly exceptional. But we need to remember that we grow in our lives what we plant in our hearts.

If you want to experience more remarkable relationships with those you are closest to, plant a row of whimsy and wonder in your friendship field. If you want an outstanding marriage, scatter seeds of awesome along the pathway. If you have kids and want your relationship with them to be outstanding, put in motion a few unlikely experiences.

Don't stand back and passively watch what happens with the people you love; lean in and tend to those important relationships. Invest in ways that will take you further in with each other, not just farther along in the timeline.

**What move can you make today to put wheels on
your desire to go deeper and further, rather than just
keeping things shallow and logging more time?**

MONEY CAN'T BUY LOVE, BUT WE STILL NEED TO DECIDE HOW WE'RE GOING TO HANDLE IT

> For the love of money is a root of all kinds of evil. Some people, eager for money, have wandered from the faith and pierced themselves with many griefs.
> **1 TIMOTHY 6:10**

I remember getting my first paycheck in high school. The minimum wage was $2.10 an hour then (I'm that old), and I had worked after classes for a month to score one hundred dollars. By my calculation, I was rolling in cash. Where would I put it all? Stocks? Bonds? Pork belly futures?

While one hundred dollars seemed like an immense amount of wealth, it was peanuts compared to the one-thousand-dollar paycheck I received when I got out of college. I felt like I should open a bank and start making high-interest rate loans. Then, when I got out of law school and started working in the justice field, I received a check for ten thousand dollars. What in the world?

With each different phase of life, it seemed there was another zero added to my definition of what was a lot of money. But thankfully, what I have found along the way is that how I deal with money doesn't have to change, no matter how many zeros are attached.

I can be wise and generous with what I'm given when I have much, and I can be wise and generous with what I'm given when I have little. Regardless of my situation, I have to consciously make a choice and decide what my interaction with money is going to be like. And you do too.

The Bible talks a lot about this. Almost two thousand verses and half of the parables Jesus told were about money. Put that up against just under five hundred verses about our faith and our prayers. Obviously, this matters a lot to Him, so we need to put some good thought into how we will approach money in our own lives.

You and I get to decide what our relationship with money is going to be.

Make a plan that honors God and execute it.
Hope without a plan is just a wish.

DON'T GO SMALL ON THE BIG THINGS GOD HAS INVITED YOU TO PURSUE

He has saved us and called us to a holy life—not because of anything we have done but because of his own purpose and grace. This grace was given us in Christ Jesus before the beginning of time.

2 TIMOTHY 1:9

We are sometimes tempted to compare what we are doing with what someone else is doing. But God doesn't want us to be like each other. He wants us to be like Him and to pursue the unique calling we are each given.

But let's get real. How do we even know what our calling is? The concept of calling is both simple and complicated. Our first calling is to Jesus. He calls our names and hopes we will not only hear Him but do something about it. We are also called to love the people around us, to be a reflection of God's heartbeat wherever we go. But what most people mean when they talk about calling is the role God has uniquely positioned each of us to play. So how do we get there?

To find more clarity about your calling, do an audit of your experiences and desires and drill down on your capabilities. What lights you up? What are you good at? What is lasting and important and meaningful and purposeful? What has worked in the past? What did you bounce back from when the wheels wobbled? These all point toward a calling.

As you go through today, ask yourself these questions and get clear on your current calling. Don't get stuck reliving or relitigating roles and opportunities you have grown out of, and don't go small on the big things God has invited you to pursue.

You are a new creation each day, and things are supposed to change over time. So expect your conversations with God also to shift over time.

Welcome those new conversations with God and the new opportunities He brings your way today.

EVEN WHEN IT'S HARD, LOVE ANYWAY

"My command is this: Love each other as I have loved you."
JOHN 15:12

If you have ever experienced a friendship where you were a lot more committed to it than the other person, you know it can be a lonely, isolating experience. These microrejections add up, and if we're not careful, we can find ourselves keeping score and focusing on what doesn't feel fair rather than celebrating what is beautiful about the other person.

If you are experiencing this, if you are feeling wronged and like you need to "give them a dose of their own medicine," pause for a moment and do the relational math again.

Jesus told His friends to love each other the way He loved them. This wasn't the butterflies-in-the-belly adolescent kind of love or the Hallmark card version either; it was the sacrificial, curious, often misunderstood kind of love Jesus expressed to everyone. Just look at how He approached Judas.

If I had one last meal to eat, I know I wouldn't have spent it with someone I knew would soon betray me. But that's exactly what Jesus did, and even when Judas went on to betray Jesus with a kiss, Jesus still loved him by giving His life for him.

Who have you been keeping score with?

Has your heart become calloused as you have tried to guard it from getting hurt?

Today, reach out to someone who has wronged you or ignored you or hurt your feelings and see what happens as you love them the way Jesus loves you.

ADDRESS YOUR MESSES SO YOU'RE NOT TRIPPING OVER THEM

"Blind Pharisee! First clean the inside of the cup and dish, and then the outside also will be clean."
MATTHEW 23:26

We all have those places in our homes or apartments or other dwelling places that get a little messy. Most of us just shut a door so we don't need to deal with it. Behind the door is a whole lot of disorganization, debris, and deferred cleaning. Addressing these messy areas is not without some amount of risk.

For me and Sweet Maria, that area is the attic. One Saturday morning, I asked Sweet Maria how I could be helpful that day. She said it would be a huge help if I got the oil in her car changed. I drove over to the local auto service center and was doing just that when she called and said, in a weak voice, "I fell out of the attic and onto the floor headfirst. How close are you?" Maria is very sturdy and not one to make a big deal out of being injured, so I immediately knew it was serious. Her fall resulted in a massive concussion and the loss of feeling in her arms and legs. We were obviously concerned while we waited for the ambulances and fire trucks to arrive.

It turns out, when you take a big blow to the head, you find your Off button. We sat at the hospital together, not knowing how things would turn out and what the new trajectory for our lives might be. After a while, though, the feeling started returning to Sweet Maria's limbs. When the doctor asked her where the biggest pain was, she pointed at me and winked, and I knew she was coming back to us. Since then, my story has been that Sweet Maria is head over heels for me.

We all have areas in our lives that need attention, and if we ignore them, sooner or later we'll trip. Ask yourself what areas you need to address, the areas you've been ignoring while issues pile up and get out of control. Then bring those areas to Jesus, so He can help you sort through them.

You don't need to fall out of an attic to figure out what your next move will be. Ask Jesus to step into the mess with you.

GOD DELIGHTS IN GOOD MISCHIEF

*If anyone has material possessions and sees a
brother or sister in need but has no pity on them,
how can the love of God be in that person?*
1 JOHN 3:17

There are a lot of great ways to prank someone and even more ways to get into some beautiful mischief. There are brilliant, generous ideas, like paying off someone's medical bill or school loan anonymously.

And then there are pranks that go far darker, like the guy in Chicago who was on the heels of a tough breakup. He bought a car for $600 and put it in his ex-girlfriend's name, then parked it where it would get parking tickets. Eventually, it had more than $100,000 in tickets. Now, that's a mean prank. Guys, don't get any ideas.

What if we put as much energy into delighting and being generous with one another as we put into our animosity toward people who have wronged us? Being generous in spirit isn't always about dropping a wad of cash on someone; sometimes it is being extravagant in terms of our time or attention or patience.

Generosity, both emotional and financial, isn't optional either. This isn't just a divine shakedown. John, the apostle, wrote to his friends that we would know the love of God resides in someone by seeing what they did with what they had.

If we see someone who is in need and it doesn't move us, it seems unlikely that God's Spirit is within us.

Who do you know who is in need today? Do the best kind of caper and blow them away with your generosity expressed in love. That's good mischief.

**The measure you give is the measure you will get—
make it a big scoop of Jesus that you offer up.**

FIGURE OUT WHO GOD MADE YOU TO BE, AND BE THAT WITH AN EXTRA HELPING OF LOVE

Each of you should use whatever gift you have received to serve
others, as faithful stewards of God's grace in its various forms.
1 PETER 4:10

We have several horses at our farm. Some are trail horses and lope along. Others are thoroughbreds and run fast. Still others are Tennessee trotters that skip on the trails like they are dancing. Horses have difference cadences, and we do too.

Some of us are early birds, and others are night owls. Those experiencing insomnia are a little of both. I know a lot of people who do many things at once and an equal number of people who do one thing at a time. Some start strong and peter out, and others begin things inauspiciously and end with a bang.

Jesus' disciples and apostles were no different. They had different backgrounds and life experiences. Some were fishermen and people with common jobs. Others were tax collectors. And then there was Judas, who was a politically tied-in person who was probably out to kill tax collectors.

Some of the people who hung around Jesus were disciples and learned from Him, and others in positions of leadership also carried His message.

We were all made differently. We operate at different speeds, approach situations in our own ways, and bring unique combinations of strengths and weaknesses, skills and shortcomings. There is not one good way to be useful to God. We don't all have to try to fit into a singular mold. God can use each one of us according to how we were made.

Find your place and your cadence in life and faith today. Understand what you bring to the table, and lead with love as you do.

NEXT TIME YOU SEE A NEED, CROSS OVER TO THAT SIDE OF THE STREET

"Which of these three do you think was a neighbor to the man who fell into the hands of robbers?" The expert in the law replied, "The one who had mercy on him." Jesus told him, "Go and do likewise."

LUKE 10:36-37

I was in Austin, Texas, for a gathering, and during the lunch break I received a phone call from two of the girls who were attending. They said their car had broken down on the highway and they didn't know who to call, but they had a copy of my book in the backseat, which had my cell phone number on it, so they thought they would give it a try. I found out where they were, and a buddy and I found them on the highway. Fortunately, it was something easy to fix, and we got them on their way as we all grinned and gave high fives.

As I drove back to the gathering, I thought about how many people I pass by every day who seem like they might be in need. It's not that I am coldhearted; I just don't want to pry or interject myself into their circumstances. Unlike the phone call I received, where I was asked for help, most times people in need either don't know how to ask or feel embarrassed to. So they get passed by.

It reminds me of the parable of the good Samaritan. There were four groups of people who interacted with the man in the parable. He had been traveling from Jerusalem to Jericho when he encountered the first group. They were robbers who took everything from him and left him for dead.

Then a priest came upon him and crossed to the other side of the road. Then a Levite (someone who worked in the temple) came upon him and did the same thing. When the various religious leaders passed by the injured man, I don't think they were trying to be mean. I bet they had lots going on, like you do.

But then the last type of person, the Samaritan, came upon the scene. The Samaritan cleaned up the injured person and even took care of his future needs. Jesus used the example of the Samaritan, an outcast in society, to demonstrate that He wants us to love the people we find.

You probably aren't like the robber, but you might find yourself, like I do sometimes, as the guy who walks to the other side of the road. Today, make a conscious choice not to avoid the person you see in need on your path.

Think of one person in need you've already encountered and offer them your hand and your help.

LOOSEN YOUR GRIP AND PREPARE FOR A POSITIVE TRANSFER

"If my people, who are called by my name, will humble themselves
and pray and seek my face and turn from their wicked ways, then I will
hear from heaven, and I will forgive their sin and will heal their land."
2 CHRONICLES 7:14

My son Adam and I are pilots. In most airplanes, both seats in the front have a yoke and foot pedals to steer the airplane. You can think of the yoke as the steering wheel that controls going up, down, and side to side and the foot pedals as the rudder that swings the tail to the left or right.

In flight, when the person in the left seat needs to tend to something or wants a break, they say to the person in the right seat, "You have the flight controls." That person is then in charge of the airplane and repeats and confirms, so there is no misunderstanding: "I have the flight controls."

This is called a "positive transfer," which is a fancy way of saying everyone in the cockpit is clear on who is flying the airplane. You can imagine the possible problems if each person in the cockpit thought the other person was flying the airplane.

It would do us all some good if we were clear about who is in charge of our lives. Sure, you can mouth the Sunday school answer and say, "God is always in charge," but take a look at your life and the decision tree you use when you are choosing your path forward. Does it look like God is in charge, or does it look like you are?

If you find yourself making your decisions first and then including God, this is an indicator that you still have the flight controls. God wants to steer the ship, but He won't rip the controls out of your hands to do it. He wants a positive transfer so everyone is certain of who is in charge.

Who is in control of your day today?

GEOCACHE REMINDERS OF GOD'S LOVE THROUGHOUT YOUR LIFE

"When your children ask you, 'What do these stones mean?' tell them that the flow of the Jordan was cut off before the ark of the covenant of the Lord. . . . These stones are to be a memorial to the people of Israel forever."
JOSHUA 4:6–7

We started a tradition in our family a long time ago where we regularly bury a jar with notes in it. We record the latitude and longitude of the location and take a photograph to keep track of where we have buried these treasures. The hope is that, someday, perhaps our kids' kids' kids will dig them up. In the jars we don't leave instructions for what they should do after finding them. Instead, in our notes we remind them of our hopes for them and of God's promises for their beautiful lives.

If you want to leave behind a lasting impact, don't tell people what to do; remind them of who they already are and who they are becoming. This is an intergenerational message worth passing along. Joshua did the same thing for the nation of Israel, but on a larger scale and with a lot of rocks. He called the people to pile up stones from the Jordan River as a memorial. And these weren't small rocks they could put in the pocket of their togas; they were stones the people had to put on their shoulders and stack where God told them to stack them. The twelve stones were to remind people forever that this was a place God had shown up for them—big time.

Reminders are important. They lift our eyes from our current situation and tap us on the shoulder. They prompt us to see what is happening now in the larger arc of our lives and to remember God's promise that He will remain present.

When God shows up in your life, why not stack a couple of rocks by your front door? When someone asks what is going on, you can tell them about all the times you have seen God show up for you.

Find a jar and geocache it or drop a note in the mail today to someone who has impacted you.

MAKE TIME FOR THE BEAUTIFUL INCONVENIENCE OF SHOWING UP

Let us consider how we may spur one another on toward love
and good deeds, not giving up meeting together, as some
are in the habit of doing, but encouraging one another—
and all the more as you see the Day approaching.
HEBREWS 10:24–25

These days there are lots of ways to connect with people. It is very efficient to be able to jump on an electronic device and see the other person's face rather than burning all the time and fossil fuels to get to them in person, but there's something missing when you do that. Even when you are talking on a device, it doesn't feel like you're together. Know what I mean?

Let's return to beautiful inefficiency in our relationships. Don't get fast food together; make it a five-course meal or go to some of the restaurants I go to where the service is lousy. They take as long to serve you food as if they were making a five-course meal, but it only costs a couple of bucks. These places that have great food and bad service are the mother load when it comes to rich conversations.

Or, pick up the phone or send an email or text to ask a couple of friends if they want to get together and bake some bread. You will find countless things to talk about while the bread rises. Talk about some of the areas in life that feel like pinch points, where things haven't come together in the way you thought they might have. These are the wonderfully inefficient conversations we need to have more of.

Jesus was completely inefficient in the way He loved people. Like most people of that day, He usually walked, and He didn't walk alone. He took others with Him. Try it. Invite somebody for a walk today and say, "Here are the three things I want to talk about: What's working? What's not working? And what are you feeling a little ambivalent about?" These questions are good for a couple-mile walk.

The best way to spur someone on toward love and good deeds is to be with them. When we are not in a hurry, when we're not being efficient in the way we love one another, we are being available to one another. Go do that today and then put a seatbelt on, because you are going to be rocked by how people will respond to you.

**Delight in the relational inefficiencies available
to you today if you slow things down.**

KEEP YOUR HEAD CLEAR SO YOU CAN FOCUS ON YOUR PURPOSE

With minds that are alert and fully sober, set your hope on the grace
to be brought to you when Jesus Christ is revealed at his coming.

1 PETER 1:13

I lost the sight in one of my eyes but, after quite a few operations, got most of it back. I was squeezed for time during the last operation because a year previously I had committed to speak at an event that same day. So we scheduled a predawn time for the operation, they put me under, and they did the work. The doctors gave me a patch, and I got a ride to the event. I was putting out the pirate vibe big time. All I needed was a peg leg and a parrot on my shoulder to complete my ensemble. I felt like I nailed the talk, because I remember people laughed a lot and I skipped off the stage as pirates do, but from what I heard later, it didn't go as well as I thought. Evidently, the anesthesia had not fully worn off. I haven't been invited back. This is what can happen when we are not fully alert.

What do you long for? Think about it by category. What do you want in your relationship with God, your closest friends, your work? This is the first step to being fully alert in the way we view our lives. Now ask yourself, *Why do I long for these things?* Alert and sober people look at the motivations underlying their desires. You might discover that these things you want were what you needed but didn't receive when you were a child. Perhaps your longings are driven by a need for approval. Or, could it be that selfishness or insecurity are playing a role in your decision tree? For many of us, including myself, we must confront the real reasons behind our longings, because they are not always apparent at first glance.

Decide what you're going to do about each of your most important and lasting longings and formulate a plan of action. When we take the steps necessary to give flight to our purposeful ambitions, we will access a deeper level of faith and meaning.

What move are you going to make today with a sober and optimistic resolve about the beautiful contribution God wants you to make?

LET PEOPLE KNOW HOW THEY LIGHT UP THE ROOM

Each of us should please our neighbors for their good, to build them up.
ROMANS 15:2

I got a little sailboat when I was young. It was called El Toro and had a mast, a tiller, and a white sail. It was about eight feet long, with enough room to fit myself and my grandmother. We spent lazy summer days sailing together on a little lake not far from her house.

She got me a captain's hat and said she was my crew, and I felt like I was the master of the seas when I was with her. She made me believe I was a good sailor and that I had what it took to keep her safe. She wasn't pretending when she said she saw me as a capable leader; she actually saw something in me that I needed to see. We can do that for one another every day.

Let the people you work with or live with or are married to know what you see in them, what special gift they bring to the room when they walk in, how your life is positively impacted because they are part of it. Some people mistakenly shy away from doing this, thinking it will come across as sappy or saccharine.

Hear this: it's not sappy if it comes from your heart. People will become who we say they are. We're wired to receive affirmation and validation. It pushes up against the negativity bias that we would otherwise default to.

Jesus saw more in people than they saw in themselves. For example, He met a woman in a desperate condition and looked past her circumstances to her heart. Another time, He met a man holding down a compromising job and looked past the employment and saw the possibilities in his life. He even saw a man nailed to a cross beside Him and said his life would not end that day but they would share eternity together.

Be the kind of person today who sees who people can become tomorrow, and don't keep it a secret.

**Call out what you see in the people around
you, and watch them light up.**

GOD WANTS TO KNOW *YOU*, NOT A BOASTFUL BLUEBERRY

"Many will say to me, 'Lord, Lord, did we not prophesy in your
name, and cast out demons in your name, and do many mighty
works in your name?' And then will I declare to them, 'I never
knew you; depart from me, you workers of lawlessness.'"

MATTHEW 7:22–23 ESV

I remember starting a nonprofit decades ago and putting on our web page that we were "saving a generation of young people." Then I paused and thought, *A whole generation? Really?* I did the quick math. There were forty-one million people in the country, and we had a school with nine kids (six of whom probably didn't want to be there). It was a bit of an exaggeration, to say the least.

I also put on our web page that we were "serving those throughout the country in the greatest need." While it was true that we were trying to be helpful and no doubt a couple of people benefitted from what we were doing, on reflection, it was as presumptuous and boastful as it was inaccurate. It wasn't malicious. I was trying to communicate that we were trying to be helpful, but I did it in a really lame way.

Why do we feel like we need to exaggerate what small efforts we are making for others? Usually we just want to let people know what we are doing, or we want supporters to know there is a problem and good is winning out over bad, right is winning out over wrong, hope is winning out over fear. These are beautiful and encouraging sentiments, but Jesus never asked us to add spin to the work He is doing in the world, big or small.

Jesus told His friends that living for God wasn't about saying the right things or even doing the remarkable, show-stopping things like telling people what would happen in the future or healing demon-possessed people or performing miracles in His name. Jesus said He isn't interested in showy efforts or exaggerations about what we are doing for Him, but instead, His interest is in knowing us. And we don't get to know someone or become friends with them by making headlines; we do it by spending time together.

Certainly, let's get to the "doing" part of our faith, not because it has the power to save us, but because the *doing* part of faith, and our dependence on Jesus as we do, is where Jesus gets to know us.

Keep all the embellishment out of today's discussions. Just enjoy being a small or large part of what God is doing in the world.

SETBACKS ARE CLASSROOMS, NOT CAMPSITES

Praise be to the God and Father of our Lord Jesus Christ, the
Father of compassion and the God of all comfort, who comforts
us in all our troubles, so that we can comfort those in any
trouble with the comfort we ourselves receive from God.
2 CORINTHIANS 1:3-4

You are going to mess up; that's just the way it is. It has always been that way and will always be that way. When you do mess up, don't be too hard on yourself. I have met people with a sincere faith who spend a weird amount of time beating themselves up.

When you fail, let yourself or someone else down, or in some other way miss the mark you were aiming for, stop hitting yourself. Remember, you are not a piñata, and when you hit yourself, it's not candy that comes out of you. It's other stuff: regret, embarrassment, jealousy, scorn. And these things eventually affect the people around you.

So don't let your mess-ups keep you from fully showing up today. What we think disqualifies us has actually prepared us to be more real, empathetic, and caring. This is what Paul was getting at when he said the way it works in God's economy is that He comforts us so that we can comfort others. He doesn't want us to bring to others the small amount of compassion we can muster on our own; He wants us to bring the comfort we have received directly from Him.

Pain is pain, but remember this: nothing is lost, not your pain or sorrow or regrets. Setbacks are classrooms, not campsites.

**Who can you comfort today who has failed big? What
increased measure of compassion and comfort can
you bring because God has comforted you?**

WE'RE ALL IN—EVERY STRANGE AND BEAUTIFUL ONE OF US

"They are still in the world, and I am coming to you. Holy Father, protect them by the power of your name, the name you gave me, so that they may be one as we are one."
JOHN 17:11

John 17 records some of Jesus' most intimate conversations with His Father. It is a chapter about protection and unity, and having His followers set apart from everyone else but not from one another. And yet, there are more than forty-five thousand different denominations, born out of disagreements about who Jesus is and what God wants of us. But here's the thing: there is a place for everyone within the body of Christ.

This makes me think of thumb wars. You clinch fingers with someone, and one person tries to pin the other person's thumb underneath theirs. You can tell a lot about the churchgoers in the room by the way they go about playing the game.

With tongue in cheek but also with a grain of truth, allow me to lead you through an exercise. Some people playing thumb wars might recite the rhyme that leads up to the game: "One, two, three, four, I declare a thumb war." These could be the Presbyterians—the rule followers—who love order and sequence and formality. Is that you? If so, you are a wonderful part of the worldwide family of friends. We need that order you bring.

Others will skip the rhyme and go in for the kill, crushing the unsuspecting person's thumb. This is how some people perceive the Baptists to be. If this offends you, loosen up. Get a puppy if you need to. We need you and all your passion and loyalty and wisdom, but we don't need you to be uptight all the time. When you are on edge, the rest of us are too.

If you were invited to play thumb wars and immediately thought, *You can't tell me what to do,* you might be the nondenominational friends who resist going along with everyone else. We need you and your independent, noncompliant spirit. Sure, it can be distracting if you go around the bend with your rejection of norms, but it can also be a beautiful reminder of the freedom we enjoy in Christ.

Today, you get to decide what part you are going to play in the symphony of God's people. God has made you uniquely for this earth and for us too. We need to learn from you, just as we need to learn from each group, as you live out your life with eyes on Jesus and a humble heart.

**One, two, three, four, it's time to play thumb
wars. What will be your move?**

THE BEST WAY TO THE BEST OUTCOME IS THROUGH KINDNESS AND LOVE

As the elect of God, holy and beloved, put on tender mercies, kindness, humility, meekness, longsuffering; bearing with one another, and forgiving one another, if anyone has a complaint against another; even as Christ forgave you, so you also must do.
COLOSSIANS 3:12-13 NKJV

We had a pinball machine dropped off in our driveway when the kids were young. Someone was closing a business and thought I would love having it, I'm not sure why. It had been hotwired, so we didn't need a pocket full of quarters to play. We could just press a button, and silver balls would start lining up to be launched. We discovered we could exert a little influence on the table by giving it a little nudge. But if we pushed the pinball machine too hard, it would flash "tilt" and the flippers would stop working. Then we were helpless as we watched the ball roll past the flippers and out of play.

People are not much different from that pinball machine. We welcome influence and small, helpful nudges in the right direction, but we resist being pushed around too much or controlled too often. Paul wrote a letter from jail to the Colossian church about this when things were not going well for them. He wanted to remind them that the way to exert the right kind of influence is to be tender and kind and humble and meek. This is the opposite of being pushy or manipulative.

It can be difficult for us to demonstrate these characteristics when we think there is a better or faster or more productive path for people to take. This is especially true when it comes to our children or other loved ones. We want to raise the volume or the consequences or the urgency to get their attention, yet when we do, we get the opposite of what we are hoping for because they hit the relational Tilt button.

Who is someone you can influence in a beautiful way today? What gentle, loving, humble, and nonmanipulative nudge in the right direction can you give that person?

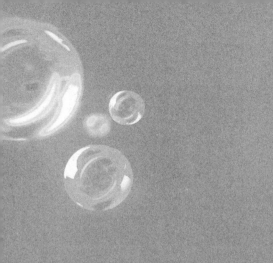

SEPTEMBER

TAKE THE LONG SHOT, EVEN WHEN IT MEANS SWITCHING TARGETS

It is for freedom that Christ has set us free. Stand firm, then, and
do not let yourselves be burdened again by a yoke of slavery.
GALATIANS 5:1

People don't walk in straight lines, and your life doesn't need to look that way either. If you're feeling defeated and disillusioned all the time, perhaps it's time to cut something loose and explore other opportunities. Aim for something lasting. Ask yourself, *What do I want to be known for long after I am gone?* Then hang a target on that.

Maybe you need to break up with some of the things that are taking your attention away from the targets you have hung in your life previously. Perhaps it is your faith that matters to you most, but you have wandered. It might be a relationship that meant everything to you, but you became distracted and drifted apart. Was there an ambition you once had that you have back-burnered, ignored, or abandoned?

You don't need page after page of proclamations to bring something you have been involved in to an end. Do yours in just two words: "I'm out." This isn't Texas Hold'em, where you have to keep most of the cards you were dealt and only get to pick a couple of new ones. Sometimes what you need is a whole new hand and a rock-solid do-over.

If you want to go all pro on this, pick an expiration date for your ambitions. Circle a go/no-go date on quitting whatever it is that isn't working for you. Then write down what you are going to do to take a step toward your target on 3x5 cards and tape them to the walls where you live. But don't let the action step you identify drift into next week or next month. Deferral is not your friend; it is your nemesis. It's not the conversation you practice in your head that has the power to change you; it is the email you actually send.

**Jesus says it is for freedom that we are set free, but
experiencing that freedom is going to require we make a
move, sometimes a bold one. What will yours be today?**

GET REAL WITH JESUS; LEAVE CANNED CONVERSATIONS FOR INTERVIEWS FOR BAD JOBS

When you ask, you do not receive, because you ask with wrong motives, that you may spend what you get on your pleasures.

JAMES 4:3

In college, I owned a Volkswagen bug. I came around a corner a little hot one day and slid out on the wet pavement. When the front tire hit the curb, it folded under the car. Kind of like the DeLorean in *Back to the Future*, but also kind of not. The reason I was in such a hurry was because I had to get to an interview for a job. I had spent the morning surfing and had changed into my best interview clothes quickly at the beach parking lot, but now I was stuck with only three working wheels on my barely working car. I called a friend and abandoned my ride.

I didn't really want the job I was interviewing for, but I did want to make rent and eat so I was eager to land it. In the interview, the hiring manager asked me about how responsible I was and whether I made it to places on time. I gave him all the right answers. I was born for this job. I wanted to be like him when I grew up. You know, thinking I was telling him what he wanted to hear. I thought I had him suckered into hiring me when I leaned forward to sign a paper he put in front of me. But the thing about surfing is there's a lot of water involved, particularly in my case, because there's a lot of falling involved. The water gets in your eyes and ears and up your nose.

When I leaned forward, all the water in my large nasal cavities came rushing out and spilled all over the paper. It was an epic case of postnasal drip. He was not impressed. I didn't get the job, but being jobless gave me more time to find a used front end for my VW bug, so there is that.

Sometimes we talk to God like we are interviewing for a job. We give Him all the answers we think He expects to hear when what He wants is for our authentic self to show up.

Let's get real with Jesus today and stop trying to present just what we think He wants. Leave the canned answers for interviews for bad jobs and the authentic ones for discussions with God.

The job of a lifetime in relationship with Jesus is yours if you want it. He doesn't want you to work for Him, He wants you to rest in Him.

KEEP YOUR HANDS IN YOUR POCKETS AND TRUST GOD

"No," he answered, "because while you are pulling the weeds,
you may uproot the wheat with them. Let both grow together
until the harvest. At that time I will tell the harvesters: First
collect the weeds and tie them in bundles to be burned;
then gather the wheat and bring it into my barn."
MATTHEW 13:29–30

I was invited to a gathering in Colorado. Most people get invited to something like this months in advance, but I got the call the day before it began. The reason was simple. All the other guests were pretty famous, and someone had canceled last minute. They couldn't find anyone else to fill in, so they invited me. When I arrived, the guests were gathering in a large room surrounded by large paintings. I recognized one of the famous prints, because my grandparents had a smaller version in their house that they had purchased at Target for four dollars, including the frame. As I looked closer at this replica of my grandparents' painting, I noticed it was askew on the wall.

My parents raised me right, so I put my hands deep into my pockets and resisted the urge to straighten it. Unfortunately, there was another guest who wasn't raised right, and he walked over and straightened the painting. When he did, all kinds of bells and alarms went off. Security guys appeared, and I half expected a guy to drop down from the ceiling on a wire. Evidently, this was the original painting and was worth millions.

It's instinctive for some of us to want to straighten out furniture and paintings and even people if we think they are a little askew. Right after the parable of the sower and right before the parable of the mustard seed is the parable of the wheat and the weeds. In modern terms, it is about someone who plants crabgrass seeds in the middle of another person's perfectly manicured putting green. But, surprisingly, when the deed is discovered, the servants are told to let the weeds grow together with the wheat, so as not to accidentally pull up the wheat. The message is to resist trying to fix it right now, with the promise that God will sort it out later.

What would it look like for you to hit pause, resist the urge to straighten someone or something out, and let the good and the bad grow together, trusting God to sort it out when the time is right?

God is going to bring more than a few opportunities your way today to engage with difficult people. Remember, people are not projects. People are people.

FANNING THE SPARK INTO A FLAME

For this reason I remind you to fan into flame the gift of God,
which is in you through the laying on of my hands.
2 TIMOTHY 1:6

Someone gave me flint and steel as a present. This is the kind of emergency gear to have with you when you need to start a fire and you've lost your matches or they got wet. Making a spark with flint is easy. But getting the spark to turn into a flame takes a great deal of focused attention and the right materials, including small sticks.

Why small sticks and not big logs? To build a fire, you need to start with smaller kindling that more easily catches the sparks. And then, as the small sticks catch and start to generate heat, making a more stable flame, the logs will light.

The same principle is true of us as we learn to exercise our gifts. If you're just starting out and feeling unsure, if you're still at the spark stage, do something small that works.

If speaking is your gift you want to develop, do it well for a dozen people before you do it for an arena full of people. If hospitality is your desired gift, host a dinner for six on your back porch, not a week away for one hundred people on an island.

Learn your craft. Give it some practice. And as you succeed with these little things, you'll be fanning that spark into a flame, eventually one big enough to light the bigger logs.

Today is your day. What are some unique
gifts God has put in your bag of capabilities?
Think of a few ways you can start small to
release those gifts. Fan your gifts today.

ASK FOR HELP BEFORE YOU HIDE

"Take my yoke upon you and learn from me, for I am
gentle and humble in heart, and you will find rest for your
souls. For my yoke is easy and my burden is light."
MATTHEW 11:29–30

When our kids were in middle school, we noticed that often the new students hadn't adjusted to using lockers yet, so they would carry all their books in their backpacks throughout the day. This earned them the nickname "turtles," because they were carrying so much with them all the time.

We do this too, more often than we should. We carry around heavy burdens on a day-to-day basis: shame, guilt, envy, hard feelings, disappointments. These things turn us into turtles, hunching under the weight of it all, and our faith gets crushed by the load. Then we go into a kind of emotional withdrawal, where we tuck our legs, tail, and head inside of our shell to protect ourselves from further crushing.

Here's the thing. When we turtle to block out all the anxiety-producing inputs in our lives, we also prevent positive inputs. This blocks all the delightful outputs that could be flowing from us that are needed to maintain healthy, authentic relationships. We might not realize it unless someone brings it to our attention, but when we turtle to self-protect, we reenforce a narrative that we are unpredictable or moody or selfish. This is not what we want to cultivate with those closest to us.

Don't just go missing emotionally. Tell people you need a little time alone to process a couple of things and you will be back. Go to Jesus with your anxieties and fears and sense of being overwhelmed. Jesus didn't say His yoke was easy because it wasn't heavy. He makes our burdens feel light because He is that strong.

**Today, make it your aim not to turtle. It will take some
work, but if you can resist the impulse, you will experience
the kind of burden-sharing Jesus talked about.**

THE TICKETS COST MORE, BUT IT'S WORTH MOVING OUT OF THE CHEAP SEATS

Therefore each of you must put off falsehood and speak truthfully
to your neighbor, for we are all members of one body.
EPHESIANS 4:25

Jesus was always inviting people to walk in the light of what is true. For many of us, this means achieving a deeper level of authenticity. It reminds me of North Carolina's state motto: "To Be Rather Than to Seem." This is a goal we should all aspire to. It doesn't matter what your faith or your family or your friendships look like on the outside; it matters what they are. If you want to get to the deeper, more beautiful, and lasting places in your relationships, let authenticity be your guide and travel companion.

You might be thinking the way to avoid feeling like you have to put up a front is to limit the number of people you're around, to give your time only to the ones you trust and feel most comfortable with. But, while it might seem counterintuitive, what I have found is the more I've made myself available to all people, both the easy and the difficult ones, the more I've been able to experience the incredible joy of being authentic and truly living for others.

I'm not just speaking from the cheap seats, either. I have made real commitments that have cost me dearly as the world sees it, but it's been completely worth it to lean into these relationships with my real self and build deep friendships.

Let the real version of you authentically show up, and you will experience a new take on your life and the lives of the ones around you who God made in His image. Doing this might feel like a stretch for you, but it is worth it, because you are worth it.

**Who is someone you can get real with today? Be honest
about what delights you and what scares you, what you
are afraid to start and what you know you must end.**

JUST DO IT: LOVE DIFFICULT PEOPLE

With the tongue we praise our Lord and Father, and with it we curse human beings, who have been made in God's likeness.

JAMES 3:9

My favorite children's movie is *Peter Pan*. There is a scene in it where Peter somehow gets disconnected from his shadow and chases after it as it bounces off the walls and ceiling until Wendy finally sews the shadow back on to the bottom of Peter Pan's feet.

This reminds me of the disconnect we sometimes have between what God calls us to do and what our instincts tell us to do. We know He wants us to love people as they are, but we struggle to do that as we wade through the waters of difficult relationships. But, like Wendy did for Peter and his shadow, we are going to need to take the version of us that wants to love people like God made them and the version of us that is ricocheting off the walls and sew them back together again.

Loving people in concept is easy but in reality is very hard. We are busy and distracted and concerned and, besides, with all the other people in the world who are nice, who has time for really difficult people? Here's something we need to remember: the people in our lives, even the ones who are the most prickly and disagreeable, are still people who have been made in the image of God. We just need to take a moment to see past all the insecurity driving their awkward conduct and silly decisions and discover the unique ways God expresses Himself through His sometimes off-putting people.

Today is the day. Who comes to mind that you can reach out to? Who is it that you have been avoiding rather than engaging? Don't just get coffee with them. That's too predictable. Take them out for a snow cone or go bowling.

Take the people who have been the subject of your conversations and make them the object of your time and interest.

IF YOU HAVE JESUS, YOU HAVE EVERYTHING

But those who seek the Lord lack no good thing.
PSALM 34:10

When I was in law school, I rented a cheap little cottage next to my favorite surf spot in San Diego for a few hundred dollars a month. It sounds charming, but truth be told, it was pretty gross. Not much worked in the house, and only one burner on the stove would light up. But that was okay because I only had one pot to cook in. Like most other grad students, I was stone broke.

I would get my one-burner stove going and cook pasta most nights for dinner. Sometimes I would throw in a stick of butter to make it healthy (not) and taste like something. I'm obviously not a foodie, but I never felt like I was lacking anything.

One of the psalms David wrote while he was on the run for his life was about this same thing. He wrote that even during a time of immense hardship, if we are chasing after God, we lack nothing. These are bold words to say when you have been threatened with death and are having to scrounge for bread just to survive.

But if David could say them in his situation, I could say the same while living with a one-burner stove. Sure, there might have been other things I was wishing for, but I had everything I needed with what I had. The same is true for you too. You've got everything you need in Jesus.

You have enough. If you find yourself wanting to add to what you have to find your joy, remind yourself it is Jesus' love that ties everything you have together. It's not pasta He gives us; it's love and patience and time and grace. And He has given us all equal amounts of these if we want to access them.

**Take stock of what you have today. What you
have is enough, and Jesus is enough.**

WHEN WHAT GOD ASKS YOU TO DO SEEMS IMPOSSIBLE, DO IT ANYWAY

Moses said, "Pardon your servant, Lord. Please send someone else."
EXODUS 4:13

Chapters 3 and 4 of Exodus record the conversations between Moses and God about Moses leading the people of Israel out of Egypt. The most generous way to describe these conversations is that Moses was hesitant, and I can understand why.

Moses had been a shepherd for decades. Even though God spoke to him through a burning bush, he was conflicted about what he should do. Moses didn't have a reputation or a following. Who was he to be leading his people? And what would the other leaders think? Besides, he could barely speak a complete sentence without messing up. Add to that, Moses had killed an Egyptian who had been beating up a Hebrew person and buried the Egyptian guy in the sand after making sure no one saw him. If you added it all up, Moses lacked pretty much all the qualifications he thought would be necessary to lead people.

We can all relate on some level to how Moses was feeling, but here's the thing. God wants us to bring our obedience, not our excuses. He wants our dependence, not our talents. He's more interested in our future than our past. Will doing what God asks of you seem impossible? Sure, it will. Do it anyway. Is He asking you to speak when you don't see yourself as very good at speaking? Perhaps. Take the leap. If you fall, if you stumble, you will fall right into the arms of Jesus all over again.

God will give you what you need to accomplish what He asks. He is not looking for us to whip out a list of excuses. He wants us to show up, and He'll do the rest.

God doesn't need another Moses, He's got you. Decide today that you will be the person God has invited you to be.

YOUR WEAKNESSES ARE PART OF THE RECIPE

For Christ's sake, I delight in weaknesses, in insults, in hardships, in persecutions, in difficulties. For when I am weak, then I am strong.
2 CORINTHIANS 12:10–11

In Greek mythology, there is a character named Achilles, who was the offspring of a bunch of hard-to-pronounce, hard-to-remember other characters. When he was an infant, someone said he would die, so his mother dipped him in a river that would make him undefeatable. When she slipped him into the water, she was supposedly holding him by the heel, so the water never got on that part of his body. Achilles would grow up to fight in many battles and, true to the promise, he never died. But eventually he took a shot to the ankle, which was unprotected, and was defeated. This is why, when we're talking about our weaknesses, we sometimes call them our Achilles' heels.

Mythology doesn't hold my attention for a host of reasons: the stories are made up, I can't pronounce the names, and I simply would rather read the stories Jesus told. Nevertheless, it is worth finding a wide spot in the road to talk about our weaknesses, our Achilles' heels. You have them, I have them, we all have them. These don't come our way because our mothers dipped us in a stream holding us by the ankle. They come because we are, at our core, in need of rescue.

Paul said it was when he was weak that he was strong. He wasn't just playing with words. Paul wanted to remind his friends that God is enough, and we don't need to hide our deep needs and flaws. Instead, we can talk about them because they show off Christ's power at work in us. Sometimes we think if we are real and vulnerable about things we aren't good at, we will make God look weak or vulnerable. But just the opposite happens. People see the power of God in our lives when they see us doing what He asks us to do in the middle of our tremendous need.

What is the weakness, the vulnerable spot, the trigger that sets you off? Let someone know about it. Then lean into it as you bring it to Jesus.

We are not an advertisement for Jesus. We are evidence of Him, and we do this best in our weaknesses, not in our strengths.

LEAN INTO THE FANTASTIC ABSURDITY OF FAITH

*For since in the wisdom of God the world through its wisdom
did not know him, God was pleased through the foolishness
of what was preached to save those who believe.*
1 CORINTHIANS 1:21

Don Quixote is a novel written by Miguel de Cervantes a few hundred years ago and is considered by many to be one of the most important books ever written. The main character frames himself as a Christian knight-errant, a knight who wanders around looking for chivalrous adventures. Don Quixote does all kinds of foolish things, like tilting at windmills, which he thinks are giants. But he also drops loads of wisdom along the way. He is the picture of faith wrapped in what seems foolish.

Isn't that exactly what it looks like to follow Jesus? Just look at how God does things. So much of the time, He chooses to do things in ways that feel completely counter to how we would do things. He even chose what seemed like pure foolishness to save the whole world, and He did it through a baby, not a famous or powerful or popular person. This is what Paul was getting at when he wrote that the wisdom of God is displayed in what seems like foolishness to save those who believe.

Many of us are looking for certainty and safety when faith only offers us a life filled with uncertainty, risk, and constantly dying to who we once were to make room for who God is turning us into. We need to remember that He has not invited us on a business trip but on an adventure with Him, which more closely mirrors Don Quixote's experience than the one often portrayed to us about what faith lived out looks like.

When we live with Don Quixote's love of honor and adventure and authenticity and whimsy, it is now commonly referred to as being *quixotic*. Not only is this a fun word to say, but as we lean into this, we reflect the ways of God, demonstrating wisdom in what is sometimes seen as foolishness.

**Roll out a little Don Quixote in your life today
and see what happens with your faith.**

CUT TO THE CHASE AND LIVE YOUR FAITH

In the same way, faith by itself, if it is not accompanied by action, is dead.
JAMES 2:17

We've all grown impatient before with someone who is rambling on without really getting anywhere in the conversation. In those circumstances, you and I are both usually hoping they will just cut to the chase. This phrase, "cut to the chase," is an idiom that means to get to the point.

Interestingly, its origins are in the silent movies. When things were dragging and movie makers didn't want people to get bored because there were no words spoken, they would drop in a chase scene. In other words, they would get to the part where something happens.

I think this is what James was getting at in a letter he wrote to his friends when he reminded them that faith has to be expressed in action. In other words, rather than spend your life just sitting back, eating popcorn, and watching or commenting on everyone else's life, get to the chase scene with your beliefs.

Get to the part where something happens. Engage with your faith and the actions that naturally flow out of it. People will understand what you believe by watching what you do.

Here's what is crazy. Jesus doesn't need our help. I wake up every morning and ask Him what I can do for Him. And every day He keeps reminding me that He doesn't need my help; instead, He wants my heart. And He wants yours too. Cut to the chase and let Him know your heart is all His.

How will you release love into the world today? How will you let people know what your faith is all about?

GOD PICKS UP THE PIECES

The LORD upholds all who fall and lifts up all who are bowed down.
PSALM 145:14

I was invited to speak at an event in the central part of Canada, which is largely farmland. The organizer had a field that could have fit fifty thousand people easily. There were countless trailers set up to house the people who would be performing and there was a huge tent where some other events would apparently happen. I made the twelve-hour trip and arrived out in the plains. It was quite a distance from the closest city, but I figured this was all part of the charm. It was truly an impressive sight to see all the infrastructure, portable toilets, first aid stations, and other preparations that had been made to accommodate the crowds.

The next morning, I was up early and eager to see the tens of thousands of people arriving for the event. I stepped out of my trailer and looked to the left and to the right. Rounding up, there was a total of nobody. The time approached when we were supposed to start, and a friend of mine, who had brought his full band up from the States to perform, seemed as puzzled as I was. Did we arrive on the wrong day? Was this the right place? Sadly, it was. Mercifully, the hosts only had me speak for a few minutes, and then I made my way back to the airport, along with my friend and his band.

Some things we try work, and others don't. Take a tip from David, the king of Israel, who reminded us that the Lord upholds all who fall and lifts up all who are bowed down. In other words, stay humble but don't lose hope. Sure, we'll get discouraged when things don't shake out the way we want, but that doesn't mean it wasn't worth trying. Do you know what the organizer did after the event flopped? The next year, they put on the same event. I wasn't there, but I bet they had at least twice as many people.

What is it you could try today that might be a big failure? Remember, we're not looking for applause or popularity; we're in search of purpose. Refuse to defer the idea you have. Take it out for a drive.

Much of what God has invited us to will have uncertain outcomes. Fail trying; don't fail watching.

WHEN CONTROVERSY SHOWS UP, BREATHE IN GRATITUDE AND BREATHE OUT GRACE

A gentle answer turns away wrath, but a harsh word stirs up anger.
PROVERBS 15:1

We all experience conflict. Take it from a lawyer, it has happened before and it will happen again, but we don't have to be dragged too far into things when disputes come our way. Every fight doesn't need to be Gettysburg. Don't let yourself get neck-deep in an argument to resolve waist-high controversies. Usually the person you're fighting with doesn't have bad intent behind their actions. Just because they were lame in what they did doesn't mean you need to be lame in how you respond.

Here are two strategies worth trying when you see controversy brewing. First, breathe in gratitude, then breathe out grace. I don't mean metaphorically. Literally take a couple of deep breaths. As you inhale, think about why you are grateful for the person and your hope for a beautiful future for them. Check yourself to see if you are looking at the action on the surface or the motive underneath. This first strategy has to do with our mindset.

The second strategy is more outward focused and is about breathing out grace. Take whatever happened and consider different explanations for it. Try this: Ask yourself what the most generous explanation is. Next, ask yourself what the most realistic explanation is. And, finally, ask yourself what the most optimistic explanation is. Here's what that might look like. Someone I know once hurt my feelings, and the most generous explanation I could come up with was that they probably didn't know that I wouldn't receive what they were doing well. The most realistic explanation I came up with was that they were having a bad day. I've had a couple of those, and I remember what that feels like. The most optimistic thought I had was that next time we would do better.

What dispute do you need to apply this to today? How does it change your perspective to think about different explanations for the surface behavior?

Don't let unresolved conflicts distract you from God's much bigger purposes for you today.

IF YOU MISSED THE BOAT, START SWIMMING AFTER IT

Sow your seed in the morning, and at evening let your hands
not be idle, for you do not know which will succeed, whether
this or that, or whether both will do equally well.
ECCLESIASTES 11:6

About seventy years ago, Art went on a drive with his friend into an orange grove. His friend wanted to build something there and wanted Art to be a part of it. But it was a long way from where everyone lived, so Art passed on buying the land. That friend was Walt Disney, and Art Linkletter turned down the chance to buy everything around what would become Disneyland. This doesn't mean Art wasn't a smart guy. It just means he didn't see what Walt Disney saw when he looked at the land.

We all miss opportunities from time to time. Maybe it seems too risky when it comes our way, or maybe we don't catch the vision for something that is still in its early stages. It's not a bad thing to be cautious, but sometimes it's worth taking a leap.

Solomon left behind some wisdom for us. He told us to sow our seed in the morning and not let our hands be idle in the evening, because we don't know how things will turn out. The next time an opportunity comes, net that butterfly or it will land near someone else. But if you missed an opportunity like Art did, don't kick yourself and don't become depressed. Perhaps you have heard the saying, "If you think your ship has sailed, start swimming after it."

We were born for a life filled with adventures and adversity and overcoming and rebounding and love and loss and learning. Quit playing it safe with your one beautiful life. Be possibility-minded, not problem-centric.

What do you do when it feels like an opportunity has passed you by and you literally or figuratively missed the boat?

**What opportunities are in front of you today
that might be worth swimming after?**

TRAVEL LIGHT—LOVE WILL NEVER WEIGH YOU DOWN

Humble yourselves, therefore, under God's mighty
hand, that he may lift you up in due time. Cast all
your anxiety on him because he cares for you.
1 PETER 5:6–7

We live down by the bay in San Diego. When the international sailing competition called the America's Cup came to town, wealthy people from all over moved into the bayfront homes for the months leading up to the big race. One guy (I'm not going to throw him under the bus, because I'm nice and he could buy and sell me twenty times) arrived at his rental house across the street from us with a huge 100-foot crane and a couple of 18-wheelers. I wondered what was inside the huge crates on the trucks and how I could climb up on top of the crane when no one was looking.

The next day, the crane started lifting huge statues from the crates and over the rooftop of the immense house and onto the bayfront in front of the house. Apparently, this guy travels everywhere with his statues. I'm lucky if I can remember to bring my toothbrush on a trip. As I marveled at how truly awful these statues were, it made me think of how I tend to travel a little heavy too. It's not statues I bring with me. It is hurts and resentments and setbacks and regrets I pack around from place to place with me.

Every time I allow these hurts to enter into my mind, I breathe new life into them and I set them in place like this new neighbor of mine did with his statues. My hurts are just less obvious fixtures in my life than his are.

What have you been packing around that you can leave behind today? It will feel uncomfortable at first, because we are so familiar with traveling with these things everywhere we go. But leave what is unhelpful behind and watch what God will do in your beautiful life.

Pack light and you will travel far.

DON'T LEAVE THE PRESENTS ON YOUR PORCH—OPEN THE DOOR!

Peter knocked at the outer entrance, and a servant named Rhoda came to answer the door. When she recognized Peter's voice, she was so overjoyed she ran back without opening it and exclaimed, "Peter is at the door!"

ACTS 12:13-14

Understand the scene: Peter has been in prison in Jerusalem and is about to go on trial. He was chained to two guards when an angel showed up in his cell, the chains fell off, and Peter started walking past guards as jail doors opened in front of him. The angel was with him until he got out to the street, then disappeared.

Peter ran from the prison to John Mark's house, where he guessed correctly that there were people gathered together. Ironically, they were praying for Peter's release when Peter knocked. One of the servants ran down to answer the door and heard Peter's voice. *Wait, what?* she must have thought. *Isn't everyone upstairs praying for Peter, hoping he will get out of jail?* Without even opening the door, she ran upstairs to tell everyone else. Certainly, her motives were not bad, but she left the gift standing at the door.

The people gathered upstairs did the same. Rather than believe it could be true that their prayers were answered, they thought it was more likely the servant had lost her mind or there was an angel at the door. As they were rifling through explanations and possibilities, Peter stood there, still knocking.

Here is why all of this is important today. First, sometimes God is at work doing things we either don't notice or don't believe. We can be so busy that we don't realize freedom has already arrived. We've all got a little bit of the servant Rhoda in us, and a bit of John Mark too. What we were praying for is already knocking at the door, and we don't know what to do about it. When our prayers are answered, we think it's crazy or come up with another lame explanation for what is occurring. We are surrounded by the miraculous every day. Don't dismiss it or ignore it, and don't leave what God has done in your life standing at the door today.

Fling wide the door and celebrate what God is doing.

READ THE ROOM

Who, being in very nature God, did not consider equality
with God something to be used to his own advantage.
PHILIPPIANS 2:6

I was asked to speak at a large gathering of men in Pennsylvania. At the end of my talk, I asked the men to stand up. We gave thanks for our time together, and I told the men to throw an arm around the guy next to them. Everyone just kind of stared back at me. In an even more enthusiastic voice, I asked the men to throw an arm around each guy on either side of them. Nothing. Then it dawned on me, most of the men were Amish and public displays of affection like this aren't done. There were plenty of beards in the room but few mustaches. I had totally failed to read the room.

This happens to all of us in various ways. A good goal is to be at least generally aware of what is going on around us and to be considerate of the people we're trying to love. Jesus demonstrated this when, even though He knew He was God, He didn't try to use it to His advantage. Rather than seizing the power that was His, He saw the people's needs and chose to release His power into their lives to help them. We, too, can be fully aware of the amount of influence we have but release that influence for others' benefit with humility and kindness.

To get to this place, we need to move from thinking too much about our own needs to considering the needs of others. This is what Jesus did every day. He had all the power, yet allowed injustice and suffering to be inflicted on Himself as He looked toward His greater purpose of helping us find our way to His love, which always focused on the needs of others.

We are all going to misread the room or misunderstand someone we meet, but if we make it our highest value to be more vigilant to the hopes, needs, and desires of the people around us, we will live richer, more engaged and inspiring lives.

Resist becoming consumed by your cares and concerns and instead think of creative ways you might use what you've been given to lift up the people around you.

What courageous step do you need to take today to tap into the power and influence Jesus already said were ours for the purpose of loving others even more deeply? How can you release what you have today into the life of a person you know who's been struggling? This is your day to make some changes.

**Who has God dropped into the blast radius
of your love and influence today?**

GOD WANTS TO HEAR YOUR QUESTIONS, WHATEVER THEY ARE

"Call to me and I will answer you and tell you great
and unsearchable things you do not know."
JEREMIAH 33:3

There is a long list of things I don't understand, like why they have armed guards at the See's Candy store. Are they keeping the candy from making a break for it or keeping diabetics out? I also don't get why there is no butter in peanut butter. And since we're talking about it, do fish get thirsty? Do they get swimmer's ear? Do they have ears?

Maybe these aren't your questions, but we all have questions about life, especially ones we'd like to ask God. Why is my pain happening? When will God answer me? Why is there suffering? Am I being punished by God? Why do bad things happen to good people and good things seem to happen to bad people? Why do other people find love when I am still looking?

Job asked why God allowed him to experience so much pain, and Jesus asked why God had forsaken Him. Mary wanted to know how she got pregnant as a teenager, Peter wanted to know if the water would hold his weight, and Abraham's wife wanted to know how she could get pregnant at ninety years old. The disciples wondered how they could feed five thousand, David wanted to know why God was hiding Himself from him, Mary asked the person she thought was the gardener where Jesus was, and Habbakuk wanted to know why God tolerated injustice.

Whatever your questions are, bring them to God. He can handle them. Take a deep dive into the Scriptures as you're looking for answers. And find wise and faith-filled people to ask for wisdom. If you wonder if what you are hearing is from God, check it out. Does it square with the Scriptures? Is it kind and supportive and encouraging? If it feels like an accusation or a bony finger pointed in your direction, that's coming from the other team. Don't let the darkness punk you.

What questions do you have for God today?
Bring them to Him; He's all ears.

GOD IS OUR SAFE ROOM

*I will say to the Lord, "My refuge and my
fortress, my God, in whom I trust."*
PSALM 91:2 ESV

Somalia is a country that has been fighting against itself for decades. There are a dozen clans at war with one another. Al Qaeda is a strong presence, and other influences abound. There is no Somalian military, and neighboring countries like Uganda provide the small amount of protection available.

When I went to Mogadishu for the first time, I stayed at the Peace Hotel, a small place behind a mountain of sandbags and razor wire. This hotel is in the green zone, which is intended to be a safe place, but is actually a very dangerous place because the bad guys know that everyone can be found there so they lob mortars in periodically. When you check into the hotel, you need to provide them with your blood type, in case you become injured, and a proof-of-life answer in case you get abducted. In these and several other ways, it is safe to say the Peace Hotel is not like the Oahu Marriott.

One interesting feature of the hotel is that there are safe rooms without any handles or hinges on the outside. Once you are inside, no one else can get in. After I checked in for the first time, at the owner's insistence, I practiced making my way to one of the safe rooms in the dark just in case there was an attack.

Knowing how to get to a safe place is a good idea no matter who you are and where you are. I envision the Peace Hotel's safe rooms when I think about how God said He made safe places and safe people to meet us there. Believe the psalmist. No fortress is as secure as the arms of God.

Who has God placed in your life who feels safe, who gets you? Who would you go to if you were really in a pickle? Where would you go? Maybe it is a faith community or a retreat center or a place you have visited before where you felt safe and welcomed and understood. Practice going to those places when you are not distracted by a crisis. Practice letting God meet you there. Even better, be a safe place for someone today.

**Every day we can create safe places for people to come and
we can be safe people who will meet them when they do.**

RECOGNIZE THE WHIMSY OF A SUNSET

From the rising of the sun to the place where it
sets, the name of the Lord is to be praised.
PSALM 113:3

I know when the sun sets. It was at 6:02 this evening. I don't know what time it will set tomorrow, but I bet it will be a time close to this. I know in the winter which way the timing of sunset will trend and in the summer how the times get later. It might sound like a small thing, but knowing what time the sun sets gives me the chance to slow down what I am doing every day and invite Sweet Maria to take in the view with me. We can do this together from our home or travel to the beach to watch the sun sink into the Pacific.

So much of the time, we are in a hurry, too rushed to watch the sunrise or the sunset. I understand why. We have twenty pounds of activities to fit into a ten-pound bag of time. But the Scriptures describe a different cadence to our days, one that involves times of introspection and prayer. What if we took to heart the idea that from the rising of the sun to the place where it sets we would be thinking about how God is in and over everything?

Imagine replacing hurry with purpose. Try changing up the language you use. Instead of saying you want to hurry less, say, "I want to see more sunsets. I want to watch for what God is doing in the world around me." Decide this will be a new habit of yours. Then, every time you check your watch, you will think about how long it is until sunset, and it will be a great reminder to wrap up your day.

This is the part where you don't merely agree but figure out when sunset is this evening and call someone you want to spend some time with. I can't think of anything more whimsical than sharing sunset moments with God and someone I care about. Let them know where they can meet you and not to be late. It is going to be one for the books, I just know it.

**Don't waste another minute. You're burning daylight and sunset.
Slow down and let God knock you off your feet with delight.**

DON'T COMPLICATE THE TRUTH

Jesus replied, "You are in error because you do not
know the Scriptures or the power of God."
MATTHEW 22:29

The Sadducees were like the Pharisees—they were the judgmental, high-browed, wealthy, powerful religious people—but they didn't believe in the resurrection or an afterlife. One day, they cornered Jesus to ask a finely pointed question about the law.

Here's the gist of what they said: "If a man died without having children, usually a brother would marry the widow and raise children with her. But what if there were seven brothers and each one married her and died? Who would she be married to in heaven?"

At first glance, what they asked sounded like an SAT question designed to test your math and deduction skills. But Jesus saw through their carefully worded hypothetical. He wasn't head-faked by the jockeying about whether there is an afterlife or not. He just pointed them back to the power of the Scriptures.

Similarly, don't take the bait when the issue de jour comes your way. Someone is going to want to know what your opinion is about every important social issue of our time. When that happens, point them toward the Scriptures and take a deep dive yourself. Race, faith, attraction, life, and death—no matter the issue, it should start with God's words rather than your opinions.

As you examine these things, don't complicate the Scriptures, but don't be ignorant of what it says. Know the Scriptures and experience the power of God in your life. Start wherever you want but look for what God's perspective is on the issues we regularly encounter.

It's tempting to be relevant and popular, but trade all of that for being true and wise, knowing what God said on the topic.

LIVING IN THE WAKE OF GRACE

Out of his fullness we have all received grace
in place of grace already given.
JOHN 1:16

When I turned sixteen, I immediately got my driver's license. I still had birthday cake on my chin when my parents took the keys out of the jar where they had done a bad job of hiding them for six months and slid them across the table. I didn't have much in the way of maturity, but I now had wheels and knew there would be many adventures ahead.

My first car was a blue Volkswagen Beetle. It had a few miles on it and a dent on the back fender, but it fit me and there was room for my backpack in the rear seat. I had planned for at least a year to go hiking in the Sierra Mountains when I started driving. With a long weekend ahead and some gas money, I hit the road a few days later. At sixteen years and four days old, I took my newfound freedom out for a spin.

The sunroof was open, and the wind blew through my fire-engine red hair as I merged into traffic. It was just me, my backpack, and Crosby, Stills, Nash, and Young playing on the 8-track tape player (I am actually that old). It wasn't long before I was a little bored and noticed there was an 18-wheeler just ahead of me in the middle lane, pulling a huge cargo trailer. I wondered whether, if I pulled up within a few feet of the back bumper, the vortex of wind created behind the truck would be strong enough to suck me, my backpack, my Volkswagen, and my flaming red hair along. And you know what? It worked.

Looking back, I learned several important lessons that day. First, I figured out why sixteen-year-olds are virtually impossible to insure. I also learned something about the power of big moving objects. And, finally, I learned that experiencing all this power would require me to move a little closer. Grace can be like that. If we are willing to get close enough to it, everyone and everything we encounter will be drawn along in the vortex it creates.

**Take your most extravagant version of grace out on
the road for a spin today and see what it can do in
your life and in the lives of the ones nearby.**

GOD GOES BEYOND YOUR IMAGINATION

As it is written: "What no eye has seen, what no ear has heard, and what no human mind has conceived"—the things God has prepared for those who love him.
1 CORINTHIANS 2:9

Do you ever feel like you do not access your imagination as much as you once did? It's not that we don't know how to imagine any longer. We just imagine different things now than we used to. Maybe when you were young you imagined what it would be like to drive a car or pilot a spaceship or raft down the Amazon or live on an island and find your food in the jungles. Then you grew up, and maybe you started imagining a car that doesn't stall on the freeway or what it would be like to pay less in taxes or have fewer deductions taken out of your paychecks.

When did we start replacing whimsy with what adults like to call reason? I wonder if we started imagining less because we feared that God wouldn't be able to deliver on our dreams.

Maybe we learned to be reasonable with our expectations and hopes and more practical with our wants. Or perhaps we felt like if we imagined too much and asked God for it, it would make Him look bad if it didn't come together. The truth is, God can't look bad, because He is infinitely and always good. Go ahead and risk it.

Take Paul's word for it that no one has seen or heard or imagined all the good things God has for us when we love Him back. What would it look like for you to begin imagining beautiful things for you and for your family? When you think of deep and lasting and impactful experiences or times when you could go deeper in your relationships together, what comes to mind? Can you imagine being more generous with your resources or time or your availability? Imagine more and let God blow your doors off.

Let love, hope, and whimsy guide your steps today. Just imagine what might happen.

STOP PUTTING IN THE MICROWAVE WHAT NEEDS TO GO IN THE CROCK-POT

I was shown mercy so that in me, the worst of sinners, Christ
Jesus might display his immense patience as an example for
those who would believe in him and receive eternal life.
1 TIMOTHY 1:16

I am not a patient man. I guess the word *patience* was not on any pages in my word-a-day calendars I would quickly flip through growing up. Perhaps Paul had the same problem as I do. He said that God put on display His immense patience when it came to Paul's shortcomings. Paul described himself as being among the worst of sinners. I can't help but wonder if being impatient was one of the undisclosed problems Paul dealt with on a regular basis. Perhaps it was the thorn he referred to that he carried with him everywhere he went—in a hurry.

One of the ways I often find myself impatient is when I'm waiting for God to develop something in my life. I want to see the end results, but growth takes time. It takes twenty days to grow a radish, seven years to grow a pear, and fourteen years to grow an avocado. Life is the same way. The things God is growing in each of our lives will take time and more than a little patience to fully develop. So while I keep putting things in the microwave, God keeps taking them out and placing them in the Crock-Pot.

What is God doing in your life? Is He giving you new desires? Are there opportunities you have not had before? Who are the new people God has intersected in your life? Some will be fun and easy relationships, and others might be more challenging, difficult ones. For each of the observations you make, ask yourself if you need to exercise a little patience to let what is small and fragile grow into something strong and mighty.

Don't rush what God is doing. Quit planting sod where God has planted seed.

Slow down today and see what God is up to. He doesn't want you to be a radish; He's making guacamole in your life.

ANTICIPATE YOUR PURPOSE

"Six days you shall labor, but on the seventh day you shall rest;
even during the plowing season and harvest you must rest."
EXODUS 34:21

Shortly after I got my driver's license in high school, I bought a beat-up Volkswagen Beetle for a thousand bucks. It's fifty years later and I still drive one. There are many differences between then and now and more than a few similarities too.

One of the similarities is that my car gas tank in high school was always on empty. Gas only cost fifty-seven cents a gallon at the time, which sounds like a bargain, but most teenagers were only making just over two dollars an hour. I couldn't afford a full tank, so I would drizzle it in by the quart.

I had to guess about how much gas was in my car because the gas gauge didn't work but the math was pretty easy: no fuel plus not much fuel is still no fuel.

These days it's not the tank in our cars riding near empty, it's our energy for the many demands competing for our time and attention. Paul warned his friend Timothy about not engaging in disputes or courting controversies. This might sound strange coming from a former trial lawyer, but as the vitriol increases, my tank rapidly empties.

We all learn how to cope when we are running low on energy and resources. One of the obvious plays is to coast as much as possible. This works better in automobiles than in relationships. A more useful idea is to take a day to rest and recharge each week. Sure, it can be a Sunday, but you can rest on Tuesday if that works better for you.

Take a break from your vocation, from distraction and controversy. Even when it seems impossible, take a day of rest and fill your tank with the faith you need to go the distance.

Rest is holy; get some.

NOT ENOUGH ROOM FOR JOY? IT'S TIME TO RENEGOTIATE THE CONTRACT

"Come now, and let us reason together," says the LORD.
ISAIAH 1:18 NKJV

Whether we realize it or not, we make social agreements with others every day when we buy food, or get the car repaired, or drop our kids off at school, or attend classes ourselves. We assume we will be treated fairly or that we will be respected or protected. We agree to pay the price for the food or the estimate we receive from the mechanic. They give us the food or the car repair, and we give them an agreed-upon amount of money. The same holds true at a school. We drop our children off, and the school keeps them safe and provides an environment for learning and growing. At the university we may attend, we pay the tuition and, if we keep up our grades, they will give us a degree.

We don't just make agreements with others; we also make them with ourselves without giving them much thought. We decide how much work we are capable of doing, how deep our relationships will go, how vulnerable we will be, what we will tolerate before we become hurt or offended, and how long we will stay in that state. Some people don't allow themselves to laugh, and others don't allow themselves to cry. These are often merely reflections and manifestations of additional agreements we have made with ourselves.

Here's my question: What if we renegotiated a couple of those agreements that aren't working well for us or for the people around us? What if we replaced some old agreements we have lived by with a couple of new agreements based on how God said He wants us to live the most current version of our lives? It wouldn't be the first time someone made some modifications to a deal. Abraham negotiated with God in Genesis about saving two cities. Jacob did the same when he was insisting on a blessing while wrestling with an angel. Perhaps it's your turn.

Here's the thing. We can't cut a new deal until we understand the existing one.

**What agreements have you made with yourself, and
what would it take to renegotiate a couple of them?**

GOD PAYS TOP DOLLAR FOR YOUR MISTAKES—REDEEM THEM TODAY!

"I have swept away your offenses like a cloud, your sins like the
morning mist. Return to me, for I have redeemed you."
ISAIAH 44:22

When I was young, most soda pop was sold in bottles, not cans, and was bought at grocery stores and in vending machines. The bottles had *redeemable* embossed on the glass. While this word was not one I was familiar with, I did know if I brought the empty bottle back, I would get a nickel from the grocery store. I would collect those bottles and exchange them for a dollar when I had twenty empties.

Without knowing it, this simple activity taught me about the term *redemption* and the hidden value in something that seems empty and worthless. I understood then that my empty bottles were still worth something and, in the same way, I understand now that the pain in my life is redeemable.

Think about your biggest setback, your most embarrassing lapse in judgment, or a big mistake you made. The regret and empty feeling you have in your gut might fool you into thinking the big mess-up wasn't worth anything and only caused you and others pain and disappointment.

Here's the thing. Nothing is wasted, not your pain or mistakes or misjudgments. They are all worth something to God. In fact, when you look at the characters and heroes in the Bible, like Adam and Eve and Moses and David and Abraham and Sarah and Jacob and Saul and Noah and a long list of other familiar names, what they had in common is they all messed up, in sometimes huge ways.

Have you really messed something up? God can redeem the dumpster fire in your life and make it a place where other people can warm their hands. Our job is recognizing the pain point, taking it to Jesus, and inviting Him to make something more beautiful out of it.

What is it you can bring to God today to watch Him redeem it?

OBEY JESUS BY LOVING PEOPLE THE WAY HE DID

"As the Father has loved me, so have I loved you. Now remain in my
love. If you keep my commands, you will remain in my love, just as I
have kept my Father's commands and remain in his love. I have told you
this so that my joy may be in you and that your joy may be complete."
JOHN 15:9–11

It's easy to fall in love. Remaining in love takes a little more intentionality. It's not a butterflies-in-your-belly thing. John 15 says the way we remain in God's love is to obey Jesus' commandments, the same way He obeyed His Father's commandments. I know, not the most exciting-sounding strategy. But the idea is not to bust our chops or be a buzzkill or wreck our fun; in fact, it is just the opposite. God wants us to experience a more complete sense of joy than we otherwise could. And to get there, we need to be God's friend and obey Him.

Depending on your upbringing and both your faith expression and experience, the idea that the God of the universe would be a friend of yours might feel unfamiliar. Yet that's how Jesus described how He wants our relationship with Him to be. Again, it's not all butterflies and unicorns and shooting stars. Jesus said the way to be His friend isn't just to pal around; it's to obey what He said. Here's the rub. Most of the time I'm better at palling around than obeying. And yet, God is infinitely patient with us when we mess up. All He asks is that we continue to get back up and start operating again out of love and obedience.

Take a quick audit of the things you are involved in and see how closely you are obeying Him. Think about Jesus' command that we love one another like He loved us and ask yourself what would need to change in what you are doing, how you are doing it, or why you are doing it to reflect the kinds of outcomes Jesus said He is looking for.

We will become what we do with our love.

**If you want to be Jesus' friend, make your core
ambition to obey Jesus by loving people the way
He did, and obey Him while you are doing it.**

COME AS YOU ARE—HE CHOSE YOU FOR EVERYTHING YOU AREN'T

Think of what you were when you were called. Not
many of you were wise by human standards; not many
were influential; not many were of noble birth.

1 CORINTHIANS 1:26

There is a myth some of us buy into that we need to have it all together before we can come to God. We think we need to achieve some level of success or approval or be the smartest or most popular person in the room to belong. Paul wanted to sort that out with his friends in Corinth. He told them it was not about how smart or influential they were. It wasn't about their last name or how powerful they were perceived to be. It was actually the opposite of these things in God's economy.

God uses the things that don't make sense to many of the people we think of as smart, and things that powerful and popular people think are a waste of time. He takes the unlikely and impossible things and makes something out of them.

All of this isn't to prove how powerful God is; He's got nothing to prove. He does this so we wouldn't boast based on what we bring to the table. We might not be the smartest kid on the block, but He still uses us. Maybe our family name isn't one like Jobs or Rockefeller, yet what we bring can be even more impactful because we aren't big shots.

I am not the smartest lawyer or the best speaker or a skilled musician and I can't play the bagpipes (although I have got to say, I could rock the kilt), yet because I am not all these other things, I can be me with all the freedom and gratefulness that accompany this comparatively simple life. God did this so I could boast about Him rather than continually making soft brags about myself. Is the same true for you?

Instead of taking inventory of all the things God has given you today, make a list of all the things you are not.

OCTOBER

NOTHING IS TOO BIG FOR FORGIVENESS

For I am persuaded that neither death nor life, nor angels nor
principalities nor powers, nor things present nor things to come,
nor height nor depth, nor any other created thing, shall be able to
separate us from the love of God which is in Christ Jesus our Lord.
ROMANS 8:38–39 NKJV

Many years ago, I brought to trial a case in Uganda against a witch doctor named Kabi who attempted the human sacrifice of a little boy. We found a judge and a courtroom and tried the case over the course of a week. In the end, Kabi was sentenced and began his time on death row at a maximum-security prison, and I began visiting him in that prison. For years, I met with him and learned from him. It would be overstating it to call myself a friend of his, because I was responsible for landing him there, but we enjoyed seeing each other. Any visitor is better than no visitors, I guess. And during that time, his interest in faith grew. One day, Kabi wrote in the Bible I had with me: "Kabi is forgiven."

It's easy to think God can forgive some of our missteps, but what about the big ones, the death-penalty-sized ones? The good news is His forgiveness is even bigger than all the evil we can imagine.

Paul wanted his friends in the Roman church to know there was absolutely nothing that could stand between them and God. This is the power of forgiveness. Nothing we do in our life, nothing in our death, not our messed-up past or screwed-up future, not big stuff or small stuff could separate us from the love of God.

Maybe you have yourself in the doghouse over something you did and now regret. God's got you covered. You are His beloved. Perhaps you are fearful about your future. He's got you, and He isn't worried a bit about it. What if something in your life feels too small or petty or insignificant to bring to the God of the universe? *Bring it*, He says from heaven. *I've got that too.*

Kabi declared he was forgiven. Maybe that's what we need to do too.

**Call out what has you feeling captured and declare
some God-given freedom over it today.**

BEING HAPPY ISN'T JUST ABOUT THE HIGHLIGHTS

May the God of hope fill you with all joy and peace in believing,
that you may abound in hope by the power of the Holy Spirit.
ROMANS 15:13 NKJV

It seems like being happy is easy for some people and hard for others. Here's the thing. Happy doesn't happen by mistake. Have you ever stepped back from the frenetic pace of your life and decided to be more available to happiness?

We spend unreasonable amounts of time trying to arrange enough circumstances or vacation days or relationships in the direction of happiness. And for good reason. Who wouldn't want to wake up laughing and then spend most of the day doing more of it? But being happy is not just about the highlights. It's about pursuing things in your life that have meaning.

Happiness involves a lot of resolve, commitment, intentionality, and a willingness to sacrifice the very comfort that some people think will make them happy. Most of the people I know who are authentically happy have a mile of strategy underneath what other people can see about how to make themselves available to those things that will give meaning to their lives.

Where we get lost in the weeds sometimes is our approach to happiness. Some dismiss happiness as idle and misdirected wistfulness and hardly worth the effort. Still others immediately dispose of the idea as a shallow and hedonistic waste of time. But I think true happiness is knowing the things you are spending your time on are things that mean something and are lasting.

If you aren't experiencing and making yourself consistently available to happiness, it might be worth taking a deep dive into figuring out why. Did you grow up in a home where smiles were frowned upon? Or did you grow up in a buttoned-down religious tradition where being happy was trivialized?

**Identify what would need to change in your life for
you to take a bold step toward happiness. It's waiting
for you with a fist full of helium balloons.**

SOMETIMES WE HAVE TO GET PAST SOME CRAZY TO GET TO GOD

Fear of man will prove to be a snare, but whoever
trusts in the LORD is kept safe.

PROVERBS 29:25

How many times have you heard the phrase, "I'm spiritual, but I'm not religious"? We all hear it a lot, and I get it. People who are part of organized religions and appoint themselves as God's spokespeople sometimes lack the skills needed to navigate even the easiest of topics and crowds. It is not lost on me that the people who want to be Jesus' lawyer are often the ones who could not advocate their way out of a relational paper bag.

I wonder if repeated encounters with these types could be a legitimate reason why so many people have been keeping a distance from Jesus or just nibbling around the edges of faith. "I'm spiritual but not religious" may be translated more accurately like this: "I like Jesus a lot, but the crazy people who are so difficult to get along with in church, you can keep them."

I am not critical of you if you see the big flaws people like me have and want a little space between us, but don't let the shortcomings of anyone keep you from Jesus. He is good when we aren't. He is humble, even though we are not. He is patient when we are too tightly wound, and He is leaning in toward us even when we are leaning back. In short, if we make it about us, we're sunk, but if we keep trusting in God, we'll be safe.

Don't settle for putting your toe in the water of faith. If grabbing your knees and doing a cannonball in the direction of faith feels like too big a leap, find a couple of safe people to draw close to and get real with about your faith questions.

**Don't miss out on the gift God has for
you hidden underneath people who are
sometimes like crumpled wrapping paper.**

WHEN THERE'S TOO MUCH GOOD, ADD ANOTHER RUNWAY

"Select from among you seven men of good reputation, full of the Spirit and of wisdom, whom we may put in charge of this task. But we will devote ourselves to prayer and to the ministry of the word."

ACTS 6:3-4 NASB

We have an airport in San Diego that is notable for two reasons. First, the angle of landing is very steep, and landing there can feel like being a dive bomber who is aiming for a small target directly below. Second, there is only one runway at the airport, which is unusual for a major United States city. This has made San Diego the busiest single-runway airport in the world.

We can feel like we are the second busiest airport in the world sometimes with the number of things that require our daily attention and need to land in our lives. Here's the thing: We can't land all the airplanes in our lives on the same runway, and certainly not at the same time. They make bad movies from that kind of storyline. Instead, we might need to build a parallel runway to accommodate a couple more planes.

Do the same with the many ambitions you are trying to land right now. Find an assistant, create a second new path for people to connect to you, or outsource or delegate a project or two. These all create new landing lanes. So does taking a vacation, jumping off social media, or not watching the news.

My friend Mark says that he always has "an heir and a spare" for his business. It is his way of saying he is building parallel runways in his life so that he can pursue things of importance to him and raise up a replacement for himself.

You are air traffic control for your busy life. How can you start creating new landing lanes today? And if you can't do that quite yet, what idea can you land today, and which other ones can you let circle the field for a little longer?

Do what the young church in Acts did and select a few people of good reputation, full of the Spirit and of wisdom, and get them on your team.

LOVE IS A GIFT, NOT A BUSINESS

So he made a whip out of cords, and drove all from the
temple courts, both sheep and cattle; he scattered the coins
of the money changers and overturned their tables.
JOHN 2:15

Picture the setting: Jesus had just done His first miracle at a wedding in Cana. From there, He and His friends walked to Capernaum. This was not a short distance and would have taken at least a day if they were hoofing it. A few days later, they headed for the temple in Jerusalem. This also was not a short distance; it's about a two-hour drive on the highway (think of walking from Tijuana, Mexico, to Disneyland, near Los Angeles). I would be beat and a little on edge after all that moving around on foot.

The Scriptures say Jesus arrived at the temple and started flipping over the tables. I didn't go to church growing up and hadn't heard all the stories, so when I read this for the first time, I wondered if it was a front flip or a back flip. When I read a little closer, I could tell that Jesus was upset and wanted to make a big deal about something. What was His point? Jesus lived His life as He did because He wanted to make disciples; in the temple courts, they just wanted to do commerce. They had cheapened what was meant to be about relationship and reverence and eternity and made it into something selfish and transactional and temporary.

Things like relationships—whether they're with God or with one another—should never be transactional. And yet too often they are. If we're honest with ourselves, a lot of the time we give love to get love. We pay attention so that people will pay attention to us. And we give away kindness in the expectation of receiving it back. If you eliminated the transactional nature of your relationships with your friends and also with God, how would your life and your faith look different?

Let's stop approaching our relationships as transactions. Show up today in anticipation and expectation of what you can bring to—and not what you can get out of—your relationship with God and the people He places in your path. Live that way today and Jesus will flip—in all the best ways.

**Don't have anything on the other side of the equals
sign in your relationships—just Jesus.**

OCTOBER 6

THANKFULNESS TURNS
SETBACKS INTO BLESSINGS

*Just as you received Christ Jesus as Lord, continue to live your
lives in him, rooted and built up in him, strengthened in the faith
as you were taught, and overflowing with thankfulness.*
COLOSSIANS 2:6–7

My father-in-law had an old wooden wagon he loved. Shortly after we got married, Sweet Maria and I brought the wagon to our house so we could restore it to mint condition. We bought the sandpaper and paint and nuts and bolts and the tools we needed and started in on the immense reconstruction project. We were so excited about the fact that we were starting. The next day, there was a storm, and a hundred-foot tree fell on the wagon. We had plenty of firewood that winter, about one hundred feet of tree and one priceless wagon's worth.

It's easy to start things. What takes a little more work is continuing with them. Unanticipated setbacks happen, and large and small failures dot the landscape of our ambitions. Trees fall on our dreams, and disappointments of every variety test our resolve. How we continue despite the resistance we encounter shapes the legacy we leave. Too often, though, something goes wrong, and we are tempted to bail on our longstanding desires by saying, "God closed a door" or "It wasn't meant to be." But what if the door God is opening is simply a different one than the one we were standing in front of? What if what God meant to happen through our circumstances is a deeper dependence on Him?

No matter your circumstance, continue to live your lives rooted and built up in Jesus, overflowing with thankfulness. Embrace the opportunities that come your way, and be curious about what God might be doing through them. Sure, you will have disappointments, but let them steel your resolve rather than off-ramp your passions.

**Don't let today's challenges break you and don't live in fear
that a tree might fall on you. Live a life so full of love and
whimsy people will think you are made of the stuff.**

LET LOVE CHANGE YOUR MIND

Do not allow this world to mold you in its own image. Instead,
be transformed *from the inside out* by renewing your mind.
ROMANS 12:2 VOICE

An inference is something someone thinks is true, whether it is or not. We draw inferences all the time by gathering information. If someone squints, we might infer there is a bright light near them. If someone is smiling, we infer they are happy. If we didn't get invited to a party, we might infer that we are not loved or that we aren't one of the cool kids. We try to make sense of thousands of events in our lives by reaching back to what we have experienced and extrapolating what the current inputs mean. It's a little like the board game Clue. After a lot of investigation, you make a guess based on everything you know or can infer and you shout out, "It was the butler in the dining room with a candlestick!"

What we infer about our lives, how we understand the various events that occur, has a lot to do with the quality of life we perceive we have. And it leads directly into who we decide we are, whether we think we are blessed or unlucky, beloved or rejected, known or forgotten. In the same way, who we believe Jesus is also comes from what we have inferred based on our own experiences. So, if you see your experiences as having been full of acceptance and grace, for example, you might conclude that Jesus is full of acceptance and grace. If you encountered people of faith who were mean or manipulative, you might infer that Jesus is unkind and not to be trusted.

But if we want to follow Scripture's call to be transformed by the renewing of our minds, we'll have to do something different. We'll have to shake up all the inferences we have drawn like a snow globe so that, when everything settles to the bottom, we can see Jesus for who He promised He is rather than how we have concluded He is from our experiences.

**Take a hard and honest look at how and why you see
God the way you do and remind yourself of the truth
that you are His cherished son or daughter.**

DON'T GET SWEPT AWAY BY ANYTHING OTHER THAN GOD'S PURPOSE FOR YOU

We demolish arguments and every pretension that sets
itself up against the knowledge of God, and we take
captive every thought to make it obedient to Christ.
2 CORINTHIANS 10:5

If you have ever stood knee-deep in the ocean, you know that when the water rushes out, the sand under your feet gets stripped away. If you aren't ready for it, the missing sand underfoot can cause you to tip over. In the same way, holding your ground can be hard, no matter where you are. It takes a strong stance and an even stronger motivation to stay upright. If your stance isn't strong or your motivation isn't immense, sooner or later you will yield to the shifts happening around and beneath you.

There is a broad range of issues out there today that are each, no doubt, important and worth spending some time on. We need to be clear about which ones we feel personally called to adopt and embrace. Doing this will require that we have our footing in solid places.

It is easy to adopt someone else's number one cause and make it your number one cause, even when it isn't. Like you, I care about many things, but none of us have the capacity to care about everything with the same level of intensity. Yet our minds are tricky things and can lead us astray. Paul told his friends in Corinth that we are to take our thoughts captive. Doing that means that we don't get swept along with the momentum of other people's zeal. Certainly, take a genuine interest in what your friends are interested in, but don't bend to the subtle expectation that you need to be as animated as they are about the issue they are most passionate about, thinking this is what makes you a good friend. You can't manufacture passion or calling; you have to walk your own path.

Pick three or four issues or causes that you feel personally moved by. Figure out what your next courageous steps will be to move the needle on those things in tangible ways.

LEAVE A LEGACY OF LOVE

One generation commends your works to another; they tell of
your mighty acts. They speak of the glorious splendor of your
majesty—and I will meditate on your wonderful works.
PSALM 145:4–7

We all have a limited period of time here on earth. When yours is coming to a close, what will you leave behind?

Have you ever noticed how some candles have a better smell when they are extinguished than when they are lit? In the same way, our legacy will be the aroma of Christ we leave in the world after we cross through heaven's veil. The most important things we hand down to the generations to come won't be cash; they will be how and who we loved.

Countless selfish, selfless, and unnoticed choices combine to create our legacy. Minimize your selfish choices. Don't settle for passing along a 401k or an old car or a painting or an heirloom. Pass along character, compassion, tenacity, and curiosity. Your life well lived will give context for the next generation to live an even more meaningful one.

Let's get practical. Make a couple of videos today for the ones you love, or start writing a book about your experiences and what you've learned along the way. Interview people on the family tree and get their unique angle on what it means to be part of your family.

Hide messages of hope and encouragement everywhere in your house. Put them in cracks in the walls and in crackerjack boxes in the pantry. And, more important than all of this, leave behind a legacy of love and faith and Jesus.

Be part of the generation that commends God's works to another and tells them about God's mighty acts. Don't wait another day to start leaving the evidence everywhere.

DON'T BUY INTO FEAR—THE GRACE OF GOD IS ENOUGH

[Jesus] replied, "You of little faith, why are you so afraid?" Then he got up and rebuked the winds and the waves, and it was completely calm.
MATTHEW 8:26

Remember the television show *Fear Factor*, where people confronted a few of their deepest fears? The show was canceled, but our fears don't get resolved as easily. We all have fears. What distinguishes us from each other is how we deal with our fears. Some people try to ignore them. This strategy might appear to be working in the short term, when what is actually happening is a boatload of deferral. Our unaddressed fears compound interest and grow in size and in the power they have over us.

Another approach is to confront our fears in small increments—not unlike inching our way into a cold lake by slowly shuffling our feet forward. Feet, ankles, and after a long period of time we might make it up to our knees. Progress is slow and unsatisfying. But the healthiest way to deal with our fears isn't to grab our knees and do a cannonball in an attempt to beat them back, it is to understand them.

Plenty of times Jesus asked people who had good reason to be fearful the reason why. He asked a couple of the men in a sinking boat, "Why are you so afraid?" A seemingly unreasonable question to a boat full of guys who perhaps knew they could not swim to shore. There was no mention of life jackets, life rings, and rescue boats. These seem like questions with obvious answers, but only until you consider the circumstance more deeply and understand that there was much more going on under the surface than in the boat.

God doesn't ask us to ignore or dismiss our fears but instead to understand them. When we figure out what our fears are attached to, we can ask God for the kind of supernatural help we need to overcome them.

Jesus doesn't force Himself or His ideas on anyone, not on me or on you or on others, even though we are all desperately in need of His involvement in our lives. Instead, He puts the ball in our court. He asks us the unexpected questions and then waits for us to acknowledge our true needs and receive what He offers: love, acceptance, and a relationship with Him.

Sometimes God will lead us into difficult situations where our fears are triggered. His hope is that we will realize our desperate need for Him.

We play the victim or the hero rather than accepting the participation He is offering us. Here's the solution. Stop aiming for fair; aim for Jesus. Let Him know you want to be well and get ready to be healed.

Now it's your call. "Why are you afraid?" God isn't confused about what the real answer is. He knows more about us than we do. He wants us to get our minds around our desperate need for Him and leave our fears in the dust, right at the feet of Jesus.

What fears do you have that you can bring to Jesus today?

SAVE YOUR BREATH

Avoid foolish controversies and genealogies and arguments and
quarrels about the law, because these are unprofitable and useless.
TITUS 3:9

I get some puzzling calls from people. I wrote a book about pursuing ambitions once and described how we need to go about finding a new habit as carving a new groove in our brains and then "going Grand Canyon on it." Someone called me, saying they thought this was evidence of what they called "an evolutionary worldview." Huh? I'm not even sure what that means. This phrase isn't evidence of an "evolutionary worldview"; it is evidence of the use of an idiom and somehow this person wanted to insert Darwin into the mix.

God used idioms all the time in the Scriptures. An idiom is simply a phrase or an expression that typically attaches a figurative, nonliteral image to a meaning. For instance, Exodus 3:8 describes a land "flowing with milk and honey." This is no more an evolutionary worldview than it is a dairy or sweetener worldview. It just means the ground there was fertile. Similarly, a term in the Scriptures like "their hearts melted," which you'll find in Deuteronomy 20, doesn't mean there was new science, new anatomy, or a new organ function or failure; it just means they were scared.

Here's my point. Some Christians can come across as myopic and critical and unnecessarily angsty about a whole range of things without realizing it. They pick at what others say and do in an effort to defend God from human imperfection. Stated differently, they pick dumb fights. When I find myself doing this, which is more often than I'd like to admit, I try to remind myself that God will use my big love expressed to others way more than my small, piercing opinions.

Let's avoid foolish controversies and arguments and quarrels because, as the book of Titus says, they are useless. If we think we need to defend God, let's do it with gentleness and respect. One without the other is just more noise.

**If you want to pick a fight, fight to see evidence of
more love, joy, and whimsy in your life today.**

DON'T ABANDON YOUR PURPOSE JUST BECAUSE YOU DON'T UNDERSTAND IT YET

The LORD will fulfill his purpose for me; your steadfast love, O LORD, endures forever. Do not forsake the work of your hands.

PSALM 138:8 ESV

Jesus said lots of things the disciples who were with Him didn't understand. There was confusion over Jesus' purpose, His friends, His miracles, His power, His Father, and what He said would happen next. Even after years of following Him, Jesus' disciples didn't fully understand who He was. They were confused about why He came as a baby and died like a criminal and why He didn't call down a million angels from heaven to save Him from being crucified. The truth is, we are all bound to be misunderstood at some point in our lives.

You might be a great communicator or a brilliant businessperson or the kindest person ever, yet there will be times when people don't understand you. It is what we do on the outside when this kind of predictable disconnection happens that tells the world about who we are on the inside. Jesus could have given in to the subtle pressure to change His plan and be the conquering king His disciples were expecting, but He didn't. He knew why He was here and what He was to do, and He wasn't going to let other people's misunderstanding of His purpose derail or distract Him from that focus.

You are going to be misunderstood. It probably happened yesterday, just happened today, and will happen tomorrow. Don't let the noise distract you from your purpose. God has given you a special gift to release into the world during your one brief time here. Trust that what isn't clear right now to the people around you might be made clear later. And if it's not, in a word, *tough*. We are not trying to build consensus around our ideas; we are here to participate in Jesus' kingdom, and this will leave more than a few people scratching their heads.

Stay the course. Let the Lord fulfill His purpose in you. Be willing to be misunderstood. God is doing bigger things than we can sometimes understand.

FIGURE OUT YOUR PASSION AND WATCH THE PIECES COME TOGETHER

For we are God's handiwork, created in Christ Jesus to do
good works, which God prepared in advance for us to do.
EPHESIANS 2:10

I don't put a lot of jigsaw puzzles together. It's an activity that lacks some of the thrill of ice blocking or axe throwing. But sometimes life itself feels like a huge jigsaw puzzle, doesn't it? Except it doesn't come with a picture on the box of what it is supposed to look like when we complete it. So we just assemble it as best we can.

Complicating things further, the unexplored and unanticipated circumstances in our lives can conspire together in ways that make it seem like all the puzzle pieces have been flipped over face down, eliminating all clues for how to solve life's puzzling encounters.

Sometimes we need to flip the pieces back over a few at a time, so we can see what we're working with, arrange similar pieces together, or even just spin a couple of puzzle pieces around to find the perfect fit.

Remember, life isn't speed chess, so don't be in a hurry to get clarity on everything all at once. The God who began good and beautiful things in your life will finish what He started. He will spin the pieces He needs to in your life to get the job done.

**What have you been trying to rush through
when you might just need to slow things
down and spin things around?**

GOOD FRIENDSHIPS CAN BE OUR REFERENCE POINTS IN THE DESERT OF LIFE

No, dear brothers and sisters, I have not achieved it, but I focus on this one thing: Forgetting the past and looking forward to what lies ahead.
PHILIPPIANS 3:13 NLT

I once set out across the Gobi Desert in Mongolia to find a small city where we were going to start a school. The Gobi Desert is a huge place and an extremely harsh environment. It is one thousand miles long and seven hundred miles wide. The temperatures range from 40 below zero to 113 above, which is a big swing you don't want to get caught in unprepared. There are few roads and no reference points, so it's easy to get off track as you are going across the sand for hours and hours. In fact, people who get lost in the Gobi are known to walk in circles either to the left or to the right, depending on which of their legs is longer.

The same happens in our lives. We get disoriented. We stray off course from the beautiful life we had imagined for ourselves. Without a reference point we can aim for, we eventually find ourselves going in circles rather than making progress. We need to find a reference point for where we are trying to go and head in that direction every day.

Find a couple of people who are intent on living amazing and engaged lives in every area, including their faith, their family, their ambitions, and their relationships. They will be fixed points you can triangulate from to find more beauty in your own life. If you want to see more waterfalls, find other people who are looking for them too. If you want to experience more joy, find a few happy and optimistic people. They may be making balloon animals or serving the poor. And if you want to go deeper in your faith, find a couple of people who are going deeper in theirs as well. Forget everything from the past that has stood between you and what will prove to be lasting in your life and fix your eyes on Jesus and what lies ahead.

Who is someone you can reach out to today who can be a fixed point and will help you take aim at the beautiful life you're looking for?

TAKE THE REINS FROM YOUR INSECURITIES AND HAND THEM OVER TO GRACE

You are a slave to whatever controls you.
2 PETER 2:19 NLT

We are all insecure and, because we are, we sometimes do lame things, even self-destructive things, to medicate these insecurities. I have a friend who is weirdly competitive. He'll post a boatload of photos and videos of things like his big house or him getting out of a helicopter. It's like he's trying to say, "I'm successful and important and am able to buy lots of stuff."

Others will post pictures of themselves at a bus stop in a conscious or unconscious attempt to show off their virtue of thriftiness. Others will make fun of people who have a sincere faith and, with an air of superiority, will tell everyone who will listen why they have it wrong.

Paul warned his friends that they were slaves to whatever controlled them. This is no less true for us. When we get hung up on projecting a certain image to feel better about ourselves or to get validation from others, we will become trapped by that image, always needing to find new green wood to burn on top. But doing this doesn't generate heat in your life, just smoke. Here's the good news: while insecurity wants us to keep track of our successes and failures, grace doesn't even write them down.

Don't let creating a perception of who you appear to be rob you of who you are. The applause is going to fade quickly, as will the accolades, and in the end, we are not the sum of our successes or our failures. We are God's kids.

Take inventory today of the things you are doing and ask yourself if it's the real version of you showing up or the curated version. And if it's the curated version of you, lay out a plan to be more authentic with God and the people around you.

**God loves you where you are and how you are.
Don't swap out the unique gift He created in
you for a version of you He never intended.**

TAKE MORE INTEREST IN WHAT YOUR LIFE MEANS THAN WHAT IT LOOKS LIKE

Humble yourselves before the Lord, and he will lift you up.
JAMES 4:10

It strikes me as a little ironic that the people who talk the most about bullies and victims are often relational bullies themselves. They are the ones who want you to believe they are above it all while they take cheap shots at the very people who have loved them with tremendous patience and kindness through their many foibles and peccadillos.

The biggest narcissist in the room will often be the one spending a weird amount of time talking about how to spot a narcissist. An attribute that gives these people away every time is that they will act like professors of things they have not been students of in their personal lives. I'm not sure why this juxtaposition occurs, and I don't have time to go back to school to learn. Perhaps they reckon if they claim the moral high ground, it will cover their tracks in the lowlands where they have been doing the very thing they are quick to opine about.

What is equally interesting, and notable, is people who are successful usually don't try to look or act like it. They don't care what their life looks like to everyone else, because they know what it means to them. They don't talk about how much money or influence they have, and they don't name-drop. They don't bring up that their business revenue has doubled or quadrupled.

It's not a false humility driving this, because what led to their success is usually a humble and confident heart. They see themselves as caretakers of what they have for the benefit of others and invite everyone in without distinction.

Identify an area in your life where you could be a little more discreet in how you describe what you have accomplished or have access to. Cultivate the kind of humility that sees yourself as a caretaker and not as a star. Do this well and people will see more of Jesus and less of you.

RECONNECT WITH YOUR AUTHENTIC SELF SO GOD CAN RECONNECT YOU TO YOUR DREAMS

Rid yourselves of all malice and all deceit, hypocrisy, envy, and slander of every kind. Like newborn babies, crave pure spiritual milk, so that by it you may grow up in your salvation.

1 PETER 2:1–2

I don't know many people who set out to fake it, but we often present ourselves to others as the person everyone expects us to be, rather than who we really are. I am a pretty upbeat guy, and people expect me to be that person when I show up. But the truth is I am also deeply introspective and can get sad and lonely too. When I show up projecting one thing just to meet people's expectations but am feeling much different, it can be disorienting. We would be wise to learn how to connect all the different versions of ourselves to who we really are.

This is what the apostle Peter was getting at when he said to off-load many of the things that make us fake or hypocritical and go for the pure and real stuff. When you feel tempted to act like someone you are not, take a moment and remind yourself that Jesus always delights in connecting the divergent parts of us back together.

It's not just God who can put us back together; we have coagency with Him to help others join the parts of their lives that are authentic and erratic. Sometimes doing this means helping them connect the best parts of their lives with the neediest parts of their story to God, who can handle all the versions of us and has promised to relentlessly pursue us all. Still, the best way for us to prepare to help others is to first do this important work within ourselves. The reason is simple. We can't tell people how to get there if we haven't summoned the courage to get there ourselves.

What in your life have you become separated from? It might be your faith or your courage or your authenticity.

**Today, ask a trustworthy friend who knows you
well to speak some truth into your life.**

WHEN YOU FEEL LIKE YOU'VE BEEN LEFT OUT IN THE COLD, GOD WILL HELP YOU BUILD AN IGLOO

"I am the Lord your God who takes hold of your right
hand and says to you, Do not fear; I will help you."
ISAIAH 41:13

Sweet Maria usually doesn't come with me to speaking events, but every once in a while she will. One time when she came with me, we checked into a hotel room that felt bigger than our own house and seemed really fancy. It was on one of the top floors of a building with views of the harbor below and the skyscrapers downtown in the distance. But, while the views were stunning, the room was freezing. They could have hung beef from the ceiling, made ice carvings, or laid Walt Disney down for his cryogenic rest in this room. We scanned the walls for a thermostat or an ice axe or an ice-cream scooper but were unsuccessful. So we called down to the desk, kind of laughing through our chattering teeth.

A nice guy came up to fix whatever was wrong, but he didn't have any luck. He came back several times, each time with another layer of clothing on, but he struck out over and over. The hotel was very apologetic but said they didn't have any other rooms to move us to. This felt like it had turned into an adventure, kind of like an unplanned trip to Antarctica where all we had on were shorts and a T-shirt. We needed to improvise.

The easiest strategy we came up with was to spend as little time as possible in our room, but at some point we would need to sleep. In desperation, we found a couple of hair dryers, made a tent in the bed, and put the hair dryers under the covers. We put the looping video of a crackling fire on the television, made lots of hot tea, and made do the best we could.

God promises that He will help us in every circumstance. But He isn't the fix-it guy trying to make our lives more comfortable; He wants them to be filled with more meaning. Let God take hold of your hand and help you.

**What steps can you take to find greater purpose in
what you are experiencing? What actions can you
take while you trust God with the outcomes?**

YOU CAN'T FAKE REAL POWER

Some Jews who went around driving out evil spirits tried to invoke the
name of the Lord Jesus over those who were demon-possessed. . . .
One day the evil spirit answered them, "Jesus I know, and Paul I
know about, but who are you?" Then the man who had the evil spirit
jumped on them and overpowered them all. He gave them such
a beating that they ran out of the house naked and bleeding.
ACTS 19:13, 15–16

In Uganda, we have operated witch doctor schools for years. We don't teach
people how to become witch doctors—they already know that. Instead, we
teach them how to read and write. We also meet with them and let them know
that if they are engaged in child sacrifice, we will take them to trial and they
will never be seen again. Sometimes I will bring one of the High Court justices
with me, just to drive the point home.

Several of the leaders in the witch doctor community have brought me gifts,
which sometimes freak me out a little. One time I was given a "magic walking
stick." I put it in the bathroom where I was staying and shoved a couple of towels
under the door, not certain what the stick might turn into overnight (I hate snakes).

At the end of our time together, we also give the witch doctors medals and
tell them that every day they have the opportunity to trade the apparent power
they have from everyone being afraid of them for real power. I tell them the
story of the seven sons of Sceva and how they attempted to do amazing things
by throwing around Jesus' name but, because they didn't really know Jesus,
ended up running away naked and bleeding after a possessed guy beat them
up. As I hang the Sceva medals around their necks, I tell them the medal has
no power and the witchcraft they use to manipulate people has no power either,
but Jesus has plenty of power if they will place Him first.

You and I aren't witch doctors trying to scare people, but sometimes titles
and positions and influence can give us the appearance of having power, but
when tested, that power can't offer lasting protection.

**Be honest with yourself. Are you using Jesus' name a lot but not tapping
into the power and protection that comes from actually knowing Him?**

GO AGAINST THE FLOW AND FIND OUT HOW FANTASTIC IT IS

Trust in the LORD with all your heart and lean not on
your own understanding; in all your ways submit to
him, and he will make your paths straight. Do not be
wise in your own eyes; fear the LORD and shun evil.
PROVERBS 3:5-7

Each of us is constantly deciding what we will do next. We decide where we'll
live, if we'll marry and who we'll marry, the job we'll take and the one we'll
quit, the car we'll buy or the bus we'll take. We decide between the cake or the
veggies (go with the cake for the win), who we will believe and who we won't,
the drive we'll take, where we'll go, and how long we'll stay.

We will make countless decisions today. Many of those choices will be
inconsequential, but others will have a lasting impact.

Perhaps the most consequential choice we could make is to choose whether
we are going to be different and follow God or go with the flow and blend in
with everyone else.

If we take the less traveled path of following God, it's not going to be a
cakewalk. It will involve pain and loss and constant sacrifice. It will also lead
to a more lasting happiness as we look further than today and keep our eyes on
the greater purpose we are choosing when we declare that we're going to serve
God and not just ourselves.

What would it look like for you to choose to serve God today? Who would
you engage with that you have been avoiding? What would you confront that
you have been ignoring?

**Declaring you are going to serve the Lord is one thing;
today is your opportunity to take it out on the road
and see what your faith will do in the world.**

KINDNESS AND LOVE WILL ALWAYS BE THE RIGHT OUTFIT

As God's chosen people, holy and dearly loved, clothe yourselves with compassion, kindness, humility, gentleness and patience.
COLOSSIANS 3:12

I heard Mark Cuban once said, "When I die, I want to come back as me." I don't know if this is a good or bad idea for him, but I don't think I would want to come back as me all over again. I didn't come to this conclusion because my nose is a little crooked, or because I have bushy eyebrows, or because my hair started turning gray in the fourth grade (it did).

I just think I would want to come back a much humbler version of myself. One that has greater empathy, is not as easily offended, and loves people who are a little prickly as if they were made in the image of God.

Jesus promised before He left that He would be coming back some day, but I haven't read anywhere that we get to do the same. Do the world a favor, and return right now as a newer, humbler version of yourself before you leave. We get to decide to do this every morning if we want to.

Paul wrote about this in his letter to the young church in the book of Colossians. He said to think of our faith like putting on clothes. He wasn't referring to socks, blue jeans, and plaid shirts. He wanted us to clothe ourselves with compassion, kindness, humility, gentleness, and patience.

It's one thing to agree there is such a thing as clothing and quite another to actually put clothes on. I promise everyone around you will notice, even if you don't, whether you put on these clothes.

What would it look like for you to clothe yourself today with the characteristics Paul talked about? How would you show up differently to your meetings and conversations and for your family and friends? It's time to suit up.

Put on your best, kindest, most joyful and authentic clothes. Don't worry about the wrinkles; they are evidence of plenty of hugs.

INVITE GOD INTO THE MESSIEST PARTS OF YOUR LIFE—HE WILL SHOW UP

When Jesus came down from the mountainside, large crowds
followed him. A man with leprosy came and knelt before him and
said, "Lord, if you are willing, you can make me clean." Jesus
reached out his hand and touched the man. "I am willing," he
said. "Be clean!" Immediately he was cleansed of his leprosy.

MATTHEW 8:1–3

There are a lot of scriptures about things that were considered "clean" and things that were considered "unclean." If you flip though the book of Leviticus, you will find an ark-load of rules about this. One of the things that made you unclean in those days was the disease of leprosy. If you were found to be a leper, you were considered unclean, the other people who had been close to you were also thought to be unclean, and holy people were supposed to avoid you. Can you imagine the surprise everyone felt when a leper came to Jesus, and Jesus touched him? *Wait. What?* they must have thought. Jesus, God in flesh, the holiest person ever to walk the earth, doing something that would be considered by every person in the culture as being unclean.

Jesus could have healed the leper from across the street and down the hill, yet Jesus didn't call it in. He had an answer for the question the leper asked about His willingness to heal, and it was this: "I am willing." Jesus is willing to enter our pain and our shame, our setbacks and letdowns, our confusion and chaos, if we will invite Him into these complicated areas of our lives.

What have you been avoiding in your life? Maybe it is a person. They don't have a disease and probably aren't considered by others as "unclean," but perhaps they are uncool, difficult, or argumentative. Maybe it is a situation in your past or present you haven't dealt with. Whatever your context, Jesus is willing. He doesn't call it in; He comes.

**We just need to find the faith today for a big ask
wrapped in a simple prayer like the leper did: "Lord,
if You are willing, You can make me clean."**

MERCY AND COMPASSION ARE NOT OPTIONAL

This is what the LORD Almighty said: "Administer true
justice; show mercy and compassion to one another."
ZECHARIAH 7:9

In some of our faith communities, there is a culture that has been either cultivated or tolerated where being curt or dismissive of people is considered by some as justified or noble or helpful. What anyone in another context would see as mean or rude or dismissive is somehow seen as virtuous or evidence of a highly informed and progressive faith. Just read some of the mean things people will write about others online while their friends cheer them on. I am not sure how we did it but having something snarky to say in some circles has been elevated as a sign of enlightenment rather than an embarrassment.

I remember reading a pamphlet in college entitled *My Heart, Christ's Home*. It is about Jesus coming to the home of our hearts and talking with us about what His hopes are for our faith as He goes from room to room.

The conversations move from the dining room to the living room to the kitchen and even to the closets. There is eventually one room that the person does not want to let Jesus in to, because it is so embarrassing to have it in the house. And yet Jesus enters, and He does it with gentleness and respect, not judgment and harsh words.

What would happen if we did the same and made a point to speak of each other well, especially where we're most tender? What if we were as understanding and compassionate as Jesus was toward the people who didn't understand who He really was?

Sure, there are going to be difficult people who make it hard to be compassionate, and people who are just plain wrong in what they believe is right, but "show mercy and compassion to one another" isn't qualified with "unless you disagree."

What can you do today in your conversations and in your online posts with people you disagree with to bring the angst down a notch?

OUR MISTAKES HIGHLIGHT OUR NEED FOR GOD

This same God who takes care of me will supply all your needs from
his glorious riches, which have been given to us in Christ Jesus.
PHILIPPIANS 4:19 NLT

I was invited to speak at an event on the other side of the country and was
running late getting out of the house. I glanced quickly at the description of the
event and figured it was a gathering of some pastors or youth workers or young,
ambitious entrepreneurs, which are all groups I love to speak to. I put on a pair
of torn blue jeans and a collared shirt and headed to the airport. At these kinds
of events, dressing comfortably is what people do, so I knew I would blend in
and they wouldn't mind if I dressed down. My clothes weren't dirty, but they
were certainly well broken in.

Five hours later, I stepped off the plane and ran to catch a ride to the venue.
I knew I was cutting it close but was confident I would make it. Plus, the youth
workers I assumed were there would understand if I was a little late. When I
got to the hotel where the meeting was happening, it was immediately evident
I was wildly underdressed for the event.

I didn't see any youth workers, only older people wearing nice clothes.
I think I saw a guy sporting an ascot like Thurston Howell, and there I was
looking like the gardener. It turns out, it wasn't a group of business hipsters or
young pastors; it was a gathering of billionaires who were doing a great deal of
good in the world.

We all make mistakes at one point or another. But God promised that
He would take care of our needs if we would depend on Him. Our mess-ups,
big and small, are all just reminders of our absolute need for Him. We don't
have to be anxious about getting things right all the time, or about presenting
ourselves the way other people might expect us to. God wants us to come to
Him just as we are, not as we wish we were. He will supply all our needs from
His glorious riches.

**What recent mistake have you made that
highlighted your need for God's help?**

SOMETIMES WE NEED TO SLOW DOWN TO LOVE WELL

Martha was distracted by all the preparations that had to be made. She came to [Jesus] and asked, "Lord, don't you care that my sister has left me to do the work by myself? Tell her to help me!" "Martha, Martha," the Lord answered, "you are worried and upset about many things, but few things are needed—or indeed only one. Mary has chosen what is better, and it will not be taken away from her."

LUKE 10:40-42

I threw my leg over my motorcycle as I reached for my helmet and quickly slipped it over my head. I put the visor down and headed out for a drive. Not much later, I was on the highway when a huge spider began crawling down my forehead, over my glasses, and down my cheek. I screamed, fogged up the visor, and hit the gas. I'm not sure why. What I should have done was find a wide spot in the road, slow down and pull over, and then work on getting the spider out of my helmet, but I did the opposite.

We all react differently to stress. Some of us freeze up, and others go faster. But whatever we tend to do when we have unresolved issues, we often end up looking like a crazy person who is thrashing around after walking through a spiderweb, while no one knows what is happening.

Martha was distracted by everything happening around Jesus and, like me, sped up. Her go-to was to hit the gas. Mary hit the brakes and sat at Jesus' feet, and Jesus said this was the better way. Stop driving faster in your life when what would allow you to love the people around you better is to slow down.

You have a lot to do—everyone does. Sometimes you need to pull over and get the spider out of your helmet first.

Is your life moving so fast that you don't have time to deal with the issues stressing you out? How can you slow down and give yourself the space for healing? As you identify these things and downshift, watch how your life will change.

Slow it down today. Bring the speed of your activities back a notch or two and experience more whimsy and joy.

PURSUE YOUR PURPOSE AND STOP WORRYING ABOUT EVERYONE ELSE

*"I have given them the glory that you gave me,
that they may be one as we are one."*
JOHN 17:22

I am not a coin collector, but I have an old coin I like because it was the first coin minted when the early colonists were in the process of forming this country. It does not say, "In God we trust," as you might expect or have an imprint of a president's head, because there were no presidents yet. Inscribed on the coin are the words, "Mind your business." It was referring to the small businesses people had in the colonies. The coin wasn't reminding people not to butt in or be nosy but to work hard. When we have our heads down working hard on something big and meaningful and laden with purpose, we will be so busy doing the important things we won't waste our time being distracted by what others are doing.

Sweet Maria Goff says, "Mind your business," in a different way. She tells me to keep my eyes on my own paper. I like that saying too. Both the coin and Sweet Maria remind me that we need to be constantly tending to our own fires rather than distracted with how everyone else's fires are burning. God delights in what He is doing in your life, even though it might look and feel a lot different from what God is doing in someone else's life right now.

On the other side of the coin are the words, "We are one." Jesus had a conversation about being one with His Father. His hope was that we would understand the oneness we see between Jesus and His Father and want that to be the way we are with one another. The coin circulated in the colonies didn't last, because no one could afford to keep minting it, but both concepts are still worth taking to the bank. Today, if you find yourself tempted to be distracted by what others are doing in their complicated lives, remember the words, "Mind your business." And as you deal with diverse and sometimes difficult people, flip the coin to the other side in your mind and remember, "We are one."

Flip the coin. Heads you win and you will pay more attention to what God wants for you. Tails you win as well because you are one with those around you.

SHARE YOUR LIFE WITH OTHERS AND LEAVE YOUR OPINIONS IN YOUR HEAD

The Spirit told Philip, "Go to that chariot and stay near it." Then Philip ran up to the chariot and heard the man reading Isaiah the prophet. "Do you understand what you are reading?" Philip asked. "How can I," he said, "unless someone explains it to me?"

ACTS 8:29–31

Faith became real to me in high school when a guy named Randy found out I was going to drop out of school and move to Yosemite. Rather than try to talk me out of the idea, he got his sleeping bag and backpack, jumped into my beat-up VW bug, and went with me. My attempts to get a job in the Yosemite Valley failed, and Randy drove home with me a few days later. I found out later that Randy had gotten married the day before we left. But when I showed up on his porch, he didn't see an interruption; he saw a kid who was about to jump the tracks. So he got in my car with me.

In Philip's story in Acts 8, someone important was reading some prophetic scriptures about Jesus coming someday. Obeying the Spirit, Philip was close by the man's chariot and asked if he understood what he was reading. Just like Randy got in my car with me, Philip climbed into the chariot.

The message of the story is simple. The Spirit will lead us, and He can use us as we show up. Philip and the eunuch eventually found some water and the eunuch decided to get baptized. And when they came out of the water, in a delightful plot twist, Philip disappeared, and the eunuch went on his way rejoicing. How cool is that?

Everything doesn't need to be our idea, and it doesn't need to go our way. I learned from Randy the power of showing up, asking the right question, getting in when invited, and staying with someone when they are confused. The best way to love people is to remain helpful and available.

If someone does ask about what you believe, keep in mind that you are not setting the hook on a tuna. Without an agenda, simply share the experiences you have had, and people will walk away changed.

PUT JESUS IN THE DRIVER'S SEAT AND LOAD UP YOUR GEAR

"But seek first his kingdom and his righteousness, and
all these things will be given to you as well."
MATTHEW 6:33

I have a good and brilliant friend who wrote a book about leaning into the most important parts of our lives. In it, he wrote about a great many things, and among them he pointed out how we make the concept of priorities plural when it should be singular. It might feel like a Sunday school answer, but we can decide today that we are going to put Jesus as the one priority, with everything else falling below that.

There is power in a clear top priority. In the book of Matthew, Jesus says to seek first the kingdom of God and all the rest will be added. If we get the priority correct, the rest will come together. But what should we do once we have settled Jesus into His place at the top of the list? How do we get clear on the next layer of life priorities, or secondary objectives, as I sometimes call them?

Drill down on your list of secondary objectives. Ask yourself, for example, how you will give that ambition of yours some wheels. Maybe it's a course you'll take or a book you will read. Or maybe you can put into action some things that will help you get closer with your family and friends. Go on a couple of adventures; put the kids in charge. If you have a good friend you want to take a journey with, split the decisions with them. Have them make all the decisions one day, and you make all the decisions the next day.

Put yourself on a schedule, maybe quarterly, to decide when you are going to get into some mischief with your family or with your friends. Then, plan out your year. Get the big stuff on the calendar, and then add actionable steps you can take to invest in your objectives while maintaining your singular superpriority of seeking God's kingdom first. Get it all written down, so you know what you're aiming for.

Step out into your next day, your next month, and your next year knowing that you have your priorities in order.

JESUS IS THE ANTIDOTE

I will meditate on your precepts and fix my eyes on your ways.
PSALM 119:15 ESV

I have been going to Uganda for more than twenty years. It is the home of the six deadliest snakes in all of Africa. I have never been a fan of things that slither, but I keep going because I believe in the work being done there by the amazing team of Ugandans we have met.

One of the creepiest of all the creepy snakes is called a black mamba. This snake won't just lie in wait for you to step on it; it will actually chase after a person who disturbs it. A black mamba can travel over the ground at seven miles per hour, which is about how fast I can run for a short distance. The good news is, these snakes are extremely shy and will do everything they can to avoid people, but encounters still happen. Knowing this will keep you high-stepping.

Another creepy snake is the anaconda. It lives in the Amazon and can grow to be over twenty feet long. If one wraps around you and starts squeezing, as they are prone to do, let's just say you won't be long for this world.

We encounter difficult people every day. Some will lie in wait, but a few will chase after us. Their intent is usually not to bite you, but their conduct will hurt you in the long run by distracting you. Theirs is a different type of venom, but it can be just as deadly. So what can we do? We can look for the antidote.

Just like one drop of alcohol on the nose can cause an anaconda to loosen its squeeze, fixing our eyes on Jesus is enough to release the hold distraction has over us.

Trusting in Jesus can guide our steps toward protection and safety, and depending on Jesus can give us the endurance we need to outrun the most persistent and sometimes toxic people in our lives.

**What is a distraction that has wrapped itself around you?
What toxic relationship can you bring to Jesus today?**

HAVE FAITH LIKE A CHILD AND WATCH HOW FAST YOU GROW

[Jesus] said: "Truly I tell you, unless you change and become
like little children, you will never enter the kingdom of
heaven. Therefore, whoever takes the lowly position of this
child is the greatest in the kingdom of heaven. And whoever
welcomes one such child in my name welcomes me."
MATTHEW 18:3-5

When the disciples were trying to help Jesus by getting everybody in line, He told them instead to help Him by not helping Him and that they needed to become more like children. Become like a child or you don't get into heaven?

This is a remarkable statement when you think about it. It isn't about doctrine or rules or dos and don'ts. It isn't about how much or how little you need to have done or the importance of what you know. It is about having a childlike faith, becoming like one of those who had some of the lowest positions in society back then.

I wonder why our standards for a ticket into heaven are so rigorous and complicated and involve so many more elements than what Jesus said would be involved.

Jesus isn't interested in our most sophisticated take on faith. There is no teacher's pet nor valedictorian of faith, just childlike belief. I think the reason is both simple and complicated. He didn't come to bring order and didn't die on a cross so we would behave better. He came to connect with us in a way a child would understand.

What could you do today to get back in touch with the simplest version of your faith? What childlike thing could you do today?

**Heaven is leaning over the rails just waiting to
see that childlike version of you arrive.**

KEEP IT SIMPLE, KEEP IT REAL

*"I tell you that for every careless word that people speak,
they will give an account of it on the day of judgment."*
MATTHEW 12:36 NASB

Can we be honest for a moment and get it out there that people in the South have a funny way of expressing themselves? It's the place where all nutty idioms get a pontoon boat and go on vacation together. For instance, have you ever heard someone say, "That pie's so good it makes me want to slap yo' mamma"? Wait, what? Slap who? It sounds like such a violent way to say "Thank you" or "Wow, this pie is good" or "Can I have another slice?" Complicating things further, there are some strange phrases to describe the things happening around you.

For instance, have you heard someone in the South talking about something they are considering and saying, "Well, I might could"? What does that even mean? On the one hand, it sounds like our foreign policy about attacking Iran. You know, we might—we could—but then I came to realize this is Southern speak for what the rest of earth calls "maybe." Or how about this one? "He's grinnin' like a possum eatin' a sweet tater." Possible translation: "He's happy"? Other possible explanation: "I own weird pets."

Someone was telling me once about how little money he had growing up and said, "I was so poor, I had a tumbleweed as a pet." Now, I'll admit, that made me chuckle.

You must agree, these are pretty funny expressions. Here's the point. When we are talking about our faith, our hopes, and our beliefs, let's not leave people scratching their heads at the unusual way we describe it. Use plain language that everyone understands. The words we use matter, and if we speak in endearing but unintelligible ways, people will miss the important point we are trying to make.

**Go love on people today, and as you do, use simple,
understandable words and even easier-to-understand
actions. One day we will be asked to account for them.**

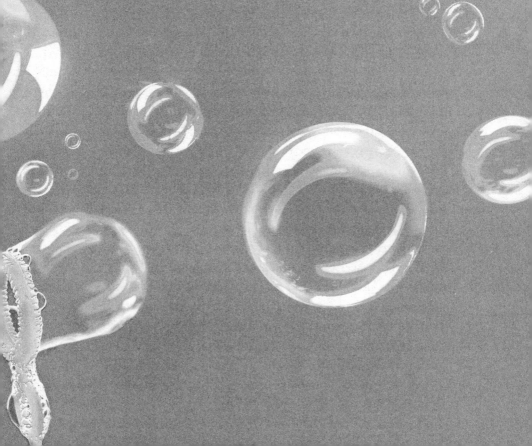

NOVEMBER

SOMETIMES LOVE IS LIKE AN UNEXPECTED ICE CREAM SANDWICH

See what great love the Father has lavished on us, that we should
be called children of God! And that is what we are! The reason
the world does not know us is that it did not know him.
1 JOHN 3:1

A few years ago, a group of girls were hiking up a mountain in the inlet near our lodge. Sometimes when we're near the radio room at the lodge, we can hear the guides checking in with base camp on how the trips are going, and we listen to see what's happening. The girls' guides were the last ones to give their report that day: "We're really having a tough time. Will you guys pray for us—over?"

The guides said morale was low but they were going to do their best and push on. The call the next day was worse. Someone had twisted their knee; another had rolled their ankle. There were also huge personality clashes among the hikers. "This is the most difficult trip we've been on. Pray for us—over." The guides called in again when they were a six-hour hike from the summit, wondering if they should just turn back. None of the kids wanted to hike anymore. But these guides were amazing and called out in the girls the strength they didn't know they had. They decided by the end of the call that they would push on the next day and hope to summit by 2:00 p.m.

I woke up early that next morning with an idea. I loaded our kids in the seaplane we use to get in and out of the remote place we live in and flew 150 miles to the nearest store. My kids piled out and ran to the grocery store with their arms waving over their heads. They jumped back in the plane minutes later with four cases of ice cream sandwiches.

We flew back over the mountaintops and found the summit in the distance. As we got closer, we could see the hikers like black dots strung together by ropes. Just as they were arriving at the summit, we flew over and threw the ice cream sandwiches a safe distance away. The hikers had no idea what was going on. We circled as they ran over. Then, they raised their arms and shouted with one voice, "Ice cream!"

Take a look and see what great love the Father has lavished on us and do the same with others. Sometimes people just need an ice cream sandwich from a stranger flying an airplane or a warm smile and a handshake from you on the sidewalk.

Who do you see around you who could use a little whimsical encouragement today?

LOVE IS SACRIFICE

This is how we know what love is: Jesus Christ
laid down his life for us. And we ought to lay
down our lives for our brothers and sisters.
1 JOHN 3:16

I traveled with a friend to a place in northern Afghanistan during a time of unrest and found myself in an open-air market. We were trying to get me into a perahan tunban, which is the traditional dress most men wear. It is basically a really long shirt with gigantic pants cinched tight around the waist.

As we were waiting for the tailor, one or two locals stopped and noticed me. Then there were twenty, then fifty encircling me. I hadn't given much thought beforehand to the current climate in northern Afghanistan, but I realized in that moment that I was in the wrong place at definitely the wrong time.

Quickly figuring out the trajectory of how things might go, my friend grabbed me by the wrist and, like a college linebacker, made a lane through the expanding crowd. We ducked around the corner and agreed, through our nervous laughter once we were in a safe place, that the situation had been more than a little uncomfortable. I told him how much protection I had felt from him and how impressed I was at how he unflinchingly pursued a solution to what could have been an immense problem.

Sometimes laying down our lives means standing up for someone else's life. Who is it you can stand beside today in their difficulties? Who is it that might be feeling like they are on the outside looking in? Maybe it is a person who was once in leadership but messed up, who was ridiculed and shunned.

It's easy to love people who are the popular, kind, fun ones. But who can you reach out to today who needs someone like you with no other agenda other than to love them?

Today is your day to lay down your life to lift someone else's up.

PLAN FOR YOUR PLANS TO CHANGE

In their hearts humans plan their course, but
the LORD establishes their steps.
PROVERBS 16:9

Things have not turned out in my life the way I expected them to. How about for you? Eve didn't see the apple coming. Noah didn't see the flood coming. Moses didn't imagine he would part the seas. Joshua didn't think he would take over for Moses. David didn't expect to become ruler, and Job didn't think he would be a victim. Jonah didn't think he would be fish bait, Paul didn't think the jail door would fall off, and Judas didn't think he would double-cross Jesus. Most of the disciples didn't think they would be followers, and the people in Sodom didn't see fire headed their way.

I'm not saying we shouldn't have plans. We should just plan on them changing. It is not the exception but the rule that things in our lives are not going to turn out the way we think they will. So let's stop acting surprised when there is a plot twist in our lives.

Here are a couple of tips for how to plan for a change in plans. First, from 1 Peter, be humble in all things. Then, listen to Paul in his letter to the Romans when he says to trust that God is working for your good, even if you don't understand what is happening and things don't turn out as expected. Finally, trust the wisdom of Solomon when he says that we can make all the plans we would like, but in the end, it will be God who decides how things will turn out.

It won't just be the big things that surprise us in life, but also the massive numbers of small things that affect our days. It is the thing that made us late, the important date we forgot to add to the calendar, or the meeting we missed. Our best strategy is to remember that God holds everything loosely while He holds us firmly.

How can you prepare your heart today for the unanticipated outcomes? The unwanted challenges? The disappointments? God has got you. It is not apathy He is asking of us but a strategy for anticipating both the unlikeliness of our circumstances and the trustworthiness of God.

Live like your days are uncertain but your future is secure.

SITUATIONAL AWARENESS—GET SOME

Show me your ways, L<small>ORD</small>, teach me your paths.
PSALM 25:4

When I was learning how to fly an airplane, one of the things drilled into me was the concept of being situationally aware. What that means is knowing what is going on around you. This is about having a full understanding of what is happening. To be situationally aware, you need to know what is ahead of you, what is behind you, and what will be intersecting you.

There is another concept in aviation called spatial disorientation. This occurs when you can't figure out where you are compared to everything surrounding you. The way to push back is to remain situationally aware. This looks like scanning the horizon in front of you from left to right. Once you take a quick look at all of it, you chunk up the sky in front of you and take a hard look at 10 percent of it at a time. The point is to start with a more general view and then focus in on more and more specific views.

It's easy to become spatially disoriented in our busy lives too. We lose track of where we are with Jesus and instead obsess over where we are in comparison with one another. When you find yourself struggling with this, scan the horizon and take a quick look at your entire life. Identify the direction you seem to be going in, what is generally working, and what isn't. Then drill down and take a hard look at specific areas in your life—chunk it up.

How are your friendships? Are they growing deeper and more meaningful? How about your faith? Does it feel dynamic and growing, or is it stagnant? Next, turn to what is going on in the cockpit of your life. What are the instruments telling you? Are you working too hard? Are you taking time to rest and go on a couple of adventures? Are you keeping track of your finances, so they don't start pushing you around?

David asked God to show him His ways and teach him His paths. We can do the same.

Do a quick audit today about what is going on in your life and bring each area to God. As you do, you will find greater clarity in your pursuit of Jesus.

FEAR WANTS TO ROB YOU
GOD WANTS TO SHIELD YOU

But you, LORD, are a shield around me, my glory,
the One who lifts my head high.
PSALM 3:3

Have you noticed there are some people who try to keep others at a distance? Are you one of them? I know sometimes I am. I come across as a happy, gregarious guy, but there is a lot of insecurity I cover up with a ton of enthusiasm. If your fear is rejection, it might show up in your being distant with people. You might unconsciously decide that if someone who didn't really know you rejects you, it would be less painful than if you had let them into your life. So we leave the real parts of us undisclosed. We think hiding behind our fears or pride or insecurities will be more effective than using God as our shield.

This reminds me of a time we had some friends show up for horseback riding at the Oaks Equestrian Center. We have three horses that wouldn't care if you lit a firecracker on top of them, but there were four of us that day so I threw a saddle on a horse that had just arrived. It was twice the size of the other horses, made lots of noises, and had smoke coming out of its nostrils. You see where this is headed. I got on the horse, and it took off running. We were doing forty miles per hour, and it was bucking so hard my ankles were over my ears. I flipped off the back of the horse and fortunately landed on my head. When my friends ran up and asked if I was okay, I sprang to my feet, laughing and said, "Of course I'm okay!" I knew I was lying and asked myself why I didn't say, "Hey, I just got my bell rung. I don't even know my name right now. Give me a moment to collect my thoughts."

Sometimes our fears and our insecurities get in the way of connecting with people and even connecting with Jesus.

I know it might be scary, but if we will bring the most authentic versions of ourselves to the world today, we will let everyone see who God created in us rather than the version our insecurities have manufactured over time.

All of heaven delights when we show up in authenticity and humble confidence of God continuing unfinished work in us.

MEAN WHAT YOU SAY TO SAY WHAT YOU MEAN

Watch the way you talk. Let nothing foul or dirty come out of your mouth. Say only what helps, each word a gift.
EPHESIANS 4:29 MSG

Paul told his friends in Ephesus to watch what they said. He wasn't saying merely to stop cussing or gossiping; he had something much more beautiful in mind.

Our words matter, and we should be thoughtful about how we use them. One way of doing that is to be intentional about using the words we really mean rather than trying to pump them up to sound better. I get it. A lot of the time, we're just trying to be enthusiastic, encouraging, or upbeat, but in doing that, we may be unintentionally misleading the people we're talking to. So, for instance, when something is simply "good," let's not say it's "awesome" or "amazing" or "unbelievable." Let's not be afraid of saying that it is good or that it is exactly what we thought it might be.

Another way we can be more mindful of our words, while also making some real progress in our connection with people, is to find the more imaginative and precise words to describe our thoughts and feelings. This will make our words count far more. For example, instead of saying, "Thank you, that was really great," say "When you did that, it made me feel like I had just jumped off a swing into a pile of leaves."

Doesn't this express something more beautiful and lasting? And rather than saying, "Thank you for the note," perhaps say, "It was like hot chocolate and warm cookies on a cold night." Can't you smell the cookies in the oven with this more imaginative response? A little whimsy can make someone smile and lighten their load.

It's a new day. Let's fill it with new and different and more meaningful words and phrases.

We don't need to inflate nor diminish our words, just find a few newer and more imaginative ones. This can be fun!

362

LOVING OTHERS IS THE BEST EVIDENCE JESUS IS ALIVE

*After his suffering, he presented himself to them
and gave many convincing proofs that he was
alive. He appeared to them over a period of forty
days and spoke about the kingdom of God.*
ACTS 1:3

The book of Acts was written by Luke to someone named Theophilus, which means "lover of God." It picks up where the Gospel of Luke leaves off. Jesus went to heaven, leaving behind the Holy Spirit as a comforter and counselor. But before He did that, Acts says Jesus left many convincing proofs that He was alive so there would be no question about it. Are you seeing them today?

We can go through our days distracted by everything going on around us, or we can live fully engaged lives where we look for evidence that Jesus is still alive. I don't see clouds in the sky that look like messages, and my faith is pretty steak and potatoes without a lot of mystical messaging from heaven. But I am constantly on the lookout for evidence that Jesus is still alive.

I don't think He stopped doing miracles after the thirty-seven in the Scriptures. He still shows up in dark moments and brings comfort. He still gives miraculous levels of perspective when it is needed. And He still brings unlikely people into our lives in miraculous ways.

Make it your mission today to find evidence that Jesus still lives. You will then start to see difficult people as people to be loved, rather than as people to avoid or problems to fix. Once you do this, you will see evidence of Jesus everywhere you go.

**Every day, in each circumstance and
with every encounter, we get to dust
for the fingerprints of Jesus.**

OBEDIENCE KEEPS OUR LIVES FROM TURNING INTO A DUMPSTER FIRE

He looked down toward Sodom and Gomorrah, toward
all the land of the plain, and he saw dense smoke rising
from the land, like smoke from a furnace.
GENESIS 19:28

The Great Fire of London occurred just after midnight on Sunday in 1666 and lasted for almost one week. It started in a bakery, which was ironically on Pudding Lane. At the time, there were a thousand watchmen walking the streets at night, and it was their job to put out fires. The person in charge immediately knew that the buildings on each side of the bakery needed to be knocked down to keep the fire from growing, but the neighbors who owned these houses pushed back so they didn't do what was necessary. As a result, the fire spread and all of London burned to the ground.

There was another fire in the Scriptures at a place called Sodom and at another one called Gomorrah. God told Abraham it was curtains for these cities because of how bad their wickedness had become. God sent two angels to destroy Sodom and Gomorrah. A great deal happened while the angels were at Lot's house, but in the end, the angels led Lot and his wife and daughters out of the city and told them not to look back. Lot and his two daughters were saved, but his wife disobeyed and looked back, and turned into a pillar of salt.

God feels so strongly about us obeying Him that sometimes He does a complete do-over. He may not rain down fire and brimstone, or continue turning people into pillars of salt, but He will do whatever it takes to get our attention. And His goal at the end is always the same: that we would be His.

All of London burned down because a fire was allowed to spread. Sodom and Gomorrah were wiped out to keep disobedience from spreading. Whether you are leading a company, a family, or a friend, all of us have many decisions to make every day.

**Put obedience at the top of this list. When it
isn't, everyone pays a high price.**

WANNA MEET JESUS? FEED THE HUNGRY

*"If you spend yourselves in behalf of the hungry and satisfy
the needs of the oppressed, then your light will rise in the
darkness, and your night will become like the noonday."*
ISAIAH 58:10

There are a lot of people who talk about what Jesus meant without doing what He did. Jesus said there were several practical things we could do if we wanted to engage with Him. At the top of the list was feeding hungry people. This also builds community as people sit together to eat, and it is something Jesus promised He would always be right in the middle of.

There was a time Al-Shabab blocked food from coming into an area in the desert outside of Mogadishu. Tens of thousands of people were encircled by Al-Shabab fighters trying to starve them out. An amazing guy and his team arranged for us to charter a plane loaded with food for thousands of people and flew it in. After we unloaded the food, we took off as fast as we could.

You may be thinking, *I can't fly to Somalia to deliver food to the hungry people.* And that may be true. But don't forget there are hungry people all around us. It sounds noble to do things while you're far away from home, and it's certainly good to help if you can, but the Scriptures emphasize helping the people close to home. Jesus told His friends to love their neighbors.

Sure, you can have neighbors across an ocean, but don't forget the neighbors across the street from you too. Not only are they more accessible to you, but you can bring them more food more often. The simple truth is that if following Jesus doesn't lead you and me to hurting and hungry people, near or far, we probably aren't following Him, or we haven't figured out how to do it the way He said to.

**Today, keep your eyes open for an opportunity to give
some food to someone who is hungry. The promise of
the Scriptures is that if you do, you will meet Jesus.**

BE PICKY WITH YOUR WORDS; DON'T GRAB THE FIRST THING OFF THE SHELF

Those who guard their mouths and their tongues
keep themselves from calamity.
PROVERBS 21:23

I received a call from a woman who had read one of my books that a friend had given her. She was polite and soft-spoken, and I told her I was honored she had taken time to call. But then I asked her what she was looking forward to, and her tone changed. She said the reason her friend had given her the book was that she was going in for brain surgery soon. Accessing the place where the tumor was located meant she probably wouldn't be able to talk after the operation. I was sad with her and asked, if it wasn't prying, what she was talking to her friends about, given that she only had a short time left to speak to them. What she said surprised me: "I'm being really picky about what I say."

Think about that for a moment. My guess is that I have many years in front of me to talk to people, and you can't shut me up most days. She, on the other hand, only had a few days left to speak and was being picky about what came out of her mouth. In that moment, I realized we all could benefit from being a little pickier about what we talk about. Certainly, every conversation doesn't need to be a mile deep, but often we settle for ones that are an inch deep and then make this the norm.

Before hanging up the phone, I set a time to connect with the woman again after her surgery. I was in Houston in the back of an Uber when the time came. I dialed her number, and it rang a few times and eventually she answered. She had lost the ability to speak, so we delighted together in the silence.

Be picky with your words. The stupid shelf is always at waist level and loaded with nonsense. Reach up a little higher in your pantry of words and find kinder ones, more thoughtful and important ones, more lasting ones.

Add a beat or two to your conversations and give yourself a chance to be a little pickier about what you have to say.

QUIT PLAYING IT SAFE, AND DANCE, DANCE, DANCE

"Be strong and courageous. Do not be afraid or terrified because of them, for the Lord your God goes with you; he will never leave you nor forsake you."

DEUTERONOMY 31:6

Life has a way of testing what we're made of. The disappointments, setbacks, and failures we face will shape us or scar us. In terms of chemistry, our bodies are made up of 85 percent oxygen, hydrogen, nitrogen, carbon, calcium, and phosphorus—all the rest is water. And the big bag of carbon and water we are each made of is only going to be on the earth for a short time, so we shouldn't waste it being afraid of what hard things might come. Steel your resolve by knowing what you believe and why you believe it, then activate what you are going to do about it.

I have a friend who always wanted to learn how to dance. Sadly, she was in a terrible accident early in her life, and after many operations, the doctors couldn't repair the damage. My friend felt the ache of being separated from her ambition and spent much of her life feeling like her dream of dancing with the ones she loved would not ever happen. Then she attended a gathering where people talked about pursuing their ambitions.

On the first day, everyone stood up and said what their ambitions were and what they were doing to go after them. My friend stood up slowly and steadied herself with her chair. She told everyone about her ambition to learn to dance and the headwinds she had faced through many surgeries. She told them she had just been released from the hospital where they cut off her foot so she could be fitted with a prosthetic, and she was going to learn how to dance.

What challenge are you facing? What ambition have you deferred?

Quit playing it safe and don't play it scared.
Be strong and courageous today.

OUR JOB IS TO LOVE PEOPLE WHILE JESUS LEADS THEM

"In the same way, let your light shine before others, that they
may see your good deeds and glorify your Father in heaven."
MATTHEW 5:16

I didn't grow up in church, but like most people, I did hear the word *evangelism* used a lot. Recently, I took a hard look to find out where the term was used in the Bible and was surprised to discover that the word *evangelist* appears in most New Testament translations only a few times. Two of the times, the scriptures refer to a particular person, like Philip or Timothy, doing the work of an evangelist, but that's it. So, why all the emphasis on evangelism?

When we know more about where words and phrases come from, we can attach more meaning to them. It turns out, the term *evangelism* comes from a Greek word that means "gospeling." That isn't a word I had heard before, but I kind of like it. This lands with me, because the gospel isn't a bunch of books or doctrine or rules, as some people are inclined to think; the gospel is a person: Jesus.

So, think of evangelism as "Jesusing." What we call evangelism isn't about cornering someone or getting in their grill to tell them what they need to believe, or that they will be facing a fiery future if they don't. It's living out faith in authentic, uncontrived ways the way Jesus did.

Remember the big moment when Jesus asked Simon Peter who people said He was? When Simon Peter answered that he thought He was God, Jesus said it wasn't men, but God, who revealed this truth to him.

Do a little "Jesusing" today. And don't worry about what happens afterward. You're off the hook.

**We don't deliver people to Jesus; Jesus draws people
to Him. We just love people while He does.**

LET YOUR LIFE BE THE MIRACLE AND THE MESSAGE

"Go," he told him, "wash in the Pool of Siloam" (this word means
"Sent"). So the man went and washed, and came home seeing.
JOHN 9:7

Modern-day Jerusalem is a large city. It has all the things you would expect in a major city: underground water, sewer systems, and well-organized roads (and a couple that aren't). Some of these roads are very old. I met Eli Shukron, one of the few archaeologists authorized to do excavations in the Holy Land, on a cold, windy, rainy day just outside the Old City in Jerusalem. He pointed out one thing after another that he had found in his digs over the decades. The most impressive was a small bell, which would have been on the high priests' robes as they went into the Holy of Holies. He found this on an almost half-mile-long road his team had excavated for five years, between the Temple Mount and the Pool of Siloam.

John tells us about a blind man who walked this same long road the day he met Jesus. After Jesus put mud on his eyes, he took a walk to the Pool of Siloam where Jesus sent him. There he washed his eyes in a ritual cleansing ceremony and found he could miraculously see.

Jesus often combines a miracle and a message. He may not have put mud in your eyes, but there may be miracles Jesus has done for you that will only be complete after you do what He told you to do next. For example, if you were given a gift and a debt was paid, perhaps Jesus wants you to do that for someone else. Or maybe someone forgave you, and the other half of the miracle is for you to forgive someone else.

If the blind guy had stayed where he was and merely agreed with Jesus that someday he should go to the pool and wash up, who knows if he would have been healed. But he did what Jesus told him to do, and it changed everything. We need to do the same.

**What is it that Jesus has repaired or healed in you and what
has He asked you to do in response? Make the call, take
the leap, let your life be the miracle and the message.**

GOD MADE YOU THIS WAY ON PURPOSE, FRECKLES AND ALL

I praise you because I am fearfully and wonderfully made;
your works are wonderful, I know that full well.

PSALM 139:14

When I was growing up, I was covered in freckles. There was a particularly mean person in my life who called me "Spot" every time I walked by, and my little insecure heart wilted a little each time. But my grandma said my freckles were angel kisses and that I shouldn't tell anyone, because they would feel bad that they didn't get as many angel kisses as I did. She knew what concerned and embarrassed me and spoke to my insecurities, which made a huge contribution to my life.

Everybody is insecure. We need to be like my grandma and find ways to speak worth and praise to the preteen kid who is trying to figure out how to fit in and the sixty-year-old who lost their confidence decades earlier when they didn't have someone like me or you in their life.

When you are feeling insecure, don't go around the bend to be mean to someone else. Being mean won't fix your insecurity—it highlights it. Today, let's work on taming our insecurity and not saying harsh things. If we take the time to understand and remind ourselves why we're doing what we're doing, it will go a long way toward changing how we react to the people around us. And we will be able to access greater love and patience and understanding than we otherwise could.

We have an important message we can pass along to the people in our lives, about how we are all fearfully and wonderfully made. Communicate this today in the warmth of your smiles, in hugs, or by taking the time to listen intently to what someone is saying. Every time you do this, you are letting people know who they are and whose they are, and that they are worth your full attention.

**We all wobble a little; the trick is to not let our insecurities
tip us over. Delight in your uniqueness today.**

GOD DIDN'T UNLOCK THE PRISON DOOR SO YOU COULD SET UP CAMP IN A DIFFERENT CELL

It is for freedom that Christ has set us free. Stand firm, then, and
do not let yourselves be burdened again by a yoke of slavery.
GALATIANS 5:1

We can experience tremendous freedom with Jesus, but we've got to really want it. Paul wrote to his friends that it was for freedom that Jesus had set them free, and they didn't need to act like they were prisoners any longer. That's another way of saying, *As to the things that have been holding you back, let them off the chain. You can live free.*

In New Hampshire, the inmates at the prisons make license plates. And get this: the slogan for New Hampshire is "Live Free or Die." The irony of this is inescapable, and yet many of us wake up each day in a prison of our own making. We are probably not making license plates, but we are making poor choices.

Some of us are shackled by our opinions about what everybody else is doing. Others overidentify with their friends' problems and feel the need to sort them out. They spend too much time distracted by lives of others instead of understanding what is happening in their own lives. Meanwhile, some of us feel stuck in our past, mired in old stories of who we once were.

Whatever and whoever you feel imprisoned by, know this: there is freedom, and you hold the keys. You don't get out of prison someday; you get out today if you want it badly enough to make some changes. You can find freedom from your old ways and rewrite the story of your life.

If you are looking for a place to begin collecting your thoughts, start with Paul's tap on your shoulder and think about what is true and noble and right and pure and admirable and excellent.

Find whatever it is that helps you reset and get to freedom. Get out of the jail you have been in and pitch a tent in that new place.

WORDS HAVE MEANING AND NAMES HAVE POWER

"The virgin will conceive and give birth to a son, and they
will call him Immanuel" (which means "God with us").
MATTHEW 1:23

There are only a couple of people I have heard of who have only a single name, like MacGyver (spoiler alert: his first name is Angus), or who are known for only one thing, like The Man in the Yellow Hat or Captain Crunch, Peppermint Patty, or The Lone Ranger (although Lone isn't really a name, but a status). While these people may have a first or last name, no one knows what they are. Jesus is another one of those names. But Jesus' name actually isn't Jesus. If we were back in His time and called the name Jesus out in a crowd, He probably wouldn't have even turned around. Here's why.

The books of the New Testament were written in Greek, and Jesus' name in Hebrew was Yeshua, which is usually Joshua in English. When words were being translated from different languages in the Old and New Testaments, they kept the Hebrew translation of Joshua for the Old Testament characters and used the Greek translation of Joshua for the New Testament, which gave us the name Jesus.

Another reason why we use the name Jesus Christ is that God was His Father. He didn't fit into the custom back then of identifying someone by who their father was, so some people used the city He came from, hence "Jesus of Nazareth," while others identified Him by His title of Messiah, which is *Christ* in Greek.

Why does all of this matter? Jesus was a man who lived. He claimed to be God and actually was God in the flesh. By whatever name you know Him, His name has power. And if Jesus' name doesn't hold any power for you, it is not Jesus you're talking about.

Live today like Jesus is the Messiah, the anointed and chosen One, and watch your life, your hopes, and your relationships change.

YOU'RE BEAUTIFUL, EVEN ON A BAD HAIR DAY

If you suffer as a Christian, do not be ashamed,
but praise God that you bear that name.
1 PETER 4:16

When something goes wrong, we get to decide whether to engage with it or ignore what just happened. Perhaps you have seen the person who gets hit by a car yet springs to their feet seemingly unfazed. Or maybe you've been with someone who endured something awful yet seemed to entirely ignore what happened. It probably seemed unnatural—because it is.

Or perhaps you have experienced drawing the ire of people around you who disagree with the things you hold close in your faith and have struggled with how to respond. This can be painful, to be sure. The apostle Peter told his friends not to be ashamed when this happens. The fix is not to merely ignore how painful it is but to praise God when it happens. But, if you are like me, my default position when I am suffering is not to thank God for all the pain in my life.

If we are going to get to the place where we praise God for the difficulties and suffering in our lives, we first need to see ourselves the way God does and live into God's name for us: His beloved. Imagine what would change if you were to own that name.

Think of the power you could access if you really believed you were that important to Him. You know the scene. Jesus is out in the desert. He gets baptized. And what does God say? "Behold, this is my beloved." And that's what He says about you and me on our best days and also on our worst ones.

What would change in your life if you started seeing yourself the way God says He sees you?

LOVE SINCERELY

Love must be sincere. Hate what is evil; cling to what is good.
ROMANS 12:9

We're all amateurs at love and acceptance. No one goes pro on loving people. And yet much of what we do is rooted in looking for places where we feel loved and accepted. To meet this need fully, the love offered must be sincere. And sincere love looks like acceptance.

A lot of us struggle with this, though, and end up giving out information more than we give out acceptance, because it feels safer. That's why we often talk about facts and historical markers at our faith gatherings rather than our life experiences, both good and bad. It might feel safer to provide exegetical interpretation of ancient Scriptures than to accept the person sitting in row three who loves someone in a different way than you would or is living with someone Jesus said they should have married.

Here's the thing, though. Accepting people, when it's done well, isn't going soft on doctrine; it's going big on Jesus. Loving people the way Jesus did doesn't make you complicit in conduct that doesn't square with your theology; it's evidence that you believe so much in what Jesus said that you're willing to act like Him and love people the way He did.

Our high calling is obedience to Jesus, not being the hall monitor of other people's conduct.

Jesus didn't avoid the people the religious people rejected. He got adjacent to them. He found them in low places of doubt, and, in the end, Jesus was lifted next to two men crucified at the same time as He was.

Perhaps the next big step for you today will be to get adjacent to people and take a genuine interest in them.

Sometimes we need to lift our eyes beyond what everyone else is looking at and see what Jesus sees. And what He sees are His kids who are desperately in need of Him.

KEEP CALM AND LOVE WELL

Post this at all the intersections, dear friends: Lead with your ears,
follow up with your tongue, and let anger straggle along in the
rear. God's righteousness doesn't grow from human anger.
JAMES 1:19–20 MSG

I was in India with my friend Moses when he shot me what I thought was a Hawaiian "hang loose" hand gesture. In surfer language, it means, "Right on," "Things are great," "Take it easy." In Hawaii, a shaka sign with a thumb and pinky finger out and three middle fingers curled in means all these things. In India, it means the person needs to go to the bathroom. Who knew? I was grinning, thinking what a nice, friendly guy Moses was as he kept signaling me and I mirrored the signal back to him.

In other places, that same hand signal can communicate someone is on the phone when they hold their thumb to their ear and pinky finger out, or it can mean someone is going to drink something if a thumb is held to the mouth. Get this: in China, it means the number six. It is no wonder we misunderstand one another so frequently. What we think we understand often isn't what was intended at all.

James tried to help his friends with predictable misunderstandings by writing to them about what he thought were the best ways to communicate with one another. He told them to be quick to listen, slow to speak, and slow to become angry. But if you poll most people, they will confirm that they don't listen first, that they talk fast and get angry easily. There is a better way, if we are willing to work on it. Listen first, speak after listening, and keep cool. If you do this, will you avoid all the communication miscues in your life? Of course not. But you will reflect the Spirit of Jesus more accurately as you interact with people.

Today is your day. Be mindful of what you are communicating and equally aware that people might misread you. Aim for clarity in your communications.

If you lead with your ears, follow up with your tongue, and allow anger to straggle behind, you will communicate a lot more of the right stuff.

MAKE SURE YOUR COMPASS IS POINTING TRUE NORTH

"Love the LORD your God with all your heart and with
all your soul and with all your strength."
DEUTERONOMY 6:5

There is a popular movie, *Pirates of the Caribbean*, that features the character Jack Sparrow. He carries a compass around with him that points toward whatever he loves the most. If you had that kind of a compass around your neck, what would it be pointing toward? I bet it would point toward your family and friends, maybe also your job and the kinds of recreation that you enjoy. Maybe it would point toward a place where you have felt wonderfully relaxed. If you were honest, what would need to change for your compass to point at all these things while at the same time pointing at Jesus?

We live in a world that wants to make our choices binary. In other words, some of us think we need to choose good or bad, in or out, up or down, this or that. This is illustrated pretty strongly in the game we used to play on long car rides, the "would you rather," where you pit two things against each other. "Would you rather be independently wealthy or totally broke with one good friend?" "Would you rather have to eat your favorite dish and nothing else every day for the rest of your life or only get to eat it once a year?"

But the truth is things are rarely binary like that. We can value both our loved ones and Jesus at the same time. We can enjoy our hobbies and love Jesus at the same time. We just have to keep it straight who comes first. So, how do you live out the command to love the Lord your God with all your heart and with all your soul and with all your strength?

Take some time today to ask yourself what and who your compass is pointing at. Is it pointing at all the things you enjoy doing or all the people you love but not pointing at Jesus?

Remember, it's okay to value the people and things God has given us. We just need to get real enough to admit when our priorities are out of order and reorient ourselves and our desires to point toward Him.

PRAY FOR OUR LEADERS, AND YES, EVEN THE ONES YOU DON'T AGREE WITH

I urge, then, first of all, that petitions, prayers, intercession and thanksgiving be made for all people—for kings and all those in authority, that we may live peaceful and quiet lives in all godliness and holiness.
1 TIMOTHY 2:1-2

On our first trip to Afghanistan, our intent was to start a school for the kids who were not being allowed—by either the rules or gender or poverty—to attend school. We had a meeting scheduled in a city in the northern part of the country, which at one time was the Taliban's capital. As we pulled up to the building, we took in the intimidating level of security and the number of people with weapons. I took comfort in knowing I was with someone well connected as we went upstairs to where we would be meeting with the governor.

We sat down in a large room with fancy chairs and a chandelier. After a short wait, the leader entered and sat down as well. But as he did, there was a 6.2-magnitude earthquake. Everything shook, and the chandelier began swaying from side to side. I turned to the leader, and I said, "You are obviously a very powerful man." He smiled, confidently looked me in the eye, and said, "Yes, I am." Before we left the meeting, this leader offered to give us land for a bigger school.

I am telling you this because God wants us to be with and pray for our leaders, not just the nice ones and the ones who agree with us, but all of them. We are surrounded by leaders. Some of them we work for; others are in local or national government. Some represent the best of what we hope for, and others will be awful. But we should pray for them and be with them if we are able to.

Not everything people who are in leadership say is entirely candid. In Afghanistan, they say the person who is not being truthful "put some onions on the news," which means they added some mistruths to the truth. Pray for them anyway. It is not a power-sharing arrangement God has invited us to. All the power is His and there is nothing left over to divide.

Lift up those who lead, both good and bad, and ask God to exercise His power in beautiful and unexpected ways in their lives.

LOVE LEAVES NO REGRETS

LORD, remind me how brief my time on earth will be. Remind
me that my days are numbered—how fleeting my life is.
PSALM 39:4 NLT

We have all heard of the observations people make on their deathbeds about what they would do differently with their lives if they had to do it over again. There is a predictability to these thoughts.

A lot of people say they would spend more time with the ones they love. They would play hooky more. Or perhaps they would break a couple of rules they had made for themselves. But here's what I think about when I hear these things. Why wait until you are about to cross over to heaven? Why not do a little more living now?

Don't just agree this is a great idea—there is no one arguing that it isn't. Instead, make a power move, and do something about it while you've still got some tread on your tires. Go out there every day with purpose, and live the big, beautiful, meaningful life faith calls us all to live.

The challenge to this is faith often tells us to go in the opposite direction of what our basic instincts tell us to do. Our primal instinct pushes us to pursue safety, self-protection, and self-interest while faith tells us to engage risk, tolerate ambiguity, and pursue Jesus. But let's not choose the path that will lead to us wishing we had done things differently when we're on our deathbeds.

Turn your limited time here on earth into your superpower. Believe the Scriptures when they say your time is limited and your days are numbered. Use these fixed points to your advantage.

**Prepare your heart like you are going
to be with Jesus soon and live each
day with purpose-filled abandon.**

LOVE GOD AND BE YOURSELF

If you have any encouragement from being united with Christ, if any comfort from his love, if any common sharing in the Spirit, if any tenderness and compassion, then make my joy complete by being like-minded, having the same love, being one in spirit and of one mind.
PHILIPPIANS 2:1–2

I don't know about you, but a couple of times each month, someone on social media will pretend to be me. I'm not sure why they do it, because I am older than dirt and am not really that interesting. Also, they are not very good at pretending to be me, so there's that. If you really want to go varsity team pretending to be me, pay off a couple of my bills, write a big check to a charity, or change the oil in my old pickup truck.

Sure, it's a little creepy when someone pretends to be us, but we do it all the time with one another without knowing it. We admire people and their God-given personalities or giftedness or unique circumstances and subconsciously try to be them. God hasn't ever asked us to be the same as anyone else. In fact, when we try to act like someone we are not, it's a form of impersonation. We are no longer the incredible, unique person God made us to be but a poor knockoff of who He made someone else to be.

If you are struggling with trying to be like someone else, someone you think is cooler or more successful or more interesting or more something else, ask God to help you stir up your most beautiful, authentic desires and live into the possibilities of the real you and what you can get done.

And if you're worried that revealing your true self will change your relationships—it will. A couple of people who aren't really your friends will drift away, but the truest relationships will remain.

Take a tip from Paul and make everyone around you joyful and complete by being like-minded, having the same love, being one in spirit and of one mind, but in your own unique way.

Today, if you want to dazzle God, go be the most genuine, authentic you the world has ever met.

379

YOUR MISTAKES DON'T DEFINE YOU, BUT THE WAY YOU LIVE DOES

Do not remember the sins of my youth and my rebellious ways;
according to your love remember me, for you, LORD, are good.
PSALM 25:7

Tommy is a friend of mine. His brother was born deaf but never learned official sign language, so they developed a rudimentary language of their own. If his brother wanted something, he would point at what he wanted with one hand as he pointed toward his chest with his other. He had heard of American Sign Language (ASL), but his family had never taken the time to learn, so the two brothers did the best they could with what they had.

In high school, Tommy got in with the wrong crowd, and by eighteen, he was in prison for doing really bad things. He got into a cycle where he would be sentenced to a term in prison, get out, and then do more bad things to land him back in. When he got out of his fifth term in prison, it wasn't long before his friends were killed by other gang members, his wife was killed in a car wreck, and his young boys were injured. Tommy tanked and this time did something that would land him in prison with a life sentence. But something was changing inside of Tommy.

Tommy enrolled in a class I teach at San Quentin about pursuing dreams and ambitions. He decided he was going to teach inmates how to use sign language, but first, he needed to learn how to do it correctly. It took some time, but Tommy completed his studies and began teaching ASL. And get this: hundreds of inmates signed up. Tommy is now the guy who teaches the incarcerated hearing population at San Quentin to communicate with the incarcerated deaf community. When I walk through the yard at San Quentin, now I see men who used to be in gangs practicing their sign language with one another.

You may not have been sentenced to prison, but you may be living in a jail of your own construction. We all have a choice to make—whether we're going to move forward and chase our ambitions or stay stuck and stagnate.

What skill or adventure have you been deferring? What could you start today that could positively impact many lives?

FAITH ISN'T CHEAP—IT'S PRICELESS

Then Jesus said to his disciples, "Whoever wants to be my disciple must deny themselves and take up their cross and follow me."
MATTHEW 16:24

I worked at a sorority during college. I would put a dinner jacket over my T-shirt and jeans and serve at a sit-down dinner each night. I learned how to pull out chairs and pick up dishes from the right and serve from the left. It was a great deal, because in exchange I could walk in the back door any time and eat anything that was still in the refrigerator. I would eat my weight in expensive sorority food, then put on my jacket the next evening and wait on tables again. This all worked out great until the sorority burned down overnight. Thankfully, everyone escaped without injuries, but my good deal went up in flames.

Some people will do anything for a good deal. They'll eat the samples at Costco for lunch and then load up on small packets of mustard, ketchup, and relish, along with one hundred napkins from the food court. They will clip coupons and sit through timeshare presentations and wait in long lines. This is all well and good if that's your thing, but sometimes getting the good deal is not the best way of thinking about living your beautiful, challenging life.

I received a call from someone who told me they wanted me to convince them over the phone of why following Jesus is a good deal. *Heavens*, I thought, *putting aside the promise of eternity, following Jesus isn't a good deal at all.* Following Jesus involves giving up everything, denying yourself every day, and taking cuts to the back of every line except the one for receiving grace. It involves suffering and denial and being constantly misunderstood, and continually dying to your lesser desires—and that's on a good day.

Faith won't be found on any bargain shelf and will cost you everything. Most things, though, are worth what they cost, and Jesus promises both that He will cost you everything and that He is worth everything.

Today, deny yourself, take up your cross, and follow Jesus. Live your life like it is as beautiful and costly as Jesus says it is.

GENEROSITY IS MORE REWARDING THAN IT COSTS

And do not forget to do good and to share with others,
for with such sacrifices God is pleased.
HEBREWS 13:16

I have met many very generous people. You probably have too. Generosity comes in as many forms as there are colors or flavors. Some people are generous with their resources and give away loads of money. Others are generous with their words, often talking about what a great job someone is doing or the beauty they see in someone's life. Still others are generous with their time. These people invite interruptions, welcome people's interactions with them, and while they may be the busiest people in the room, they don't show it and live lives marked by tremendous availability.

Many of us, on the other hand, prefer to be efficient with our time and resist interruptions, and it makes sense why. Our minds are engaged in something and, after an interruption, we need to retrace our steps just to remember where we were in our thought processes so we can return there. But I wonder if another reason we don't like to be interrupted is that this gives us little time and opportunity to control the conversation.

I picked up the phone one afternoon, and the person on the other end said, "Hello, Bob? I'm so surprised you answered." "How come?" I asked. "I heard you were dead," she said with a laugh. *Tell me you're not reading tomorrow's newspaper,* I thought to myself and grinned. You never know what you're going to get when you make yourself available to people. But in truth, most people who reach out just want to know if they matter enough for us to give them our attention. They may be asking a question about something, but the unspoken question they have is how important they are to us.

Don't miss the opportunity to give the people who intersect your life a huge shot in the arm by giving them your full attention. Putting down what you are doing and giving someone your attention the way Jesus did communicates volumes about who you are.

**Look for opportunities to surprise someone with how
free and generous you are with your love.**

REFRESH YOUR FAITH

Do not merely listen to the word, and so deceive yourselves.
JAMES 1:22

I was in Flint, Michigan, a place that later became known for its awful water system, which was in disrepair and had caused damage to so many. It was a sunny spring morning, and the weather report indicated it would in the mid-seventies that day. I stepped outside in my short-sleeve shirt and found the roads in every direction had been freshly salted. *What in the world?*

It was a head-scratcher. It turns out the winter that year had been exceptionally mild, and the amount of salt they would get the following year to melt the snow on the roads was dictated by the amount of salt they used that year. So they salted the roads, even when they didn't need to.

I wonder if we do the same thing at our faith gatherings. Here's what I mean. We tell the same stories, teach the same lessons, and cover the same topics with the same people over and over, whether we need to or not. Don't get me wrong, these stories are good and true and important, but even with an infinite universe of examples, metaphors, and engaging topics surrounding us, we still lock in on a couple of stories and overuse or overteach them. It's like Flint thinking they were helping by salting roads that didn't need it.

For decades I have met with eight guys on Friday mornings. It's not a Bible study but a Bible-doing group. This is not a distinction without a difference. We don't want to read or tell the same stories over and over and then merely agree with Jesus again. In doing so, we would just be salting snow-free roads. We want to do what Jesus did, risk the ways He risked, be compassionate in the ways He was compassionate.

Tell a couple of new stories today. Find a few new Bible verses that are important to you, and instead of merely talking about them, go do something about them.

Don't just salt the same roads when the snow has already melted.

WHEN THINGS GO WRONG, ARE YOU GONNA ASK GOD FOR A BAILOUT OR A BIGGER PADDLE?

For it is God who works in you, both to will
and to work for his good pleasure.
PHILIPPIANS 2:13 ESV

When Sweet Maria and I were still dating, I heard she was going to a Young Life camp called Oakbridge to lead ten high school girls who were volunteering at a weekend women's camp. I'm no dummy, so I immediately rounded up ten high school guys to volunteer at the camp, so I would have a reason to be near Maria without looking like a stalker. I was leaning in, not bailing out on my ambition. I hoped that God was at work in some way.

On the first night, an elderly woman's pacemaker stopped, and she face-planted in her spaghetti. But I knew how to do CPR, so until the ambulance arrived, I pumped on her chest and blew into her mouth—and it worked. It wasn't quite a Lazarus-level thing, but it was close enough to get Sweet Maria's attention. I'm guessing she thought, *This guy isn't much to look at, but he can be useful in a pinch.*

Thirty-four years later, we found out Young Life had put Oakbridge up for sale, so we bought it. The camp smelled like three hundred fourteen-year-old boys had lived there for forty years without ever taking showers, but we leaned in once again, hoping God was at work. We stripped the walls down to the studs, put some air fresheners out, moved a couple of walls around to make suites, and turned it into a topflight resort and retreat center.

We were so excited to throw the doors open. I started blowing up the balloons—then COVID hit. We had sixty thousand square feet of empty buildings on hundreds of acres, but we couldn't open. We had more tumble-weeds blowing through than people, and we were losing a stunning amount of money. But we kept leaning in, wondering if God still might be at work on something we couldn't quite see.

A version of this happens to all of us. We have a terrific idea we can't wait to release into the world, and it seems like everything is going just great—right up until it doesn't. This isn't just a small part of life, it is how much of life works. It's a relationship that falls apart, it's the job or the internship that ends, or the car that breaks down, or the break you inexplicably don't get. When this happens, we each get to decide whether to bail out or keep leaning in.

What kind of strategy can you commit to in advance of when these predictable setbacks happen?

Instead of giving God a list of all the things you think you need, take inventory today of what you've already got.

LIVE INTO YOUR TRUE PURPOSE

Do your best to present yourself to God as one approved, a worker
who has no need to be ashamed, rightly handling the word of truth.
2 TIMOTHY 2:15 ESV

When we are performing for others, we are no longer ourselves and instead
are just another sword swallower at the circus. The trick to stop performing
and start living more authentically is to find out what you feel a unique sense
of satisfaction doing and can envision yourself devoting boatloads of time and
energy toward.

Many of us make our lives work by operating only within our current
capabilities rather than responding to our deeper purposes. And a lot of people
would be happy for us to continue doing just that. People who identify us by
our capabilities to be a lawyer or a singer, for example—and whose livelihoods
are connected to our continuing to do what the previous versions of us have
done—can directly or indirectly steer us toward continuing to do what we're
merely capable of, rather than having us welcome the new and truer versions
that might be stirring within us.

Perhaps you need to make some changes in your life to sync up more fully
with the person God created you to be. Let the previous versions of you go,
and ask God to help you live into the bright future He has for you as a new
creation. Then repeat this to yourself every morning: "New day; new me." We
don't go to sleep having one career and wake up with a new one (unless you call
your boss and quit at 2:00 a.m.). Live in anticipation of the cumulative effect
of small daily changes you make. The world can't wait to meet the person you
are becoming.

Take away what you are known for, and whatever is left is who you are.
For instance, if you are a talented musician, envision what your life would look
like if you took away music. If you are a lawyer, what would your life look like
if you took away your reputation as a hot-shot lawyer? If you are known as a
famous chef, take away all the cooking, and what is left?

**We do not have value because of what we can
do, but because we are loved by God.**

GO CRAZY WITH COURAGE—IT ONLY TAKES A FEW SECONDS

All hard work brings a profit, but mere talk leads only to poverty.
PROVERBS 14:23

You are going to ask someone today, "How are you?" To which you will probably receive a predictable response. It's a North American greeting and it's how we roll, but it doesn't need to be the way you engage with people. The only way to fully give and receive love is to come out from behind the facade of an "everything's great" nonresponse. Sure, it sounds like it checks the right box, but it lacks substance and won't serve you well in the long term. Replace this prefabricated reaction with a more courageous one and say, "Actually, I'm in need of attention" or "I need a hug" or "I'm feeling a lot of rejection recently." Doing this is going to take some courage.

Somebody sent me a movie called *We Bought a Zoo*. The movie is about a widowed dad who buys a failing zoo. At one point, the father is trying to explain to his teenage son how life works, and he tells him that twenty seconds of insane courage and unreasonable bravery will change everything. Hover over that idea for a second. What if all it takes is twenty seconds to move away from our shallow relationships and into deeper, more real connections?

Perhaps you will dig deep and decide it would take twenty seconds of insane courage to be authentic with someone and say, "I know you did not intend this, but it actually hurt my feelings when this thing happened." Maybe you need twenty seconds of courage to meet with your boss and tell them you have changed in ways the job has not and then quit. Or, it might be a relationship you need to part with. Thank them for all the good they brought your way but let them know the relationship needs to change. It's going to take some guts and grit to lean into relational authenticity like this, but you are worth it and so are they.

What will be your power move today? It's probably going to take about twenty seconds of insane courage to get there. Just twenty seconds.

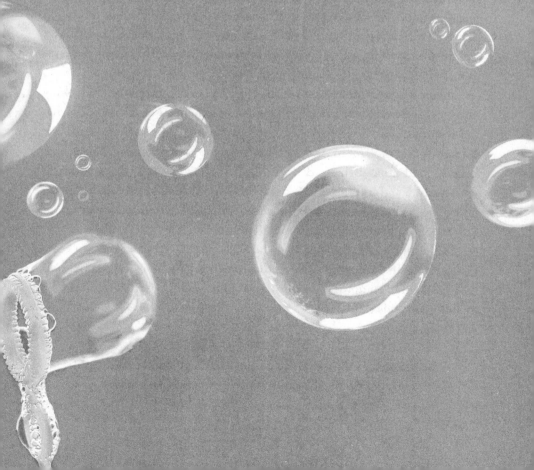

DECEMBER

LIVE IN ANTICIPATION OF HOW GOOD IT CAN GET

The creation waits in eager expectation for
the children of God to be revealed.
ROMANS 8:19

People who lead beautiful, purposeful lives have several things in common. One of them is that they live in constant anticipation. But it's hard living in anticipation if you are in a continual state of consternation, frustrated with many things that happen from day to day. That's why the mindset we bring to each day matters.

Every day we get to decide how we will show up. Will we overindex those disappointments that will predictably come our way, or will we entirely ignore them and pretend they never existed? These unhealthy extreme reactions bracket a good one. What if, instead, we lived in anticipation and expectation that God will do terrific, amazing, unanticipated things? Some of those things will be unexpectedly painful and others remarkably beautiful, but we can rest in knowing God can make something of either.

In one of the opening scenes in the New Testament, people began looking for Jesus, and the Scriptures say the people were in great expectation of what was to come. They had heard about a person named John who was out in the wilderness and thought to themselves, *Is this the One?* It wasn't much later that Jesus showed up and changed everything. Expectation was the precursor to Jesus' arrival, and it still is. His arrival and our anticipation are usually closely linked. So, let me ask you, are you living in great expectation and anticipation? Or are you shuffling your feet through life?

Paul captured this anticipation when he said that "creation waits in eager expectation." In a beautiful word picture, one translation says "the entire universe is standing on tiptoe, yearning to see the unveiling" of what God is going to do for His kids (TPT).

What about you?

What are you living in anticipation of? If you can't see it right now, get up on your tiptoes and look a little harder.

BIG PLANS REQUIRE BIG PLANNING

Be very careful, then, how you live—not as unwise but as wise,
making the most of every opportunity, because the days are evil.
EPHESIANS 5:15–16

Ezekiel was an Old Testament prophet who asked the question, How then shall we live? when considering the problems all mankind faces. How we live is a function of many things, but at the top is who we are and what we do. At some point we need to figure out how God wired us from the factory and where we are going to throw our energy.

For example, are you a do-one-thing-at-a-time person, or are you a little more like me and are a do-lots-of-things-at-once person, who then goes with the opportunities that are working out the best? There is no judgment toward either approach, only wisdom in thinking through if the approach you have adopted is serving God, you, and the people around you well. Paul cautioned his friends in Ephesus to be wise when they decided how they were going to live.

To be sure, there are pluses and minuses with both the one-thing-at-a-time approach and the many-things-at-a-time approach. If you bet all the chips on one single thing at the time and there is an unexpected or unanticipated delay, you might burn a lot of time waiting for that obstacle to clear before making the kind of contribution you had in mind. On the other hand, if you have several things started and one hits a snag, you can go with the fastest pony you've got that is still in the race with the fewest impediments.

Consider having a couple of high-value tasks in play. Sure, it makes a great "against all odds" story to talk about someone who stayed with one thing for decades without any progress until the breakthrough came. But wouldn't it also be a great story to talk about all the things you were able to accomplish during those decades while you were waiting on that idea to break through?

Don't let all the slow-moving ideas be like slow ponies
staying in your barn and eating all your hay; find one
or two you can take out for a gallop right now.

WHERE HAS GOD PLANTED YOU? SINK YOUR ROOTS IN EVEN DEEPER.

Peter said to Jesus, "Rabbi, it is good for us to be here. Let us put up three shelters—one for you, one for Moses and one for Elijah."

MARK 9:5

We have all been on a vacation or at a retreat that was deeply meaningful and thought, *I wish I could just live this way every day. Let's sell everything and move here.* We feel this way because we connected with something deeply important to us, or we saw ourselves and others from a new camera angle we enjoyed, or perhaps we uncovered and engaged an important part of who we are at the core. It's more than just having an experience we enjoyed and would like to repeat; it felt like we traded in the life we were living for a better version.

When Jesus took Peter, James, and John to what most scholars think was Mount Tabor, they also experienced something unforgettable. They saw Jesus in a way they had never seen Him before, and two other heroes of the Scriptures, Elijah and Moses, showed up too. This experience made Peter want to stay up on top of the mountain, because it connected with something new and important and core to who he was becoming. Who wouldn't want to set up shop there and not leave?

God wants us to experience massive amounts of His love and acceptance. If you experience this somewhere, soak it in and then read the room and God's heart. He doesn't want you to camp out; He wants you to run home to the community where He has placed you, changed. There you can wring every drop of what you have learned out on the people you are called to live life with. It's good to experience God in new places, but don't set up camp there. Return to the vineyard God has planted you in and sink your roots in even deeper.

Who are your people?

Gather some wonderful experiences and return home to your people.

IF AT FIRST YOU DON'T UNDERSTAND, ASK AND ASK AGAIN

[Jesus] said to them, "Do you still not understand?"
MARK 8:21

I'm not always hip to contemporary words and phrases and what they mean. I was on an airplane once, and someone was trying to get their luggage in the overhead compartment. They said to me, "I'm going to move your bag. Are you down with that?" *Huh? Does this person want me to take my bag down out of the overhead?* I wondered. "Sure, you can take it down if you'd like to." She shook her head and said, "No . . . are you down with me moving your stuff?" After four or five rounds, the nickel dropped, and I understood what she was asking me. Maybe I should have an urban dictionary in my back pocket to bail me out in a pinch.

Not long after that, I heard someone talking about an athlete and calling him a "goat." Really? The eat-my-sweater barn animal kind of goat? Did he mean this athlete is agile? Or that he had hooves and creepy eyes? It is embarrassing to admit, but I only found out later that it means "Greatest Of All Time." Who knew? The answer seemed evident to everyone—except me.

This sort of thing happened all the time to Jesus' disciples. They often didn't understand what He said. You are probably familiar with the time when Jesus fed thousands of people with a couple of loaves and fish. After that miracle happened and the disciples left with Jesus, they realized they didn't have any bread with them, which is more than ironic, don't you think? Jesus told them to watch out for the yeast of the Pharisees and Herod. They thought He was talking about who not to buy bread from, but He was talking about not being deceived.

If you want to be the GOAT at living out your faith, you will need to dig a little deeper to understand what Jesus is saying. Keep asking questions about the parts you don't understand. Jesus knew this would happen often and He drops people in our path to help us along.

Today, think of something in the Gospels you've always wondered about and dig deep for the truth.

BELIEVE IN MIRACLES LIKE YOU BELIEVE IN YOUR NEXT BREATH

> When he had gone indoors, the blind men came to him, and he
> asked them, "Do you believe that I am able to do this?" "Yes, Lord,"
> they replied. Then he touched their eyes and said, "According to
> your faith let it be done to you"; and their sight was restored.
> **MATTHEW 9:28–30**

Jesus performed miracles in several different ways. Sometimes He touched people and healed them. Think here of the blind man, the lepers, the sick woman, and the paralyzed man. Other times, all it took was for people to be close to Him, and that did the trick. For example, there was a wedding Jesus attended where He turned the water into wine for everyone. Another time He healed an official's son because He was nearby, and He even cast demons out of people who were in His vicinity. Still other times, Jesus said the miracle healings were attributable to someone's faith or the faith of their friends. Think here of the man lowered through a roof and the centurion's servant.

What we believe is a great predictor of our behavior and of God's power in our lives. That's why Jesus asked people all the time, right before He healed them, if they believed He could do it. The problem is, a lot of us don't know the specifics of what we believe. What do you believe Jesus is capable of doing in your life and in the lives of your friends?

Make a list of the things you believe about Jesus and what He can do. Before you make grand predictions, start with the basics. Do you believe you are loved by God? What about the miraculous? Do you see miracles as something you could experience, or do you see them as something that happened a long time ago for someone else? It's easy to think about what God could do in someone else's life. Get real about what you think He can do in yours. Do you believe He can change your circumstances or heal your damaged relationships?

Quit playing it safe.
We were created to believe.

REPLACE YOUR TO-DO LIST WITH A LEGACY LIST

Because so many people were coming and going that they did
not even have a chance to eat, [Jesus] said to them, "Come
with me by yourselves to a quiet place and get some rest."
MARK 6:31

We can be busy without being productive. I'm not pointing fingers at you, because you know who you are already. That's why you are fidgeting in your chair and tapping your fingers on the table or are the one listening to this book on tape because you are doing several things at once. It's easy to confuse a lot of activity with a purposeful life. Don't take the bait. Do what lasts; let the rest fall away.

But how do you know what should be getting prioritized in your life, so you're not just being busy but being purposeful? I struggle with this myself, so I get it. Try this. Get rid of your to-do list and replace it with a legacy list. Think of the way you want to be remembered and what characteristic traits you want to develop in yourself to get there. Do you want to be known for your courage? Your curiosity? Your compassion toward others? Think of what steps you will need to take or what activities you will need to involve yourself in to move toward developing those character traits you want to inform your legacy.

For those of you who are overly busy, what do you think would happen if you took your level of activity down a notch or two? Maybe three? Do you think this would sink you into a deep depression? Or perhaps you think you will run out of money if you aren't working tirelessly on the next big deal?

I am betting the bank it is more likely you will find more meaning and purpose and resolve. Sure, you might need to tighten your financial belt a little if you cut out some of the hustle, but you'll feel great about yourself while you chill out. Find a quiet place and rest.

**Take time to rest, which can bring clarity about the
legacy you want to leave and how to go about doing it.
Then begin working on your legacy list today.**

DON'T BE A SHERIFF; BE A LOVING FRIEND

"If your brother or sister sins against you, rebuke them; and if they repent, forgive them. Even if they sin against you seven times in a day and seven times come back to you saying 'I repent,' you must forgive them."

LUKE 17:3-4

We all have setbacks in relationships. Maybe things were rock solid in your relationship but somehow along the way things got wonky. Perhaps this person did something underhanded or deceptive or hurtful. You had hoped you had simply misunderstood something, but when you blew the foam off the top, there was no conclusion to reach other than that you had been betrayed on purpose by someone you trusted. So, what is your next move?

Some think that following Jesus means you just suck it up; you absorb the body blow and take the pain and disappointment like a champ. This isn't what Jesus said. Jesus said that if someone sins against you, your move is to rebuke them. This heavy, religious-sounding word simply means expressing your disapproval.

Jesus said the next move is theirs. If they repent, which is another religious word that means they immediately go in the opposite direction of their previous behavior, then forgive them. Not only that, but if they blow it in the same way or a new way and they change directions again, forgive them again and again.

There are people you will get sideways with who will stop doing mean things if you call them out. But they won't take the next step to move in a new direction. Give them a little time; it's embarrassing for all of us when we mess up. Let them know there is a path forward. Don't play the victim. Just be available and loving.

This model Jesus gave us for resolving disputes is not to be punitive but to take a more complete approach. Don't hold people accountable; hold them close. Holding people accountable sounds like you are taking on the role of a sheriff or hall monitor of someone's behavior, and it rarely works. By contrast, holding people close almost always works. God didn't design us to live in community so we would constantly be correcting one another; He wants us to love one another.

Who do you need to reach out to today to have a heart-to-heart? Be courageous. You are worth it, and they are too.

DON'T BE PERFECT, BE REAL

[The blind man] looked up and said, "I see people; they look like trees walking around." Once more Jesus put his hands on the man's eyes. Then his eyes were opened, his sight was restored, and he saw everything clearly.

MARK 8:24–25

In law school, they teach you never to ask a question you don't know the answer to. There was a man who was blind, and Jesus spit into the dirt and rubbed the mud in the blind man's eyes. After He had done this, Jesus asked the man, "Do you see anything?" I don't think Jesus was asking a question He didn't know the answer to. And I'm sure the man felt conflicted about what to say to Jesus, because his eyesight hadn't been healed. I can imagine him stuttering with uncertainty as he said, "I see people, but they look like trees." If Jesus had put mud in my blind eyes and it didn't work, I would have been tempted to lie, because I wouldn't want Jesus to look bad. But when we're not truthful and authentic, we make our faith look weak. Here's the point. Keep it real with God. Jesus didn't have a problem with people who were confused about their faith; He just didn't want people to fake it.

The story doesn't end after the first touch. Jesus touched the man's eyes again, and his sight was fully restored. This wasn't a miracle that misfired. I bet Jesus wanted to know if the man could be truthful and authentic enough to admit that he needed Jesus to touch him again. Don't we all need a second touch?

Think of it this way. We have the story of our lives and the truth of our lives. You might think they would be the same, and they should be, but over time and with enough distraction they can be very different. We need to resist the urge to hide who we really are and the important questions we still have. Too many people are living life cautiously, like they have signed a nondisclosure agreement.

If you're struggling right now, give someone a call who is safe and knows you, and tell them how you can identify with the blind guy. Then tell Jesus about the things that are still a little fuzzy where you need a second touch.

EMPTY THE WORRIES AND FILL YOUR POCKETS WITH WHIMSY

"Do not worry about tomorrow, for tomorrow will worry about itself. Each day has enough trouble of its own."
MATTHEW 6:34

I have lots of pairs of pants. In all of them, I have cut out the left pockets. The things I want to hang on to that are useful to me, like car keys, I keep in the right pocket, and the things that end up in the left pocket simply fall away.

It's easy to accumulate concerns and worries, biases, and false beliefs. Let these be left-pocket things. In your mind, move them from your right pocket, where you have been carrying them around, to your left. Are there controversies and misunderstandings or opinions you hold closely that, if moved to your other pocket, would better serve you and the people around you? Are there worries you have been carrying around that are dogging you? Move them eighteen inches to the left and let them go.

Let's get even more practical about what we move from the right pocket to the left pocket. Some of us are working so hard to provide for our families that we are not providing what they need most, which is us.

If you are up for a bold experience, write your resignation letter today. Address it to your boss, put a stamp on it, and give it to the person you love the most. Tell them that if your job ever gets in the way of your relationship with them or your relationship with God, to mail the resignation letter. Writing this letter is like moving those portions of your career that are interfering with the more important parts of your life from the right pocket to your left.

What is it you are going to keep in your right pocket, and what things do you need to move to your left pocket and let go of?

SOMETIMES THE BEST PART OF THE MOVIE IS THE END

All the people were wailing and mourning for her. "Stop wailing," Jesus said. "She is not dead but asleep." They laughed at him, knowing that she was dead. But he took her by the hand and said, "My child, get up!" Her spirit returned, and at once she stood up. Then Jesus told them to give her something to eat.
LUKE 8:52–55

You can imagine the scene. A little girl has died, and it happens to be the daughter of one of the religious leaders in the area. Jairus had tried everything, as any good father would, and he ended up with Jesus, asking for help—but then the news came. It was over.

We may not have lost a child, but we have all come to what appeared to be an end. Maybe it was the end of a career, or the end of a relationship, or the end of a legal battle. You put absolutely everything you had into it, left nothing on the table or in reserve, and then—it was all over. There was nothing more to do, no Hail Mary pass to throw, no more effort required, no more hope for an alternate ending.

Jesus' response to Jairus was to make an impossible statement. He told Jairus his daughter would be healed. Perhaps it felt to Jairus that Jesus was naïve; that was certainly the reaction of the people gathered at Jairus's house who laughed at Jesus. Sometimes the extraordinary promises Jesus makes to us seem laughable in the midst of tragedy. But then Jesus said the words "Get up." The same words He spoke to a man sitting by a pool, waiting for years to be healed. And then the miraculous happened.

What is it that seems to have come to an end in your life? Certainly grieve the loss, but also trust the seemingly impossible promises of Jesus. He may be asking you to get up and walk into a new life.

BE LOVE AND LOW-MAINTENANCE

*Humble yourselves, therefore, under God's mighty
hand, that he may lift you up in due time. Cast all
your anxiety on him because he cares for you.*

1 PETER 5:6–7

Do you have high-maintenance people in your life who have maneuvered their way into being adjacent to you? You don't need to point to them if you are sitting in the same room right now; we'll keep it our secret. Let's have some straight talk about difficult people.

Sometimes people who have made a career out of helping people have also overindexed their own highly refined list of perceived needs. So they surround themselves with lots of helpers. They hire cupbearers, and the cupbearers have assistants, who also have assistants. You know the type. They arrive with their entourage and expect you to bend to their will and their eccentric demands. The odd part is that most of the highest-maintenance people I know don't think they are difficult at all.

Here's where the dividing line is, and also a way forward. You can be aware of your needs without expecting the people around you to meet them. Sure, you can give a lot of input on, for example, what food you are served. If you are a soy-only, vegan, extra-virgin, no carbs, gluten-free person, great. Most people want you to be pleased and are happy to go the extra mile for you. Just double check and make sure you aren't overdoing it on what you can control as a reaction against feeling like you can't control anything, and then putting all that dysfunction on someone else and a day of running around just to buy yourself some momentary relief.

Make your goal today to be high impact in the areas of love, encouragement, and gratitude, and to be low maintenance for other people. Make a parallel ambition to serve others with love and patience without losing yourself as you do.

**We all have needs. Delight in them,
vet them, and then manage them.**

LIVE IN HOPE LIKE IT'S CHRISTMAS MORNING

*Now faith is confidence in what we hope for and
assurance about what we do not see.*
HEBREWS 11:1

When our family was getting ready for Christmas when the kids were little, they had a hard time waiting as they counted down the days. You too? Sweet Maria and I would take one of our little Santa decorations and set him at the end of the hallway. We would inch him forward each day, and by Christmas Eve, Santa would be under the tree. This worked great until the anticipation became just too much for our kids, and they started moving Santa all the way down the hallway to speed up the arrival of Christmas. Every day, Sweet Maria and I would patiently move Santa back to the right spot and inch him forward again. We didn't say to our kids, "You aren't doing this right. Stop trying to fast forward to Christmas." Instead, we delighted in knowing they were living in absolute anticipation and delightful expectation. God feels the same way about us.

What are you anticipating? I remember in junior high school I hoped for a date—but it never happened. What I wanted in high school was the same—a date—but it never quite happened then either. I squeezed four years of college into five years, and I still wanted the same thing, but once again, it never happened. When I met Sweet Maria, it was like all the decades of waiting collapsed in one moment. As soon as what I'd been longing for arrived, all the waiting didn't matter. This is the stuff eternity is made of.

Figure out what you're hoping for, and then get comfortable living in expectation. Santa didn't move as quickly down the hallway as my kids hoped, but he was still moving in the right direction and eventually got there every time. God doesn't always give us specifics about how things will work out, but what He will often give us is a direction He hopes we will move toward.

Live in constant expectation of what God might have for you today.

Know what you're hoping for and have confidence in what you haven't seen yet, knowing that God is over the moon about you.

JOY IS THE REWARD FOR LOVING SACRIFICE

Jesus said, "Truly I tell you, this poor widow has put more into the treasury than all the others. They all gave out of their wealth; but she, out of her poverty, put in everything—all she had to live on."

MARK 12:43–44

I have mites. It feels like I have admitted to a troublesome medical problem, but that's not what I mean. I actually have two ancient coins that are called mites. Think of a mite in today's values as a couple of bucks or about six minutes of someone's time. This would be pocket change for most people today (if people carried change in their pockets any longer), but Jesus told a story about a widow who had just two mites. She was as generous as she was needy, and Jesus used her as an example to reveal a truth about the relationship we have to money.

I don't know about you, but it's easy for me to contribute out of the extra amounts of my gifting or time or energy that I have. But Jesus flipped it. He said if I give what comes from a surplus, it won't matter as much as if it came from the little I have that's not extra. Here is the kicker: the point of the story of the two mites isn't that God wants us to pony up what we should but, rather, that we need to be cheerful givers, just like the poor widow.

I bet you are generous—me too. But Jesus is talking about the power of sacrificial giving and what we can access in our lives if we will take the risk. Keep in mind there was not a follow-up story about how everything changed in the widow's life after she gave everything she had. The next verse isn't about how she got a new house and new wheels like she might on an Oprah show. We never even learn her name. My guess is that she continued on with her beautiful, sacrificial life and learned boatloads about her faith as she did.

What is it that you have the least of but can make available? Is it your time? Is it your cash? Is it your ability to pursue people who are more than a little prickly? Take a step in that direction today, and I will bet you two mites that it will change you.

**Take inventory of what you've got and make it
your life's work to clear the shelves.**

GOD WILL RELENTLESSLY PURSUE YOU

"While he was still a long way off, his father saw him and was filled with compassion for him; he ran to his son, threw his arms around him and kissed him. . . . 'Bring the fattened calf and kill it. Let's have a feast and celebrate. For this son of mine was dead and is alive again; he was lost and is found.' So they began to celebrate."
LUKE 15:20, 23–24

Most of us have experienced that terrifying moment at the grocery store or at Disneyland or at the mall when you lose track of the people you came with. In that moment, you feel a rush of fear as you realize, *I'm lost. I'm alone.* These feelings beg the question: "Will I ever be found?"

Most of us will learn how to control these emotions as we grow up, but they never go away entirely. Later in life, something else might happen that triggers the *I'm lost, I'm alone, I'm abandoned* trifecta of fear again. So what do we do when that happens?

The parable of the lost son follows the parable of the lost sheep and the lost coin. In each of these parables, something is lost in great pain and then is found again with great joy. These are all stories about value and the diligence of the search for the thing of value. In the case of the son, the father runs to him and throws his arms around him, and there is a great celebration that follows.

You are of tremendous value to God, and so are the people who are in your orbit. Sometimes when we feel most lost to the people we love, we find we had only been misplaced for a short time. We have a Father in heaven who will relentlessly pursue us. Remind yourself about your value today.

Remind yourself about what God likes about you. Don't stop there; let the people adjacent to you know how valuable they are too.

INTENTIONAL INTERACTIONS CAN BE SHORT AND SWEET

Watch your words and hold your tongue; you'll save yourself a lot of grief.
PROVERBS 21:23 MSG

We all know someone who talks before they think about what they are saying. The polite way to frame this is that these people are "verbal processors." It's a nice phrase, but stating it plainly, some people just run their mouths, talking too much and not thinking about what they are about to say before they say it.

We come up with ways to explain and accommodate this kind of behavior by giving a quick eyeroll when a predictable misplaced sentence is dropped into an otherwise beautiful conversation. Lacking the interpersonal skills to be mindful of what you are saying, who you are saying it to, or knowing why you are saying it is not a hall pass for people who are not reading the room.

The fix is not for us to be the policemen of people's interactions. Instead, we need to take the opportunities that come to make sure the least socially aware person in the room doesn't hijack the conversation. When they do, don't get mad. Get busy and come up with a strategy that will serve them and you and everyone within earshot.

If you are in a group of people, put some parameters on the responses when you ask questions. For example, "In three sentences, tell us what your most impactful thought is on this." If they jump the rails, you can say with a laugh, "This sounds like we are going longer than three sentences. Land your idea with one last sentence." Doing this doesn't mean you are rude; it means you are aware.

Why does all this matter? We save ourselves a lot of grief as we watch what we say. Pay attention to what comes out of your mouth for an entire day. Is it small talk? Work talk? What words of encouragement did you have for others?

Let's tame our tongues for the benefit of the ones around us.

Make it so that people start assuming every conversation with you will leave them feeling acknowledged and cared for.

YOUR INBOX IS FULL OF MESSAGES FROM GOD

He said, "O man greatly loved, fear not, peace be with you; be strong
and of good courage." And as he spoke to me, I was strengthened
and said, "Let my lord speak, for you have strengthened me."
DANIEL 10:19 ESV

Before the internet was a thing, I used to love receiving and sending letters. I would run to the mailbox each day to see what the mail carriers had dropped off. I remember having a laugh with the mail carrier once when I raised the red flag signaling outgoing mail and had a cardboard box full of inflated beachballs with stamps and addresses on them.

The New Testament is made up of what we call twenty-seven books, but twenty-one of those are actually letters. Nine are letters from Paul to churches, four are letters from Paul to individuals, and eight are more general letters. Think about how thin the New Testament would be if you took away all the letters written to individuals and faith gatherings. God dropped off the mail in these books of the Bible and said they were messages meant for us, even if they were letters addressed to others.

The letters in the Bible include lasting ideas to influence us about the way we live, the way we love one another, and the way we connect with God. These letters are not just about pointing out problems; they invite us to lift our eyes and see things the way God does, to change what we need to in our lives so we can discover a new and better and more beautiful and lasting way forward.

Today, be a modern-day Paul and write a note to someone. Let them know what you appreciate about them, do a little self-disclosure about your shortcomings, and then encourage them to set their sights a little higher on Jesus.

**Find a piece of paper and a pen. You don't need a quill,
an ink well, and a wax seal. If you need postage, let
me know and I'll hook you up with a stamp.**

LEAD WITH YOUR WEAKNESS

If I must boast, I will boast of the things that show my weakness.
2 CORINTHIANS 11:30

I have been to Uganda dozens of times over more than twenty years. I never take the malaria meds. I mean, what are the chances I will get malaria? It turns out the odds were 100 percent for me because I got malaria. I ended up in the hospital for quite a while with a particularly aggressive strain that is a people killer.

I dropped twenty pounds, which was cool, but I now have a tremor in my left hand. Usually, it's mild and unnoticeable, but when it gets going, I could whip eggs with it. Sometimes when I am speaking, for no particular reason, it will just go off, and I will put my left hand in my pocket so it doesn't draw too much unnecessary attention.

We all find ways to cope with the physical, emotional, and relational weaknesses we are dealing with. We are trained not to show our weaknesses. We do things to hide them that often go unnoticed by others, but we know what is really going on. The psalmist wrote that if we cast our cares on the Lord, He will sustain us. That makes sense to me.

If we show up in relationships talking about our accomplishments and victories and recognitions, no one will be impressed. In fact, these brag fests will cost us deeper conversations and deeper relationships that might otherwise be available to us.

Alternatively, if we show up for the same conversation and choose to be vulnerable about our setbacks and failures and other burdens, we invite relationship and depth to our conversations. Show me someone who has cultivated a reputation for humility, authenticity, and love born out of weakness and I will show you someone who has strong relationships with God and the people around them.

Today reach out your weak hand, not your strong one, to the people around you and watch what God will do with the beautiful authenticity this unlocks for you.

BE A STUDENT AND A TEACHER

Be shepherds of God's flock that is under your care, watching over them—not because you must, but because you are willing, as God wants you to be; not pursuing dishonest gain, but eager to serve; not lording it over those entrusted to you, but being examples to the flock.
1 PETER 5:2-3

You might be surprised to hear the origin of the word *mentor*, which comes from an old-world story in *The Odyssey*. In short, as the story goes, a king left for war, leaving his wife and son behind in the care of someone called Mentor, who was supposed to give loads of training and protection to the king's wife and son. Mentor didn't do his job, and a Greek goddess shapeshifted and showed up to take over in providing training and guidance. This is all pretty weird stuff, and what followed was more than a little messy, but so is the task of mentoring.

Having a mentor can be a helpful thing, but I think I prefer something a little different than the traditional idea of mentoring. What would happen if we got back to the best parts of doing life together, where older brothers exchanged ideas with but also learned from younger brothers and older and younger sisters did the same? Here's the thing. You can be that person who both educates and learns. You can be both the professor and the student.

It is a subtle difference, but when you gather with the friends you hope to learn from, make your time about living with tremendous anticipation of learning rather than the expectation of teaching. Here's what I mean. Expectation is how you hope things will turn out. Anticipation is different. It is for people whose resting position is leaning forward. Anticipation doesn't just look around the corner; it looks well over the horizon. Yes, you will likely share the lessons you have learned in the past along the way, too, but come leaning in and ready to learn.

Stop trying to find a mentor; find a friend who helps you lean forward and look further.

WHEN LIFE THROWS YOU A HURRICANE, MAKE SALTWATER TAFFY

We rejoice in our sufferings, knowing that suffering produces endurance, and endurance produces character, and character produces hope, and hope does not put us to shame, because God's love has been poured into our hearts through the Holy Spirit who has been given to us.
ROMANS 5:3–5 ESV

I am a soft touch for most candy, but my go-to is saltwater taffy. In the summers, we live far away from everybody at the end of an inlet in Canada. There is a camp nearby, and the kids from the camp will paddle by in their kayaks. For decades, I have been throwing saltwater taffy to them with great delight.

Not only am I a fan of the taffy and will regularly sneak a couple of pieces out of the bag, but I am a bigger fan of the story behind saltwater taffy, because it was about making a bad thing a really good thing. It was the late 1800s when a huge storm hit Atlantic City, New Jersey. The waves crashed in through the windows of a candy store, ruining everything. The next day, rather than throwing his hands in the air, the owner put up a sign, saying, "Saltwater Taffy For Sale," and the rest is history.

We are all going to face setbacks, and these can be a real body blow when they happen. Some people will bail out when the resistance comes, and others will innovate. Be one of those people who makes saltwater taffy out of waterlogged candy.

Whether it is a financial or relational setback you are experiencing, or even one involving an unfulfilled dream or your faith, take stock of what you have, like the candy store owner did, and figure out what you can make out of the pieces you have been left with. Remember, your suffering produces endurance, and endurance produces character, and character produces hope.

God promises He will use us. Our job is to figure out what unexpected pieces He has already given us.

WE EACH HAVE GIFTS—KNOW YOURS

*Now eagerly desire the greater gifts. And yet I
will show you the most excellent way.*
1 CORINTHIANS 12:31

When I was growing up, my parents got me a clarinet because they thought it would be a cool instrument to play. Pro tip to all parents here: it's just not. I wanted a guitar, because the guys I knew who played those seemed to have all the girls swooning. With my clarinet, the best I could hope for was to charm a cobra out of a woven basket if I ever made it to India. And that was not what I was going for.

Whether we realize it or not, most of life is deciding what we want most, what it is we will choose to throw our energy into. Paul wrote to his friends in Corinth about the importance of various spiritual gifts, and how these are different reflections of the Spirit of God in the world.

For example, there are gifts of wisdom or healing or speaking in a spiritual language or the gift of discerning what it means. Paul said to go for the greater gifts. He told other friends to aim for God's highest and best. As you are choosing what gifts you will let off the chain in your life, choose the ones with the greatest lasting impact.

Sometimes, as you think about what gifts to pursue, you start to compare yourself with other people and the cool gifts you're seeing them operate in. But Paul said we should think about it like a body, where all the different parts need to find a way to operate together and not envy what another part is doing. When you choose what you are going to do, don't become distracted by what others are doing. Remember, God never compares what He creates.

God wants us to pursue our greater giftings, but we need to decide what we will do with our lives and our faith. Quit waiting for a plan to drop from heaven. And don't merely stumble into the choice of what you will do.

**God will use people who know
their purpose. Know yours.**

DON'T TELL ANYONE—SHOW THEM

Then [Jesus] ordered his disciples not to tell
anyone that he was the Messiah.
MATTHEW 16:20

San Quentin prison was built right on the San Francisco Bay with an epic view of the surrounding areas. There are approximately three thousand men incarcerated there at any one time. It takes a lot of prison cells to house the thousands of incarcerated men who are part of this gated community, and despite its location on the bayfront, only thirty-five of the cells have windows.

We were at San Quentin one day helping the inmates make a documentary. One of the interviews they wanted was of me and the warden at the highest point in the facility, which is a ten-story building. We piled out of the elevator together in what was clearly something special for the inmates, as they were not allowed into this part of the prison. The guy holding the camera stopped when we stepped out onto the balcony and started weeping. "Hey, are you okay? What's up?" I asked. He said he had been next to the water for twenty-five years. He had learned about the bay, he smelled the salt air every day, he was able to hear the ferries go back and forth in front of the prison every day, but he had never seen the water.

Someone asked me what I thought was the best way to let people know about Jesus. I think my answer after that day on the balcony at San Quentin is to show people the water. Every kind expression shows people the water; every selfless act of love shows people the water. I am often asked what my favorite Bible verse is. It always feels like I'm supposed to pull out one of the classics and repeat it with meaning as I stare toward the sky with my hands gently pressed together. But my favorite is Matthew 16:20: "Don't tell anyone." I don't think Jesus was saying to keep it a secret who He was, but instead was encouraging us to show people the water rather than tell people what we believe is true.

**Today, who can you show the water to in a
humble act of love and service?**

KNOW WHO YOU'RE TRAVELING WITH AND WHO YOU'RE TENDING TO

One of them, the disciple whom Jesus
loved, was reclining next to him.
JOHN 13:23

Jesus had twelve disciples, but three of them, Peter, John, and James, were closer to Him than the others. John referred to himself six times as "the disciple Jesus loved." We all have an inner circle of people we are hugely invested in and do life with. These are our fixed points, and we should be deeply grateful for their various contributions to the way we see and experience the world. There are also other people in our lives at varying levels of closeness, and we would be wise to decide ahead of time the ways we will make ourselves available to them.

There are as many ways to approach this as there are words, but here's one way to start. Sort the people in your life into two large categories: people you are traveling with and those you are tending to. Certainly, we are all both traveling with and tending to one another in many respects because we occupy the same planet spinning through space at the same time, but for this exercise, think of the relationships you find to be personally or professionally engaging.

Maybe you find that you always leave a conversation with someone seeing greater possibilities, encouraged to make needed changes, and affirmed in who you are and what you are about. This would be someone you are traveling with. Or maybe you have someone in your life who has a particular relational or emotional challenge and has needs beyond what most people have. This might be someone you are tending to. This is a good thing because God does His best work in community.

Another way to know who you are traveling with and who you are tending to is by asking yourself some clarifying questions:

Does the person pursue you? That's a traveler.

Does the person expect you to make the plans, fix the problems, and carry the conversations? This is someone you are tending to.

Once again, both categories of people are equal in the eyes of God who created them, but it's important to know what your needs are and how much energy you have, and to figure out who to allow in closer based on that assessment. This way we can both receive what we need and give what we are gifted to give.

Today, assess one relationship you assume to be with a traveler and one you would guess to be someone you are tending to. Were you right?

IF FAITH WEREN'T A PARADOX, IT WOULDN'T BE FAITH

"For whoever wants to save their life will lose it, but whoever
loses their life for me and for the gospel will save it."

MARK 8:35

The Bible is a long list of paradoxes. If you are unfamiliar with this word, a paradox is a statement that seems contradictory at first but may still be true. Think of a paradox as a different way to think of things. Here are some examples from Scripture: God exalts the humble and humbles the exalted; the greatest are the least; the first are the last; the sorrowful rejoice; the poor are rich; the weak are strong; we give to receive; we are wise by being fools; we deserve judgment but get grace; we have ears but don't hear and eyes but don't see; God demonstrates His strength in our weakness; we keep our lives by losing them; and Jesus who was the King of the universe with all power came as a helpless baby who would grow up and die so we could live.

See what I mean? Much of faith is paradox and navigating these sometimes mind-bending plot twists. The kind of faith Jesus talked about is impossible without the embrace of paradox.

Someone asked me once what it felt like to be a Christian, and I told them it was equal parts confidence and confusion. I am confident of God's love for me, and at the same time the truths Jesus left us with are often confounding. Following Jesus means spending the rest of our lives trying to live out the paradoxes of faith and also fully understanding that our faith means hovering over the same paradoxes that make real faith seem impossible. This, in a word, is also a paradox.

Take one paradox each day from the list above and reflect on it. Figure out whether you accept the premise and the promise contained in each of them. Expect to encounter some intellectual and emotional pushback as you consider each one. If you didn't, it wouldn't be a paradox.

Life is full of push and pull, up and down, in and out. Keep spinning the puzzle pieces to discover what God has for you in all of it.

TURN YOUR QUESTIONS INTO TREASURES AND YOUR FEAR INTO HOPE

But Mary treasured up all these things and pondered them in her heart.
LUKE 2:19

The story in the Bible when God sends an angel to Nazareth, a small town at the top of a hill just west of the Sea of Galilee, is a familiar scene, but let's hover over it for a moment. We don't know for sure how old Mary was at the time, but she was probably a teenager when the angel told her not to be afraid. My bet is that she was afraid. Who wouldn't be? Then the angel announced she would give birth to a son and that her son would have King David's throne and would reign over Jacob's descendants. One more thing, there would be a kingdom established that would never end.

Wow and yikes! The angel's announcement would have been a big one for anyone, but particularly to a teenager from a small village in Israel. Mary now knew that she was going to have a baby and that her Son would be King of the universe. Yet right in the middle of quite a bit of certainty, there remained a boatload of ambiguity.

While Mary's soon-to-be-mother status was unique to her, it is typical for all of us to be cast into circumstances where we have a few square feet of fixed points in our lives surrounded by acres of questions with answers as scarce as hens' teeth. The Scriptures say that Mary took in all these mysterious things and treasured them up in her heart. Here's the thing. There is a lot to hold in your heart too. It doesn't matter who you are. If you are breathing, you have stored up a lot in your heart. Hopes, happiness, expectation, disappointments, all of it.

The question is how you will respond to the biggest questions in your life. Will you store them up, confident that God will let you in on them later? Or will you freak out or turtle under the weight of uncertainty?

With all the mysteries and unknowns in your life, what would it look like for you to treasure up in your heart the ambiguity God allows?

SOMETIMES THE FANCIEST GIFTS COME IN CRUMPLED WRAPPING PAPER

Now after Jesus was born in Bethlehem of Judea in the days of
Herod the king, behold, wise men from the East came to Jerusalem,
saying, "Where is He who has been born King of the Jews? For we
have seen His star in the East and have come to worship Him."

MATTHEW 2:1-2 NKJV

How do the people you love wrap the presents they give? There are people who crease every corner like they are bending sheet metal. You know the ones—every fold is perfect. Next, one perfectly square piece of clear tape or a gold-foiled circle with the family crest embossed on it is perfectly aligned at the center of every fold. Finally, a perfect red ribbon turns into a flourish of some unknown red flower with gold accents. Then there's the other way to wrap things. It's the way I have seen plenty of guys do it. They take a sheet of used newspaper, or a paper bag, crumple it around whatever they are wrapping, wrap a couple of feet of Scotch tape around it, and call it good.

Here's the reason I am writing about this. Sometimes God wraps presents like a guy. Sure, He could send perfect people with virtuous intentions and large amounts of self-awareness our way, crease all their emotional and relational corners, and put a bow on top. But God often wraps His best gifts in imperfect people and less-than-ideal circumstances. That's why, when Jesus was born, God didn't need a stage or a rolled-out red carpet. Instead, He picked a manger, and through that humble manger everything changed forever.

Maybe things in your life have not turned out the way you were hoping. If there is a gift under the crumpled dreams in your life, it's hard to see what it is. Or, perhaps everything has turned out for you picture perfect, neatly creased and perfectly presented—but I doubt it. Here's why God doesn't always perfectly wrap the gifts He gives us: He wants us to see beyond the circumstances and to want Him, not the gift.

**From our family to yours, we wish you a season filled with
Jesus, the gift of God to each and every one of us.**

JESUS HEARS OUR SINCERITY AND SHOWS US MERCY

"If my people, who are called by my name, will humble themselves
and pray and seek my face and turn from their wicked ways, then I will
hear from heaven, and I will forgive their sin and will heal their land."
2 CHRONICLES 7:14

I remember my first bee sting and my first day at school, but I don't remember the first time I let someone down. I know for certain it happened that I disappointed someone, and judging from the frequency with which I currently let people down, it must have happened early on. Somehow, as children, we can metabolize someone else's disappointment in us and move on, but as we get older, we become harder on ourselves and less resilient. We become less willing to let ourselves off the hook for our failures and less willing to let others out of relational jail for theirs. At the very time you would think we would have more grace for others who fail, given the number and magnitude of our own mess-ups, in an unlikely plot twist we seem to have less.

Think of the two guys on the crosses next to Jesus on the day that Jesus was crucified. I have often wondered what some of the angry people I have met in our faith gatherings would say to them. Jesus didn't say anything to the criminal who was cursing Him, which is a good reminder to us that we do not need to swing at every person who gets in our grill. The conversation Jesus had with the other criminal was a brief one. He just told the guy He would see him in heaven. Jesus didn't ask what the criminal was in for, or if he felt bad about it, or his position on any of the many issues we seem to quarrel about. Jesus didn't trade His sacrifice for the criminal's regret. He just heard his sincerity and showed him mercy.

There are people in your life who are a lot like the first criminal and want to distract you by calling you out. You don't need to engage with them. There will be other people who have messed up and just need an understanding word from you. If you encounter that person today, give them a hug and tell them you forgive them.

**Jesus stepped out of heaven so we could climb into
it. Bring a few people with you when you do.**

LOVE INEFFICIENTLY

Love is patient, love is kind. It does not envy, it does not boast, it is not proud. It does not dishonor others, it is not self-seeking, it is not easily angered, it keeps no record of wrongs.

1 CORINTHIANS 13:4–5

I remember falling in love with Sweet Maria and wanting her to feel the same way about me. It was only the first day we had met, but I'm a planner. First, I would make sure she knew what my name was. Then, I would dazzle her in every way possible. Unfortunately, it seemed that every great idea I had for getting time alone together blew up on the launch pad, and after weeks of great plans, all I had managed to do was spend some time with her and her roommates. It was hardly the over-the-top beginning to the romance I had in mind. Looking back, I can see God's hand in all of this. Maria didn't want a surreal experience that could not be replicated years later; she wanted to know if I was someone she could do life with.

Resist the urge to impress. If you are able to pull this off, people are going to find their way to you, because they believe in who you are, what you are about, and what you are doing. The best and most self-aware of these people will have no agenda for loving you. They simply desire to enjoy as much time together as possible in whatever context is available. These kinds of relationships are worth a standing ovation, so don't forget to give them one.

But don't just avoid trying to impress people. Be equally aware of not allowing your relationships to be merely convenient. Be wonderfully inefficient in the way you love the people in your life. Show up in person; make the drive. Try this: aim for having at least two shared unimpressive experiences each week, and then buckle up and watch the quality of your relationships shoot through the roof.

Remember all the things that love is: patient, kind, not envious or boastful or proud. It honors people, isn't self-seeking, nor easily angered, and it doesn't keep track of people's mess-ups.

Are you ready to be love today? Here we go!

GO FOR COMMUNITY; NOBODY NEEDS ANOTHER CLIQUE

"When you give a banquet, invite the poor, the crippled, the lame, the blind, and you will be blessed. Although they cannot repay you, you will be repaid at the resurrection of the righteous."
LUKE 14:13–14

Nobody likes a clique. They feel exclusive, judgmental, and anything but humble. One of the crazy things about cliques is that nobody who is in one thinks they are in one. I don't know the dictionary definition of a clique, but in layman's terms, it's a group of people who intentionally block others out and use exclusivity to hide their underlying insecurities. They seem to make their own rules, and, over time, they perfect the subtle art of acting superior within the safety of similarly insecure people. In an odd twist, why is it the ones who come across as superior and self-confident are some of the most insecure, weirdly competitive people we've met?

It is possible to have relationships with a group of people with shared experiences and values but not form an off-putting clique that excludes people because they don't meet the unspoken social metrics of the group. This is what Jesus did every day when He ate dinner with unlikely people, avoided those who claimed to be powerful, touched lepers, and told stories about fathers who pursue lost sons.

The good news is we can adopt practices and habits that let people know they have access to us and that there is no secret handshake or gatekeeper or a vote on how cool someone is before they can be included. Why not flip the script the way Jesus did and blow everyone's minds with your availability?

Who could you reach out to today to let them know you consider them part of your posse? The popular people have lines out the door of people who want to be with them.

Go be Jesus to someone who has felt like an outcast. You'll know who they are because they are probably sitting all alone.

TIME IS YOUR MOST PRECIOUS CURRENCY

*There is a time for everything, and a season for
every activity under the heavens.*
ECCLESIASTES 3:1

Simplifying our lives can be hard to do. If you are anything like me, the allure of doing everything that presents itself to you can be irresistible. However, simplifying is about settling down, sorting through the chaos, and acknowledging you only have so much time available each day and that it is time to exert more agency over it. Consider your time as a precious resource, a currency you can spend only once. Where do you want to invest the greatest portion of this invaluable and limited resource? The trick is to identify and then choose those things that matter the most.

I practiced law for more than thirty years, and here's the crazy part: I can't remember having lost a case. Isn't that nuts? Maybe I did and put it out of my mind. My winning streak wasn't because I was a great lawyer; it was because I was a great picker. I would only pick cases nobody could lose. Apply this principle to your life and pick what you are going to spend your time on.

Here's a trick I use annually. I clear the slate, return the odometer to zero, and then start adding just a few things back into my life. Try it. If faith is the most important thing to you, make God the first thing you add back in. Family might follow next, trailed by a close group of friends. The fourth thing you add back in might be a few of the colleagues you work with.

Resist the urge to make the list too long or to be influenced by others as you are picking. Having three or four solid priorities is more powerful than scattering attention among endless activities. You will know you have it wrong if you find yourself adding what is a high priority to someone else but is irrelevant to you.

This is your opportunity to prepare for the next season by unburdening yourself of the things that hold you back and focusing instead on the things that truly matter.

Today is your day to reset and reprioritize.

WE ALL NEED A LITTLE—A LOT OF— HELP FROM OUR FRIENDS

When I am afraid, I put my trust in you. In God, whose word I praise—
in God I trust and am not afraid. What can mere mortals do to me?
PSALM 56:3-4

I'm not big on raw fish. A friend of mine is a famous chef and made a delicacy for me to enjoy. He splashed a little orange juice on the top of some raw fish and said this juice was going to "cook" the fish. I was looking for a Bunsen burner or a couple of pine logs I could set on fire. I may be old school, but pouring a little orange juice on a fist full of dead fish is not cooking in my book. It felt like I was participating in an episode of *Fear Factor* as I politely got a spoonful of this delicacy into my mouth and swallowed hard. *God, I'll get it down if You keep it down*, I said in a sincere foxhole prayer.

We all find work-arounds when we're in a sticky spot, whether it's with what we eat or what we do. Even Disney has work-arounds. Did you know that many of the United States flags at Disneyland do not respect the protocols we have for our flags, like only flying them during the day or lighting them up at night or flying at half-mast when appropriate? There are just too many flags at Disneyland to be raising and lowering them every day, so they needed a work-around. They made their American flags to have only forty-seven stars rather than fifty stars. They look like United States flags, flap like United States flags, and have stripes like the United States flag, but they are not official flags. Problem solved, while not disrespecting the otherwise required protocols.

Work-arounds help uncomplicate our complicated lives. Some of these can be incredibly positive and helpful and lasting. Others can just defer difficulties to another day and become avoidance techniques that aren't helpful at all. What are your best work-arounds for fear and insecurity? Do you medicate these emotions with activities or substances that prevent you from fully dealing with them? Or do you face them head-on and work your way through them?

Find a friend or two, perhaps even a counselor, to talk with about your work-around tendencies. This is the courageous work Jesus invites us to, and He promises He will be with us in all of it.

GET HUMBLE, BE ROOTED, AND GET READY BECAUSE IT'S ABOUT TO GET GOOD

I pray that you, being rooted and established in love, may have power, together with all the Lord's holy people, to grasp how wide and long and high and deep is the love of Christ, and to know this love that surpasses knowledge—that you may be filled to the measure of all the fullness of God.
EPHESIANS 3:17–19

There is a tradition in Northern Uganda that is the culmination of the courtship process. The young man who wants the family of the daughter to give their blessing gets a couple of buddies together, and they crawl on their hands and knees toward the house of the girl's parents in a beautiful humble act. When they arrive, they are completely ignored as part of the ceremony, and a conversation about the girl's dowry starts. The young man will offer sugar and cattle and grain and, if royalty is involved, the skins of certain animals. If things stall, the young man has to pay the girl's mother to put in a few good words for him. If things break down, the young man and his friends need to crawl away and start all over again.

This tradition has been ongoing for millennia, and in our time in Uganda, I have pitched in quite a few cattle to move things along for my friends. Once an agreement is reached, a curtain that everyone pretends they don't know has been hiding the family from the young man is dropped and a huge celebration happens.

Paul wanted his friends at Ephesus to know he was praying they would realize that Christ wanted to dwell in their hearts through faith. It wasn't more sugar or cattle or grain or even animal skins they needed—it was more love. Love holds the keys to understanding just how big Jesus' love for us is.

God wants to do immeasurably more in your life than you can even imagine.

Today, make it your goal to be humble, be rooted, and remain established in love, and then buckle up as you see what amazing thing God has in store for you.

ACKNOWLEDGMENTS

Behind any book of substance is a core of people who delight in doing the quiet, important heavy-lifting work necessary to get general ideas turned into words and then into pages and then bind these pages to make them available to us. Two good souls, Janene MacIvor and Jessica Rogers led the charge for a larger circle of friends at my publisher, Thomas Nelson. They worked in tight formation with the rest of the publishing team to make this book happen. Huge thanks to Mark Schoenwald, Don Jacobson, Andrew Stoddard, Merry MacIvor, Mallory Collins, Meg Schmidt, John Andrade, and Lisa Beech for your patience, tenacity, and resolve to release words that matter into the world. You could each be running a small country, but instead, you have devoted your careers to getting books into the hands of people in the hopes that they would lead more purposeful and meaningful lives filled to the brim with love and intention.

I want to thank my lifelong friend and literary agent Bryan Norman for his role as the guiding force behind all my writing. If Bryan wasn't part of my life, none of these books would be part of yours. Thank you also to my friend Dominick Dom and my daughter Lindsey Goff Viducich for your many contributions to the book that were so helpful.

There are countless other people who have contributed in large and small ways to the words and stories in this devotional. Calling them out by name to thank them would require that I append a telephone-book-size list here, and space does not allow. Beyond my immediate family who are constant sources of influence, including my father who is my next door neighbor, I want to publicly acknowledge some of the heroes who I get the honor of interacting with and whose lives are a constant inspiration to me.

My assistants Stephanie and Katie have navigated with grace and poise all the many challenges I have thrown their way.

Taylor Hughes, you kept things fun; and Dr. Rick Parker, you kept me alive.

Thank you to the Love Does Team, led by my friend Jody Luke, who have been constant encouragers while they continue to serve communities in war-torn countries around the world. Also, our team at the Oaks Retreat Center who lead with love every week, hosting new friends and helping them on their journeys, as do my friends at OnSite led by my buddy Miles Adcox.

Thank you also to the happy band of friends called the Champions of Love and its ring leaders Stéphane and Brenda. You love people the way Jesus did and are living out the important parts of faith every day.

These acknowledgments would not be complete without a shout-out to the guys I have met with every Friday morning for thirty-six years of "Bible-doing."

Finally, to you, the reader. Thank you for wanting to go deeper in your faith. Doing this takes guts and grit and more than merely acknowledge you, I applaud you. You are the ones who will live the kinds of lives, guided by love, which is the best evidence people will have that Jesus is still alive.

NOTES

INTRODUCTION

1. C. S. Lewis, *The Pilgrim's Regress: Wade Annotated Edition* (Wm. B. Eerdmans, 2014), 156.

MARCH

1. Karin Akre, s.v. "schadenfreude," *Britannica*, updated June 3, 2024, https://www.britannica.com/topic/pride-human-behavior.
2. *Psychology Today*, "Schadenfreude," accessed June 26, 2024, https://www.psychologytoday.com/us/basics/schadenfreude.

JUNE

1. Anxiety and Depression Association of America, "What Are Anxiety and Depression?" updated October 25, 2022, https://adaa.org/understanding-anxiety.

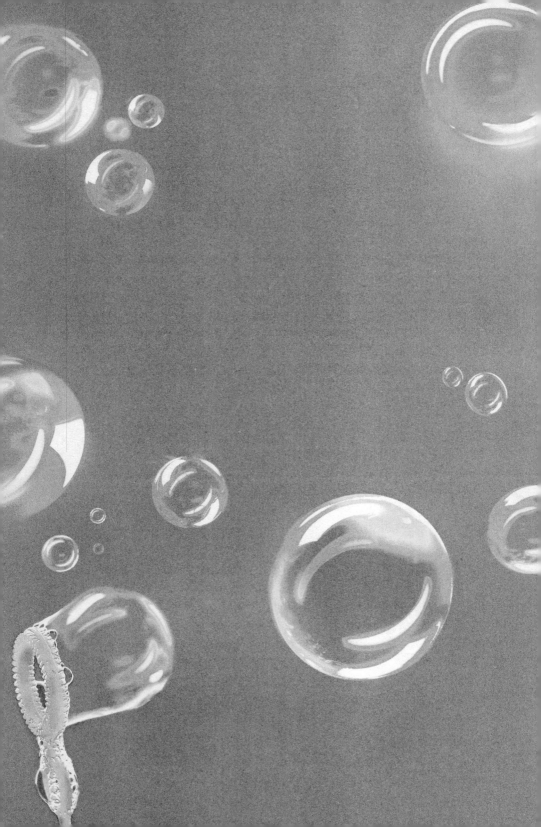

ABOUT THE AUTHOR

Bob Goff is the *New York Times* bestselling author of *Love Does*; *Everybody, Always*; *Dream Big*; *Undistracted*; *Live in Grace, Walk in Love*; *Catching Whimsy*; and *Love Does for Kids*. He's a lover of balloons, cake pops, and helping people pursue their big dreams. Bob's greatest ambitions in life are to love others, do stuff, and, most importantly, to hold hands with his wife, Sweet Maria, and spend time with their amazing family. For more, check out BobGoff.com and LoveDoes.org.

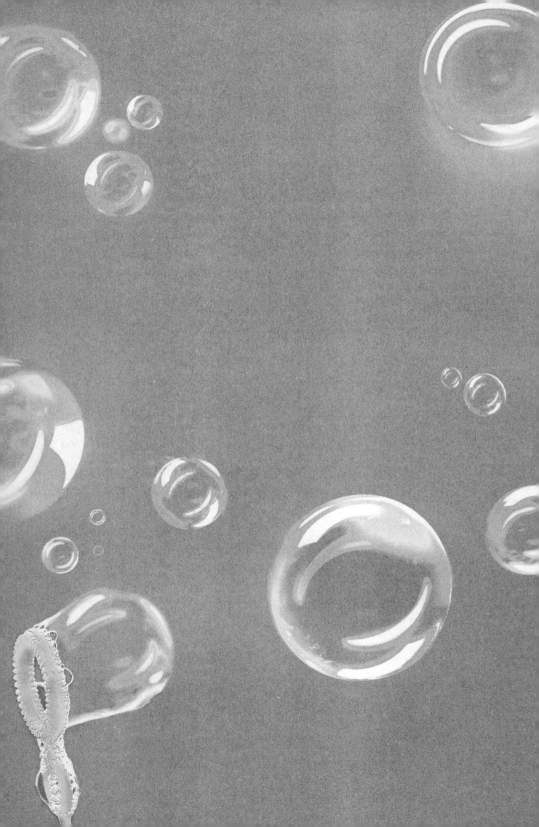

CONNECT WITH BOB

Bob's passion is people. He'd love to hear from you if you want to email him at info@bobgoff.com. You can also follow him on Instagram and X: @bobgoff. Here's his cell phone number if you want to give him a call: (619) 985-4747.

Bob is available to inspire and engage your team, organization, or audience. To date, he's spoken to more than two million people, bringing his unique perspective and exciting storytelling with him. He is a personal coach and hosts various workshops at The Oaks, a retreat center in Southern California.

To learn more about coaching, Bob's workshops, or inquire about speaking opportunities, check out bobgoff.com.